INFORMAL INTRODUCTION TO ALGOL 68

Informal introduction to ALGOL 68

C. H. LINDSEY
Department of Computer Science, University of Manchester

S. G. van der MEULEN
Computer Department, University of Utrecht

1973

NORTH-HOLLAND PUBLISHING COMPANY — AMSTERDAM · LONDON
AMERICAN ELSEVIER PUBLISHING COMPANY, INC. — NEW YORK

© IFIP, 1971

All Rights Reserved. No part of this publication may be reproduced, stored in a retrieval system or transmitted, in any form or by any means, electronic, mechanical, photocopying, recording or otherwise, without the prior permission of the Copyright owner.

Library of Congress Catalog Card Number: 78−148532
ISBN: 0 7204 2048 2

First revised reprint 1973

Published by
NORTH-HOLLAND PUBLISHING COMPANY − AMSTERDAM
NORTH-HOLLAND PUBLISHING COMPANY, LTD. − LONDON

Distributors for the U.S.A. and Canada:
American Elsevier Publishing Company, Inc.
52 Vanderbilt Avenue
New York, N.Y. 10017

PRINTED IN THE NETHERLANDS

To the uninitiated reader

ACKNOWLEDGEMENTS

The Authors wish to thank Prof. Dr. A. van Wijngaarden and the other authors of the ALGOL 68 Report, and also the many members of WG 2.1 and others in the computing community who have read this Introduction in draft form, for their encouragement and helpful criticisms of the text. They also wish to acknowledge the official support accorded to this work by IFIP TC–2 and WG–2.1, and the assistance given by the Mathematical Centre, Amsterdam in reproducing the earlier drafts.

PREFACE

Publication of this volume represents a major step in making accessible to the international computing community the operational content of the "Report on the Algorithmic Language ALGOL 68". The Report itself is, of course, an unparalleled accomplishment in the literature of programming languages *as a defining document*. The complexity of the topic, however, necessarily disqualifies such a completely rigorous treatment from consideration as a general pedagogical device; hence the present volume.

As noted by the authors, this book "is not – and is not intended to be – a primer for the programming novice". This is as it should be. The original Report addresses those who must understand every nuance of the language; primarily language designers and compiler implementers. If implementations of ALGOL 68 are to be other than academic exercises, there is a pressing need to acquaint the set of people who write computer programs as a routine part of their daily lives with the essential elements of the language. This book can do just that.

The algorithmic language, ALGOL 68, stands as a major product of the International Federation for Information Processing, an organization now in its second decade, counting among its members the national information processing societies from thirty-two countries spread over all six of the world's inhabited continents. Among the principal activities of the Federation is the work of Technical Committee 2, Programming Languages, and its Working Group 2.1, ALGOL. The initial effort of WG 2.1 stemmed from the development of the algorithmic language ALGOL 60, and since 1964 under the Chairmanships of Prof. Dr. W.L. van der Poel and, most recently, Prof. Dr. M. Paul, this group of international experts, including the authors of the present work, has been engaged in the design and development of ALGOL 68. During this time, until his recent election as an IFIP Vice President, the entire enterprise has been carefully shepherded by Prof. Dr. H. Zemanek as Chairman of the parent Committee, TC-2.

While the present book is wholly the work of the two authors, it has been extensively reviewed in manuscript by the Working Group and has the status of a working paper within the group. It follows that the accuracy with which it represents ALGOL 68 is far higher than might be apparent from its cover.

Every effort has been made to insure that the book contains a comprehensive, accurate and readable introduction to the language. Having had the opportunity to observe this effort closely from my present position as Chairman of TC-2, I can assure the reader that the authors have been successful in this endeavor.

T.B. Steel, Jr.
Woodland Hills, Calif.
November 30, 1970

The Report referred to throughout this book is published as follows:
  A. van Wijngaarden (Ed.), B.J. Mailloux, J.E.L. Peck, C.H.A. Koster, Report on the Algorithmic Language ALGOL 68, Mathematisch Centrum, MR 101, Amsterdam, 1969;
  also in Numerische Mathematik 14, 1969, pp. 79–218;
  also in Kibernetika, Vol. 6, 1969, and Vol. 1, 1970 (in English and Russian).

0. VERY INFORMAL INTRODUCTION TO ALGOL 68

0.0. Aims and methods

The "Report on the Algorithmic Language ALGOL 68" (hereafter referred to as the "Report") is a document officially sponsored by the International Federation for Information Processing. It seeks to define, in a rigorous manner, a machine-independent programming language known as ALGOL 68.

This "Informal Introduction to ALGOL 68" seeks to describe rather than to define. If you have some difficulty in understanding the Report, it is our hope that you will find our informal treatment more palatable, even though this may have been achieved at the expense of rigour. It is the "companion volume" referred to in Section R 0.1.1 of the Report. (We shall always precede our references to the Report with such an R. All other references are to other parts of the Introduction.)

This Introduction, however, is not — and is not intended to be — a primer for the programming novice. The "user" to whom we address ourselves is assumed to be a "programmer", i.e. someone who is able to write, or at least to read, a text in some machine-independent programming language which is on a level not too much below, for instance, ALGOL 60. Our aim has been to describe the whole of ALGOL 68, and this Introduction may also, therefore, have some merit as a work of reference — provided that it is always understood that the official Report is the final arbiter in all matters of doubt.

Since ALGOL 68 is a highly recursively structured language, it is quite impossible to describe it until it has been described. So that you can read this Introduction without tying your own mental processes into a recursive knot, it has been laid out to a certain pattern, which we ask you to follow. Please, therefore, start by reading once or twice the "Very Informal Introduction" (Sections 0.1 to 0.12 following), in which we try to give a broad survey of what is in this language — mainly by the way of small examples and plain explanations. After that, we shall tell you what to do next.

    if *you think you know it all already*
    then goto *What to do next*   **comment** *Section 0.13* ¢
    fi

0.1	A simple program
0.2	The primitive modes, denotations
0.2 .1	**bool**
0.2 .2	**int**
0.2 .3	**real**
0.2 .4	**char**
0.2 .5	**bool**, **int**, **real** and **char**
0.3	**goto** and repetition
0.4	The creation of new modes, multiples
0.4 .1	Multiples
0.4 .2	New mode indications
0.4 .3	Multiples with flexible bounds, **strings**
0.5	The value of a unit
0.5 .1	The value of a formula
0.5 .2	The value of a conditional clause
0.5 .3	The value of a serial clause
0.5 .4	The value of a closed clause
0.5 .5	The value of a constant
0.6	A more involved program
0.7	Routines and procedures
0.7 .1	Procedures without parameters
0.7 .2	Procedures with parameters, routine denotations
0.7 .3	Examples of procedure declarations
0.8	The creation of new modes, names and values referred to
0.8 .1	Identity declarations in the strict language
0.8 .2	Procedures, values and references
0.8 .3	The switch
0.8 .4	Procedures as formal parameters
0.8 .5	Pointers (variable names)
0.8 .6	Identity relators, the cast, coercion
0.9	The creation of new modes, structures
0.9 .1	**complex** values, vectors etc.
0.9 .2	**bits** and **bytes**
0.9 .3	Structures with mixed mode fields, chains etc.
0.10	Routines and operators
0.10.1	Operations on boolean operands
0.10.2	Formulae
0.10.3	Operations on arithmetic operands, the standard prelude
0.10.4	Operations on **complex** operands
0.10.5	Operations combined with assignations
0.10.6	Operations on **strings**
0.10.7	The library prelude option
0.11	The creation of new modes, **long** -- **long** modes and **unions**
0.11.1	The **long long** -- **long** modes
0.11.2	United modes
0.11.3	Conformity relators
0.12	Other distinctive features
0.12.1	Local and global generators, stack and heap
0.12.2	The ordinary **case** clause
0.12.3	The conformity **case** clause

0.1. A simple program

(E1)   **begin**   **real** x, y, z ;
                    read (x) ; read (y) ;
                    $z := (x+y) / 2 - sqrt(x \times y)$;
                    print (z)
    end

This piece of text represents a program, and as such it defines a sequence of actions to be performed by a computer. This sequence of actions is termed "the elaboration of the program". We shall briefly outline the elaboration of E1 :

1. Three identifiers x, y and z for **real** variables are declared. That is to say that somewhere in the memory of our computer, in the "stack", three locations for **real** values are reserved. These values are referred to by the names $\hat{x}$, $\hat{y}$ and $\hat{z}$ (i.e. by their "addresses") which are also entities (values) in the computer. It thus appears that a 'variable' consists of a value associated with the name which refers to it. You may consider the identifiers x, y and z as the representatives in the programtext of the names $\hat{x}$, $\hat{y}$ and $\hat{z}$. The technical term for this relationship is "to possess":

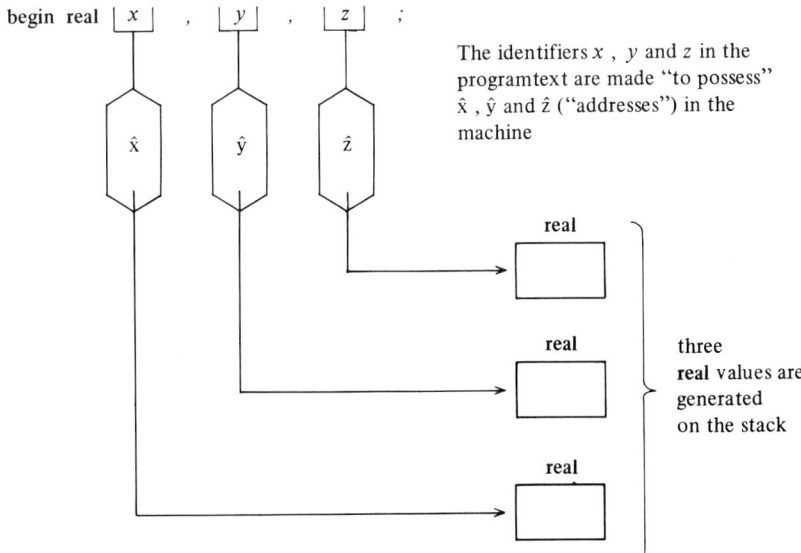

The identifiers x, y and z in the programtext are made "to possess" $\hat{x}$, $\hat{y}$ and $\hat{z}$ ("addresses") in the machine

three **real** values are generated on the stack

The names $\hat{x}$, $\hat{y}$ and $\hat{z}$ "refer to" **real** values (see also Section 0.8).

2. Next, from a punched tape, or punched card or some other medium, two numbers are read in and assigned to *x* and *y*. That is to say, these numbers are converted into the proper bit-patterns in the private internal number-system of the computer, which subsequently are stored in the locations corresponding to the names x̂ and ŷ :

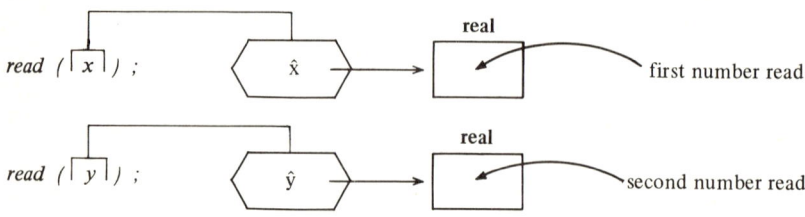

3. Then, the difference between the arithmetic and geometric mean of these values is calculalated and assigned to *z*, so that we find this difference in the location corresponding to ẑ :

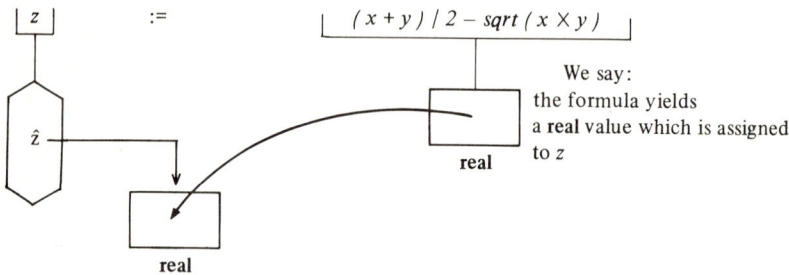

4. Finally, this value, referred to by ẑ , is reconverted into humanly recognizable graphics and is printed by some device:

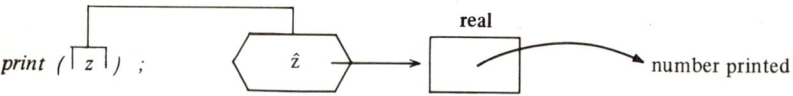

Summing up we have:

1. Three identity-declarations.
2. Two input statements.

Ch.0.1   VERY INFORMAL INTRODUCTION TO ALGOL 68   5

3 An assignation. To the left of the becomes-symbol := we find the destination z, and to the right a 'formula' whose value is to be assigned to that destination.

4. An output statement.

The three identity-declarations in the first line are separated by comma-symbols. This means that they are elaborated "collaterally", which is a technical term stating that the order of their elaboration is not prescribed.

The collateral declaration in the first line, the input statements in the second, the assignation in the third, and the output statement in the last line are separated by go-on-symbols (represented by semicolons). This means that they are elaborated "serially". This again is a technical term stating that the order in which these phrases are elaborated is explicitly prescribed to be the textual order: one after the other. They form a 'serial clause'.

The piece of text E1 might very well be part of a larger program. The meaning of the identifiers x, y and z (and consequently the existence of the names $\hat{x}$, $\hat{y}$ and $\hat{z}$ and of the **real** values referred to by them) is, however, "local". This technical term states that the "scope" of their declarations is limited to the serial-clause between **begin** and **end**, which define a 'closed clause'. If outside this closed-clause (or inside another closed-clause contained within it) other identifiers x, y and z should be declared, then these have nothing to do with those declared in example E1. We say, therefore, that the "original meaning" of x, y and z applies only to that part of the program text.

The standard input procedure *read* accepts as actual parameter not only the name of a **real** value, but also (amongst many others) a 'row display' like (x,y).

Consequently, line 2 may be replaced by:

> *read ((x,y));*   Observe that we again give precisely one actual-parameter to *read*; instead of one name, one row-display of names.

Instead of the two phrases 3 and 4 we may write, in one statement:

> *print (z := (x+y)/2 − sqrt (x×y))*

Instead of the begin-symbol **begin** we may write an open-symbol *(* ; instead of the end-symbol **end** we must then write a close-symbol *)*. Thus E1* below is, at least in its effect, completely equivalent to E1:

(E1*) (real x , y , z ; read ((x,y)) ;
        print ($z := (x+y)/2 - sqrt(x \times y)$)
)

0.2. The primitive modes, denotations

The **real** in E1 specifies a mode (i.e. it specifies that $\hat{x}$, $\hat{y}$ and $\hat{z}$ will refer to values which belong to a certain class). An infinite number of distinct modes (disjunct classes of values) is provided in this language. They are, however, all derived from five primitive modes (which form the basis of the entire mode system): boolean (**bool**), integral (**int**), real (**real**), character (**char**) and format (**format**). In this section we shall briefly discuss **bool**, **int**, **real** and **char**. A **format** is a value which controls input and output.

For all primitive modes we have 'denotations': symbols or sequences of symbols possessing a specific value in such a mode.

0.2.1. bool

There are two boolean values, denoted by the symbols **true** and **false**.

If (in E2 below) C is a piece of program (maybe a serial-clause, maybe as simple as an identifier) yielding a boolean value, then this value is either **true** or **false**. In a 'conditional clause' like:

(E2)   if C then $Ctrue$ else $Cfalse$ fi

first of all C is elaborated, being the condition between **if** and **then**. The then-clause $Ctrue$ between **then** and **else** is elaborated only if the condition yielded **true**. The else-clause $Cfalse$ between **else** and **fi** is elaborated only if the condition yielded **false**.

The symbols **if** and **then**, **then** and **else**, **else** and **fi** enclose serial-clauses in which new identifiers of local scope may be declared as in a closed-clause (they form a pair of brackets, so to speak). Observe that the whole conditional-clause is enclosed between **if** and **fi**. The else-clause may be absent, in which case the then-clause is closed by **fi**; the then-clause must always be there.

For **if** we may also write (, for **fi**) and for **then** as well as for **else** we may write | . Now E2 looks like:

(E2*)   (C | $Ctrue$ | $Cfalse$)

which may be a fine notation to use in a formula, where either the value of $Ctrue$ or the value of $Cfalse$ is to be yielded (see 0.5.2).

0.2.2. int

There will be many integral values, denoted by:

0 1 2 3 4 5 6 7 8 9 10 11 12 --- --- 2147483647 ---

How far can we go? The Report does not answer this question. It depends entirely on the implementation. It is, however, prescribed that we can always know the largest integral value by an "environment enquiry" *max int*, which is a standard identifier possessing the largest integral value in a specific implementation (see also 0.11).

Observe that there is no sign preceding an integral-denotation. Of course you may write:

+1   −37   −1000   +534711   −513617   etc.

but then the + and the − are monadic-operators applied to the value denoted.

0.2.3. real

There are many real values, which can be denoted in many styles:

3.1415927 or *31415927$_{10}$−7* or *0.31415927$_{10}$+1* or *.31415927$_{10}$1*

instead of the symbol $_{10}$ you may also use *e* : *31415927e−7*

0.9 .9 9.0 100.0 0.0 1$_{10}$2 10$_{10}$10 1$_{10}$−10 1$_{10}$0 ---

The class of real values in the finite memory of a concrete computer is finite by necessity; it is an implementation dependent image of the mathematical concept "real number system". The largest real value in a certain implementation can be obtained by the environment enquiry *max real* and the smallest real value which can be usefully compared with *1.0* from *small real*. (See also 0.11).

Observe again that there is no sign preceding a real-denotation. Of course you may write:

+1.0   −37$_{10}$−4   −31415927$_{10}$−7   etc.

but then the + and − preceding the real-denotation are monadic-operators applied to the value denoted.

0.2.4. char

There is a prescribed minimal set of graphics in which we find all (small) letters, the digits and some other tokens. The class of character values is at least this minimal set; specific implementations, however, may extend it.

A character-denotation consists of the character denoted between two quote-symbols:

"a" "b" "c" --- --- --- "x" "y" "z"
"0" "1" "2" "3" "4" "5" "6" "7" "8" "9"
"." "$\overline{10}$" "," "(" ")" "+" "-" --- ---

Specific character-denotations are:

" "   the space-symbol   (see 0.4.3)
"$\overline{\bot}$" or "!" or "i"   the plus-i-times-symbol   (see 0.9.1)
"$\underline{1}$" and "$\underline{0}$"   the flip-symbol and flop-symbol   (see 0.9.2)

0.2.5. bool, int, real and char

(D1)   bool p, q ;
           int i, j, k, m, n ;
           real a, b, x, y ;
           char c ;

By these declarations the identifiers p and q possess boolean variables; i, j, k, m and n possess integral variables; a, b, x and y possess real variables, and c possesses a character variable. That is to say the names $\hat{p}, \hat{q}, \hat{i}, \text{---}, \hat{a}, \text{---}, \hat{c}$ refer to boolean, integral, real or character values as specified by the declarers bool, int, real and char.

In this Informal Introduction, identifiers will occasionally occur out of context from their declarations. Unless otherwise specified, these identifiers will be assumed to have been declared as listed in D1 (or D2, D3, -- hereafter). The complete set is listed in Appendix 2.

For boolean values operators are defined: ∨ (or), ∧ (and), ⌐ (not), yielding boolean values. Boolean values can be compared = (equal), ≠ (not equal) ; the result of a comparison is also a boolean value. The monadic operator abs, however, when applied to a boolean value, yields an int : abs p is 1 if p is true, abs p is 0 if p is false. This can be expressed concisely as the conditional-clause ($p \mid 1 \mid 0$) .

Many operators are defined for integral and real values : + (addition), − (subtraction), × (multiplication), / (division), ÷ (integral division, defined for integral values only), ↑ (to the power), etc. The result is an integral value when both operands are integral (except division which always yields a real value); in all other cases the result is real.

Integral and real values can be compared : <, ≤, =, ≠, ≥, > ; the result is a boolean value.

The monadic operator **abs**, when applied to an **int** or a **real** *ir*, yields
(ir < 0 | −ir | ir).

The monadic operators **round** and **entier** (integral part of) serve to transfer a **real** into an **int**. The transfer of an **int** into a **real** is implicit in the language (no operator is needed to control this transfer); you may write:

$$x := i$$

but you must write:

$$i := \mathbf{round}\, x \quad \text{or} \quad i := \mathbf{entier}\, x$$

Each character value corresponds to an integral value; no two different characters correspond to the same **int**; the actual correspondence is to be defined by the implementation. The **int** corresponding to a **char** is obtained by applying the monadic operator **abs** (**abs** *c* yields the integral value corresponding to *c*).

Character values can be compared as if they were integral values and by the same operators; in fact their **abs** values are then compared.

Character values are the materials from which strings are composed (see Section 0.4.3).

0.3. **goto** and repetition

Suppose we want to input many pairs of numbers *x* and *y* and we want to do the algorithm E1 that many times. Let the input start with an integral number $n > 0$, which fixes the number of pairs following. Then the program might be:

(E3)   **begin**   **int** *n*,
         real *x*, *y*, *z*;
         read (n) ;
  again : *read ((x,y))* ;
         print (z := (x+y)/2 − sqrt (x × y)) ;
         n := n−1 ;
         if $n > 0$ **then goto** *again* **fi**
      end

1. The reason we declared *n* was to count the number of pairs, and it is quite natural to read this *n* immediately after its declaration. In this language it is allowable to put statements between declarations, so that the order of the second and third lines may be reversed. But then a go-on-symbol must of

course follow the declaration of *n* (the order of elaboration of **int** *n* and *read (n)* is not arbitrary):

> **int**   *n ;*
> *read (n) ;*
> **real**   *x , y , z ;*

4. The identifier *again* defines a 'label' signposting a point in the program where we want to **go to** from elsewhere. Labels are only allowed beyond the declarations (i.e. it is not allowed to write a label in a serial-clause where a declaration follows).

6. The **int** value referred to by ñ is decreased by *1*. Operations of this kind, combined with assignment to the same variable, occur so often that we have got special operators for the most frequent cases; they combine subtraction (or addition, multiplication, division etc.) with assignment. We may write:

> *n* **minus** *1*   or   *n* −:= *1*   instead of   *n := n − 1*

7. The go-to-symbol **goto** is completely redundant in this language. Instead of:

> **if** *n* > *0* **then goto** *again* **fi**

you may write:

> **if** *n* > *0* **then** *again* **fi**

and consequently:

> *(n* > *0 | again)*

6,7. We may now combine the phrases 6 and 7 into one phrase:

if *(n* **minus** *1)* > *0* **then** *again* **fi**	The brackets around *n* **minus** *1*
or:	are obligatory because **minus** is
((n −:= *1)* > *0	again)*	of lower priority than > .

A cycle like *((n* −:= *1)* > *0 | again)* occurs so often in algorithms that we have a special construction for it (which is, however, a specific case of a much more general construction; see 0.6). Instead of:

> *again:*   *read ((x,y)) ;*
> *print (z := (x+y)/2 − sqrt (x×y)) ;*
> *((n* −:= *1)* > *0 | again)*

we may write:

>   to *n* do begin *read ((x,y)) ;*
>   *print (z := (x+y)/2 − sqrt (x×y))*
>   end

The only difference between the two (but be aware of it) is that in the first construction the operation *n* −:= *1* exhausts *n* until *0*, while in the second the value of *n* is not changed (the counting is done in a copy, hidden from the programmer).

Of course we may, if we wish to do so (see 0.7.1), bring the declaration **real** *x , y , z ;* into the closed-clause following the **do**. And thus the piece of program below is as good as equivalent to E3:

(E3*)   begin   int *n ; read (n) ;*
                     to *n* do begin real *x , y , z ; read ((x,y));*
                                         print (z := (x+y)/2 − sqrt (x × y))
                                end
           end

or, using open- and close-symbols instead of **begin** and **end** :

(E3*)   (int *n ; read (n) ;*
              to *n* do (real *x , y , z ; read ((x,y)) ;*
                         print (z := (x+y)/2 − sqrt (x×y))
)
)

0.4. The creation of new modes, multiples

One of the interesting features of this language is the possibility of deriving new modes from the primitive ones, as many as you need. The method whereby new modes are created is such that they can, in their turn, be used to create further modes in a perfectly systematic manner. Some of these derived modes, such as **string** , **compl** (complex) , **bits** and **bytes** are standard in the language (i.e. being declared in the standard-prelude, they are permanently built in).

In this section, we shall briefly outline the construction of multiple values (multiples). Other constructions (procedures, structures, references, unions and further derived modes) will be outlined in following sections. You will find a more systematic treatment in Chapters 1 and 2.

0.4.1. Multiples

Suppose you want to use a row of n **reals** named a, then you may declare, for instance:

(E4) $[1:n]$ **real** a ;   The lower-bound of the row is 1, the upper-bound of the row is the value of n.

Now you have at your disposal n **real** values on the stack:

$a[1], a[2], \cdots, a[n]$

In fact you have got more than this, you have got n names:

$â[1], â[2], \cdots, â[n]$

to which you can assign new values as in the case of simple variables:

$a[i] := a[i] + x$
$a[i] := a[n-i]/a[j]$ etc.

If you want to use a square matrix of $n \times n$ **reals** (a row-of-row-of-real) named A, then you may declare, for instance:

(E5) $[1:n,1:n]$ **real** A ;

Now you have at your disposal $n \times n$ **real** values on the stack:

$A[1,1], A[1,2], \cdots, A[1,n], A[2,1], A[2,2], \cdots, \cdots, A[n,n]$

In fact you have got $n \times n$ names of **real** values to which you can assign new values:

$A[i,j] := A[i,k] \times A[k,j]$
$A[i,j] := A[j,i] / (i+j)$ etc.

(D2) $[1:n]$ **real** $x1, y1$; $[1:n]$ **int** $i1$;
           $[1:m,1:n]$ **real** $x2$; $[1:m,1:n]$ **int** $i2$;
           $[1:n,1:n]$ **real** $y2$;

By E4 and E5 we declared the identifiers a and A to possess the names $â$ and $Â$ respectively (see also 0.1). The name $â$ refers to a [ ] **real**, a row-of-real; the name $Â$ refers to a [,] **real**, a row-of-row-of-real. That is to say that a possesses a [ ] **real** variable and A possesses a [,] **real** variable in much the same way as, for instance, x possesses a **real** variable and p a **bool** variable.

Ch.0.4.1 VERY INFORMAL INTRODUCTION TO ALGOL 68 13

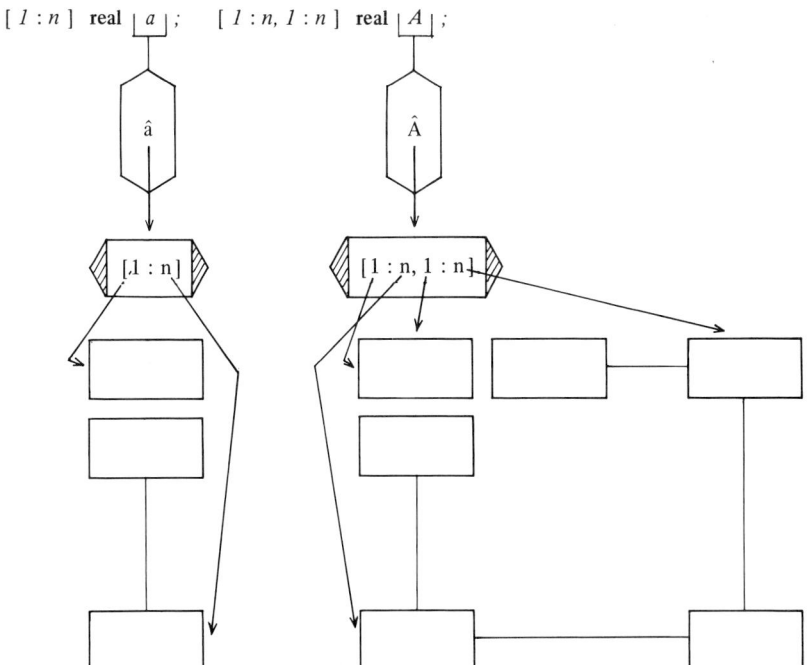

Now the question arises as to whether we may assign, for instance:

$a := x1$
$A := y2$

the answer is yes, and it does exactly what you should expect it to do:

$a[1] := x1[1], a[2] := x1[2], \cdots, a[n] := x1[n]$

and:

$A[1,1] := y2[1,1], A[1,2] := y2[1,2], \cdots, \cdots\cdots, A[n,n] := y2[n,n]$

provided, of course, that the bounds to the left and to the right of the becomes-symbol are compatible. Also an input-statement like:

read (y2)

does what you would expect:

read ((y2[1,1], y2[1,2], ···, y2[1,n], ···, ······, y2[n,n]))

Where â is a name referring to the whole of the multiple value:

$$a[1], a[2], \cdots, a[n]$$

the 'slice' $a[2:5]$ possesses a name referring to a part (a slice) of that multiple value, namely:

$$(a[2], a[3], a[4], a[5])$$

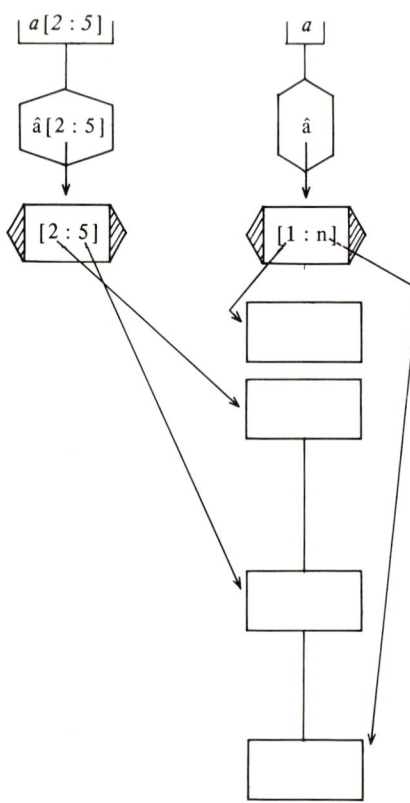

In much the same way $A[i, \ ]$ possesses a name referring to the multiple value:

$$(A[i,1], A[i,2], \cdots, A[i,n])$$

Therefore, even assignments like:

Ch.0.4.2   VERY INFORMAL INTRODUCTION TO ALGOL 68   15

$$a[2:5] := x1[n-3:n];$$
$$A[i, \ ] := a;$$
$$A[i, \ ] := y2[,j]$$

etc. do exactly what they suggest. For further discussion see 1.5.1 and 5.5.1.3.

Moreover, operators acting upon multiple values and slices may also be defined (see, for example, 8.5), so that we can then write clauses like:

$$a := x1 + y1;$$
$$A := y2 \times A$$

0.4.2. New mode indications

Once you have decided to create a new mode, you may want to give this new class of values a distinguishing mark (we do not say "name", because that is a technical term in this language with a very specific meaning, see 0.1 and 0.8). You may define a new 'mode indication' by declaring:

(E6)   **mode column** = $[1:n]$ **real** ;
       mode matrix = $[1:n,1:n]$ **real** ;

And now, in the context of these mode-declarations:

(E4*)   **column** a ;   is equivalent to E4 : $[1:n]$ **real** a ;

(E5*)   **matrix** A ;   is equivalent to E5 : $[1:n,1:n]$ **real** A ;

You might be allured into declaring **matrix** as **mode matrix** = $[1:n]$ **column**. This, however, is not allowed. Once a mode is declared to be "row-of", you cannot derive further row-of modes from it. The only way to declare a multi-dimensional multiple, is by $[h:k,---,m:n]$. In this language you will find only a few restrictions of this kind (but see 2.5.1).

0.4.3. Multiples with flexible bounds, **strings**

In E4 and E5 the bounds (the lower-bounds 1, and the upper-bounds n) are fixed at the elaboration of the declaration and cannot be changed afterwards, but on some occasions you might wish to do just that, although this may be expensive in some implementations (the storage allocation at run time is more complicated than in the case of fixed bounds).

Bounds which may be changed after the declaration of the multiple are termed "flexible" (**flex**):

(E7)   [*m* :*n* **flex**] **real** *fa* ;   the lower bound is fixed to the value of *m*; the upper-bound is set to the value of *n* but may be changed later.

[*m* **flex** :*n* **flex**] **real** *faf* ;   both the bounds are flexible.

Flexible bounds are particularly useful in the case of **string**s, which are built into the standard-declarations of the language (which is why one may expect a reasonably efficient implementation of, in particular, this flexible bound application). A **string** is a row-of-character with a flexible upper-bound:

(D3)   **mode string** = [*1* :*0* **flex**] **char** ;
       string *s* ;

The mode-declaration D3 states that the lower-bound of a **string** will always be *1*; the upper-bound, however, is declared to be flexible. The identity-declaration **string** *s* (which is equivalent to [*1* :*0* **flex**] **char** *s*) declares *s* to possess a name *ŝ* referring to a row-of-character, which is empty to begin with (the flexible upper-bound is set to *0*). As soon as you assign to *s*, the upper-bound gets the new value required:

(E8)   *s* := "*the␣upper-bound␣becomes␣26*" ;
       s := "*the␣flexible␣upper-bound␣now␣becomes␣39*" ;
       s := " " ;   the **string** is empty again.

By the way, you have just met three string-denotations. Observe that the denotation for the empty string is " ", and for the space is "␣".

For **string**, being a built-in mode, several operators are defined, such as <, ≤, =, ≠, ≥, > (to compare them) and + (to concatenate them).

If the value of *s* is "*this␣is␣the␣begin*", then the outcome of the assignation:

(E9)   *s* := *s* + "*␣and␣this␣is␣the␣end*."

or (which is the same):

(E9*)   *s* **plus** "*␣and␣this␣is␣the␣end*."

may speak for itself.

0.5. The value of a unit

So far we have met identifiers and denotations as the objects in this language that possess a value of some mode. They are, however, only specific cases of a 'base'; and a base is in its turn a specific case of the more general concept of a 'unitary clause' (or 'unit' for short). In this section we shall show you over some unitary-clauses and pay some attention to the values they may possess. The complete and systematic treatment will be found in Chapter 5.

0.5.1. The value of a formula

A formula is a unit. For example:

$$x + y \;,\quad (x+y)/2 \;,\quad (x+y)/2 - sqrt\,(x \times y)$$

A formula defines a (more or less compound) computation, which usually yields (i.e. delivers on the stack) a value of some mode. We then say: "the formula possesses (upon elaboration) the value", or "yields the value".

In the example above, we met:
identifiers x and y, units (bases) possessing variable values (names);
a denotation 2, a unit (base) possessing a constant value;
and another kind of base $sqrt\,(x \times y)$, which is the 'call' of a procedure delivering a value: the square root of the value of the formula $x \times y$ (for procedure calls see Section 0.7).

Different operators may have different priorities. The implied bracketing in the example above is:

$$\underbrace{(\,x+y\,)/2}_{\text{left-operand}} \;-\; \underbrace{sqrt\,(\,x \times y\,)}_{\text{right-operand}}$$

The 'left-operand' and the 'right-operand' of the subtraction are elaborated collaterally. That is to say that there is no prescribed order for getting the value of the left-operand and getting the value of the right-operand (see also 0.1). The same applies again to the elaboration of the left- and the right-operand in the formula $(x+y)/2$.

Hence, an implementor is perfectly entitled to optimize the elaboration of formulae. For example:

$$y1[\textbf{round}\;sqrt(a \times b)] + i1[\textbf{round}\;sqrt(a \times b)] \times x1[\textbf{round}\;sqrt(a \times b)]$$

The implementor may elaborate **round** *sqrt (a × b)* only once (for reasons explained in 3.7.1), and elaborate the multiplication *i1* [*k*] × *x1* [*k*] before accessing *y1* [*k*]; that is to say that there is no prescribed order of elaboration "from left to right".

0.5.2. The value of a conditional clause

A conditional-clause is a unit:

if *p* **then** $31415927_{10} - 7$ **else** $27182818_{10} - 7$ **fi**

possesses upon elaboration the **real** value of its then-clause or of its else-clause, depending upon the value of its condition. You may assign it to a **real** variable, or use it in a formula:

$x := 1 / (p | 31415927_{10} - 7 | 27182818_{10} - 7)$

If a conditional-clause yields a variable then you are perfectly entitled to use it in a destination (to the left of a becomes-symbol):

if *p* **then** *x* **else** *y* **fi** := *3.1415927*

or:

(p | x | y) := *3.1415927*

0.5.3. The value of a serial clause

A serial-clause (see 0.1) may also possess a value, although it is not (yet) a unit. It may be used, however, to make a unit. For example, a closed-clause, which is a unit (see 0.5.4), contains a serial-clause, and a conditional-clause (another unit) may contain three of them.

The value of a serial-clause, then, is the value of its final (completing) unit. The serial-clause:

num +:= *1* ; *read (x)* ; $x > 0$

(see E10 below) possesses the value of its final unit $x > 0$, which is a **bool** value. Now consider the program:

Ch.0.5.3   VERY INFORMAL INTRODUCTION TO ALGOL 68

(E10)   **begin**
        int *num* := 0 , *pos* := 0 , *neg* := 0 , **real** *absum* := 0 , *x* ;
        again: *absum* **plus**   **if** *num*+:=1 ; *read (x)* ; $x > 0$
                               then *pos* +:=1 ; +*x*
                               else *neg* +:=1 ; −*x*
                               fi ;
              if $x \neq 0$ **then** *again* **else** *ready* **fi** ;
        ready: *print ((num , pos , neg , absum))*
        end

1. A variable may be initialized on the very occasion of its declaration:

    int *num* := 0 , *pos* := 0 , *neg* := 0 , **real** *absum* := 0 , *x* ;

is equivalent in its result to:

   int *num* ; *num*:=0 ; **int** *pos* ; *pos*:=0 ; **int** *neg* ; *neg*:=0 ;
   real *absum* ; *absum*:=0 ; **real** *x* ;

2–4. The value of the condition is $x > 0$, a value which is delivered on the stack after the completion of the statements *num*+:=1 and *read(x)*. Likewise, the value of the then-clause is +*x* and the value of the else-clause is −*x* ; but only one of the two serial-clauses is elaborated, leaving a value on the stack to be added to *absum*.

As in example E3*, we may use **do** and, not knowing beforehand how often we shall **do** it, we may omit **to** *n* :

(E10*) **begin**
         int   *num* := 0 , *pos* := 0 , *neg* := 0 , **real** *absum* := 0 , *x* ;
         do (*absum* **plus**   **if** *num*+:=1 ; *read(x)* ; $x > 0$
                                then *pos* +:=1 ; +*x*
                                else *neg* +:= 1 ; −*x*
                                fi ;
               if *x* = 0   **then** *ready*   **fi**) ;
         ready: *print ((num , pos , neg , absum))*
         end

It may happen that a serial-clause does not yield a value, because its final unit does not leave a value on the stack (the root of this will be shown in 0.7). We then say: "this serial-clause yields void". For example:

   real *x* , *y* , *z* ; *read ((x,y))* ; *print (z := (x+y)/2 − sqrt (x×y))* yields void, because the output statement *print* (although it delivers humanly recognizable graphics on some printing device) does not leave a value on the stack. If, however, we want this serial-clause to possess, for example, the name of the value printed (from which that value may then be obtained), then we simply make z its final unit:

real x , y , z ; *read ((x,y))* ; *print (z := (x+y)/2 − sqrt (x × y))* ; z

0.5.4. The value of a closed clause

A closed-clause (see 0.1) is a unit and as such it may be used in formulae and in assignations. The value of a closed-clause, if any, is that of its constituent serial-clause:

$x2[i,j]$:= (**real** x , y , z ; *read ((x,y))* ;
   print (z := (x+y)/2 − sqrt (x × y)) ;
   z)

The value of a closed-clause may also be a name, and then you are entitled to use it in a destination (see also 0.5.2); provided, of course, that the name yielded does not happen to be local to the clause:

(**real** x , y , z ; *read ((x,y))* ;
   print (z := (x+y)/2 − sqrt (x × y)) ;
   if $z > 1$ **then** m **else** n **fi**)   **plus** *1*

Under certain circumstances it may be annoying to have to arrange a closed-clause in such a way as to deliver the value required, because there may be more than one candidate for the final unit. In such cases a 'completer' may help. A completer is the symbol **exit** (or .); the unit preceding a completer is (by definition) a completing (final) unit of the closed-clause. You may take a completer as a suppositious close-symbol.

For example, suppose you want a closed-clause to read a block of n pairs of real numbers and to deliver **false** if there is no pair in the block in which the difference between the arithmetic and geometric mean is greater than *1*, but to deliver **true** and to print the first such pair if this is the case. This may be programmed as follows:

Ch.0.5.5 VERY INFORMAL INTRODUCTION TO ALGOL 68 21

(E11) $p := ($ **real** x, y, z ;
         to n **do** $($ $read$ $(\,(x,y)\,)$; $z := (x+y)/2 - sqrt\,(x \times y)$;
                  if $z > 1$ **then** $stop$ **fi** $)$;
         false exit
         $stop$: $print$ $(\,(x,y)\,)$;
         true $)$

(For other examples in which a completer is used, see E27* in 0.7.3 and E63 in 0.12.3).

0.5.5. The value of a constant

To conclude this bird's-eye view, we consider an extremely simple kind of unit, the constant. You may declare:

(E12)   **real** pi = 3.1415927

The thus declared identifier pi possesses a **real** value (and not a **real** variable), in much the same way as the denotation 3.1415927 possesses that value. You cannot assign to pi (it not being a variable): $pi := 2.7182818$ would be as nonsensical as is $3.1415927 := 2.7182818$. Beware of the slight notational distinction between E12 and:

(E12*)   **real** $pivar$:= 3.1415927

To $pivar$ you may assign any other **real** value ($pivar$ being a **real** variable). For the notational matter, see 0.8.

Declarations of constants enable the programmer to enforce efficient compilation, for example in accessing the elements of multiple values. Compare E13 and E13* below:

(E13) $(\ W$ **plus** $w[i]$;
          Swx **plus** $w[i] \times x[i]$;
          $Swx2$ **plus** $w[i] \times x[i] \times x[i]$;
          $Swx3$ **plus** $w[i] \times x[i] \times x[i] \times x[i]\ )$

In E13 an element such as $w[i]$ and $x[i]$ has to be pulled many times out of a multiple value, which may be rather time consuming.

(E13*) $(\ $**real** $wi=w[i]$, $xi=x[i]$; **real** $wixi=wi \times xi$; **real** $wixi2=wixi \times xi$;
         W **plus** wi ;
         Swx **plus** $wixi$;
         $Swx2$ **plus** $wixi2$;
         $Swx3$ **plus** $wixi2 \times xi\ )$ (see also E14)

In E13*, an element is never taken out of a multiple more than once. Of course, you could have achieved most of this efficiency equally well by declaring the proper local variables : **real** $wi := w[i]$, $xi := x[i]$; etc, but then you would still have to go via the names when getting the values referred to (which may take longer in some implementations). In the form of a constant, you have the desired values most readily at hand.

The importance of the constant declaration, however, is to be found at another level; in Chapter 1, we shall see that in all identity-declarations a constant is declared (see also 0.7 and 0.8), and the constant declaration is nothing more nor less than the life-line of the formal − actual correspondence.

0.6. A more involved program

Before embarking upon routines and other new modes that actually make the new language, it is worthwhile to dwell on the subject of primitive declarations and multiple values for just one section more. Many of the (until now only) newly dressed features of the language will be found in full swing in the more involved example E14 below. Although it is the program that matters here, it may acquire a not too artificial setting in the following context:

Suppose the input starts with an integral number n, which fixes the number of pairs of measurements following. The first **real** f of each pair is a factor, accounting for environmental influences on the target measurement, which is the second **real** x of the pair. There may be other (not measured) influences on x, which is why we are not particularly interested in the correlation of the two. We therefore confine ourselves to the computation of the mean, dispersion and momental skewness of the x's, weighted by the (more or less normal) distribution of the f's. Preceding the (f,x)-couples, but following n, we input another pair of **real**s *eps* and *ups*; all x's below *eps* or above *ups* are to be discarded as being certainly out of range (as a result of punching errors, for instance).

We briefly survey the program E14 (the numbers in the margin refer, as usual, to the linenumbers in the program text):

2---. In any place in a program text, even "inside" an identifier, comments may be inserted. A comment begins with the comment-symbol **comment** or ¢ and ends with the next occurring comment-symbol: ¢ *this is the beginning of a comment, and this is the end*: ¢ .

4,10,22. **for** *i* **to** *n* **do** (as well as **to** *n* **do** and **do** , see 0.3 and 0.5.3) is a specific case of the general construction:

for *i* **from** *start* **by** *step* **to** *stop* **while** *condition* **do** *doclause*

The controlled integral variable *i* is implicitly local to the construction (it has nothing to do with a possibly declared other *i*). If the controlled variable *i* does not occur in the *doclause*, then you may omit **for** *i*. If *start* is *1*, you may omit **from** *start*. If *step* is *1*, you may omit **by** *step*. If you do not want to stop at a certain value of *i*, you may omit **to** *stop* (see also E10*). If the condition is **true**, you may omit **while** *condition*.

22,28. You are allowed, at your own risk, to jump over declarations. Here it is harmless to do so, because we want to leave the doclause when *fi* = *0*. On purpose (to demonstrate the construction) we have not written down the most natural expression. A label has to be followed by a unit. Here we want to do "no action at all" after the label *finish:*. Therefore we write **skip**, the "dummy statement" in this language.

11,12,13.   The construction :   or, in the abbreviated notation:

          if *C1* **then** *C1true*   (*C1* | *C1true*
          elsf *C2* **then** *C2true* |: *C2* | *C2true*
          elsf *C3* **then** *C3true* |: *C3* | *C3true*
                    else *C3false* | *C3false*
          fi   )

is shorthand for the nested conditional-clauses:

          if *C1* **then** *C1true*
                    else **if** *C2* **then** *C2true*
                              else **if** *C3* **then** *C3true*
                                        else *C3false*
                                        fi
                              fi
          fi

There are many other convenient contractions of this kind, and not only for conditional-clauses (the repetitive statements, discussed under 4,10,22 in this section, may also be regarded as a kind of "contraction").

33–39. The statement *print* is a very accommodating output carrier. It accepts almost everything you may invent to output,

VERY INFORMAL INTRODUCTION TO ALGOL 68   Ch.0.6

be it a lay-out procedure like:	*new line*	,
or a string-denotation like:	*"number_of_measurements:_"*	,
or a variable like:	*n , below , above ,*	etc.
or a unit like:	*sqrt (varf)*	,
or a row-display of them all.		

1–40. In the example E14 we are very strict about the use of variables and constants: we never use a variable when a constant suffices (i.e. when we do not assign to it). Of course, you could declare all identifiers to possess variables; in some implementations, however, a constant declaration might be slightly more efficient. Pay also some attention to the use of comma-symbols (collateral elaboration of declarations and row-displays) and go-on-symbols (serial elaboration).

```
(E14)    begin
  2)        int   n ;           read (n) ;           ¢ number of measurements ¢
  3)        real  eps , ups ;   read ( (eps,ups) ) ; ¢ eps ≤ x[i] ≤ ups ¢
  4)        [1:n] real f , x ;  for i to n do
  5)                 read ( (¢factor¢ f[i] , ¢measurement¢ x[i] ) ) ;
  6)        int   below := 0, ¢ number of measurements rejected, too small ¢
  7)              above := 0, ¢ number of measurements rejected, too large ¢
  8)        real  Sf    := 0, ¢ Sum factors accepted ¢
  9)              Sf2   := 0; ¢ Sum squared factors accepted ¢
 10)        for i to n do ( real xi = x[i] ;
 11)                 Sf    plus   if xi<eps   then below plus 1 ; f[i] := 0
 12)                              elsf xi≤ups then f[i]
 13)                                          else above plus 1 ; f[i] := 0 fi ;
 14)                 Sf2   plus f[i] ↑ 2 ) ;
 15)        int   N = n − below − above ;
 16)        real  Af    = Sf / N ;              ¢ mean factor ¢
 17)        real  varf  = Sf2/N − Af×Af ;       ¢ variance of the factors ¢
 18)        real  W     := 0 ,   ¢ total Weight ¢
 19)              Swx   := 0 ,   ¢ Sum weighted measurements ¢
 20)              Swx2  := 0 ,   ¢ Sum squared weighted measurements ¢
 21)              Swx3  := 0 ;   ¢ Sum cubed  weighted measurements ¢
 22)        for i to n do ( real  fi = f[i] ; if fi = 0 then finish fi ;
 23)                        real  xi = x[i] , wi = exp ( −(fi−Af)↑2/(2×varf) ) ;
 24)                        real  wixi , wixi2 ;
 25)                        W     plus wi ;
 26)                        Swx   plus (wixi := wi × xi ) ;
 27)                        Swx2  plus (wixi2 := wixi × xi ) ;
 28)                        Swx3  plus  wixi2 × xi ;      finish: skip ) ;
```

29)   ¢   first   ,   second   ,   third   moment about 0   ¢
30)   real Ax = Swx /W , Ax2 = Swx2/W , Ax3 = Swx3/W ;
31)   real varx = Ax2 − Ax↑2 ; real sdx = sqrt (varx) ;
32)   real skx = (Ax3 − 3×Ax×Ax2 + 2×Ax↑3) / (2 × varx × sdx) ;
33)   print ((new line ,
34)   "number.of.measurements:." , n , "below:." , below , "above:." , above ,
35)   new line , new line ,
36)   "mean.factor:." , Af , "dispersion:." , sqrt (varf) ,
37)   new line , new line ,
38)   "normal.mean:." , Ax , "dispersion:." , sdx , "skewness:." , skx)
39)   )
40)   end

0.7. Routines and procedures

A concept of fundamental importance in programming is the "routine", a unit that can be activated from different places in the program, under different circumstances and in different incarnations when elaborated recursively. Moreover, routines may have a provision for formal-parameters, to which the actual-parameters are then supplied when the routine is activated.

Routines, and also their names, may be possessed by identifiers; we then speak about 'procedures'. In this language, a routine may also be possessed by an operator. Procedures and operators are to be distinguished in that they are declared and activated differently. We have procedure declarations (they are, however, nothing more than particular cases of identity-declarations) and we have operation-declarations in which operators are made to possess routines. Procedures are activated by "calling" them, and operators by applying them in formulae. In this section we shall consider procedures; for operators see 0.10.

0.7.1. Procedures without parameters

With the aid of the symbol **proc** we can derive new modes from already defined ones (as we did with the aid of the symbols [and] in 0.4). We thus obtain one of many possible **proc** modes, the simplest of which is the procedure-void (without parameters, not delivering any value).

Suppose we want to turn the algorithm E1* into a procedure. This algorithm is defined by a unit (a closed-clause); we declare it as a **proc** in the following way:

(E15)   **proc** E = ¢void¢ : (**real** x, y, z ; $read\,(\,(x,y)\,)$;
                    $print\,(\ z := (x+y)/2 - sqrt\,(x \times y)\,)$
) ;

In this identity-declaration, the identifier E is declared to possess (constantly, see also 0.5.5) a value of the mode **proc**. During elaboration of the declaration, the unit after ¢void¢ : is not elaborated. It is transformed into a routine, a piece of code which is equivalent to that very unit; the : preceding the open-symbol serves that purpose. You may conceive the function of the symbol : (in this syntactic position) as follows:

: makes of the unit it precedes a value, the mode of which is **proc** (procedure-void) .

The procedure E does something for you: it reads two numbers, does some computation with them and finally prints the result. However, it does not, and it cannot, deliver any value; E is declared to be a procedure delivering void. To emphasize this fact, we inserted the comment ¢void¢ in front of the : .

For those who are accustomed to the "procedure body" (a well known concept in some other programming languages), the alternative writing:

(E15*)   **proc** E = ¢void¢ :   **begin**   **real** x, y, z ;
                            $read\,(\,(x,y)\,)$;
                            $print\,(\ z := (x+y)/2 - sqrt\,(x \times y)\,)$
                        end ;

may be more familiar.

Within the context of the declaration E15, we can call this procedure. Consider:

(E16)   **begin**   **int** n ; $read\,(n)$; **to** n **do** E **end**

Right after **do** we find E. By virtue of its declaration, E is a unit of the mode **proc**. The elaboration of a unit of the mode **proc** is (in this syntactic position) the elaboration of the unit it possesses. Therefore, the piece of program above is, at least in its effect, equivalent to E3* (see 0.3).

We often want a procedure to deliver a value. For example, E could do just a little more and yield the value printed. Inside the closed-clause this value is referred to by $\hat{z}$. We already know how to get a closed-clause to deliver a specific value (0.5.4). Now, by prefacing it with **real** : , we arrive at the declaration of a **proc real** :

(E17)   **proc real** Ez = **real** : (**real** x , y , z ; read ((x,y)) ;
                      print (z := (x+y)/2 − sqrt (x×y)) ;
                      z) ;

The mode **proc real** is derived from **real** as, for instance, was $[1:n]$ **real** . The function of **real** : (in this syntactic position) may be conceived as follows:

real : makes of the unit it precedes a value, the mode of which is **proc real** (procedure-real) .

Within the context of E17, it is not difficult to understand the effect of the following piece of program:

(E18)   **begin**   **int** n ; read (n) ;
                int less := 0 , morequal := 0 ;
                to n **do** (print (newline) ; Ez < 1 | less | morequal) **plus** 1 ;
                print ((newline , newline , less, morequal))
        end

The Ez in the formula $Ez < 1$ is a unit of the mode **proc real**. The elaboration of a **proc real** unit is (in this syntactic position) the elaboration of the routine it possesses; that routine yields a **real** value, and consequently Ez yields that **real** value.

0.7.2. Procedures with parameters, routine denotations

Even more important than procedures without, are procedures with formal-parameters. The actual-parameters are then supplied when the procedure is called, as we have already done on several occasions when calling the standard procedures read , print and sqrt .

We now declare an identifier D to possess a procedure with two **real** parameters delivering a **real** value, a **proc** (**real** , **real**) **real** :

(E19)   **proc**(**real**,**real**)**real** D =   (**real** a , **real** b) **real** : (a+b)/2 − sqrt(a×b) ;

This is, indeed, a tedious expression. Fortunately, it is full of redundancies and may be (and, of course, always is) abbreviated to a more appetizing one:

(E19*) **proc** D = (**real** a , b) **real** :   (a+b)/2 − sqrt (a×b) ;
1		2
3

1. This is the formal-parameters-pack. The formal-parameters *a* and *b* are both specified to be of mode **real**. The actual-parameters have to match this mode. There are, however, certain facilities in this respect. If, for instance, the name of a **real** is supplied, then its value will be taken; if an **int** is supplied, then it will be transformed into a **real**.

2. The prefix **real** : requires that the routine is to deliver a **real** value, when elaborated.

3. The whole sequence of symbols to the right of the equals-symbol = is a 'routine denotation'. It denotes a routine in much the same way as, for instance, *3.1415927* denotes a certain **real** value. The routine denoted is equivalent to some closed-clause with a provision for (in this case) two **real** parameters. This equivalence, and in particular the elaboration of a call in which the actual parameters are then supplied to match these formal-parameters, is the subject matter of 1.2.3 and 4.2.2.2. It will suffice, here, to state that *a* and *b* , as formally declared in our example E19, will be **real** constants in the routine (when, for instance, *x* and *y* are supplied as actual-parameters, then the constant declarations **real** *a = x* , *b = y* ; will be elaborated). That is to say, the actual-parameters are elaborated once, to supply their **real** values. In other programming languages this phenomenon may be known as "call by value" (see also 0.8.2 and 0.8.4).

Within the context of the declaration E19, the algorithm E1, for example, could be programmed in the following way:

(E20)   **begin**   **real** *x* , *y* , *z* ; *read ((x,y))* ;
　　　　　　 print (z := D(x,y))
　　　 end

The assignment E11 (see 0.5.4) could look like:

(E11*)   *p := (* **real** *x* , *y* , *z* ;
　　　　　 to *n* **do** *(read ((x,y))* ;
　　　　　　　　 if *D(x,y) > 1* **then** *stop* **fi** *)* ;   *false* .
　　　　　 stop: *print ((x,y))* ;　　　　　　　　 *true)*

An example of a procedure with a parameter not delivering a value is:

(E21)   **proc** *skip* = *(* **int** *n)* :
　　　　　　　　 (**real** *x* ; **to** *n* **do** *read (x))* ;

which skips *n* numbers on the input tape. To emphasize the fact that *skip* yields void (does not deliver a value) we may insert the comment ¢**void**¢ :

(E21*) proc *skip* = (int *n*) ¢void¢ : (real *x* ; to *n* do *read (x)*) ;

See also Appendix 4 (superlanguage features).

0.7.3. Examples of procedure declarations

We have four kinds of procedures:

1) without parameters, not delivering any value (procedure-void) ;
2) without parameters,   delivering a   value ;
3) with   parameters, not delivering any value ;
4) with   parameters,   delivering a   value .

Examples:

    proc *skiptozero* =   ¢void¢ : (real *x* := *1* ;
                                          while *x* ǂ *0* do *read (x)*)

¢ *which was a* proc ¢ ;
    proc *nexttozero* =   real : (*skiptozero* ;
                                          real *x* ; *read (x)* ; *x*)

¢ *which was a* proc real ¢ ;
    proc *skipto*   = (real *a*) ¢void¢ : (real *x* := *a*−*1* ;
                                        while *x* ǂ *a* do *read (x)*)

¢ *which was a* proc (real) ¢ ;
    proc *nextto*   = (real *a*)   real : (*skipto (a)* ;
                                          real *x* ; *read (x)* ; *x*)

¢ *which was a* proc(real) real ¢ ;

In the standard prelude of the language, we find declarations for the proc (real) reals *sqrt* , *exp* , *ln* (the natural logarithm), *cos* , *arccos* , *sin* , *arcsin* , *tan* , *arctan* . Moreover there is a proc real *random*, which delivers the next pseudo-random real value after *last random*, from a uniformly distributed sequence on the interval [0,1) (i.e. $0 \leq random < 1$); to this proc real belongs the real variable *last random* which is initialized to the value *0.5*. Finally we find in the standard prelude a constant declaration real *pi* = c *a* real *value close to* π c . (See 1.3.2 for the significance of the special comment-symbol c).

To these we subjoin:

(D4)   proc *ncos* = (int *i*) real : *cos (2×pi×i/n)* ; ¢ *a* proc (int) real ¢
           proc *nsin* = (int *i*) real : *sin (2×pi×i/n)* ; ¢ *a* proc (int) real ¢
           real *e* = c *a* real *value close to the base of natural logarithms*,
                  i.e. 2.718281828459045 c ;

Another example of a **proc/int/real** declaration is:

(E22) **proc** *fac* = *(* **int** *n)* **real** :
          if $n > nmaxfac$
          then *faclarge (n)*
          else **int** $f := 1$;
                for *i* **from** 2 **to** *n* **do** *f* **times** *i* ; *f*
          fi ;

where *nmaxfac* is an implementation dependent integral constant which is related to *maxint* in the following way:

(E22*) **int** *nmaxfac* = *(* **int** $n, f := 1$;
                    for *i* **while** $f \leq maxint \div i$ **do** *(* $n := i$; *f* **times** *n* *)* ; *n* *)*;

and *faclarge* is another   **proc/int/real**

(E22**) **proc** *faclarge* = *(* **int** *n)* **real** :
              c *depending on nmaxfac* :
              stirlings formula with correction factor ,
              sqrt ($2 \times pi \times n$) × *(n/e)* ↑ *n* × *corr (n)*
              or some series expansion for 1 / gamma (n) ;
              see "Handbook of Mathematical Functions"
              edited by Milton Abramowitz and I.E. Stegun
              Sections 6.1.37/38 and 6.1.34 **c** ;

The **proc/int/real** *fac* , as declared in E22, attempts to deliver the exact **real** equivalent of *n*! as long as this value remains $\leq maxint$ (the critical value of *n* is possessed by the constant *nmaxfac*); otherwise, a **proc/int/real** *faclarge* is called to give a reasonable approximation.

Formal-parameters may be of any mode and procedures may deliver a value of any mode. The time has not yet come for the more arresting examples, which is why we confine ourselves to two simple ones. Both of them will put in another appearance in 0.8.2, because their efficiency can be improved. The starred example numbers refer to the unstarred numbers in Section 0.8.2.

(E26*) **proc** *maxindex* = *(* [1:] **real** *a)* **int** :
                      (**int** $j := 1$;
                      for *i* **from** 2 **to** *upb a* **do**
                      if $a[i] > a[j]$ **then** $j := i$ **fi** ; *j* *)*;

In E26* we see the declaration of a procedure with a row-of-real parameter, delivering an **int**, a **proc/[ ]real/int** ; *maxindex* delivers the index of the maximal element in a given row (if there are more "maximal elements", then the lowest of their indices is delivered).

Ch.0.8   VERY INFORMAL INTRODUCTION TO ALGOL 68   31

In a formal-parameter it is allowable to omit one or more bounds; the actual-parameter then may have any value in this bound (this has nothing to do with flexible bounds: if a bound in a formal-parameter is not specified, this simply means that the value of this bound is dictated by the actual-parameter; if, to the contrary, the formal-parameter specifies a bound, then the actual-parameter has to match that value, if not, an error message may follow).

The monadic operators **upb** and **lwb** yield the (actual) values of the upper-bound and lower-bound respectively; being declared in the standard-prelude of the language, they are permanently built in and are applicable to all kinds of multiples. If they are applied to a multidimensional multiple, they are dyadic operators (so that, for instance, 2 **upb** $x2$ yields the second upper-bound of the row-of-row-of-real $x2$).

In E26* the lower-bound is specified to be 1 and the actual row has to match this requirement; therefore, inside the routine the lower-bound is known to be 1. The value of the upper-bound, on the contrary, is not specified; inside the routine its actual value is yielded by the formula **upb** a .

The **proc**(**char**,**string**)**bool** *match* , declared below, delivers **true** if the character formally possessed by c occurs in the given **string**; if not, then the value of *match* will be **false**. In this routine we make use of a completer (see 0.5.4):

(E27*)   **proc** *match* = (**char** c , **string** s) **bool** :
           (**for** i **to upb** s **do**
            if $c = s[i]$ **then** *yes* **fi** ; *no*:   **false exit**
                             yes: **true**   ) ;

0.8. The creation of new modes, names and values referred to

It is time to reconsider the identity-declaration:

(E23)   **real** x ;

because it is not so innocent as it looks.

You might already have suspected this, knowing what its elaboration achieves (see 0.1):

a location for a **real** value is reserved in the memory
of our computer (on the stack);
this **real** value is referred to by a name x̂
(i.e. its address);
this name x̂ is now in the program text possessed by
the identifier x .

In the program text, the identifier x thus represents a **real** variable, which is a **real** value associated with the name referring to it. What is "variable", of course, is not the name (the location, the address) but the value referred to. The name cannot be changed by the program, it is possessed by x and this relation is an indissoluble alliance. Nevertheless, a "name" is a value as well, and consequently it must have a mode. The mode, then, of the name x̂ is **ref real** (reference-to-real).

The symbol **ref** plays a role in declarations as do the symbols [and] and **proc** (and some others which we shall meet soon): they assist in the creation of new modes. We now come to the unmasking of E23. It is a "contraction" (abbreviation) of:

(E23*)   **ref real** x = **loc real** ;

which expresses more strictly what happens during the elaboration of the declaration:

the identifier x is made to possess a **ref real**
(the name of a **real**) which refers to a **real** value
on the stack which is to have a **loc**al "scope" determined by the
range in which E23* occurs.

The point to remember in E23 is the hidden fact (unfolded by E23*) that, on declaring a variable, two values are involved:

1)   a **ref real** which is constantly possessed by the identifier,
      but refers to

2)   a   **real** which is variable.

By E23* (or E23 which is the abbreviated form of E23*), a **real** value is generated on the stack. The **loc real** to the right of the equal-symbol is termed a "local generator". Getting ahead of Section 1.2.2.3 we may depict this generation happening as follows (see also 0.12.1):

Ch.0.8   VERY INFORMAL INTRODUCTION TO ALGOL 68   33

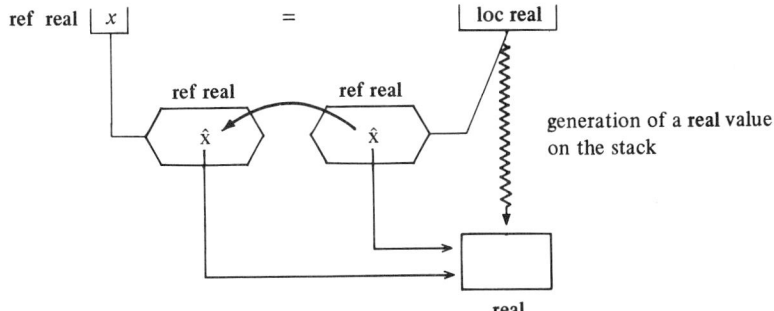

The result of this generation process is:

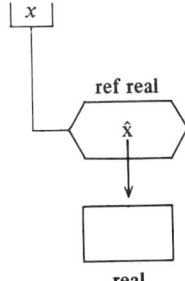

which is the same as the situation depicted in 0.1. For a more systematic treatment see Chapter 1.

The result of the declarations E12 and E12* (see 0.5.5) can be depicted as follows:

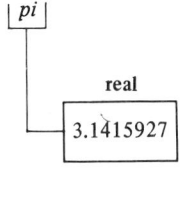 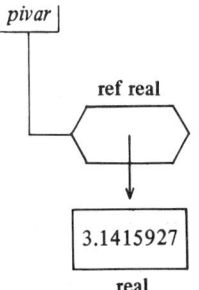

To *pi* no other value can be assigned, *pi* being a constant.

To *pivar* any other value can be assigned, *pivar* being a variable.

0.8.1. Identity declarations in the strict language

The contraction E23 of E23* is, of course, introduced because exactly this kind of identity-declaration occurs most frequently in programs. Moreover E23 is the manner after which this kind of declaration is written down in most existing programming languages.

Nevertheless, E23* is the proper sequence of symbols as defined by the syntax of this language; it is a phrase in the "strict language" (the language defined by the syntax). E23 is its equivalent phrase in the "extended language", which is brought into existence mainly to facilitate the programmer's life. We shall for all practical purposes be using the extended language. You should, however, always bear in mind the strict form of any extension (which, by the way, is in most cases an abbreviation):

extended language :	strict language :
bool p ;	**ref bool** p = **loc bool** ;
int n ;	**ref int** n = **loc int** ;
real x, y ;	**ref real** x = **loc real** ,
	ref real y = **loc real** ;
char c ;	**ref char** c = **loc char** ;
$[1:n]$ **real** $x1$;	**ref** [**either** : **either**] **real** $x1$ = **loc** $[1:n]$ **real** ;

(for the mysteries of **either**, see 2.5.2.1)

string s ;	**ref string** s = **loc string** ;
	which develops into:
	ref [**either** : **either**] **char** s = **loc** [1 : 0 **flex**] **char** ;
real $pivar := 3.1415927$;	**ref real** $pivar$ = (**loc real** $:= 3.1415927$) ;
real pi $= 3.1415927$;	**real** $pi = 3.1415927$;

The declaration of a constant is the same in the extended as in the strict language, being already in the fundamental form of an identity-declaration.

proc $sinh$ =	**proc** (**real**) **real** $sinh$ =
(**real** a) **real** :	((**real** a) **real** :
$(exp(a) - exp(-a))/2$;	$(exp(a) - exp(-a))/2$) ;

0.8.2. Procedures, values and references

One of the implications of the extremely fruitful concept of a reference ("name") as a mode in this language is that we have been given a quite natural way of declaring (amongst many other very useful constructions):

I   variable procedures,
II   formal-parameters which refer to, rather than possess, the values which are topical ("actual") when the procedure will be called,
III   procedures delivering a name (a reference to a value).

We discuss briefly these three applications of the concept of a name by giving some examples.

I)

By declaring:

(E24)   **mode fun = proc (real) real ;**
               fun f **;**

the identifier f is declared to be a variable **fun** (to possess the name referring to a routine of the mode **proc(real)real**). E24 is the contraction of the strict form:

(E24*)   **ref fun** f **= loc fun ;**

which develops into:

        ref proc (real) real f **= loc proc (real) real ;**

Within the context of this declaration, we may assign any **fun** routine to this **fun** variable. For example:

        $f := ln$

Now the call:

        $y := f(x)$ is the call $y := ln(x)$

while after the assignment:

        $f :=$ **(real** a**) real** $: a \times ln(a) - a$

the same call becomes:

        $y := x \times ln(x) - x$

II)

Even more important is the specification of a formal-parameter to be a name:

(E25)   **proc** *readf* = (**ref real** *a*) **real** : (*read(a)* ; *a* := *f(a)*) ;

E25 declares the formal-parameter to be a **ref real** (the name of a **real**) to which, consequently, a **real** value can be assigned. This happens two times in the procedure: first the value of the number read is assigned to *a* (by the call of the procedure *read*), and then the *f* of that value is assigned to *a*. If we now call this procedure, for example:

$$y := readf(x) - y$$

then the formal — actual correspondence results in:

ref real *a* = *x* ;

i.e. the formal name *â* is made to refer to the same **real** value as the actual name *x̂*. The call *readf(x)* thus results in assigning to *x* the *f* of the value read. Which **fun** is then applied depends (in the context of E24) on the **fun** assigned to *f*.

In other programming languages, a **ref** parameter may be known as an "output parameter". In contradistinction to the more or less domesticated term "call by value" in ALGOL 60 (see 0.7.2), this could be termed "call by reference". For an equivalent of the ALGOL 60 term "call by name" see 0.8.4.

We are now in a position to improve on the examples at the end of 0.7.3. The effect there was that value parameters require a copy of the actual rows to be made on the stack. We shall now show how to do this better:

(E26)   **proc** *maxindex* = (**ref** [*1*:] **real** *a*) **int** :
       (**int** *j* := *1* ;
       for *i* **from** *2* **to upb** *a* **do**
       if *a*[*i*] > *a*[*j*] **then** *j* := *i* **fi** ; *j*) ;

Now, in the call *maxindex(x1)* , only the name *x̂1* is given to the procedure: **ref** [*1*:] **real** *a* = *x1* . The access to the [ ] **real** referred to by *x̂1* thus runs via the formal name *â* to that very [ ] **real** and not (was the case in 0.7.3) to a copy of it.

(E27)   **proc** *match* = (**char** *c* , **ref string** *s*) **bool** :
       (**for** *i* **to upb** *s* **do**
       if *c* = *s* [*i*] **then** *yes* **fi** ; *no*: **false** .
            yes: **true**) ;

Now, in the call *match("?", text)* , in the context of the declaration **string** *text*, the character *"?"* is copied onto the stack, but the name *text* is given to the procedure instead of a copy of its value.

III)

An example of a procedure delivering a name is:

(D5)   **proc ref real** *xory* = **ref real** : **if** *random* $<$ *0.5* **then** *x* **else** *y* **fi** ;

If we now assign:

    xory := *3.1415927*

then it depends on the value delivered by *random* to what destination we actually assigned.

A more substantial example is:

(E28)   **proc** *maxelmnt* = (**ref** [*1*:] **real** *a*) **ref real** :
                                (**int** *j* := *1* ;
                                for *i* **from** *2* **to upb** *a* **do**
                                if *a*[*i*] $>$ *a*[*j*] **then** *j* := *i* **fi** ; *a*[*j*]) ;

Compare E28 with E26. In E28, *â*[*j*] is a name referring to a maximal element of the actual row, when the procedure is called. If you want to assign a new value to the maximal element of, for instance, the row *x1*, then you could do it by a call of *maxindex* :

    x1 [*maxindex(x1)*] := *y*

but also, and more directly, by a call of *maxelmnt* :

    maxelmnt(x1) := *y*

0.8.3. The switch

In most programming languages you will find some provision "to compute a label". Let

    L1: , *L2*: , *L3*: , *L4*: , *L5*: , --- , *here*: , *there*: , *again*: , *alarm*:

be labels. Then you may want to compute an **int** *i* which decides to which label you shall jump. In this language you will not find a specific feature of this kind; it is, however, all in the game of **procs** and names of **procs**.

Suppose you want to compute a jump to one of the five labels *L1*: , --- , *L5*: . Then you may declare a row of 5 **procs** *switch* :

(E29)   [1:5] **proc** *switch* = (**goto** *L1* , **goto** *L2* , **goto** *L3* , **goto** *L4* , **goto** *L5*) ;

which may be abbreviated (the **goto** being a redundant symbol in this language) to:

(E29*)   [1:5] **proc** *switch* = (*L1* , *L2* , *L3* , *L4* , *L5*) ;

The expression to the right of the = is a row-display of **proc**s, which is (by virtue of E29) constantly possessed by the row-of-procedure-identifier *switch*. Consequently, a call:

switch [*i*]

results in a call of the *i*th element of this row, the elaboration of which is a jump to the *i*th label. If for instance *i* = *3*, then the call *switch* [*i*] results in:

goto *L3*

However, in this language an identifier may be declared to refer to a value of any mode, in particular to a [ ] **proc**. Moreover, a row may be declared to have a flexible upper-bound (see 0.4.3 on **string**s). Putting these two concepts together, we arrive at the following useful construction:

(E30)   **mode switch** = [*1:0* **flex**] **proc** ;
    switch *hop* , *skip* , *jump* ;

All three identifiers then possess **ref switch**es (**switch** variables), to which any row of jumps may be assigned. For example:

hop := (*L1* , *L2* , *L3* , *L4* , *L5*) ;
skip := (*L1* , *L5*) ;
jump := (*here* , *there* , *again*) ;

Now, if again *i* = *3*, the call:

hop [*i*]   results in   **goto** *L3* ,
skip [*i*]   results in (as you may hope) some error message,
           i being out of the range of the [*1:2*] **proc**
           possessed by the row-display *(L1,L5)* ,
jump [*i*]   results in   **goto** *again* .

We may, however, assign other values to *hop* , *skip* and *jump* ; or to their elements. For example:

jump [*3*] := *here* ;
skip := *hop* ;
hop [*2:4*] := *jump* ;

Ch.0.8.4   VERY INFORMAL INTRODUCTION TO ALGOL 68   39

After these assignments, supposing again that $i = 3$, the call:

    hop [*i*]   results in   **goto** *there* ,
    skip [*i*]   results in   **goto** *L3* ,
    jump [*i*]   results in   **goto** *here* .

Pay some attention to the assignment:

    jump [*3*] := *here*

The elaboration of this assignment ensures that *here* will be assigned to *jump* [*3*] as a value of the mode **proc** (in much the same way as in E15, for instance, the routine was not elaborated). For further discussion of this rather delicate matter see 5.2.1.

To an element of a **ref switch**, you may assign any **proc** (not necessarily as simple as an unconditional jump); for example:

(E31)   *hop* [*2*] := ¢**void**¢ : (**int** *n* ; *read(n)* ;
              if *n* = *0* **then** *print* ("*value_read_was_0...*
                      we_start_again") ;
                  goto *again*
              else *print (n)* ;
                  (*n* ≤ *5* | *skip* [*n*] | *alarm*)
            fi)

0.8.4. Procedures as formal parameters

Compare:

(E32)   **proc** *choice1* = (**real** *a)* ¢**void**¢ : (*a* < *0.5* | *x* **plus** *a* | *y* **plus** *a*) ;
            choice1 (random)

with:

(E33)   **proc** *choice2* = (**proc real** *a)* ¢**void**¢ : (*a* < *0.5* | *x* **plus** *a* | *y* **plus** *a*) ;
            choice2 (random)

In the call *choice1 (random)*, the identity-declaration **real** *a* = *random* will be elaborated. Hence, the **proc real** *random* is called only once and its value (< *0.5* or ≥ *0.5*) is added to *x* or to *y*.

In the call *choice2 (random)*, the identity-declaration **proc real** *a* = *random* will be elaborated. Hence, the **proc real** *random* is inside the routine possessed by *a* and will be called once in the condition and again in the then-clause or in the else-clause, depending on the value yielded by the condition (i.e. *random* will be called twice in E33).

The construction E33 is similar to what in ALGOL 60 is known as "call by name"; it has, nevertheless, nothing to do with the concept of a name in ALGOL 68 (in which it is an application of the principle that any mode may occur in a formal-parameter, in particular also a **proc real**).

Compare also:

(E32*)   *choice1 (x−y+ncos(k))*

and:

(E33*)   *choice2 (x−y+ncos(k))*   ¢ see D4 in 0.7.3 ¢

In E32*, the formula $x-y+ncos(k)$ will be elaborated once in the elaboration of the identity-declaration **real** $a = x-y+ncos(k)$. Depending on the condition, this value (inside the routine possessed by *a*) will be added to *x* or to *y*, so that the result of the call will be:

$x := x + a$ i.e. $x := x +$ ¢ the value of ¢ $x-y+ncos(k)$

or

$y := y + a$ i.e. $y := y +$ ¢ the value of ¢ $x-y+ncos(k)$

In E33*, on the contrary, the formula $x-y+ncos(k)$ will be transformed into a **proc real** (we call this "proceduring", see 4.2.2.1) and as such it will (inside the routine) be possessed by the **proc real** identifier *a*. Hence, the formula will be elaborated twice (once in the condition and again in the then-clause or in the else-clause). The two successive elaborations, however, yield the same value, which is why the two calls E32* and E33* have the same result (though E32* is the more efficient one).

However, compare now:

(E32**)   *choice1 (x − y + ncos(k* **plus** *1))*

and:

(E33**)   *choice2 (x − y + ncos(k* **plus** *1))*

Each elaboration of the formula $x - y + ncos(k$ **plus** $1)$ has a side effect on *k* ($k := k+1$) and therefore the two calls will not have the same result; in E32** the formula being elaborated once, and in E33** twice.

Another construction in which we find a procedure as formal-parameter (in ALGOL 60 circles known as "Jensen's device") is:

(E34) proc SIGMA = (ref int i, int a, b, proc real fi) real :
                   (real value := 0 ;
                     for k from a to b do
                     (i := k ; value plus fi) ;
                     value) ;

calls of which may be:

$$y := SIGMA\ (\ j\ ,\ 1\ ,\ n\ ,\ x1\ [j]\ )\ ;$$
$$y := SIGMA\ (\ j\ ,\ -m\ ,\ +m\ ,\ ncos(j)\ )$$

A call of *SIGMA* assigns to the **ref int** formal-parameter i ; i.e. the two calls have a side effect on the **ref int** actual-parameter j. In the first call the unit $x1\ [j]$, in the second call the unit $ncos(j)$ will be transformed into a **proc real** (will be "procedured").

A more or less equivalent construction in this language is:

(E34*) proc SUM = (int a, b, proc(int)real fun) real :
                   (real value := 0 ;
                     for i from a to b do value plus fun(i) ;
                     value) ;

calls of which may be:

$$y := SUM\ (\ 1\ ,\ n\ ,\ (\text{int}\ j)\ \text{real} : x1\ [j]\ )\ ;$$
$$y := SUM\ (\ -m\ ,\ +m\ ,\ ncos\ )$$

It is worth your while to find out why we have to give the **proc(int)real** denotation *(int j)real: x1[j]* as actual-parameter in the first call, and why *ncos* would do in the second call. Compare also the calls of *SIGMA*.

0.8.5. Pointers (variable names)

Until now, names have always appeared as being constantly possessed by identifiers. By:

real x ;

or, in the strict form:

ref real x = loc real ;

we declared x to possess constantly a **ref real** (the name of a **real**). Only the **real** value referred to could be changed and never the name $\hat{x}$.

You may, however, also want to declare identifiers to possess variable names, i.e. references to names. It may be clear immediately that such an identifier will then possess a reference-to-reference. We thus declare:

(D6)   **ref real** *xx* , *yy* ;

or, in the strict form:

(D6*)   **ref ref real** *xx* = **loc ref real** ,
        ref ref real *yy* = **loc ref real** ;

This collateral declaration generates on the stack two **ref real**s (two locations for names of **real**s), which simply means that via such values on the stack you can refer to other values (**real**s):

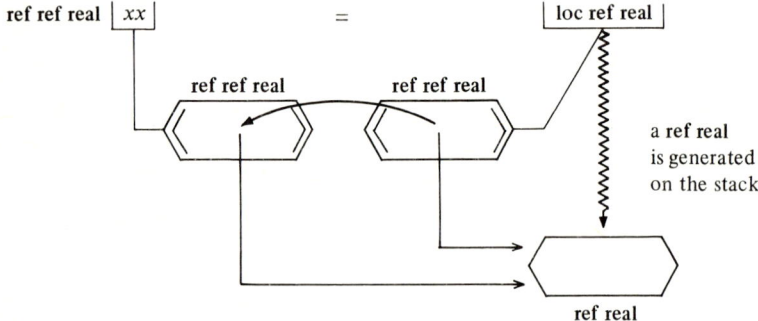

The result of D6(*) is:

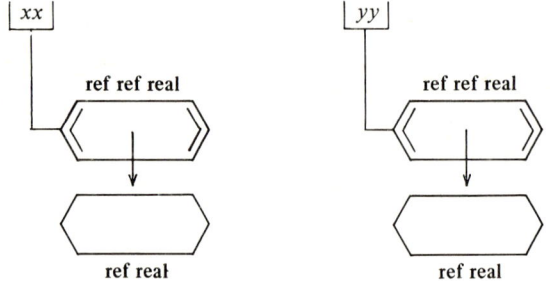

Consider now:

(E35)   *xx* := *y*

After this assignment, the value of *xx* (i.e. the **ref real** referred to by x̂x̂) is the name ŷ (i.e. the **ref real** possessed by *y*):

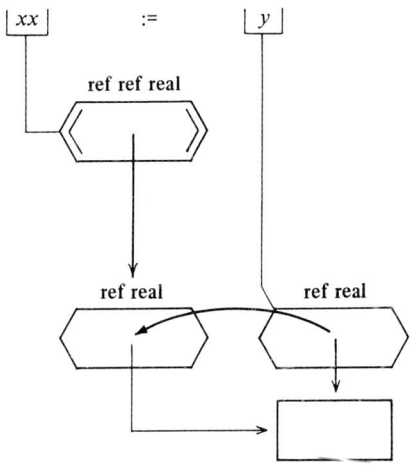

Observe that an assignment always takes place at the highest level possible. Now the call:

$y := sqrt(xx)$

results in: $y := sqrt(y)$, while after the assignation:

(E35*) $xx := x$

the same call results in

$y := sqrt(x)$

In computer oriented programming this is known as "indirect addressing" (in a certain location in the memory one finds the address of another value). In some other programming languages (in particular in assembly languages) a **ref ref** may be known as a "pointer" (i.e. by D6, *xx* and *yy* possess "pointers" to **real** variables, addresses of addresses of **real** values).

0.8.6. Identity relators, the cast, coercion

Where names are values in this language and may be manipulated as all other values (see 0.8.5), you may want to ask whether two names of the same mode are the same name. Neither the equals-symbol = , nor its negation ≠ can serve this purpose, because they are operators defined to compare values of certain modes only (and these values are mostly not names). To compare names, we have the identity-relators :=: (or **is**) and :≠: (or **isnt**). For example, after the assignation:

$$y := x$$

it is most certainly **true** that

$$y = x$$

but it is also **true** that nevertheless:

(E36) y **isnt** x or $y :\neq: x$

because y and x possess different names (references to different locations on the stack).

(E37*) y **is** x **or** y or $y :=: x$ **or** y

however, is **true** or **false** depending on the value lastly yielded by random (see D5 in 0.8.2) and independently of whether $y = x$ or $y \neq x$.

Observe also that after the assignations:

$$xx := y \ ; \ yy := xx$$

or, in one phrase:

$$yy := xx := y$$

nevertheless:

$$yy :\neq: xx \quad \text{or} \quad yy \ \textbf{isnt} \ xx$$

because yy and xx possess different names (the mode of which is **ref ref real**); reconsider E36 and its motivation.

One might now be disappointed that after the assignation $yy := xx := y$, nevertheless yy **isnt** xx. In the nature of things it must be possible to get an answer to whether names assigned to different pointers are the same. But then the right question must be asked, and this question lies one level of reference below the question $yy :=: xx$.

We could go down one level in reference by declaring, for instance, the **proc/ref ref real/ref real**

proc *the name assigned to* = *(***ref ref real** *aa)* **ref real**: *aa* ;

and then we get undoubtedly the proper answer when we call this procedure to the left and to the right of the identity-relator:

the name assigned to (xx) :=: *the name assigned to (yy)*

The **ref real**: in front of the reference-to-reference-to-real-unit *aa* "coerces"

Ch.0.9   VERY INFORMAL INTRODUCTION TO ALGOL 68   45

this unit to deliver its reference-to-real value. Fortunately, it is not necessary to declare such a monstrosity of a procedure. You may write:

(E38)   *(*ref real: *xx)* :=: *(*ref real: *yy)*

The technical term for **ref real**: followed by a unit, is 'cast'; the reference-to-real-cast of that unit. A cast, in general, coerces the unit it precedes to deliver a value of the mode it dictates (if possible). It is worthwhile to reconsider now the function of the prefix **real**: in E19* (in Section 0.7.1). We have already made frequent use of casts in routine-denotations, when we dictated the mode of the value to be delivered.

The cast may also be used to assign a value to the name assigned to a pointer:

(E39)   *(*ref real: *xx)* := *y*

comes, in the context of E35*, to the same as:

$$x := y$$

You might ask now why we did not meet the cast at a much earlier stage; why, for example, we did not have to write:

$a := ($real: $b)$, which, by the way, is correct ALGOL 68

The answer is that in all current situations where it is clear from the context what you want, your computer will be so kind as to coerce your units to your will. As a matter of fact, "coercion" is the technical term for the provision that:

> when no ambiguities make trouble,
> your units will be implicitly coerced to the mode you
> apparently require.

The time has not yet come to discuss all the slings and arrows of coercion. Here we set a pointer to 1.1.6 and another one to 5.1.0.

0.9. The creation of new modes, structures

Besides the multiple, you will find in this language another system that gives you control of a collection of values, and that is in the form of a structured value (or "structure" for short). The individual values in a multiple are its "elements", the individual values in a structure are its "fields". The elements in a multiple are all of the same mode, $[1:n]$ **real** , $[1:0$ **flex**$]$ **char** ,

[*1:5*] **proc** etc.; the fields of a structure on the contrary may be of different modes, although there are very useful (even standard) applications where the field modes are the same.

0.9.1. **complex** values, vectors etc.

By declaring:

(D7)   **mode compl** = **struct** (**real** *re* , *im*);   ¢ another built in mode, like **string** ¢

or:

   mode compl = **struct** (**real** *re* , **real** *im*) ;   ¢ the strict form ¢

or:

   struct compl = (**real** *re* , *im*);   ¢ another contraction ¢

a new mode **compl** (complex) is defined consisting of two **real** values; one of them is selected by the field-selector *re*, the other by *im*. Although field-selectors look the same as identifiers, you must not confuse them.

Now the identity-declarations:

(D8)   **compl** *w* , *z* ;

declare *w* and *z* to possess the names *ŵ* and *ẑ* which refer to structures as defind in D7 (i.e. *w* and *z* are **compl** variables).

The fields of *w* and *z* (the real and imaginary part of these complex variables) may be selected as follows:

(E40)   *x* := *re* **of** *z* ; *y* := *im* **of** *z* ;

The *re* **of** and *im* **of** select the field in much the same way as, for instance, [*i*] , [*i,j*] etc. select the element in a multiple. There is, however, an important distinction: the selection of a field may be done at compile time, whilst the selection of an element in a multiple usually involves computation and, consequently, can then only be done at run time.

After the declarations D8, the identifiers *w* and *z* possess **ref compl**s; the situation may be depicted as follows:

Ch.0.9.1   VERY INFORMAL INTRODUCTION TO ALGOL 68   47

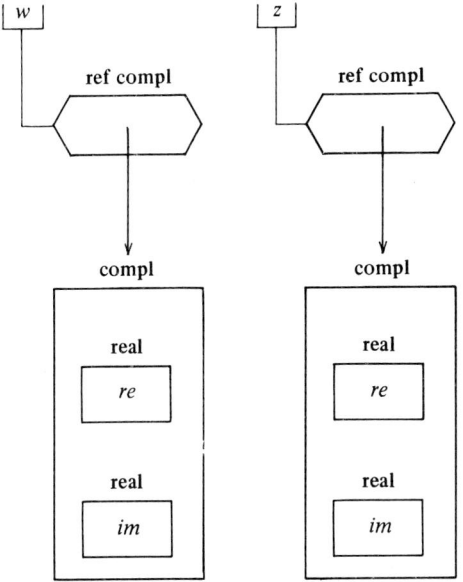

The result of the assignation:

$z := w$

should be obvious. You may, however, also assign:

(E41) $z := (x , y)$

which amounts to:

re **of** $z := x$, im **of** $z := y$

The (x , y) in this context is a structure-display, the counterpart of a row-display.

The mode **compl** is built into the standard declarations of the language, and operators = , ≠ , + , − , × , / , ↑ , and a monadic operator **conj** are declared for it with the meanings to be expected. Moreover, we have (monadic) operators **re** , **im** and **abs** which deliver a **real** when applied to a **compl** , and an operator ⊥ (or **i**), which may be pronounced as plus-i-times, which makes a **compl** of two **real** operands:

$z := x \perp y$ or $z := x$ **i** y

amounts to:

$$z := (x, y)$$

(see also 0.10.4).

As from **int** to **real**, there is automatic "widening" from **real** to **compl** (and via **real**, from **int** to **compl**). The assignation:

$$z := x := i := 1$$

results in $i = 1$, $x = 1.0$, $z = (1.0, 0.0)$

Other examples of new modes defined by structures with fields of the same mode might be:

(D9)   **mode vec** = **struct** (**real** *xcoord*, *ycoord*, *zcoord*) ;
        mode rational = **struct** (**int** *numerator*, *denominator*) ;
        vec *v1*, *v2*, *v3* ;
        rational *r1*, *r2*, *r3* ;

These modes, however, are not built into the standard declarations. If you want to use them for new kinds of operands, then you have to declare operators for them; this can easily be done (see 0.10.7, 8.4.1 and 8.4.2).

0.9.2. bits and bytes

In the standard declarations you will also find:

(D10)   **mode bits** = **struct** ([1 : *bits width*] **bool X**) ;
        mode bytes = **struct** ([1 : *byteswidth*] **char X**) ;

Here we have a structure with only one field, a row-of-boolean and a row-of-character respectively. Moreover, the field-selector makes a queer face in both structures: the **X** is an (abortive) attempt to print an unprintable letter, which has been invented specially to prevent you from actually selecting the field (in particular the elements of the row) on your own account.

The point is that both **bits** and **bytes** are defined to enable the programmer to take advantage of certain (hardware-) features of the machine on which the language is implemented. A **bits** will be something pretty close to a machine word and the environment enquiry *bits width* is then the wordlength. A **bytes** may be a memory unit in which a certain number of characters can efficiently be stored; a **bytes** may be considered as a string of fixed length *bytes width*.

Operators are defined for **bits** and **bytes** reflecting the most current machine operations.

For **bits** we have = and ≠ to compared them, and ∨ (disjunction),

∧ (conjunction), ↑ (shift), **abs** (from **bits** to **int**), **bin** (from **int** to **bits**), an operator **elem** (selects a certain bit from a **bits**) and some others.

For **bytes** we have the comparison operators as for **strings**, **elem** as for **bits** and a transfer from **string** to **bytes**.

(D11)   **bits** *t* ; **bytes** *r* ;

declares *t* to be a **bits** variable, and *r* to be a **bytes** variable.

For **bits** we have a separate denotation, consisting of a sequence of flip-symbols **1** (the equivalent of **true**) and flop-symbols **0** (the equivalent of **false**). If we assign:

(E42)   *t* := **1011100100001**

and **bits** width is, say, *32* then *t̂* refers to a machineword (a **bits**):

000000000000000000001011100100001

The value of **abs** *t* is now *5921* (conversely, the value of *t* is **bin** *5921*).
If we now assign:

t := *t* ∧ **111111**

then the value of *t* becomes **100001**. Then, after the assignation:

t := *t* ↑ *3*

the value of *t* is **100001000**, so that *28* **elem** *t*, i.e. *(bitswidth−4)* **elem** *t*, is **true**, but *29* **elem** *t* is **false**.

If we want to consider the **bytes** *r* as a **string**, then we may apply the cast **string:**. e.g.

s **plus** *(* **string:** *r* *)*

Just to demonstrate **bits** and **bytes**, we consider the following example:

(E43)   **proc** *compose string* =
           (**bits** *select* , **ref** [*1*:*bits width*] **bytes** *phrase* *)* **string** :
               (**string** *s* ;   ¢ initialization is not necessary, because
                                    the flexible upper-bound is set to *0* at
                                    the declaration (see D3 in 0.4.3) ¢
                 for *i* **to** *bitswidth* **do**
                 if *i* **elem** *select* **then** *s* **plus** *(* **string:** *phrase* [*i*] *)* **fi** ;
                 s *)* ;

For an application of this procedure see the following section.

0.9.3. Structures with mixed mode fields, chains etc.

The really interesting feature of structured modes is, however, that you can collect values of different modes into them. For example:

(E44)   **mode book** = **struct** (**string** *text* , **int** *index*) ;
              book *Report on the Algorithmic Language ALGOL 68* ;

Now the field:

    text **of** *Report on the Algorithmic Language ALGOL 68*

contains the **string**: "*may_be_difficult_for_the_uninitiated_reader.*" [see R 0.1.1], and:

    index **of** *Report on the Algorithmic Language ALGOL 68*

might be the point where you really got stuck.

There is, however, another

    book *Informal Introduction to ALGOL 68* ;

which also contains the **string** denoted, but in quite another context. May this other **book** help you to proceed at the *index* **of** referred to above.

An important implication of the concept of mixed mode fields is that you can make a field refer to another structure of that same mode. In this way chains (lists, queues, etc.) can be defined in a most natural manner. For example:

(E45)   **mode volume** = **struct** (**string** *text* , **int** *index* ,
                            ref volume *companion* , *next*) ;
                volume *Report* , *Informal Introduction* ;

The assignation:

(E46)   *companion* **of** *Report* := *Informal Introduction*

has been made. Until now, there is no *next* **of** *Report* , neither *companion* nor *next* **of** *Informal Introduction* . To express this, we assign:

(E47)   *next* **of** *Report* := *next* **of** *Informal Introduction*
                      := *companion* **of** *Informal Introduction* := **nil**

where **nil** is the same as "a reference to no value at all".

We may speak about:

    text **of** *companion* **of** *Report*

which is the text under your very eyes at this moment.

Ch.0.9.3   VERY INFORMAL INTRODUCTION TO ALGOL 68   51

It is important to comprehend the mode of the *companion* and *next* fields of *Report* and *Informal Introduction*. The identifiers possess **volume** variables and their mode is **ref volume**. Likewise, and this is the important point, *companion* of *Report* possesses a **ref volume** variable, and so its mode is **ref ref volume**; hence, *companion* of *Report* is a "pointer". From this it follows that in E46 the name *Informal Introduction* has been assigned to this pointer, not its value (indeed, you will not find the *text* of *Informal Introduction* in the *Report*, but via the pointer *companion* of *Report* you find a reference to that text). A more complete discussion of this rather delicate matter will be found in Sections 1.4.3 and 5.4.2.

To conclude, we consider two examples in which names will be assigned to **ref** fields.

In the context of the declarations:

> $[1:n]$ **bits** *acceptable* ,
> $[1:n , 1:bitswidth]$ **bytes** *new notions* ,
> **volume** *your algol Y ;*

you might have an inspired input in new notions. Then, but only after a critical evaluation of the row *acceptable*, you could elaborate:

> *your algol Y* := *("" , 0 ,* **nil** *,* **nil** *) ;*
> **for** *i* **to** *n* **do**
> *text* **of** *your algol Y* **plus**
> *compose string (acceptable*$[i]$ *, new notions*$[i,\ ]$ *) ;*

You may then try to elaborate:

> **if** *(***ref volume**: *next* **of** *Report)* :=: **nil**
> **then** *next* **of** *Report* := *your algol Y* **fi**

If [see R 6.0.2.a] the assignation is initiated, it may be interrupted without being resumed, or halted; if not then it will be completed and then you had better start to compose the *text* **of** *companion* **of** *next* **of** *Report*.

(E48)   **mode card** = **struct** *(* **int** *value ,* **string** *colour , picture ,*
                  ref card *next) ;*
      mode deck = **struct** *(* **int** *number ,* **ref card** *one) ;*
      $[0:51]$ **card** *card ;*
          deck *myhand , yourhand ;*

52 VERY INFORMAL INTRODUCTION TO ALGOL 68 Ch.0.9.3

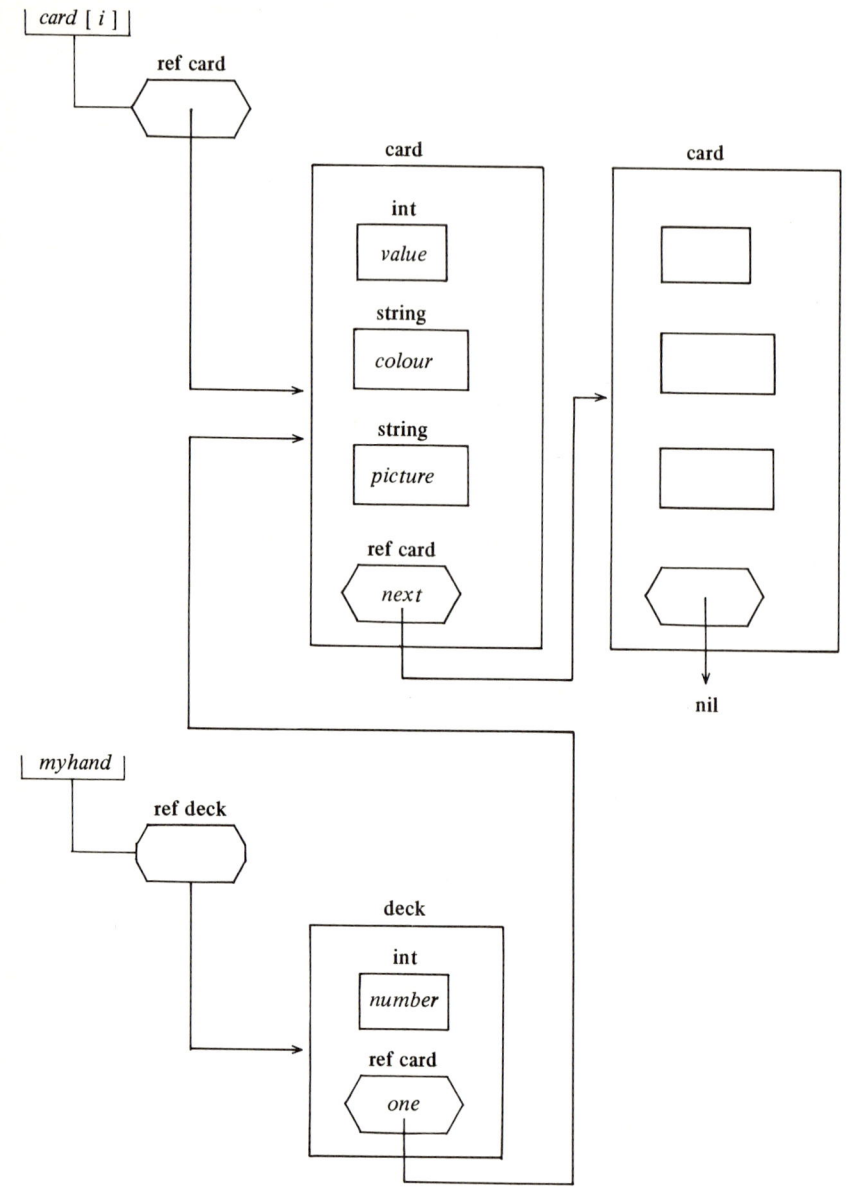

In E48 we declared 52 **cards** and two **decks**, each of which may refer to a certain **card** by its field *one* of *myhand* (*one* of *yourhand*). Which **cards** you and I then have in our hands may now follow from the fields *next* of *card*[*i*] ; *number* of *yourhand* may be the number of **cards** you have in your hand.

Leaving the value, colour and picture of the **cards** for what they are, we may assign:

(E49) for *i* from *0* to *51* do *next* of *card*[*i*] := *card*[*(i+1)* mod *52*] ;
yourhand := (*52*, *card*[*0*]) ; *myhand* := (*0* , **nil**)

where **mod** is a standard operator yielding the value of the left-operand modulo the right-operand. We thus arranged our 52 **cards** in a circular chain and you have them all in your hand.

You may now remove a **card**, say *card*[*37*], by:

next of *card*[*36*] := *card*[*38*]

and give it to me:

one of *myhand* := *card*[*37*] ;
next of *card*[*37*] := *card*[*37*]   ¢ we made *card*[*37*] selfreferring ¢

which you could have done in one statement:

one of *myhand* := *next* of *card*[*37*] := *card*[*37*]

You may give me another **card**:

next of *card*[*28*] := *card*[*30*] ;
next of *card*[*37*] := *card*[*29*] ;
next of *card*[*29*] := *card*[*37*]

We may administer these two events by:

number of *yourhand* **minus** 2 ;
number of *myhand* **plus** 2

0.10. Routines and operators

A routine may be possessed by an operator (see 0.7). An operator is represented by a symbol, such as:

+ − × / ÷ ↑ ↓ ∨ ∧ ⌐ ⊥ < ≤ = ≠ ≥ >   etc.

or by an indicant (representing a symbol), such as:

> **over up down or and not** i **lt le eq ne ge gt**
> **plus minus times div** **upb lwb** **re im** etc.

You can make as many indicants as you need:

> **add sub mul quot pow**
> **nor con parl perp** a b c m n o p etc.

We have to distinguish between two kinds of operators:

1) monadic: the routine has one formal-parameter;
 a monadic operator is always applied to the operand to its right (prefix notation),

2) dyadic: the routine has two formal-parameters ;
 a dyadic operator is always applied to the operand to its left (the left-operand) and to its right (the right-operand), (infix notation).

The monadic operators always have a higher priority than all the dyadic ones; for the latter nine priority levels are provided. The priority of a newly defined indicant is declared by a priority-declaration:

> **priority** o = *3 ;*

An operator will normally be used to deliver a value. The natural use of operators is in formulae. Routines possessed by operators are therefore always routines with either one or two formal-parameters, usually yielding a value. Operation-declarations look like procedure-declarations; the only difference lies in the use of **op** instead of **proc**.

In this section we shall confine ourselves to taking over some of the operation-declarations from the standard-prelude [R 10.2]. They may speak for themselves and reading them is one of the ways of learning the language. At this point (or at a point a little further on in this section), you might decide to try some close reading in R 10.1, R 10.2 and R 10.3. Anyhow, the examples we give here illustrate how to declare and use your own operators.

0.10.1. Operations on boolean operands

[R 10.2.2]

> **op abs** = *(* **bool** *a)* **int** : if *a* then *1* else *0* **fi** *;*
> **op** ⌐ = *(* **bool** *a)* **bool** : if *a* then **false** else **true fi** *;*

op ∨ = *(***bool** *a,b)* **bool**: **if** *a* **then true else** *b* **fi** ;
op ∧ = *(***bool** *a,b)* **bool**: **if** *a* **then** *b* **else false fi** ;
op = = *(***bool** *a,b)* **bool**: *(a* ∧ *b)* ∨ *(⌐a* ∧ *⌐b)* ;
op ≠ = *(***bool** *a,b)* **bool**: *⌐(a = b)* ;

These declarations express neither more nor less than the fundamental truth tables of elementary boolean algebra. You might subjoin in your own library (it is not in the standard-prelude):

op impl = *(***bool** *a,b)* **bool**: *⌐(a* ∧ *⌐b)* ;

You then have to declare a proper priority for this new dyadic operator.

Pay some attention to the definition of equality of two **boolean** operands: the first occurrence of the symbol = is the operator to be defined; the second occurrence is the equals-symbol which is part of all identity- and operation-declarations.

0.10.2. Formulae

Routines possessed by operators are activated by the formulae in which those operators occur. Compare, for instance:

op ∨ = *(***bool** *a,b)* **bool**: **if** *a* **then true else** *b* **fi** ;
proc *or* = *(***bool** *a,b)* **bool**: **if** *a* **then true else** *b* **fi** ;

Both ∨ and *or* possess (different instances of) the same routine. Therefore, the formula *p* ∨ *q* delivers the same value as the call *or(p,q)* .

There is, however, a very important distinction between the elaboration of a formula and that of a call. In a procedure-call it is the procedure-identifier (irrespective of the actual-parameters) which appoints the routine to be activated. In a formula, the mode of the operands, as well as the operator itself, is taken into account. In a procedure-call your computer will be so kind as to coerce (if possible) your actual-parameters until they match the modes required by the formal-parameters (**int**s may be widened into **real**s and **real**s into **compl**s etc.). In formulae this kindness is restricted. There may be many different occurrences of the same operator-token, possessing different routines depending on the (then necessarily different) modes of the formal-parameters. Therefore, the modes of the actual operands have a firm vote in the election of one of the routines nominated under the same operator.

Moreover, the same symbol may occur as a monadic as well as a dyadic operator, even in the same formula. It is always immediately clear from the context which of these two possibilities applies.

Let there be declared:

(E50.0)   **proc** eq = *(***compl** a, b*)* **bool**: **abs** a = **abs** b ;
(E50.1)   **op** = = *(***compl** a, b*)* **bool**: *(re* **of** a = *re* **of** b*)* ∧ *(im* **of** a = *im* **of** b*)* ;
(E50.2)   **op** = = *(***real**   a, b*)* **bool**: a ≤ b ∧ a ≥ b ;
(E50.3)   **op** = = *(***int**   a, b*)* **bool**: a ≤ b ∧ a ≥ b ;
(E50.4)   **op** = = *(***bool**   a, b*)* **bool**: *(a ∧ b) ∨ (⌐a ∧ ⌐b)* ;
(E50.5)   **op** ⌐ = *(***bool**   a   *)* **bool**: *(a | false | true)* ;
(E50.6)   **op** ⌐ = *(***bool**   a, b*)* **bool**: a ∧ ⌐b ;

Now:

    w = z   invokes E50.1
    x = y   invokes E50.2
    i = j   invokes E50.3
    p = q   invokes E50.4

but:

    eq(w,z)⎤
    eq(x,y)   all three call E50.0   ⎡because w and z are **ref compl**s ⎤
    eq(i,j)⎦   ⎢x and y will be widened⎥ to
                                                                   ⎣i and j   will be widened⎦ **compl**

however:

    eq(p,q)   is undefined, because a **bool** cannot be coerced to **compl**

but:

    *eq(***abs** p , **abs** q*)*   calls E50.0 , because **abs** p and **abs** q yield
                                    ints which will be widened to **compl**

and in:

    ⌐p ⌐⌐q   ⎫   the first   occurring ⌐ is monadic, and invokes E5◦
      or   ⎬   the second occurring ⌐ is dyadic , and invokes E5◦
    (⌐p) ⌐ (⌐q)⎭   the third   occurring ⌐ is monadic, and invokes E5◦

Apart from possessing a routine, operators also have a certain priority which determines the parsing of the formula in which they occur. By inserting brackets in a formula, a different parsing can be obtained from that required by the "natural" priorities; in fact, priorities serve to avoid brackets.

Take, for instance, the formula *(a ∧ b) ∨ (⌐a ∧ ⌐b)* . The operators ∧ and ∨ have different priorities (**priority** ∧ = *3* , ∨ = *2*); consequently, the brackets are superfluous: *a ∧ b ∨ ⌐a ∧ ⌐b* yields the same value, though in a less transparent manner.

The monadic ¬ is of higher priority than any dyadic operator and therefore the brackets in, for instance ¬(a ∧ ¬b) are essential.

0.10.3. Operations on arithmetic operands, the standard prelude

Maybe a certain amazement will fall upon you in Sections 10.2.3, 4 and 5 of the Report. You will find there declarations such as:

[R 10.2.3.h]   op + = (int a,b) int : a − − b ;
[R 10.2.3.m]   op ÷ = (int a,b) int :
               (b ≠ 0 | int q := 0 , r := abs a ;
                 while (r := r − abs b) ≥ 0 do q := q + 1 ;
                 (a < 0 ∧ b ≥ 0 ∨ a ≥ 0 ∧ b < 0 | −q | q)) ;

and even worse, because you will also meet tokens not belonging to the language such as **L** , **P** , **Q** , **R** , **E** etc. which provide a kind of shorthand for the standard-prelude only.

These definitions of arithmetic operations (the meaning of which will be known to every programmer) have nothing to do with machine efficiency. To the contrary, their justification lies in the fact that they "fix the semantics" by defining all operations in terms of a certain minimal set of primitive operations [R 2.2.3.1 c,d]. Agreement with the choice of this set and whether you like this method or not is a matter of taste (maybe even of philosophy); it has nothing to do, however, with the language defined. This is entirely a problem of how to define a language.

Moreover, being equivalent to some closed-clause, a routine defines a series of processes in a computer and it is explicitly stated in the Report [R 1.1.6.h] that any of these processes may be replaced by any process which causes the same effect. Consequently, an implementor is perfectly free to supply means for generating (more) efficient machine code, whenever he is able to do so. In particular, for the routines occurring in the standard-prelude (and also in the library-preludes, see 0.10.7), he can generate efficient machine code himself, taking advantage of every specific machine feature (most machines will have single commands for addition and integer division and, unless he is a maniac, your implementor will not follow the routines in the standard-prelude to the letter).

0.10.4. Operations on **complex** operands

[R 10.2.7]   **mode compl** = **struct** (**real** re , im) ;

58 VERY INFORMAL INTRODUCTION TO ALGOL 68 Ch.0.10.5

```
op  ⊥     = (real   a,b) compl:   (a,b);
op  re    = (compl a) real:        re of a;
op  im    = (compl a) real:        im of a;
op  abs   = (compl a) real:        sqrt( re a ↑ 2 + im a ↑ 2);
op  conj  = (compl a) compl:       re a ⊥ − im a;
op  =     = (compl a,b) bool:      re a = re b ∧ im a = im b;
op  +     = (compl a,b) bool:      ¬(a = b);
op  +     = (compl a) compl:       a;
op  −     = (compl a) compl:       − re a ⊥ − im a;
op  +     = (compl a,b) compl:     ( re a + re b )⊥( im a + im b );
op  −     = (compl a,b) compl:     ( re a − re b )⊥( im a − im b );
op  ×     = (compl a,b) compl:     ( re a × re b − im a × im b )⊥
                                   ( re a × im b + im a × re b );
op  /     = (compl a,b) compl:  (  real d = re( b × conj b );
                                   compl n = a × conj b;
                                   ( re n / d )⊥( im n / d ));
op  ↑     = (compl a , int b) compl:
                                   ( compl p := 1;
                                   to abs b do  p := p × a;
                                   ( b ≥ 0 | p | 1/p )       );
```

We could subjoin another operator to this set, which the authors seem to have forgotten: the monadic **i** (or ⊥ which is, however, a less appropriate representation in this case):

(D12) op i = (int a) compl: (0 , a);
       op i = (real a) compl: (0 , a);

Instead of $x \perp y$ (or x **i** y) you could then also write $x +$ **i** y, which is closer still to the usual mathematical notation.

0.10.5. Operations combined with assignments

[R 10.2.11]

```
op plus   = (ref real a , real b) ref real:  a := a + b;  ¢ or +:= ¢
op minus  = (ref real a , real b) ref real:  a := a − b;  ¢ or −:= ¢
op times  = (ref real a , real b) ref real:  a := a × b;  ¢ or ×:= ¢
op div    = (ref real a , real b) ref real:  a := a / b;  ¢ or /:= ¢
```

Ch.0.10.6   VERY INFORMAL INTRODUCTION TO ALGOL 68   59

The first formal-parameter has to be **ref**, because we want to assign to it. The value delivered has also been declared to be **ref**, and some consequences of this are shown in 6.3. These operators are declared for all arithmetic operands (**int**, **real** and **compl**).

0.10.6. Operations on **strings**

It is instructive to unravel the operations on **strings**, in particular to find out the kind of ordering defined by the routine possessed by $<$.

[R 10.2.10]   **mode string** = [$1:0$ **flex**] **char** ;

    op $<$ = (**string** a, b) **bool** :
        (**int** m = **upb** a, n = **upb** b ;
        int p = ($m<n$ | m | n), **int** i := 1 ; **bool** c ;
        if $p<1$
        then $n \geq 1$
        else *again* : **if** $c := a[i] = b[i]$ **then**   **if** (i **plus** 1) $\leq p$
                                                                                   then *again* **fi**
                                                                                   fi ;
                if c **then** $m<n$ **else** $a[i] < b[i]$ **fi fi**
        fi
    );
    op $\leq$ = (**string** a, b) **bool** : $\neg(b<a)$;
    op = = (**string** a, b) **bool** : $a \leq b \wedge a \geq b$;
    op $\neq$ = (**string** a, b) **bool** : $\neg(a = b)$;
    op $\geq$ = (**string** a, b) **bool** : $b \leq a$;
    op $>$ = (**string** a, b) **bool** : $b < a$;
    op + = (**string** a, b) **string** :
        (**int** m = **upb** a, n = **upb** b ; [$1 : m+n$] **char** c ;
        $c[1:m] := a$; $c[m+1 : m+n] := b$;
        c) ;
    op plus = (**ref string** a, **string** b) **ref string** : $a := a + b$;

0.10.7. The library prelude option

The operation-declarations considered thus far belong to the standard-prelude of the language, i.e. they are built in. You will also find in the standard-prelude all environment enquiries and all declarations for formatless and formatted input and output (which therefore are also built into this language).

Nothing, however, prevents you from subjoining to this standard-prelude a set of home made declarations. Of course you are free to declare such new things in your own particular-program; but, as soon as you want to apply them in several programs, or you want to enable others to use them, or you have reason to expect that more efficiency may be acquired, then you can go to your implementor and ask him to make the whole set an as efficient as possible extension of the standard-prelude, i.e. a 'library prelude'. In that way an arbitrary number of problem oriented dialects may be defined. For some possible examples see 8.4 and 8.5.

The possibility of subjoining library-preludes to the standard-prelude contributes in no small measure to the flexibility of this language and the concept of a 'library prelude option' is one of the basic concepts of ALGOL 68.

You should, therefore, never accept an implementation in which library-preludes cannot be coded efficiently or in which the attachment of one or more library-prelude(s) to the standard-prelude cannot easily be done.

0.11. The creation of new modes, **long** --- **long** modes and **unions**

On most modern computers you will find, if not in the hardware then in the standard software, provision for double and maybe even multilength arithmetic. In many cases this comes to two or more machine words treated as though they were one.

In a concrete computer, all instances of values of all modes will be stored as bit-patterns. Whether a specific bit-pattern may correspond to a value of a specific mode or not is mainly a matter of how the standard software may interpret that piece of binary information. That is to say the interpretation of bit-patterns and also the arrangement, size and structure of their locations in the memory is entirely a matter of software.

In this language, the possibility of multilength arithmetic is reflected in the **long** --- **long** modes (0.11.1), and we have united modes (**unions**) reflecting the poly-interpretability of bit-patterns (0.11.2 and 0.11.3). To what extent available hardware features will be used for these further derived modes and to what extent (and how) they will be simulated by software provisions is entirely a matter of implementation.

0.11.1. The **long long** --- **long** modes

The prefix **long** plays a role in the creation of new modes in much the same way as [ ] , **struct** , **proc** and **ref** do; the **long**, however, may stand only in front of **int** , **real** , **compl** , **bits** and **bytes** and of all long modes derived from these.

In the standard-prelude you will find the environment enquiries:

    int *int lengths* = **c** the number of different lengths of integers **c** *;*
    int *real lengths* = **c** the number of different lengths of reals   **c** *;*
    int *bits widths* = **c** the number of different widths of bits   **c** *;*
    int *bytes widths* = **c** the number of different widths of bytes   **c** *;*

stating to what extent the long feature is implemented for **int**s, **real**s, **bits** and **bytes** respectively.

Now, if we declare, for instance:

    long long long long long long long int *iiiiiiiint ;*

but *int lengths* = *3* , then the value of our *iiiiiiiint* will be treated as if it had been declared:

    long long int *iiiiiiiint ;*

Hence, *int lengths* = *3* means that your implementor will distinguish only three kinds of integral values: **int** , **long int** and **long long int** . The same applies to **real** (and, consequently, to **compl**), **bits** and **bytes**. The number of **long**s characterizes the degree of discrimination with which the value is kept in the computer.

In the language the prefix **long** also turns up in denotations:

    iiiiiiint := **long long long long long long long** *0*

In the standard-prelude you will also find the environment enquiries:

    long int   *long max int* = **c** the largest long integral value **c** *;*
  long long int *long long max int* = **c** the largest long long integral value **c** *;*

etc.

  long real *long max real*   = **c** the largest long real value **c** *;*
  long real *long small real*   = **c** the smallest long real value which can be usefully compared with **long** *1.0* **c** *;*

etc.

For the arithmetic modes (**int**, **real**, **compl** and their **long**s) we have a monadic operator **leng** which makes the operand one **long**er, and a monadic operator **short** which takes away one **long**. There is no automatic transfer between different **long**s of the same basic mode.

For example:

(E51)   **proc** *INPROD* = (**ref**[*1*:] **real** *a*, *b*) **real** :
         (**long real** *value* := **long** *0.0* ;
         for *i* **to** (**upb** *a* < **upb** *b* | **upb** *a* | **upb** *b*) **do**
         value **plus leng** *a*[*i*] × **leng** *b*[*i*] ;
         short *value*) ;

If, in a call of E51, the upper-bounds of the actual rows are not equal, then, by **for** *i* **to** (**upb** *a* < **upb** *b* | **upb** *a* | **upb** *b*) **do** , the routine will compute the innerproduct on the assumption that the row with the lesser number of elements may be treated as if it were supplemented with zero elements.

0.11.2. United modes

United modes (**union**s for short) are brought into existence to enable the programmer to specify locations in which values of different modes can be stored, and to dispose of the names which refer to such accommodating locations. In particular, with the aid of **union**s you can define routines which accept actual-parameters and (or) yield a value of one of several possible modes.

The mode-declaration:

(E52)   **mode strint** = **union** (**string** , **int**) ;

   or:

(E52*)   **union strint** = (**string** , **int**) ;

declares a **strint** to be a value of either the mode **string** or the mode **int**. It is important to know that this does not define a new kind of value; a new mode has been declared. The values in this mode, however, are **string**s or **int**s (see also Section 1.6.1).

The identity-declaration:

(E53)   **strint** *year* ;

declares *year* to possess the name of either a **string** or an **int**. In particular here, do please remember that the strict form of E53 is:

Ch.0.11.2   VERY INFORMAL INTRODUCTION TO ALGOL 68   63

(E53*)   **ref strint** *year* = **loc strint** ;

A **ref strint** is, most certainly, a new mode (i.e. it is neither a **ref string**, nor a **ref int**), it is a **ref union (string , int)**. A "strint", on the contrary, does not exist as such (being a **string** or an **int**).

You may now assign to *year*:

(E54)   *year* := "*1968*"

as on another occasion:

(E54*)   *year* := *1968*

Observe, that in the context of:

(E55)   **string** *text* , **int** *numb* ;

neither the assignment *text* := *1968* , nor the assignment *numb* := "*1968*" , is allowed.

The assignations E54 and E54* may be depicted as follows:

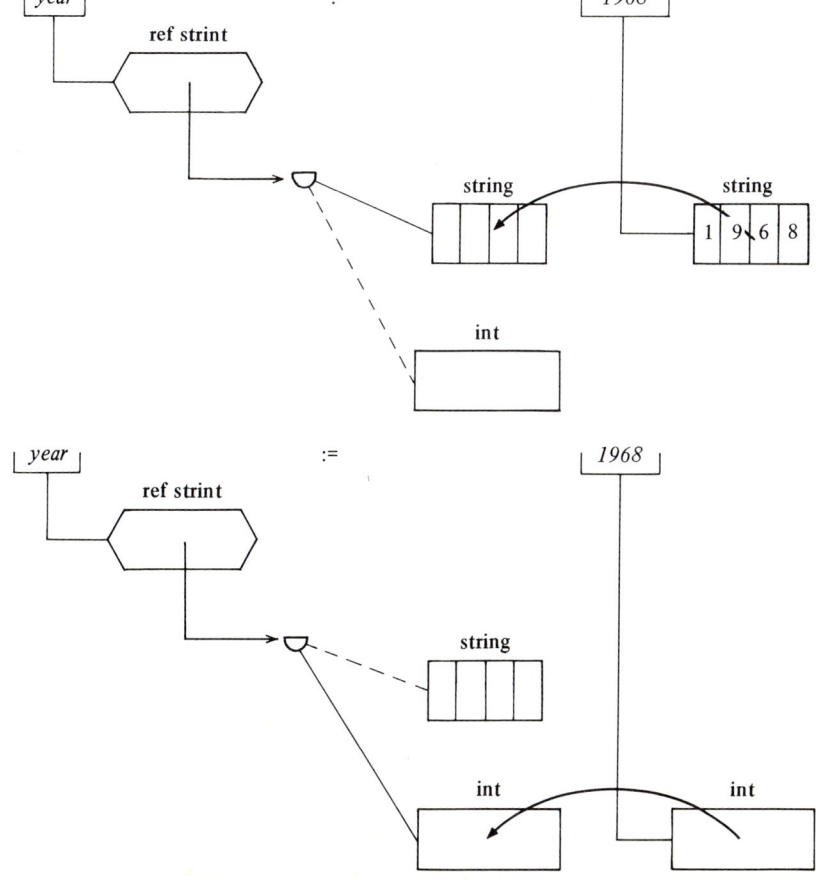

0.11.3. Conformity relators

Once you have declared a united variable, you may want to ask the mode of the value assigned to it. It may be clear that this requires mode checking at run time. However, this is in fact the only situation where, in this language, run time mode checking is inevitable and for no other reason than that the programmer has explicitly asked for it.

In the context of E52 --- E55 you may write:

(E56)   **if** *text* :: *year* **then** *Ctrue* **else** *Cfalse* **fi**

The unit *text* :: *year* possesses upon elaboration the value **true** if *year* refers to a **string** (which is the case, for instance, after the assignment E54): otherwise its value is **false** (which is the case after E54*).

The symbol :: or **ct** (conforms to) is one of two conformity-relators. The :: does not compare values (as, for instance, does =), it does not compare names (as, for instance, does :=:). The conforms-to-symbol :: compares modes only (without regard to the values): *y* :: *x* is **true**, even though *y* **isnt** *x* and *y* ≠ *x* may well be **true**.

More serviceable is the other conformity-relator ::= or **ctab** (conforms to and becomes), which combines the function of :: with assignment (provided that the modes conform).

The expression *text* := *year* is not a correct assignment in this language, not even when the modes conform. Therefore the conforms-to-and-becomes-symbol ::= is indispensable:

(E57)   *text* ::= *year*

might be paraphrased as follows:

> **if** *text* :: *year* **then** ¢ text := year ; ¢ **true**
> **else** ¢ no assignment ¢ **false fi**

An example might be:

(E58)   **proc** *deliver* = *(***ref string** *s* , **ref int** *i* , **strint** *si)* **bool** :
                    (s ::= *si* ; *i* ::= *si) ;*
            deliver (text , numb , year)

The call delivers the actual value of *year* to the right destination. The value of *deliver* is **true** or **false** depending upon the mood of the year.

An example of a procedure yielding a value of one of two possible modes may be (in the context of the declarations E22* and E22**, see 0.7.3):

Ch.0.11.3   VERY INFORMAL INTRODUCTION TO ALGOL 68

(E59*)   **mode** intreal = **union** (**int** , **real**) ;

(E59)   **proc** *factorial* = (**int** *n*) **intreal** :
         if $n > nmaxfac$
         then *faclarge (n)*
            ¢ in which case a **real** value is yielded ¢
         else int $f := 1$;
            for *i* **from** 2 **to** *n* **do** *f* **times** *i* ; *f*
            ¢ in which case an **int** value is yielded ¢
         fi ;

The difference with E22 is that any call of the there declared **proc** (**int**) **real** *fac* yields a **real** (the **int** computed in the else-clause is widened to **real** because such is required by the real-cast), so that you can not know whether the value delivered was an exact factorial or not. A call of the **proc** (**int**) **intreal** *factorial*, on the contrary, yields an **int** or a **real** and you can find out which of the two was the case.

     Beware, however, of a pitfall.
     You cannot assign:

         $y := factorial (m)$

nor:

         $i := factorial (m)$

because an "**intreal**" can neither be assigned to a **ref real** nor to a **ref int**.
     You should declare, for instance:

         intreal *ir* ;

Then you may assign:

         $ir := factorial (m)$

and then, by

         $y ::= ir$

or (and) by:

         $i ::= ir$

you can find out. See also 0.12.3.

0.12. Other distinctive features

In our sightseeing trip we visited almost all the places in this language worthy to be posted up in computer centres and other programming offices. We regret our inability to design a concise poster for formatted input and output for which we may refer you to Section 7.6. To conclude these very informalities, we briefly discuss a few other distinctive features:

0.12.1. Local and global generators, stack and heap

We know already that by an identity-declaration like:

>   **ref real** x = **loc real** ;

a **real** value is generated on the stack. A more careful consideration of the unit to the right of the equals-symbol brings out the following (see also 5.7.2 and R 8.5.1):

> The actual-parameter **loc real** is a 'local generator'.
> It generates, on the stack, a **real** value (its "side effect", so to speak) and it possesses upon elaboration the **ref real** name $\hat{x}$ which refers to that newly generated **real**.
> The identity-declaration then causes this name $\hat{x}$ to be thereafter possessed by the identifier x .

As soon as the elaboration of the range to which the thus generated **real** value was **loc**al is completed (i.e. as soon as we leave that range), the **real** value ceases to exist. Not only the relation between x and the **ref real** value it possesses ceases to hold, but also the **real** value it referred to vanishes as the stack contracts.

Besides the stack, this language supposes another storage allocation regime, the "heap", in which values may be generated which remain there as long as some name refers to them.

By an identity-declaration like:

(E61)   **ref real** hx = **heap real** ;

a **real** value is again generated, and the unit **heap real** possesses (upon elaboration) its name. However, the 'global generator' **heap real** generates its **real** value not on the stack, but in the heap. This value then may exist beyond the context of the identifier hx; for instance, because a **ref real** in a still wider range refers to this **real**. The heap storage allocation regime presupposes garbage collection (see 5.7.2.2) at run time, which may be time consuming. For examples of heap generators, see 8.5 and 8.7.

Ch.0.12.2   VERY INFORMAL INTRODUCTION TO ALGOL 68   67

Local- (and global-) generators, being units which generate values and possess their names, may also occur individually. As an interesting example of the use of a generator outside identity-declarations, consider the following phrases in which a triangular matrix is generated:

(E61) $[1:n]$ **ref** [ ] **real** T ;
         $i := 1$;
generate row: $T[i] :=$ **loc** $[1:i]$ **real** ;
         if $i < n$ **then** i **plus** 1 ; *generate row* **fi** ;

By its declaration T possesses a **ref** $[1:n]$ **ref** [ ] **real**, that is the name of a row of n names each referring to a [ ] **real**. In the cycle we generate n [ ] **reals** of increasing length and assign their names to the elements of T.

You might be allured into writing a repetitive statement:

for i **to** n **do**
$T[i] :=$ **loc** $[1:i]$ **real** ;

but that would be exactly the kind of thing you cannot do with a local-generator. A repetitive statement stands for a closed-clause, and each row generated within it ceases to exist immediately after the elaboration of that clause. You may, however, use a global-generator:

(E61*) $[1:n]$ **ref** [ ] **real** T ;
         for i **to** n **do**
         $T[i] :=$ **heap** $[1:i]$ **real** ;

and now the rows generated in the heap are not thrown away, because names in a wider range still refer to them. You should, however, ask your implementor how much inefficiency is introduced by using global-generators in such cases.

Observe that T is declared to possess a 1-dimensional row of names: $T[i]$ possesses the name of a [ ] **real**, $T[i,j]$ is undefined. If you want to access the $[i,j]$ th element of the triangular matrix, you must write:

$T[i][j]$

you then access the jth element of the row referred to by the ith element of T (for further discussion, see 5.7.2. E14).

0.12.2. The ordinary **case** clause

In the routines for *fac* (E22 in 0.7.3) and *factorial* (E59 in 0.11.3) a rather lengthy computation has to be performed when the actual-parameter is $\leq$ *nmaxfac*. In such cases it will certainly be more efficient to take a mathematical table and to give these values as constants to the routine.

Let *maxint* be $2^{32} - 1$ (= 4294967295), so *nmaxfac* (see E22*) will be 12. We could now set about it as follows:

```
if  n =  0 then 1
elsf n =  1 then 1
elsf n =  2 then 2
elsf n =  3 then 6
elsf n =  4 then 24
elsf n =  5 then 120
----------------------------------------
elsf n = 12 then 4790 01600
else faclarge (n)
fi
```

which is not only a long expression, but obviously also inefficient. If, for instance, $n \geq 12$, then we have to do 13 tests before we arrive at the required value or the call *faclarge (n)*.

For such cases we have the "**case** clause" which occurs in the new fashion below of the declaration E59:

(E62)   **proc** *factorial* = *(* **int** *n)* **union** *(* **int**, **real** *)* :
         case *n+1* **in** *1 , 1 , 2 ,*
                        6 , 24 , 120 ,
                        720 , 5040 , 40320 ,
                        3 62880 , 36 28800 , 399 16800 ,
                        4790 01600
         out *faclarge (n)*
         esac ;

The expression may speak for itself (if not, then see 3.2.4.3). Though semantically equivalent to the **if** -- **then** -- **elsf** -- **then** -- **elsf** -- -- **else** -- **fi** construction discussed above, it will (in all respectable implementations) not have its lengthy testing disadvantage. The **case** clause should not only be regarded as a convenient abbreviation for a long expression, but also as a mandate to the implementor to generate efficient code (respecting of course the official semantics).

case , **in** , **out** and **esac** are other representations of respectively the **if** - , **then** -, **else** - and **fi** - symbols. Another notation for the **case** clause above is, therefore:

Ch.0.12.3   VERY INFORMAL INTRODUCTION TO ALGOL 68   69

(E62*)   proc *factorial* = (int *n*) union(int, real) :
                 (*n+1* | *1 , 1 , 2 , 6 , 24 , 120 , 720 , 5040 , 40320 ,*
                          3 62880 , 36 28800 , 399 16800 ,
                          4790 01600
                          | *faclarge (n)*
) ;

Between the **in** and the **out** we may write any sequence of units, separated by comma-symbols. Between the **out** and the **esac** any serial-clause is allowed:

   case *i* **in**   (*m* **plus** *1* ; *x1*[*n*]) , (*n* **plus** *1* ; *y1*[*m*]) ,
                (*k* **plus** *1* ; *x2*[*m*,*n*]) ,
                (*m* := *n* := *k* := *0* ; *x* + *y*)
         out   *print* ("*something‗wrong‗with‗i*") ; **goto** *alarm*
   esac

If there is no danger of *i* being out of range, then we may omit the **out** and the serial-clause following.

0.12.3. The conformity **case** clause

In 0.11.3 we discussed how to deal with the value yielded by the **proc**(int)intreal *factorial*, declared in E59. Its value is either an **int** or a **real** which is, however, held in a location of the mode **union**(int, real), which is why it can neither be assigned to a **ref int** nor to a **ref real**. In the context of the declarations:

   union (**int** , **real**) *ir* ; **int** *i* ; **real** *r* ;

we can go about it as follows:

   ir := *factorial* (*m*) ;
     if *i* ::= *ir* **then** ¢ computation using *i* ¢
     else *r* ::= *ir* ;   ¢ computation using *r* ¢
     fi

If there are more modes possible, then we arrive of course, at anotherr **if** -- **then** -- **elsf** -- **then** -- **elsf** -- -- -- **else** -- **fi** construction. For these (with conformity-relations in the conditions) we have the specific "conformity **case** clause", which runs as follows:

   ir := *factorial* (*m*) ;
   case *i* , *r* ::= *ir* **in** ¢ computation in a unit using *i* ¢ ,
                      ¢ computation in a unit using *r* ¢
   esac

If not all possible modes are catered for in the expression after **case**, then we may write a serial-clause after **out** and before **esac**, dealing with the situation of unforeseen modes.

As a final example consider:

(E63)   **proc** *GAMMA* = (**union**(**int**, **real**, **compl**) *u*) **union**(**int**, **real**, **compl**) :
   begin int *i* , **real** *r* , **compl** *c* ;
      case *i* , *r* , *c* ::= *u*
      in (**if** *i* ≤ *0* **then** *finish* ¢ undefined value ¢ **fi** ;
         case *i*   **in** *1* , *1* , *2* , *6* , *24* , *120* , *720* , *5040* ,
                  40320 , *3 62880* , *36 28800* , *399 16800* ,
                  4790 01600
            out *faclarge (i−1)*
         esac) ,
         (¢ algorithm for the gamma-function with a **real** *r* ,
           yielding a **real** value ¢) ,
         (¢ algorithm for the gamma-function with a **compl** *c* ,
           yielding a **compl** value ¢)
      esac exit
      finish : **skip end** ;

0.13 What to do next

The remainder of this Introduction contains, in a two-dimensional way, eight (or seven) chapters (please now refer to the table of contents). The eight horizontal chapters are:

   1. BASIC CONCEPTS
   2. DECLARATIONS
   3. CLAUSES
   4. ROUTINES
   5. UNITARY CLAUSES
   6. STANDARD PRELUDE
   7. TRANSPUT
   8. EXAMPLES

The seven vertical chapters are:

.1 FUNDAMENTALS
.2 PROCEDURES AND NAMES
.3 OPERATORS
.4 STRUCTURES
.5 MULTIPLE VALUES
.6 UNIONS
.7 DISTINCTIVE FEATURES

Thus the horizontal chapters are subdivided into seven sections ".1" through ".7". Likewise, the vertical chapters are subdivided into eight sections "1." through "8.".

You may read row-wise:

> **for** *i* **to** *8* **do**
> **for** *j* **to** *7* **do** *elaborate section* [*i,j*]

or you may read column-wise:

> **for** *i* **to** *7* **do**
> **for** *j* **to** *8* **do** elaborate section [*j,i*]

The latter (vertical) route is the more didactic one, for those who wish to learn the language. The horizontal one (along which this Introduction has been bound) is more appropriate for those who wish to survey the essential principles of the language as a whole. In particular, the first chapter on **BASIC CONCEPTS** is a survey of the main part of the basis on which the language was "orthogonally designed" [R 0.1.2]; i.e. the generalised concept of "mode", and all its consequences.

If you are now in some doubt as to which route is for you, then take our suggestion — read horizontally in Chapter 1 until you find the waters beginning to get a little deep: then return to 2.1 and read by the vertical route thereafter.

1. BASIC CONCEPTS

1.1. Fundamentals

You write or read a 'particular program' which is embedded in an environment consisting of the 'standard prelude' (with 'standard postlude') and a 'library prelude option' (with 'library postlude option').

The standard-prelude is a comprehensive selection of features, generally accepted as a standard environment for a modern programming language. A library-prelude is a continuation of the standard-prelude. It may contain more specific features you would like to have at your disposal in certain classes of problem. The implementation is supposed to cater for some provision which enables you to subjoin one or, ideally, a selection of library-preludes.

The whole constitutes a 'program'.

1.1.1. Objects

A program may be parsed into a tree of "external objects" (such as identifiers, operators, denotations, indications, declarations, clauses etc.) and as such, by "elaboration", it defines a sequence of "actions" in a "computer" (be it a human being or an automaton). These actions are performed on "internal objects", presumedly somewhere in the human mind or in the memory of his automaton. Each internal object (in the sequel often "object" for short) has three relevant attributes:

1) it is of some "mode",
2) it is a particular instance of a value of that mode,
3) it has some location.

1) The mode specifies how the object is built up from basic material (bits, or the little grey cells in your brain) and to what kind of entities (numbers, characters, records, names etc.) it is related. Partly this is a matter of implementation (the building of a real number for example), partly this construction may be specified by the program in terms of modes already defined (for example the building of a complex number as an ordered pair of real numbers). In the program text a mode may be indicated by a bold faced word, which is then to be considered as one indivisible symbol (e.g. **amode**). Such a mode-indication may be regarded as the badge of some class of "values".

Ch.1.1.1   BASIC CONCEPTS   73

2) Some modes define but a few values (e.g. a **bool** can only be **true** or **false**), some quite a lot (e.g. **int** and **real**), some in principle an infinity (e.g. **string**); but there may be any number of instances of any particular value within the automaton, and such an "instance of a value" of some mode is an internal object.

3) An object is to be found somewhere, and this somewhere is its location (its address in the memory). The physical address is none of your business, but in many cases you will certainly want to have control of that location (for example you may wish to supersede the object by another instance of a value, or to enter its location in some chain), that is you may wish to refer to that object. As far as the location is concerned, there are two possibilties:

3a) The internal object is "possessed" by an external object (an identifier, an operator, or a denotation). In that case you cannot control its location (because it may well be concealed in the object code) and you have to take it as it arises in the elaboration of the program, in which it is a "constant".

3b) The internal object is, by elaboration, "referred to" by another internal object. In that case its location is at your disposal as a "name", i.e. as an object of another (!) related mode. Such a location mode is a reference-to (**ref**) mode. A **ref amode** object (a name) refers to an **amode** object.

You may visualize the interrelation of the concepts mode, value and name (which are of fundamental importance in this language) by drawing boxes in a "paper computer".

Boxes of the same shape then represent objects of the same mode. Each box holds an instance of a value (not necessarily different from the instance in another box). Names may come into the picture by drawing boxes of another shape, holding those names.

The relation "to refer" between two internal objects is depicted by an arrow pointing from the name to the object referred to by that name:

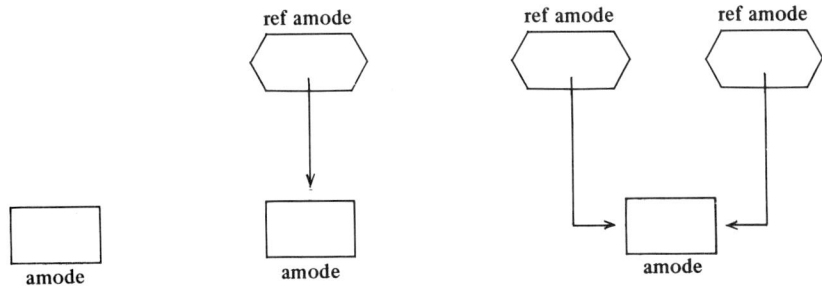

We shall presently show you how actions may be depicted in our paper computer. They will always achieve the effects defined by the hypothetical computer in the Report (but sometimes by a marginally different method).

1.1.2. Identifiers

To distinguish between objects of a given mode, we use identifiers. An identifier is a sequence of letters and digits with a leading letter, like *mar1lyn* and unlike *1marlyn*.

The meaning of an identifier is defined in an identity-declaration; the only exception is the label-identifier which is defined as such when it occurs as a label in the program text.

1.1.2.1. Simple declarations

By declaring:

(E1)   **amode** *object1* , *object2* , *object3* ;

three internal objects are generated in the memory, each of them being an **amode**. The three identifiers are then made to possess the names (**ref amode** objects) referring to the **amode** objects generated. Therefore they are known as **ref amode** identifiers. In a picture: three boxes come about, each of them holding the name (location) of another box of the mode **amode**.

Now, *object1* , *object2* and *object3* are external objects, being constituents of the program. By the identity-declaration E1 each of them is made to possess an internal object. The relationship between an identifier and the object it possesses cannot be changed; and the object thus possessed (in this case a name) cannot be changed.

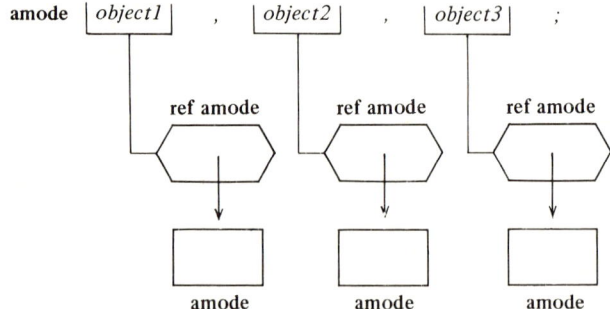

The relation "to possess", between an identifier and an internal object, is depicted by a line from the external to the internal object.

Ch.1.1.2.2   BASIC CONCEPTS   75

This is nothing new. In many other programming languages the proper relation between an identifier and its variable value is exactly the same, although perhaps you were never aware of it.

1.1.2.2. Assignation, collateral elaboration

If *mar1lyn* and *mar2lyn* are likewise declared to be **ref amode** identifiers (consequently possessing **ref amode** objects), then by assigning:

(E2)   *object1* := *mar1lyn* ; *object2* := *mar2lyn*

the value referred to by *object1* (*object2*) is "superseded" by the value referred to by *mar1lyn* (*mar2lyn*). Nothing happens to the names possessed by the identifiers. The value referred to by the LHS (Left Hand Side) becomes a copy of the value referred to by the RHS (Right Hand Side). The copy-action "to make a new instance of" is depicted below by a bowed arrow originating from the object to be copied and pointing into the location of the copy:

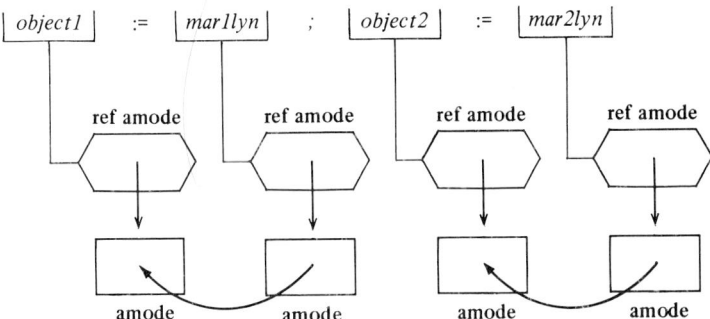

Again this is nothing new. In most other programming languages the process of "assignment to a variable" takes place in exactly the same way.

In an assignation the LHS (the 'destination') and the RHS (the 'source') are elaborated "collaterally", i.e. there is no prescribed order for the actions of getting the name (the **ref amode**) in the LHS and getting the value (the **amode**) in the RHS. Consequently, if these two actions should happen to have any side effect upon each other (in the case of more involved assignations this could occur), then the result of the assignations is "undefined" (i.e. not defined by the Report alone).

In E1 also we met a collateral elaboration. In fact E1 defines three identity-declarations, the declaration of *object1*, of *object2* and of *object3*; and these three declarations are elaborated collaterally.

1.1.3. Phrases, serial and collateral elaboration

The piece of program text:

(E3)   **amode** *object1 , object2 , object3 ;*
                  object1 := mar1lyn ;
                  object2 := mar2lyn

is a simple case of a serial-clause. The "constituents" separated by semicolons are 'phrases' which may be either 'declarations' or 'clauses'. The semicolons represent the go-on symbol. The action defined by the phrase following a go-on-symbol begins after the completion of the action defined by the phrase preceding it.

As we have already pointed out, the identity-declaration:

amode *object1 , object2 , object3*

is a collateral-declaration. In fact it is an abbreviation for the phrase:

amode *object1 ,* **amode** *object2 ,* **amode** *object3*

The comma-symbols achieve the collateral creation of the objects.

Besides collateral-declarations we may have serial-declarations, for example:

amode *object1 ;* **amode** *object2 ;* **amode** *object3*

and the go-on-symbols achieve serial creation of the objects (one by one). Eventual side effects (which in the case of more involved declarations could occur) now act precisely as prescribed by the order of elaboration thus defined.

Embracing a serial-clause by "*(*" or "**begin**" and "*)*" or "**end**", we obtain a closed-clause:

(E4)   *(* **amode** *object1 , object2 , object3 ;*
             object1 := mar1lyn ; object2 := mar2lyn ;
             XXXXX *)*

By "XXXXX" we denote here and in the sequel an arbitrary constituent valid in the context.

By closing a serial-clause, a 'range' is demarcated (see also 3.1.5). A range has much in common with what in some other programming languages is known as a block; in particular it defines the "scope" of the values (names) created by the declarations within it.

A clause may or may not possess a value of some mode. For example, the clause:

$$object1 := mar1lyn$$

possesses the value yielded by the LHS (and not, as you might have expected, the value yielded by the RHS), that is the **ref amode** object possessed by *object1*. An assignation yields the name in its LHS.

Correspondingly, a serial-clause may possess a value of some mode. If so, then it is the value possessed by the clause which completes its action.

The same applies to closed-clauses.

For example, if XXXXX in E4 yields by elaboration an **amode** object, (and *marilyn* is declared to be a **ref amode** identifier) then:

(E5)   *marilyn* := *(amode object1 , object2 , object3 ;*
                   object1 := mar1lyn ; object2 := mar2lyn ;
                   XXXXX)

is a perfectly sound assignation. It assigns the value yielded by E4, which is the value yielded by XXXXX, to *marilyn*.

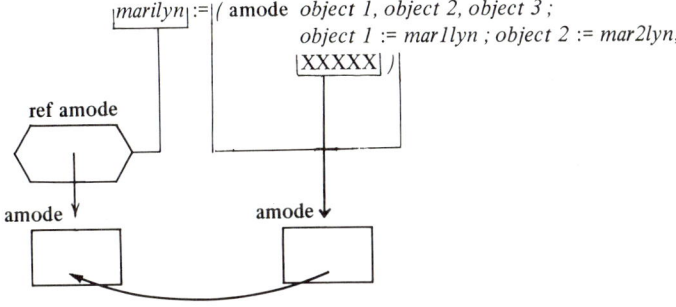

1.1.4. Routines

An internal object of fundamental importance is the "routine", to be considered as equivalent to a sequence of symbols which is the same as some closed-clause. A routine may or may not have formal-parameters, and may or may not deliver a value of some mode. A routine may be possessed by a routine-denotation, which is rather close to what in some other programming languages is known as "a procedure-heading with procedure-body".

In this language not only an identifier, but also an 'operator' may be declared to possess a certain routine.

A routine may be activated:

a) in a 'formula' by means of the operator possessing the routine,
b) or else by means of the identifier possessing (or, which may also be the case, referring to) the routine, i.e. by a 'call'.

By declaring:

(E6)   **op** ◊ = (**amode** *formal1* , *formal2*) **amode** : XXXXX ;

the indication "◊" is declared to be an operator, possessing the routine denoted by the right hand side of the equals-symbol "=". In this routine-denotation, XXXXX is some clause defining the action, using the formal-parameters *formal1* and *formal2*. The **amode** : preceding it expresses that the clause is to deliver an **amode** value.

By virtue of this declaration, the clause:

(E7)   *object3* := *object1* ◊ *object2*

results in:

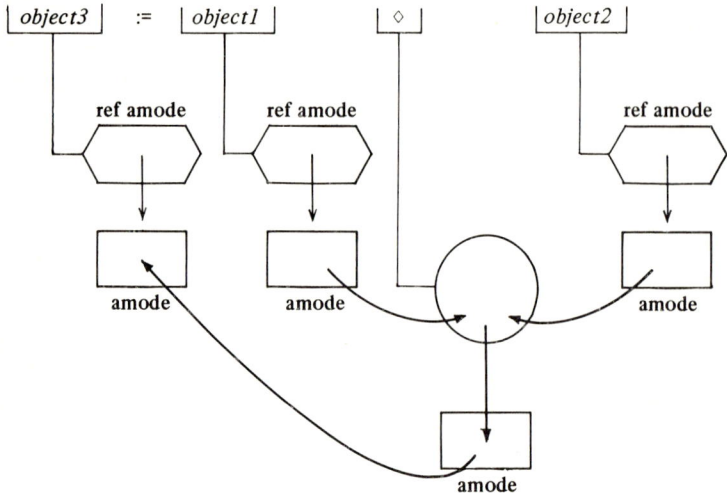

The routine possessed by ◊ is depicted by a circle.

In E7 again, the LHS and the RHS are elaborated collaterally. The RHS is a formula in which both 'operands', *object1* and *object2*, are in their turn elaborated collaterally (corresponding to the fact that the formal-parameters in E6 appear in a collateral-declaration). Formulas are described more fully in 1.3 and 5.1.3.

Ch.1.1.5 BASIC CONCEPTS 79

By declaring:

(E8)   **proc** *function* = (**amode** *formal1* , *formal2* , *formal3*) **amode** : XXXXX ;

the identifier *function* is declared to possess the routine denoted by the RHS. In this routine-denotation, XXXXX is some clause defining the action, using the formal-parameters *formal1* , *formal2* and *formal3* .

By virtue of this declaration, the call:

(E9)   *marilyn* := *function* (*object1* , *object2* , *object3*)

results in:

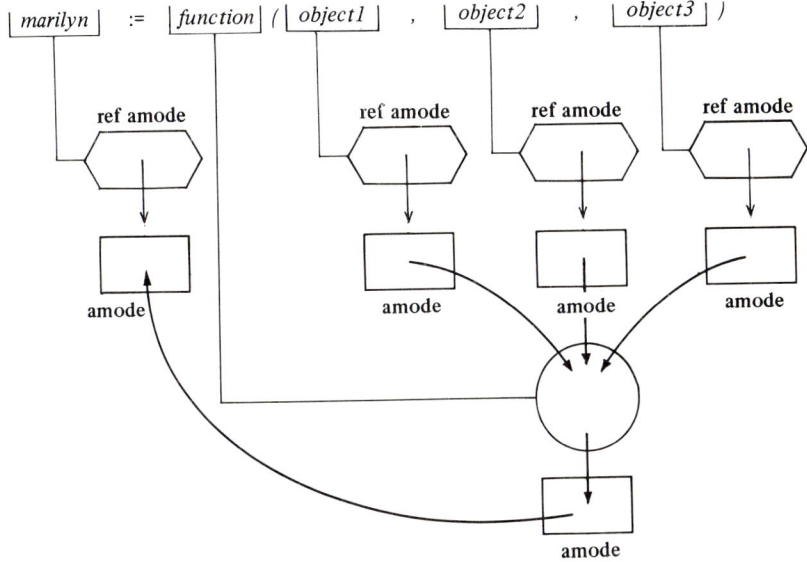

Again, the LHS and the RHS are elaborated collaterally, as are the three actual-parameters *object1* , *object2* and *object3* on the RHS, by virtue of the collateral-declaration of the formal-parameters in the routine.

1.1.5. Defining and applied occurrences

Consider the assignation:

(E5*) *marilyn* := (**amode** *object1* , *object2* , *object3* ;
$\qquad\qquad\quad$ *object1* := *mar1lyn* ;
$\qquad\qquad\quad$ *object2* := *mar2lyn* ;
$\qquad\qquad\quad$ *object3* := *object1* ◊ *object2* ;
$\qquad\qquad\quad$ *function* (*object1* , *object2* , *object3*))

To *marilyn* is assigned the value of a closed-clause. The outmost "(" and ")" enclose a serial-clause consisting of a collateral-declaration, followed by three consecutive assignations, in the last of which the RHS is a formula, followed by the call of a procedure delivering an **amode** value. This value delivered by *function* is the value yielded by the closed-clause and consequently the value assigned to *marilyn*.

It might be worth your while to try to visualize the elaboration of E5* in one picture, in the same way as we did for the separate constituent phrases. You will meet then several "occurrences" of the identifiers *object1* , *object2* and *object3*, the first of which are the "defining occurrences" in the declaration **amode** *object1* , *object2* , *object3*. All other occurrences of these identifiers are "applied occurrences". Here we have a relation between two external objects, the technical term for this relation is "to identify": the second occurrence of *object1* identifies its defining occurrence. You might depict this relation by an arrow pointing from the applied occurrence to its defining occurrence.

1.1.6. Coercion

Every external object has, independent from the particular syntactic position in which it stands, an "a priori" value of some a priori mode. In order to make it fit its particular context, the external object may be "coerced", that is "forced to possess a value of another mode": its "a posteriori" mode and a posteriori value.

For example, the a priori mode of *mar1lyn* in E2 is **ref amode** (by virtue of its declaration), and thus its a priori value is a name (of an **amode** object). Now, by the assignation process as described in 1.1.2.2 ("getting the value" on the RHS), the a posteriori mode of *mar1lyn* must here be **amode** (we want the **amode** value referred to, and not the name). In this particular context *mar1lyn* must be "dereferenced", which is one of the eight basic coercions in this language.

Observe that *object1* in E2 (the LHS of this assignation) is not dereferenced, but in E7 (in the syntactic position of an **amode** operand) as in E8 (in the syntactic position of an **amode** actual-parameter) it is.

Another example of coercion is "widening", implicit change from mode **int** to mode **real**. Once you know what the term is about, you will find quite a lot of coercions in other programming languages, although perhaps they are not always so well defined if at all [see R 8.2].

In a language in which the basic concepts are extended as far as possible, one must inevitably be very clear and precise on the subject of the actions concealed in the language. It is dangerous to presume actions to be implicit without stating exactly why, where and how. Of course, one could have supplied a certain number of operators, expressing explicitly the desired transitions from a priori to a posteriori mode and value. But then you would have been coerced into writing *object1* := **DEREFERENCE** *marllyn* and *object3* := **DEREFERENCE** *object1* ◊ **DEREFERENCE** *object2* or some such, and very soon you would encounter much more miserable constructions (see 5.1.0.2).

In ALGOL 68 at least eight rather offensive monadic operators of this kind are incorporated in the syntax, being implied by the syntactic position of the external object to which they otherwise ought to have been explicitly applied. This, indeed, complicates in no small measure the syntax. However, once you have mastered that part of it [the whole of R 8], you will appreciate that the burden is taken away from your shoulders. Apart from that, coercion has one great charm: it does exactly for you what you want, but could easily have forgotten. You will feel happy that you can write $x := i$ instead of $x :=$ **WIDENTOREAL DEREFERENCE** i. For a systematic discussion of all the coercions, see Chapter 5.

Vertical readers, please turn to 2.1.

1.2. Names and declarers

1.2.1. Strict and extended language

The syntax defines which sequences of 'symbols' form a 'program'. A program becomes a "proper program" under the constraints given by the "context conditions", and then it is a proper program in the "strict language".

The semantics define which actions (on internal objects) a computer is supposed to perform when elaborating a proper program.

The strict language, defined thus by syntax and semantics, is in some respects a bit grim and tedious; fortunately it can be sweetened by that modicum of syntactic sugar that suits the taste of the user. Chapter 9 of the Report is the sugar basin.

In this Informal Introduction we are going to use a frank amount of syntactic sugar (as a matter of fact we did it already in Section 1.1); there will be no milk however; we always want to see what is on the bottom of our constructions.

A sweetened program is a proper program in the "extended language" and the technical term for syntactic sugar is "extension". The ingredients of extensions are extra-tokens, and the ritual of proper sugar supply is the replacement of certain sequences of symbols by certain other sequences of symbols, in most cases leading to convenient abbreviations and a more readable text.

The extensions mainly concern declarations, repetitive statements and conditional-clauses. In the latter two, some rather opaque closed-clauses are replaced by more transparant constructs. The most used declarations can be "contracted" to more intimate forms; this is very comfortable, provided that in all circumstances you realise what is behind the screens. In particular, never confuse the abbreviated (contracted) forms with the strict forms.

If you are becoming suspicious that some extensions were invented to make ALGOL68 look more like some other programming languages, then you are quite right.

1.2.2. Identity declarations

1.2.2.1. Syntax

In the strict language, an identity-declaration (defining the meaning of an identifier within its range) consists of an equals-symbol "=" with a formal parameter on its left and an actual-parameter on its right:

 formal-MODE-parameter = actual-MODE-parameter

(The "MODE" stands for an arbitrary mode. In the syntax you will find a number of production rules starting with MODE, generating an infinity of different modes. MODE is a so-called "metanotion"; the capitals express that there are separate production rules for it. You may forget this remark; everything will become clear in the sequel.)

A formal-MODE-parameter consists of a formal-MODE-declarer followed by a MODE-identifier. The formal-MODE-declarer determines the mode of the internal object which will be possessed by that identifier:

	formal-parameter declarer:	identifier:	this identifier is a:
	amode	*thing*	amode-identifier
	ref amode	*name*	reference-to-amode-identifier
ref	ref amode	*pointer*	reference-to-reference-to-amode-identifier

etc.

The actual-MODE-parameter yields an internal object to be possessed by the MODE-identifier of the formal-parameter. There are several possibilities for an actual-parameter:
1) any clause yielding the required mode (1.2.2.2.1 and 2)
2) a local-generator (1.2.2.3)
3) an initialized local-generator (1.2.2.4).

1.2.2.2.1. Constants

(E1)   **amode** *thing* = *marllyn* ;

The actual-parameter *marllyn* is a simple case of a clause and it possesses a **ref amode**; *thing*, however, is declared to be an amode-identifier (by the actual declarer **amode**). Consequently, *marllyn* must be dereferenced to yield an **amode** value and what happens is:

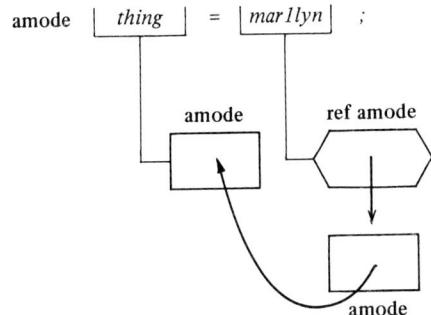

Now, by this declaration, *thing* is made to possess a new instance of the value referred to by *marllyn* when the declaration was elaborated. You can never assign to such a *thing*, because it is not a name. You may consider *thing* as a constant and indeed, whatever may happen to the **amode** value referred to by *marllyn*, *thing* always possesses the instance of an **amode** value it got from *marllyn* at its declaration. "Constant" is to be understood as "constant until next elaboration of the declaration"; then it may get a different value from *marllyn*.

Instead of *marllyn* we may write any clause yielding, after the proper coercions, the required mode:

(E1*)   **amode** *thing* = XXXXX ;

which may be depicted as follows:

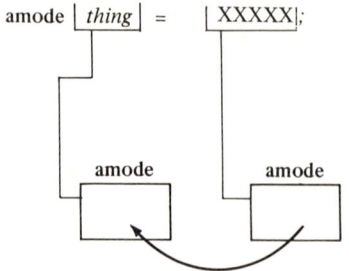

1.2.2.2.2. Equivalences

(E2)   **ref amode** *name* = *marllyn* ;

Although here again, as in E1, the actual-parameter is a strong unitary-clause, this is a story completely different from E1.

The formal-declarer in E2 is **ref amode**; and where the formal-declarer determines the mode of the object to be possessed by the newly declared identifier, an instance of a reference-to-amode value is required from the actual-parameter.

The a priori mode of *marllyn* happens to be reference-to-amode. Consequently no dereferencing of the actual-parameter is needed. The identifier *name* is made to possess a new instance of the name possessed by *marllyn*.

What happens is:

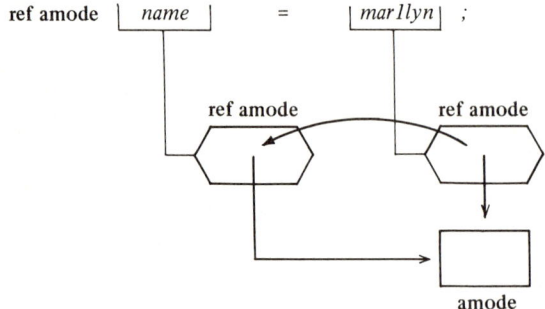

The result of the elaboration of E2 is that we have got two different identifiers, *name* and *marllyn*, both possessing different instances of the same name and consequently referring to the same internal **amode** object.

Ch.1.2.2.3   BASIC CONCEPTS   85

Assigning to *name* or to *marllyn* has the same result (supersedes the same **amode** value); different identifiers but the same variable value.

In some other programming languages this phenomenon is known as "equivalence". In this language "equivalence" is only a particular case of a general (and extremely fruitful) construction.

1.2.2.3. Local generators

Usually we want an identity-declaration to create the name of a new object (we want to define a new variable). Then we choose for the actual-parameter a 'generator'. A generator "generates" a new object; a local-generator creates a new object on the "stack"; an amode-local-generator creates a new **amode** object on the stack.

On creating a new object, the generator yields its name. We may even say that a generator "possesses" the name of the newly created object, but then we have to bear in mind that on every elaboration (on each occurrence) of a generator, a new object is created, and consequently a new name is possessed by it.

The new object created by a local-generator ceases to exist when the range in which it occurs has been elaborated up to the hilt.

A MODE-local-generator consists of the local-symbol "**loc**", followed by an actual-MODE-declarer; the amode-local-generator is **loc amode**. **loc amode** generates an **amode** object on the stack and possesses its name on that special occurrence. We shall depict the creation of the **amode** object by a special kind of arrow:

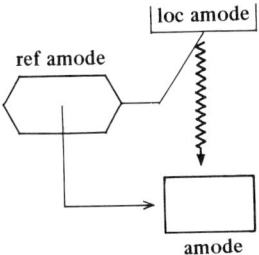

Now consider the identity-declaration:

(E3)   **ref amode** *aname* = **loc amode** ;

What happens is essentially the same as in E2:

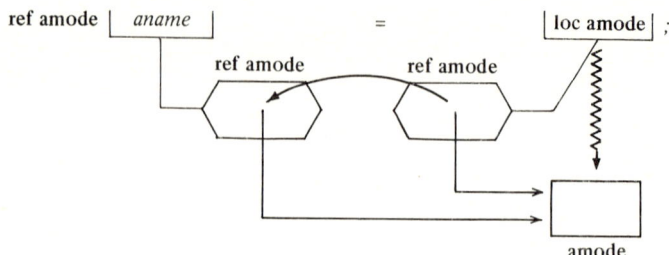

The identifier *aname* is made to possess an instance of the name possessed by **loc amode**, and consequently it refers to the newly created **amode** object on the stack.

Of all identity-declarations this is the only kind that occurs in most other programming languages. By an extension it may be written in the contracted and more familiar form:

    amode *aname* ; Although this is a very convenient abbreviation for a very frequent kind of declaration, never forget that the identifier thus declared possesses a **ref amode** object.

  contracted form: strict form:

(E3*) **amode** *aname* ; (E3) **ref amode** *aname* = **loc amode** ;

We may also simplify the picture, and forget about the local-generator. We then return to the picture of 1.1 E1:

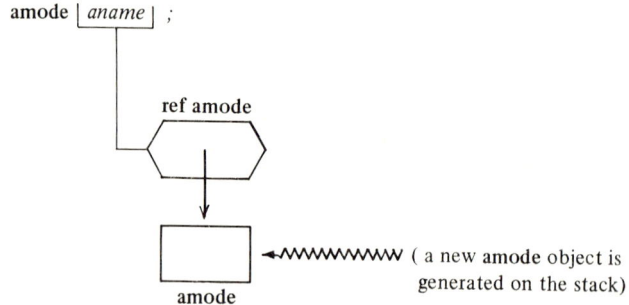

(a new amode object is generated on the stack)

A collateral-declaration like:

    amode *object1* , *object2* , *object3* ;

Ch.1.2.2.4 BASIC CONCEPTS 87

is a contraction of:

> **ref amode** *object1* = **loc amode** ,
> **ref amode** *object2* = **loc amode** ,
> **ref amode** *object3* = **loc amode** ;

1.2.2.4. Initialized declarations

We often wish to assign an initial value to a newly generated variable. Now consider the assignment:

(E4)   **loc amode** := *marllyn*

This is, of course, a perfectly correct assignation. What happens is:

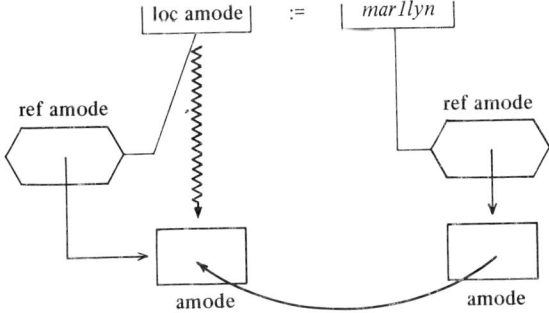

The local-generator possesses the name of the newly created **amode** object, which is initialized to the value referred to by *marllyn*; *marllyn*, of course, is dereferenced (compare 1.1.E2). So far so good, but we cannot do much with it, because no external object in the whole program is made to possess the name of our new **amode**.

However, an assignation possesses the value yielded by its LHS (see 1.1.3) which is **ref amode**. We may now consider E4 as a special case of a reference-to-amode-clause (compare E2) and write:

(E4)   **ref amode** *aname* = **loc amode** := *marllyn* ;

And see what happens:

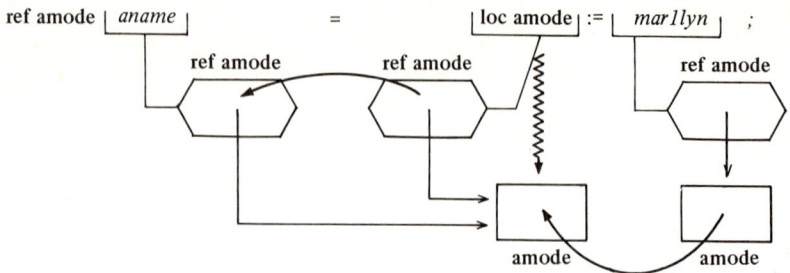

By the same extension used in E3*, this may be written in the more familiar form:

(E4*)   **amode** *aname* := *marllyn* ;   Please, do not confuse this with **amode** *thing* = *marllyn* ; (see E1).

1.2.2.4.1. The concept of a variable

Syntactically, a 'variable' is a reference-to-MODE; a name.

Semantically, the object which is in fact "variable" is the object referred to.

Informally, we may choose an intermediate position and regard the pair of objects, consisting of an instance of a value and the name referring to it, as a variable:

1.2.2.4.2. Names of names

Going up one stair of references, we can generate variable names:

Ch.1.2.2.5   BASIC CONCEPTS   89

(E5)   **ref ref amode** *pointer* = **loc ref amode** *;*

by extension:

(E5*)   **ref amode** *pointer* ;   Observe that again one **ref** is embezzled; *pointer* is made to possess a **ref ref amode** value.

What happens is:

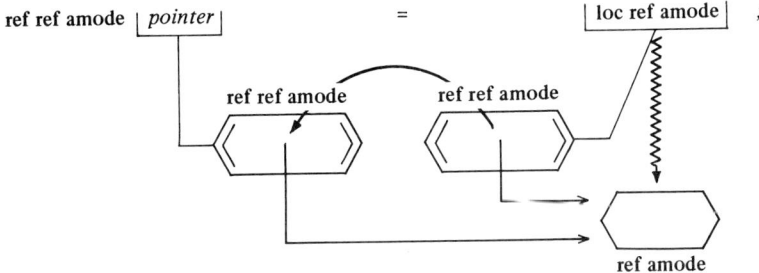

This is essentially the same as E3. The generator **loc ref amode** generates a name on the stack. Such a **ref amode** on the stack may, by assignment to *pointer*, become an instance of a name referring to an **amode** object on the stack. In this way, "indirect addressing" is another fruit of the general concept of an identity-declaration.

1.2.2.5. Casts

Consider the assignment:

(E6)   *pointer* := *marllyn* ;

Here the value referred to by *pointer* (a **ref amode** object) is superseded by the value possessed by *marllyn* (its a priori value; of course there is no dereferencing in this syntactic position; the required mode is **ref amode**).

What happens is:

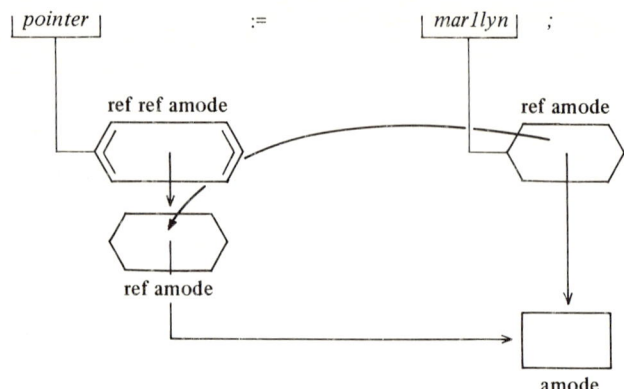

Now the value referred to by *pointer* refers to the value referred to by *marllyn* (describing indirect addressing in a natural language always leads to muddling sentences). Observe the resemblance with the situation in E2, we do the same thing at one reference level higher.

We could also have achieved this in the declaration of *pointer*, again by an initialized declaration.

(E6′)   **ref ref amode** *pointer* = **loc ref amode** := *marllyn* ;

or, still always by the same extension:

(E6*)   **ref amode** *pointer* := *marllyn* ;

To make things workable on the higher reference-to-something levels, we often need dereferencing in syntactic positions where coercion cannot do it for us; for example in the LHS of an assignation. In a reference-to-reference-to-MODE, we have at least two name levels, and we have to make clear which name is meant (how far down we want to assign). In E6′ (*pointer* := *marllyn*) the value assigned is the **ref amode**.

Now suppose we want to assign the **amode** value of *object1* ◊ *object2* to the variable referred to by *pointer* (which is, after E6, the variable *marllyn*). We cannot do it without further preface, *pointer* is one **ref** above the level at which we want to assign.

Now the "preface" is a remarkable little magic wand termed a 'cast', which provides in many situations where coercion fails. We have already used a cast on two occasions (1.1.E6 and 1.1.E8) when we wrote:

amode : XXXXX

Ch.1.2.3   BASIC CONCEPTS   91

There we required an **amode** value to be yielded from XXXXX.
If we now write:

(E7)   *(ref amode : pointer) := object1 ◊ object2*

the LHS becomes a closed-clause yielding a **ref amode** value from *pointer* (dereferencing it once), which is (after E6) the variable possessed by *marllyn*.
What happens is:

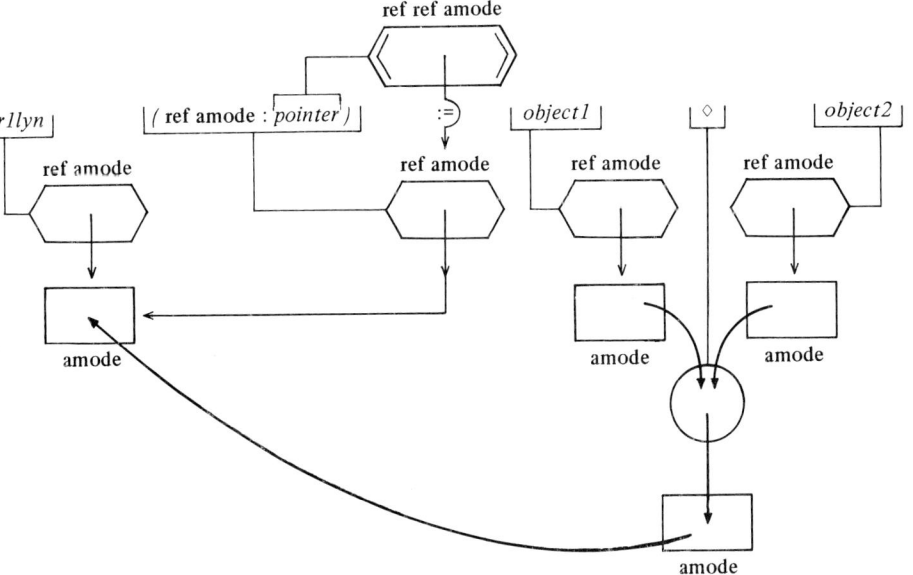

1.2.3. The notion MODE

In this language a mode is something you can define (declare) yourself in terms of other, already defined, modes (see 1.3.3.1). In the Report [R 1.2.1] you will find a set of production rules for "MODE", defining an infinite number of possible modes. They are all derived from five PRIMITIVE modes:

bool , char , int , real , format   (see also Section 2.1.1)

(Occasionally, we shall follow the syntactic style of the Report, as we already did on some occasions, writing for instance "reference-to-reference-to-MODE-identifier". We do so just to point out that for these "notions" exist certain production rules in the syntax, by which they are defined ultimately as sequences of symbols. You can have some confidence that the intuitive meaning of these notions is in good accordance with their syntactic coherence and the meaning imposed upon them by the semantics of the language. Certain parts of notions are written in capital letters. For such "metanotions" exist separate (meta) production rules, defining them in terms of other notions. Some of these metanotions stand for an infinite number of other notions, which is the case with "MODE". Some others cover only a finite number, which is the case with "PRIMITIVE", the production rule of which is:

>   PRIMITIVE :   boolean ;   character ;   integral ;   real ; format.

this simply means that:

>   PRIMITIVE may be boolean or character or integral or real or format.

There is no reason to worry about the syntax, but in the long run you might appreciate our attempts to break you softly to the syntactic saddle and the metanotional stirrups of the Report.)

In this Informal Introduction "**amode**" stands for "a mode" (you may conceive **amode** as a declarer for some, not specified, MODE). We shall also use indications like **bmode, umode, zmode**. For all these declarers you may substitute any MODE-declarer derived from the PRIMITIVEs, with the assistance of the symbols:

ref	(this section and 2.2)
proc	(this section and 4.2.1)
struct	(Sections 1.4.1 and 2.4.1)
"[" and "]"	(Sections 1.5.1 and 2.5.1)
union	(Sections 1.6.1 and 2.6.1)
long	(Sections 1.7.1 and 2.7.2)

We have already met *marilyn* and her sisters *mar1,2,3lyn* who all possess **ref amode** objects. We shall soon meet also their cousins *marUlyn, marVlyn* and other *mar*-vellous ladies. However, we shall in the sequal substitute for **amode** other declarers (even **ref amode**), and all the girls will then follow the new fashions. We trust that you will recognise them in their other moods.

1.2.3.1. **proc** modes

In this section we consider the case in which we substitute for **amode** the declarer of a procedure with parameters delivering a value or not. We mainly

BASIC CONCEPTS

do so to elucidate further the principle of identity, which is the main subject of 1.2. A more complete discussion of declarations in which procedures are involved will be found in 4.2.

All values of mode PROCEDURE are routines. A routine is a sequence of symbols which is the same as some closed-clause. In a call this closed-clause is activated. In a routine we can make use of formal-parameters; the actual-parameters are then supplied when the routine is activated. It is not without reason that the LHS of an identity-declaration is denominated as the "formal-parameter", and the RHS as the "actual-parameter". The fact is that the identity-declaration states very precisely what happens when an actual-parameter is supplied, be it in a procedure call or in an operation in a formula.

A routine can be denoted by a routine-denotation, in much the same way as, for instance, "**true**" may denote the value of this sentence. In the denotation of a routine with formal-parameters we find the formal-PARAMETERS-pack, a sequence of formal-parameters separated by comma-symbols "**,**" or go-on-symbols "**;**".

Declarers for procedures with parameters (see also 4.2.1) have the form:

not delivering a value:	delivering a **zmode** value:
proc (umode **)**	**proc (** umode **)** zmode
proc (umode , vmode **)**	**proc (** umode , vmode **)** zmode
proc (umode ; vmode **)**	**proc (** umode ; vmode **)** zmode
proc (umode , vmode , wmode **)**	**proc (** umode , vmode , wmode **)** zmode
etc.	etc.

"**(**" , "**)**" and the sequence of declarers between them form the virtual-PARAMETERS-pack.

Each declarer in the virtual-PARAMETERS-pack corresponds to a formal-parameter in the formal-PARAMETERS-pack in the routine-denotation:

e.g. corresponding to **umode** ⇒ **umode** U
corresponding to **umode** , **vmode** ⇒ **umode** U , **vmode** V etc.

We now reconsider:

(E1)   **amode** *thing* = *marllyn* ;

We take for **amode** the declarer:

(E8.1)   **proc (** umode , vmode **)** zmode

and for *marllyn* the routine-denotation:

(E8.2)   *((* umode *U* , vmode *V)* zmode : XXXXX *)*

in which we find the formal-PARAMETERS-pack *(* umode *U* , vmode *V)*, corresponding to the virtual-PARAMETERS-pack *(* umode , vmode *)* in E8.1.

We thus obtain the procedure declaration:

(E8)   **proc** *(* umode , vmode *)* zmode *thing* = *((* umode *U* , vmode *V)* zmode : XXXXX *)* ;

which, by extension, may be written in the more intimate form:

(E8*)   **proc** *thing* = *(* umode *U* , vmode *V)* zmode : XXXXX ;

The routine possessed by E8.2 is the closed-clause:

(E8.2*)   *(* umode *U* = ~ , vmode *V* = ~ ; zmode : XXXXX *)*

The "~"s are only there as locum tenens for the actual-MODE-parameters; we will, very soon, get rid of them.

The result of the elaboration of the procedure declaration E8* is that *thing* is made to possess a (new instance of) the routine E8.2*. Observe that the closed-clause is not elaborated, but transformed into a **proc** *(* umode , vmode *)* zmode. The result of the elaboration of E8* may be depicted as below:

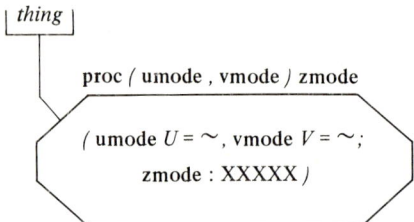

1.2.3.2.1. The supply of the actual parameters (call by value)

Calling the *thing* of E8*, we have to supply an actual-umode-parameter and an actual-vmode-parameter. Let *marUlyn* be a **umode** variable and *marVlyn* a **vmode** variable. If we now "parametrize" *thing* by writing the actual-PARAMETERS-pack *(* marUlyn, marVlyn *)* right behind *thing*, we obtain the procedure call:

(E9)   *thing (marUlyn , marVlyn)*

The elaboration of this call effectuates (in the routine possessed by *thing*)

Ch.1.2.3.2.1 BASIC CONCEPTS 95

the replacement of the "~"s by the corresponding actual-parameters. (The Report states more precisely that this trick is done to a copy of the closed-clause possessed by *thing*). The result is the closed-clause:

(E10)   (**umode** $U = marUlyn$, **vmode** $V = marVlyn$; **zmode** : XXXXX)

This closed-clause is then elaborated, yielding a **zmode** value which is possessed by the call:

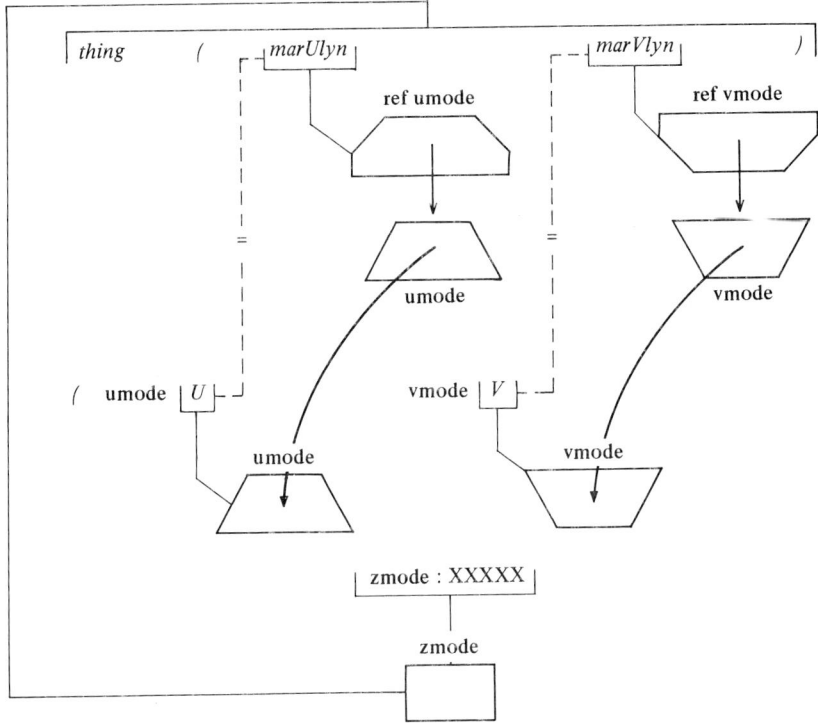

If, for instance, *marZlyn* is declared to be a **zmode** variable, then you may assign:

(E9*) $marZlyn := thing (marUlyn , marVlyn)$

which, in fact, elaborates into:

(E10*) $marZlyn := ($ **umode** $U = marUlyn$, **vmode** $V = marVlyn$; **zmode** : XXXXX $)$

1.2.3.2.2. The supply of the actual parameters (call by reference)

Observe that in E10 you cannot assign to the formal-parameters U and V; the identity-declarations in E10 are of type E1; U and V are constants, instances of the values referred to by *marUlyn* and *marVlyn* respectively. This situation has some similarity to "call by value" in some other programming languages.

If you want to assign to a formal-parameter, you have to declare it to be a reference-to-MODE; the replacement action then leads to an identity-declaration of type E2 (equivalence, two names referring to the same instance of a value).

Consider, for example, the procedure declaration:

(E11)   **proc** *(* **ref zmode** *,* **umode** *,* **vmode** *) assign thing* =
        ((**ref zmode** *Z ,* **umode** *U ,* **vmode** *V): Z :=* XXXXX *)*

or, abbreviated:

(E11*) **proc** *assign thing* = *(* **ref zmode** *Z ,* **umode** *U ,* **vmode** *V) :*
        Z := XXXXX *;*

The call:

(E12)   *assign thing (marZlyn , marUlyn , marVlyn)*

elaborates into:

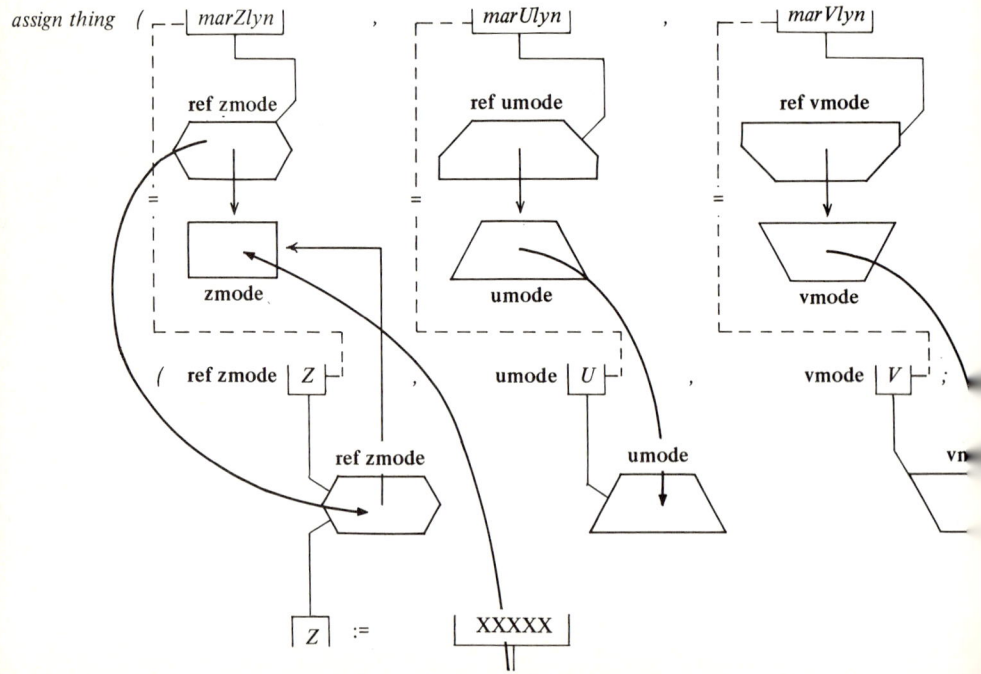

Ch.1.2.3.2.3 BASIC CONCEPTS 97

The call E12 is equivalent to the closed-clause:

(E12*)   (**ref zmode** Z = *marZlyn* , **umode** U = *marUlyn* ,
          vmode V = *marVlyn* ; Z := XXXXX)

It is important to observe that the first identity-declaration is of the type E2. Its effect is that, by its elaboration, the formal-parameter Z is made to possess a new instance of the name possessed by the actual-parameter *marZlyn*. The result is that Z and *marZlyn* both refer to the same **zmode** value. Consequently, assignation to Z within the routine has the same result as assignation to *marZlyn* and, although the scope of the name possessed by Z is limited to the closed-clause (the routine), the value referred to still exists when the elaboration of the routine is completed. This is exactly what we wanted to achieve.

Conforming to the domesticated terminology of a "call by value", we might refer to the elaboration of a reference-to-MODE-parameter as a "call by reference".

The second and third declarations make U and V to possess constants, new instances of the values referred to by *marUlyn* and *marVlyn* respectively; these actual parameters are "called by value".

1.2.3.2.3. The supply of the actual parameters (other possibilities)

Now we know exactly what happens to the actual-parameters in a procedure call, we shall find no difficulties in other applications of the principle of identity. For example:

Suppose you want to call *assign thing*, but you are only interested in the elaboration of the routine (for its side effects, for instance) but not in the implied assignation to the first parameter. Then you may call:

(E13)   *assign thing (* **loc zmode** , *marUlyn* , *marVlyn*)

which elaborates into:

(E13*)   (**ref zmode** Z = **loc zmode** , **umode** U = *marUlyn* ,
          vmode V = *marVlyn* ; Z := XXXXX)

and see what happens. The first identity-declaration is now of type E3; Z is made to possess a variable of local scope. The value in which you were not interested is assigned to this local variable and disappears when the elaboration of the routine is completed.

Suppose the value of, for instance, *marVlyn* does not matter under some circumstances, and you have no **vmode** value at hand in the range where you want to call *assign thing*. Then you may call:

(E14)   *assign thing (marZlyn , marUlyn ,* **skip** *)*

Now, when this call is elaborated, the textually third "~" in the routine is replaced by **skip**. A **skip** happens to be a very docile little dud, it always delivers an undefined value of the required mode without any further action.

1.2.4. Summary

For their importance in this language, we review briefly the constructions E1, ---, E6. Make them to possess internal objects in your own memory:

recommended form:					strict form :			
amode *thing*	= *mar1lyn* ;				**amode** *thing*	= *mar1lyn*	;	(E1)
ref amode *name*	= *mar1lyn* ;			**ref**	**amode** *name*	= *mar1lyn*	;	(E2)
amode *aname*	;			**ref**	**amode** *aname*	= **loc amode**	;	(E3)
amode *aname*	:= *mar1lyn* ;			**ref**	**amode** *aname*	= **loc amode** :=		
						mar1lyn	;	(E4)
ref amode *pointer*	;		**ref**	**ref**	**amode** *pointer*	= **loc ref amode**	;	(E5)
ref amode *pointer*	:= *mar1lyn* ;		**ref**	**ref**	**amode** *pointer*	= **loc ref amode** :=		
						mar1lyn	;	(E6)

And remember:

(E1)   *thing* does not possess a name and you cannot assign to it (provided, however, that **amode** does not happen to be a mode-indication for a **ref bmode**).

(E2)   *name* possesses the same name as *mar1lyn*; assignation to *name* has the same result as assignation to *mar1lyn* and vice versa.

(E3)   *aname* possesses a new name, different from all other names (that is what the local-generator achieves) and you can assign to it.

(E4)   *aname* possesses a new name (variable) and is initialized by assigning the value referred to by *mar1lyn* to it.

(E5)   *pointer* possesses a reference to a name (a variable name or name of a name); you can assign a name to it.

(E6)   *pointer* possesses a reference to a name and is initialized to refer to the name possessed by *mar1lyn*.

Vertical readers, please turn to 2.2.

1.3. Indicants, modes and operators

1.3.1. Representations

A 'program' is defined to be a sequence of symbols. Consider for example:

>**begin real** $x, y, z;$
>$read\ (x);\ read\ (y);$
>$z := (x + y)/2 - sqrt(x \times y);$
>$print\ (z)$
>
>**end**

This piece of program begins with the symbol "**begin**" followed by the sequence "**real**" "x" "," "y" "," "z" ";" "r" "e" "a" "d" "(" "x" ")" ";" and so on. Typographical display features, such as blank space, change to new line, and change to new page have no significance in the language. Strictly speaking "**begin**", "**real**" "x" "," etc. are not themselves symbols; they rather represent them.

In the Report the representation(s) of symbols is strongly suggested, rather than explicitly prescribed. For the benefit of available charactersets, other representations may be chosen for a specific implementation of the language; one and the same implementation might even accept different representations from different input-devices. The given piece of program could for example look like:

>'$BEGIN$ '$REAL\ X, Y, Z;$
>$READ(X);\ READ(Y);$
>$Z := (X + Y)\ /\ 2 - SQRT\ (X \times Y)\ ;$
>$PRINT(Z)$
>
>'END

or even:

>'$BEGIN$' '$REAL$' $X, Y, Z.,$
>$READ(X).,\ READ(Y).,$
>$Z\ ..= (X + Y)\ /\ 2 - SQRT\ (X * Y).,$
>$PRINT(Z)$
>
>'END'

In principle a program in this language can be represented in a 48 - characterset.

On the other hand, if small letters and capitals are both available, one could for instance reserve the capitals for the construction of representations for special symbols such as the begin-symbol, the real-symbol etc. If suitable tokens are available one could also choose other representations for the go-on-symbol and the becomes-symbol and the example might then look like:

$$\begin{aligned}
&BEGIN \ REAL \ x, y, z \Rightarrow \\
&\quad read(x) \Rightarrow read(y) \Rightarrow \\
&\quad z \leftarrow (x + y) \ / \ 2 - sqrt \ (x \times y) \Rightarrow \\
&\quad print(z) \\
&END
\end{aligned}$$

In this Informal Introduction we shall always follow the suggestions of the Report [see R 3.1.1], but we shall occasionally use capital letters in identifiers even though they are not obligatory for all implementors. Where the Report suggests alternatives, we shall follow our own taste which may, however, depend upon the context. A complete list of the alternatives suggested by the Report is given in Appendix 1.

1.3.2. Symbols, indicants and comments

In this language a rather extensive set of symbols is required, and moreover, we need some expedient for constructing an arbitrary number of 'indicants' (new symbols).

The Report does not state explicitly what is or may be an 'indicant'; this is entirely a matter of representation and there you are free, be it by the grace of your implementor.

A decisive point of course is the set of characters, types and marks producible by your input equipment; or, to state it more precisely, distinguishable by the input devices on your computer. If this happens to be you, then there is hardly any problem, thanks to the productive power of human handwriting and the perceptive qualities of the human eye. With an automaton there may, however, be some difficulty. Usually its senses are only able to distinguish a rather small set (some power of two) of different combinations of punched holes or magnetized spots in some material. In that binary form usually at least one font of letters (we represent them in lower case), ten digits, the punctuation marks ".", ",", ":", ";" and "'", one pair of brackets "(" and ")" and a more or less generally accepted set of marks, such as "+", "−", "×" (or "*"), "/" and "=", can be represented. In more favourable cases, the equipment may afford more luxury in the form of a second case of letters and/or some selection of types such as "<", ">", "[", "]", "∨", "∧" and perhaps even "¬", "↑", "$_{10}$" etc. In particular an underlining "_" and a vertical stroke "|" may be available and can be used to assist in the construction of other tokens like, for instance, "≠", "≤", "≥" etc.

Nevertheless, this language needs much more than all the marks mentioned, and thus, even for the representation of the finite set of required symbols, an expedient to construct symbols from available marks appears to be essential. The usual way to do this is by "stropping". The strop mechanism may be open- and close-apostrophes, or an apostrophe used as "bold face shift", or underlining, or bold type face, or even (if you are willing to sacrifice them) the use of upper case letters (i.e. the capitals):

"*begin*"   is an identifier or 'tag'   (see 1.4)

but:

" '*begin*' ", " ' begin " , "**begin**" , "*begin*" or "*BEGIN*"

might be used as a stropped word to represent a certain symbol.

Here we adopt stropping by bold type face. In this notational convention, a sequence of marks like "**notification**" is to be considered as one indivisible symbol and definitely not as a sequence of the symbols "**not**" , "**if**" , "**i**" , "**c**" , "**at**" , "**i**" and "**on**", even though "**not**" , "**if**" , "**i**" and "**at**" happen to be proposed representations for required symbols, and "**c**" and "**on**" very well might be some other indicants. Whether you want to consider such a construct as an ill chosen representation (in particular if such a splitting happens to make sense) or not is related to your inclination to meditate on problems concerning the amount of blank paper needed to separate spots of ink. Anyhow, you will be wasting your time, because your implementor hardly has any choice other than to dictate here something pretty close to a well shaped blank space, even in spite of the fact that blank space, change to a new line and the like have no meaning in this language.

We now assume ourselves able to construct as many symbols as we need. For example "**not**" for "¬" and "**i**" for "⊥" if we are unable or unwilling to produce or use "¬" and "⊥" on our input equipment. In particular we are now in the position to introduce as many indicants as we want, and we really need them for:

1)   MODE-mode-indications   (see 1.3.3.1)

for example we used **amode** as an amode-mode-indication

2,3)   operators and PRIORITY-indications   (see 1.3.3.2 and 3)

Of course, by the grace of your implementor, you might still be free to take, for example, "?" even for a mode-indication, but we shall never do so.

For the representation of an operator, however, it may be a good thing to use "+", "×", "∧" etc. if the action defined can be considered as an "addition", "multiplication" or "conjunction" in some technical sense. For the rest we shall use stropped words for operators as well.

A particular role is played by the comment-symbol represented by "**comment**", "**co**", "#" or "¢" and, maybe in certain implementations, by "**pr**" or "**pragmat**". These symbol(s) serve to step outside the language for a while.

A 'comment' consists of two comment-symbols enclosing an arbitrary sequence of characters, marks and types, not containing **comment**, ¢, **co**, #, **pragmat** or **pr**. Comments can be inserted at any place in a program, if such is desirable even "inside" an identifier, but not inside a character or string denotation (5.1.1.1 and 5.5.1.1).

A specific implementation may distinguish human comments, between two **comment**s or ¢s, from pragmats between two **pragmat**s or **pr**s.

A (human) comment then serves to supply additional human information for the possibly human reader.

A pragmat may contain a message for a specific compiler (for instance to inform it to compile in some special mode or sub-language or to subjoin the program to some library or something), or for an operating system (for instance to inform it concerning certain required equipment or availability of hardware features, certain libraries etc.). A pragmat will usually be subject to the rules of a specific command language.

Consider the following program:

    pr *ALGOL68* **pr**
    begin   **comment** *this example is based on the*
                  report on the algorithmic language
                  algol68 section 2.3.c; end of **comment**
            proc pragmat *NONREC* **pragmat** *pr = (: pr) ;*
            p¢*we now call this procedure* **cor**
            comment *if NONREC means "nonrecursive compilation",*
                whatever that may be, then we got into
                trouble #
    end pr *RUN* **pr** ¢ ??? ¢

In the standard-prelude (the standard declarations) of the Report a special comment-symbol "c" is used to express that the comment should be replaced by a representation of an actual-declarer or closed-clause suggested by that comment [R 10. step 10]. In this Informal Introduction we shall follow this convention. (e.g. in 3.7.2.E5).

1.3.3. Other declarations

Besides the identity-declaration (1.2) we have:

1) mode-declarations   (1.3.3.1)
2) operation-declarations (1.3.3.2)
3) priority-declarations (1.3.3.3)

Each of these defines the meaning of indicants.

1.3.3.1. Mode-declarations

A mode-declaration has the form:

mode MODE-mode-indication = actual-MODE-declarer

For example, in:

(E1)   **mode pram** = **proc** (**umode** , **vmode**) **zmode** ;

the pram-mode-indication **pram** is declared to stand for the actual-declarer, which is **proc** (**umode** , **vmode**) **zmode**, and now, by declaring for example:

(E2)   **ref pram** *puvz* = **loc pram** ;

or, by the usual contraction:

(E2*)   **pram** *puvz* ;

You declare *puvz* to possess a name referring to a value of the mode **pram**, which is a routine with a **umode** and a **vmode** as parameters, delivering a **zmode** value:

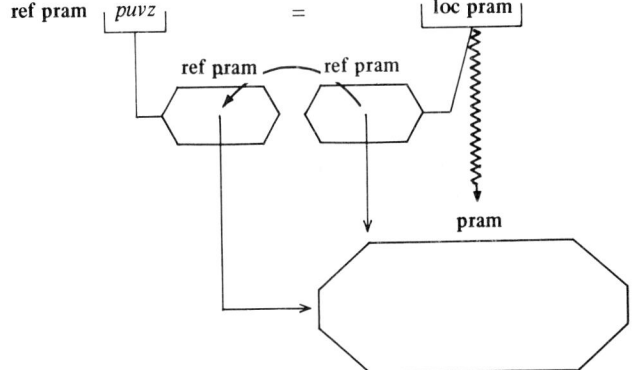

We may now assign to the procedure variable *puvz*, for example:

(E3) *puvz* := *thing*

where *thing* is declared as in 1.2.3.1.E8 to possess a **proc** *(umode , vmode)* **zmode**. What happens in the elaboration of E3 is:

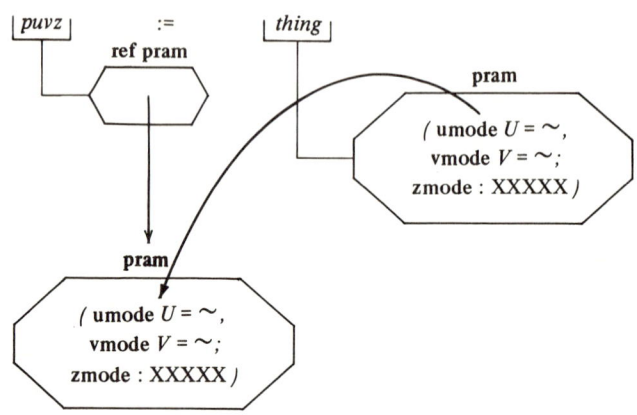

In fact we are now repeating the things we discussed in 1.2.

By virtue of the mode-declaration E1, the identity-declaration E2 "develops" into:

(E2**) **ref proc** *(umode , vmode)* **zmode** *puvz* =
    loc proc *(umode , vmode)* **zmode** ;

"to develop" is a technical term, which should be distinguished from "to elaborate".
In "elaboration", actions on internal objects are performed;
In "development", a mode-indication is replaced by its actual-declarer.

(One could say that "elaboration" is performed by the object code (at run time), while "development" is an action of the compiler.)

(In E3 the semantics of the language state that the **pram** possessed by *thing* is copied into the **pram** referred to by *puvz*. As in other situations where copying is prescribed, one should remember an important remark in Section 1.1.6.h of the Report: "Any of these processes may be replaced by any process which causes the same effect". In particular where routines are manipulated, the implementor usually has other expedients at his disposal which "cause the same effect" as copying. The same applies to many other situations of this kind, particularly where copying is involved.)

You may declare a mode-indication as a convenient abbreviation for certain declarers (as, for instance, was the case in E1 and E2). You could do without them in these situations, at the price of time and ink.

There are, however, very interesting and important situations in which mode-declarations are indispensible for expressing certain essential interrelations of objects in the memory. Some of these more involved mode-declarations will be used in other sections (see 1.4).

Circular mode-declarations like:

mode amode = amode ;
mode amode = bmode ; mode bmode = cmode ;
                          mode cmode = amode ;
mode amode = ref amode ;

might bring the compiler into difficulties and are apparently of no use. Consequently, they are excluded by the declaration condition (one of the context conditions). However, there are constructions which might puzzle you at first sight, because they have an appearance of circularity (in fact are circular in some aspect), but nevertheless are very useful and can (easily) be implemented. Of course, such mode-declarations are not excluded.

It is, however, not so easy to separate the sheep from the goats, which is why the declaration condition is really awkward in its formulation [R 4.4.3 and 4.4.4]. Don't invest too much time in it; the confidence that all useful and logically coherent mode-declarations are allowed is fully justified.

1.3.3.2. Operation declarations

There are two kinds of operators:
monadic, declared as:

(E4) **op** (**umode**) **zmode** m = ((**umode** U) **zmode** : XXXXX) ;

or, by extension:

(E4*)   **op** m = (**umode** U) **zmode** : XXXXX ;

and dyadic, declared as:

(E5) **op** (**umode** , **vmode**) **zmode** ◊ = ((**umode** U, **vmode** V)
                          zmode : XXXXX) ;

or, by the same extension:

(E5*)   **op** ◊ = (**umode** U, **vmode** V) **zmode** : XXXXX ;

Observe the resemblance to procedure declarations. Instead of declarers like **proc (umode) zmode** and **proc (umode , vmode) zmode** we have here **op (umode) zmode** and **op (umode , vmode) zmode**.

The result of the elaboration of an operation-declaration is that the operator is made to possess a (new instance of) the routine. For example, E5 (E5*) elaborates into:

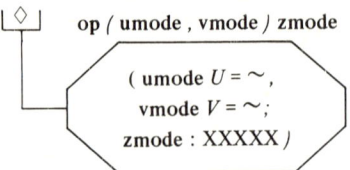

In contrast to procedures, an operator can only be defined to possess a routine and not to refer to one. Consequently, the strict forms (as in E5) are never of any practical use, and we shall never write one again.

If *marZlyn* is declared to be a **zmode** variable, then the assignation:

(E6) *marZlyn* := *marUlyn* ◊ *marVlyn*

elaborates into:

(E6*) *marZlyn* := (**umode** U = *marUlyn* , **vmode** V = *marVlyn* ; **zmode** : XXXXX)

The closed-clause in E6* is then elaborated, yielding a **zmode** value which is possessed by the formula:

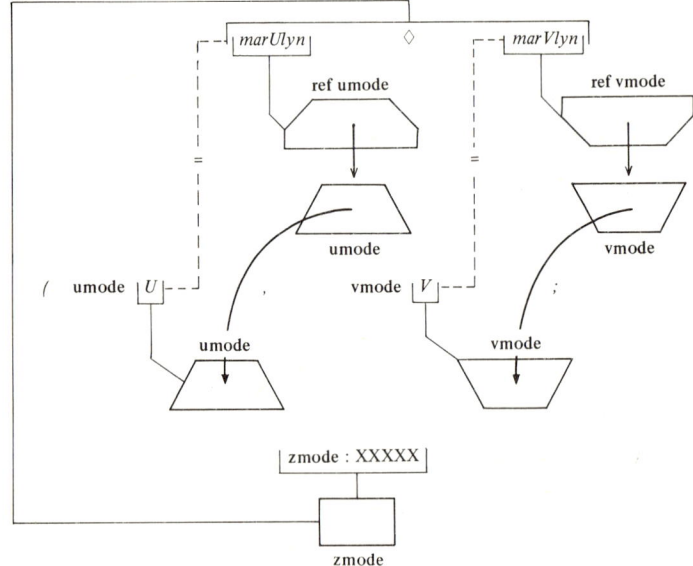

Ch.1.3.3.3 BASIC CONCEPTS 107

Observe that this picture is almost identical to the picture of Section 1.2.3.2.1.

There is, however, a fundamental contradistinction to procedures. For one and the same operation-indication (sloppy: "operator"), more than one declaration may occur within the same range. Which one then applies depends entirely on the mode(s) of the operand(s) in the particular formula in which the operator is applied.

For example:

(E7)   op m = (amode A) amode : XXXXX ;
(E8)   op m = (bmode B) bmode : WWWWW ;
(E9)   op ◊ = (amode A1 , A2) amode : XXXXX ;
(E10) op ◊ = (bmode B1 , B2) bmode : AAAAA ;
       amode am , am1 , am2 ; bmode bm , bm1 , bm2 ;

```
am1 := m am2 ;         ⇒ E7 applies
bm1 := m bm2 ;         ⇒ E8 applies
am  := am1 ◊ am2 ;     ⇒ E9 applies
bm  := bm1 ◊ bm2 ;     ⇒ E10 applies
```

Observe that it is determined during the elaboration of the formula which operation-indication (operator), i.e. which routine, applies.

1.3.3.3. Priority declarations

All monadic-operators have the same, the highest, priority.

For dyadic-operators nine priority levels can be declared by a priority-declaration of the form:

priority ◊ = NUMBER-token

in which "NUMBER-token" produces one of the nine digits "*1*" to "*9*".

In a formula with dyadic-operators of equal priority like:

(E11)   am ◊ am1 ◊ am2 ◊ am

the implied bracketing is:

(E11*) ((am ◊ am1) ◊ am2) ◊ am

Priority-declarations may impose another (implied) bracketing:

(E12)   **priority** ○ = 6 , ◊ = 7 , × = 8 ;

the bracketing implied in the formula:

(E13) $A \times B \diamond C \times D \circ E \diamond F \circ G \times H \diamond I \times J \times K \circ L$

is:

(E13*) $((((A \times B) \diamond (C \times D)) \circ (E \diamond F)) \circ ((G \times H) \diamond ((I \times J) \times K))) \circ L$

Unless explicit bracketing requires otherwise, monadic-operators are elaborated first, i.e. they have the highest priority:

(E14) $am := \mathbf{m}\, am1 \diamond \mathbf{m}\, am2$

is parsed like:

(E14*) $am := (\mathbf{m}\, am1) \diamond (\mathbf{m}\, am2)$

Of course it would have been possible (and in fact has been investigated) to declare different priority levels for different monadic-operators. However, it makes matters very awkward without much gain. The main root of this smallness of gain is that, if **m1, m2, ---, mn** were monadic-operators with different priorities, nevertheless only one parsing is conceivable for the formula **m1 m2 --- mn** *operand*, namely:

$$(\mathbf{m1}\,(\mathbf{m2}\,(\,---\,(\mathbf{mn}\, operand\,)\,---\,)))$$

The gain can thus be found only in combination with dyadic-operators. There is only one situation in which you might feel sorry (see 5.1.3).

Vertical readers, please turn to 2.3.

1.4. Stowed values, structures

1.4.0. STOWED values

In this language values (one or more) can be STOWED (i.e. collected) to form a value of a new mode. The metanotion "STOWED" stands for:

1) structured-with-FIELDS

or

2) row-of-MODE

corresponding to two entirely different systems of collecting:

1) into a "structured value"   (this section)
2) into a "multiple value"   (section 1.5).

In a multiple value you collect values of essentially the same mode, its "elements", each of which can be selected by a specific integer, its index. The mode of a multiple value is row-of-MODE and covers the concept of "array" (or "vector", "matrix", "dimension", etc.) in other programming languages.

In a structure you collect values of (not necessarily) different modes, the 'fields' of the structure, each of which can be selected by a specific field-selector. Structured values cover what in other programming languages are known under a variety of names like "records", "lists", "trees", "queues", "chains", etc.

The important feature of structures is that values of different modes may be collected into them. In particular, one or more of the fields may be references to other values, in which way lists and trees of all kinds may be constructed.

Another important feature, however, is that the selection of a field in a structure may very well take place at compile time, whereas the index of an element in a multiple value is usually determined (computed) at run time. Therefore, even in situations in which multiple values are the only possibility in many other programming languages, in this language you will often use structures instead. A good example is the **compl** (see Section 2.4.4).

Finally, the general concept of MODE allows you to build multiple values the elements of which are structures, and vice versa to build structures the fields of which are multiple values.

1.4.1. Enumeration by tagging

By a mode-declaration like:

(E0) **mode triple** = **struct** (**umode** *first* , **vmode** *second* , **wmode** *third*) ;

triple is declared to indicate a new class (mode) of values, each of which is structured with three fields, a **umode** field *first*, a **vmode** field *second* and a **wmode** field *third*. *first*, *second* and *third* are the field-selectors.

Syntactically a selector is a sequence of letters and digits with a leading letter. It may look like an identifier but it is not. It is important to recognize clearly its function:

> A field-selector as such does not possess any internal object.
> A field-selector is part of a declarer or of a selection.

A **triple** object, as declared by E0, may be visualized as a box with a **umode**, a **vmode** and a **wmode** box within it, the fields of the **triple**. These fields can be "pulled up" by their field-selectors *first*, *second* and *third*. We might imagine a piece of cord between the field and its tag:

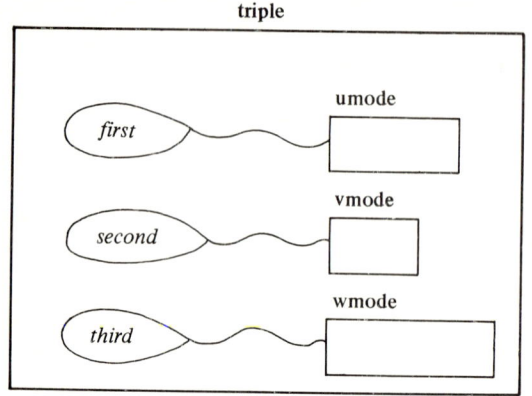

It is important to bear in mind that *first*, *second* and *third* are not names referring to the fields (see 1.4.1.1)

Merely to simplify our drawings we shall often write the selectors inside the boxes:

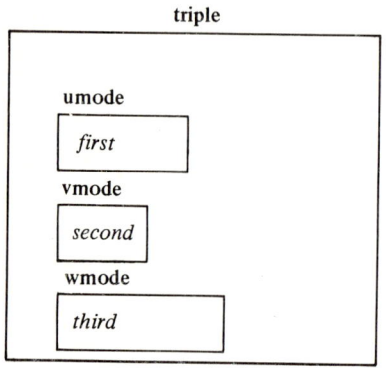

warning :   our drawings serve to visualize internal objects and matters of elaboration;
  please do not confuse the selector in the box with the instance of a value in it.

1.4.1.1. Structured constants

We now reconsider the three fundamental identity-declarations E1, E2 and E3 of Section 1.2, in which we substitute systematically **triple** (as declared in E0) for **amode**:

(E1)   **triple** *thing* = *marllyn* ;

By E1, *thing* possesses a new instance of the **triple** value referred to by *marllyn* (which is of mode **ref triple**):

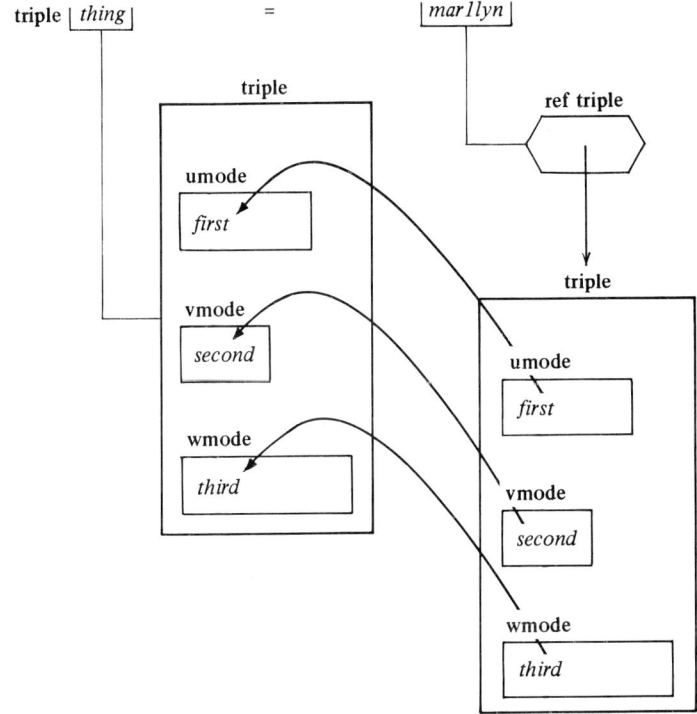

By this declaration *thing* possesses a **triple** object and its fields can be selected separately by pulling them up by their tags:

first **of** *thing*	selects	the **umode** object ,
second **of** *thing*	selects	the **vmode** object ,
third **of** *thing*	selects	the **wmode** object .

Because *thing* does not refer to a **triple**, but possesses one, you cannot assign to it. Consequently you cannot assign to its fields *first* **of** *thing*, *second* **of** *thing* and *third* **of** *thing*, which in their turn possess the fields of *thing*.

In the declaration E1, *marllyn* is dereferenced, because *thing* is required to be of **triple** mode, and its fields are copied into the **triple** *thing* thus defined; the supersession is a triple action (three fields are copied). But, in the range of this declaration, whatever may happen to the fields of the **triple** referred to by *mar1lyn*, nothing can happen to the fields of the **triple** possessed by *thing*. You may select them, you cannot change them; *first* **of** *thing* etc. are not names.

1.4.1.2. Names of structures

By the declaration:

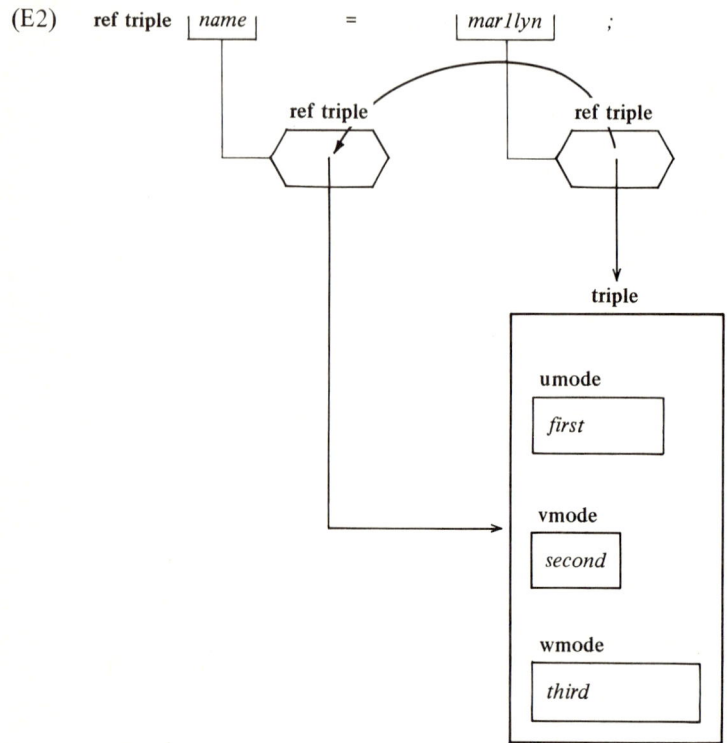

mar1lyn is not dereferenced (see 1.2.E2) as in E1, because the formal-declarer requires a **ref triple** value.

Clearly, *name* is a name, referring to the same **triple** object as *mar1lyn* (two identifiers referring to the same internal **triple**).

You may assign to *name*, for example:

(E2*)   *name* := *mar2lyn*

by which assignation the **triple** object referred to by *mar2lyn* is copied into the **triple** object referred to by *name* (and *mar1lyn*).

Ch.1.4.1.3   BASIC CONCEPTS   113

Moreover you can assign to the names:

> *first* **of** *name* , *second* **of** *name* and *third* **of** *name* .

For example, the assignation E2* is equivalent to the collateral assignation:

(E2*)   (first **of** *name*   :=   *first* **of** *mar2lyn* ,
             second **of** *name*   :=   *second* **of** *mar2lyn* ,
             third **of** *name*   :=   *third* **of** *mar2lyn*)

Recapitulating:

> *first* **of** *thing* , *second* **of** *thing* and *third* **of** *thing*
> possess the fields of the **triple** possessed by *thing* ,

but:

> first **of** *name* , *second* **of** *name* and *third* **of** *name*
> possess names which refer to the fields of the **triple**
> referred to by *name* .

1.4.1.3. Creation of new structures

A new **triple** variable can be declared (see 1.2.E3) by means of a local-generator:

(E3)   **ref triple** *atriple* = **loc triple** ;

or by the usual contraction:

(E3*)   **triple** *atriple* ;

What happens is essentially the same as in 1.2.E3:

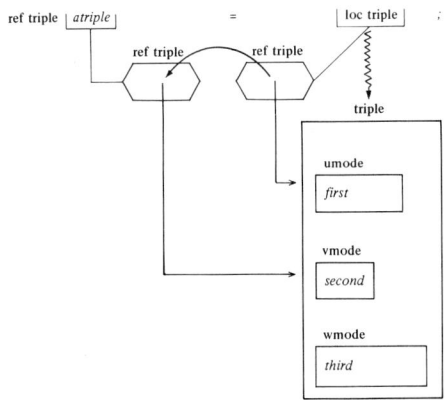

Of course you can also initialize a thus declared new **triple**:

(E4)   **ref triple** *atriple* = **loc triple** := *marllyn* ;

or by the usual contraction:

(E4*)   **triple** *atriple* := *marllyn* ;

You are not required by the syntax to declare a new mode like **triple** (E0) before you give identity-declarations; that is, you may very well declare:

(E3**)   **struct** (**umode** *first* , **vmode** *second* , **wmode** *third*) *atriple* ;

In most cases, however, you will spare time and ink by a mode-declaration. Moreover, if you use structures to construct lists etc., the mode-declaration is indispensable (see 1.4.3).

1.4.2. Different objects in one box

The fields of a structure may be of different modes, but could also be the same. In the latter case it is often a matter of efficiency (or even convenience) whether you declare them in a structure or in a multiple value. You can stow as many values in a structure as you wish, but you have to enumerate them in the declaration by tagging the fields explicitly. The number of fields in a structure is determined statically (at compile time). The minimum number is one, the maximum depends only on your perseverance in writing them down.

Of course the field-selctors in one structure must all be different. However, if it suits you, you may very well use the same sequence of symbols as a field selector in different structures or even elsewhere as an identifier.

Just to give you some impressions, consider:

(E5)   **mode threeofakind** = **struct** (**amode** *one* , *two* , *three*) ;

which is a contraction of:

(E5*)   **mode threeofakind** = **struct** (**amode** *one* , **amode** *two* , **amode** *three*) ;

and may even be written as:

(E5**)   **struct threeofakind** = (**amode** *one* , *two* , *three*) ;

And consider further:

(E6)   **mode couple**   = **struct** (**man** *one* , **wife** *two*) ;

Ch.1.4.2   BASIC CONCEPTS   115

(E7)   **mode largebox** = **struct** (**amode** *one* , *two* , *three* ,
                              bmode *first* , *second* , *third* , *fourth* ,
                              fifth , *sixth* ,
                              cmode *a* , *b* , *c* , *d* , *e* , *f* , *g* , *h* , *i* , *j* , *k* ,
                              l , *m* , *n* , *o* , *p* , *q* , *r*, *s* , *t* , *u* ,
                              v , *w* , *x* , *y* , *z*) ;

Now consider the identity-declarations:

(E8)   **threeofakind** *one* , *two* , *three* , *four* , *five* , *six* , *seven* , *eight* ;
        couple   *romeo and juliet* , *tristan und isolde* ,
                          daphnis et chloe ;
        largebox   *a* , *b* , *c* , *d* , *e* , *f*, *g* , *h* , *i* , *j* , *l* , *m* , *n* , *o* , *p* , *q* , *r* ,
                          s , *t* , *u* , *v* , *w* , *x* , *y* , *z* ;

and observe that there are no ambiguities in:

(E9)   *one* **of** *two* , *two* **of** *three* , *one* **of** *one* ,
        two **of** *romeo and juliet* , *one* **of** *daphnis et chloe* ,
        one **of** *t* , *t* **of** *t* , *o* **of** *o* , *a* **of** *b* ,
        etc.

There is no restriction on the modes of the fields in a structure; every mode is allowed (including structures, see 1.4.4). Consider, for example:

(E10)   **struct surprisepacket** = (**umode** *umode* , **vmode** *vmode* ,
                                      zmode *zmode* ,
                                      proc (**ref zmode** , **umode** , **vmode**) *proc*) ;

and the identity-declarations:

(E11)   **surprisepacket** *S* , *S1* , *S2* , *S3* ;

and the assignments:

(E12)   *umode* **of** *S1* := *marUlyn* ;
        vmode **of** *S2* := *marVlyn* ;
        proc   **of** *S* := *assign thing* ;

By virtue of E11, *proc* **of** *S* is a procedure variable, a reference to a **proc** (**ref zmode** , **umode** , **vmode**) to which we assign in E12 the compatible routine possessed by *assign thing* (see 1.2.E11*). If we now parametrize *proc* **of** *S* (1.2.3.2.1), it will be dereferenced to yield a routine which can be called (this will be discussed in 5.2.1). For reasons to be discussed later (5.5.1.3.E25) we must put brackets around *proc* **of** *S* before parametrizing it.

Now you may fish out what happens by elaboration of the call:

(E13)   (proc of S) (zmode of S3 , umode of S1 , vmode of S2)

1.4.3. Chaining

By declaring a field of a structure to refer to (to be the name of) another value, you can chain this structure to that other value. If, in particular, this other value is of the same mode as the structure, we are able to chain values of the same mode (i.e. to construct "queues", "lists", "trees" etc.).
Consider:

(E14)   mode box = struct (amode *value* , ref box *next*) ;

This mode-declaration is one of those which have an appearance of circularity (see 1.3.3.1). You might think that it develops into:

> mode box = struct (amode *value* ,
>   ref struct (amode *value* ,
>   ref struct (amode *value* ,
>   ref struct (etc. ad infinitum

This, however, is not the case. By the declaration condition (one of the context conditions [see R 4.4.4]) the **box** textually contained in **ref box** *next* in E14, is "shielded" by the **ref**, that is the compiler does not develop this indicant (in this syntactic position).
Consider the identity-declarations:

(E15)   box *A* , *B* , *C* , *D* ;

The result of their elaboration will be:

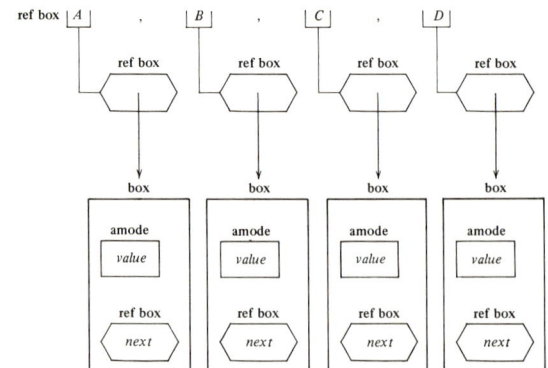

Ch.1.4.3   BASIC CONCEPTS   117

Observe that the field tagged *next* is of the same mode as the names possessed by A, B, etc. There is not a tittle of infinity about the size of these boxes.

Let us first assign:

(E16)   *value* of A := *mar1lyn* ;
        value of B := *mar2lyn* ;
        value of C := *mar3lyn* ;   *mar3* and *4lyn* are **ref amode**s
        value of D := *mar4lyn* ;   like their sisters (see 1.1.2.2).

Because A refers to a **box**, *value* of A refers to its **amode** field. Consequently, *value* of A possesses a **ref amode** value and thus is an **amode** variable, which is why we can assign *mar1lyn* to it. The four *mar lyn*s are dereferenced and their **amode** values are copied into the *value* of fields of the **boxes** referred to by A, B, C and D respectively.

Much more interesting is to see what happens when we assign:

(E17.1)   *next* of A := B ;

By the same reasoning as above, *next* of A refers to the **ref box** field of the **box** referred to by A. Consequently, *next* of A possesses a **ref ref box** value and thus is a **ref box** variable (is a variable name). Therefore B in the RHS of the assignment is not dereferenced (for syntactic reasons explained in 5.4.2) and the value possessed by B is copied into the field *next* of the **box** referred to by A:

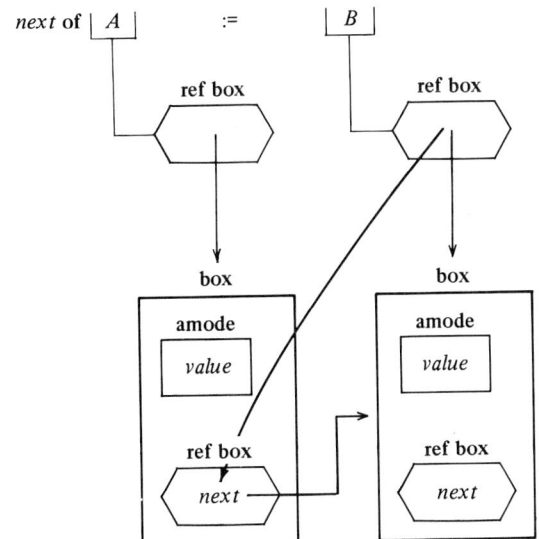

The result is that we have chained the **box** referred to by A to the **box** referred to by B via the *next* **of** field of the **box** A.

Similarly:

(E17.2)   *next* **of** $B := C$;
(E17.3)   *next* **of** $C := D$;

Finally, we want to express that D is the last **box** in the chain. Then we must give a special value to its *next* **of** field, recording this fact. Such a value is **nil**, which is "a name referring to no value":

(E17.4)   *next* **of** $D := $ **nil** ;

What we have achieved by the assignations E17 is:

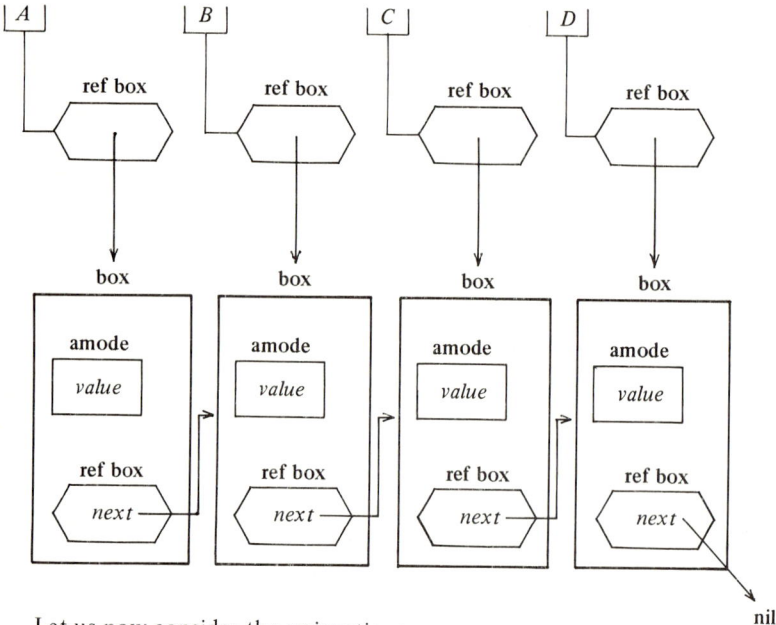

Let us now consider the assignation:

(E18)   *value* **of** *next* **of** *next* **of** *next* **of** $A := $ *marilyn*

   next **of** A refers to B ,
   next **of** B refers to C ,
   next **of** C refers to D ,

consequently, *value* **of** *next* **of** *next* **of** *next* **of** A refers to the **amode** field of the **box** referred to by D. It thus appears that E18 was a rather complicated way of prescribing:

(E18*)   *value* **of** *D* := *marilyn*

In a mode as declared in E14 we can build single threaded lists. Of course we can chain in much more complicated ways.
For example:

(E19)   **mode node** = **struct** (**amode** *mainvalue* ,
                           proc (**amode**) **amode** *function* ,
                           ref node *north* , *east* , *south* , *west*) ;

(E20)   **node** *P, Q, R, S, T, U, V, W* ;

We may assign:

(E21)   *mainvalue* **of** *P* := *marilyn* ;
        etc.
        function **of** *P*   := (**amode** *A*) **amode** : XXXXX ;
        etc.

(E22)   *north* **of** *P* := *Q* ; *east* **of** *P* := *R* ; *south* **of** *P* := *S* ; *west* **of** *P* := *T* ;
        north **of** *R* := *U* ; *east* **of** *R* := *V* ; *south* **of** *R* := *W* ; *west* **of** *V* := *R* ;
        north **of** *S* := *P* ; *east* **of** *T* := *P* ; *south* **of** *Q* := *P* ; *west* **of** *U* := *Q* ;
        north **of** *W* := *R* ; *east* **of** *Q* := *U* ; *south* **of** *U* := *R* ; *west* **of** *R* := *P* ;
                               east **of** *S* := *W* ;   *west* **of** *W* := *S* ;

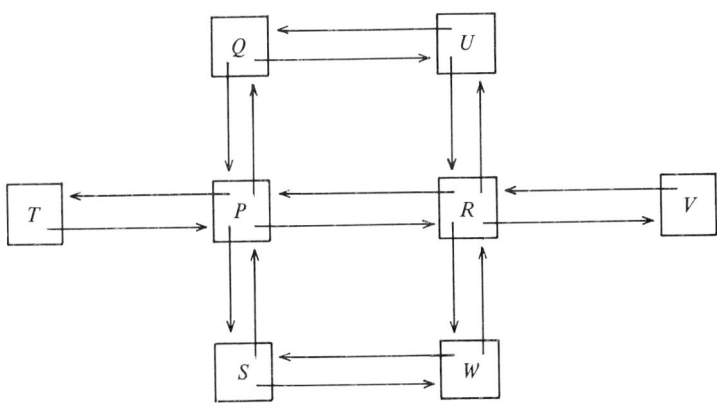

You might now like to meditate on expressions like:

(E23)   *function* of *W* := *((amode A) amode* :
        if *mainvalue* **of** *W* = *A*
        then *mainvalue* **of** *north* **of** *W*
        else *(function* **of** *V)(mainvalue* **of** *east* **of** *W)*
        fi *)*

1.4.4. Pandora's boxes

A field of a structure may be another structure with a field which may be another structure and so on:

(E24)   **mode pandora** = **struct** *(amode a , pando p) ;*
(E25)   **mode pando**   = **struct** *(amode a , pan   p) ;*
(E26)   **mode pan**   = **struct** *(amode a , * **ref pandora** *next) ;*

By virtue of E25 and E26, E24 develops into:

(E24*) **mode pandora** = **struct** *(amode a ,*
                              struct *(amode a ,*
                                    struct *(amode a ,*
                                          ref pandora *next*
) p
) p
) ;

Intentionally, we chose the selectors of the fields of **pandora** and its inner fields somewhat confusingly, just to point out that such is allowed (though it may be not wise).

(E27)   **pandora** *P ;*

Now observe that:

a **of** *P*	refers to an **amode** value ,
a **of** *p* **of** *P*	refers to an **amode** value ,
a **of** *p* **of** *p* **of** *P*	refers to an **amode** value ,

but:

a **of** *p* **of** *p* **of** *p* **of** *P*	is meaningless

as are:

next **of** *P*	because a **pandora** has no *next* of field ,
next **of** *p* **of** *P*	because a **pando** has no *next* of field ,

Ch.1.4.4 BASIC CONCEPTS 121

but:

>*next* **of** *p* **of** *p* **of** *P*   refers to a **pandora**

as do also:

>*next* **of** *p* **of** *p* **of** *next* **of** *p* **of** *p* **of** *P* ,
>*next* **of** *p* **of** *p* **of** *next* **of** *p* **of** *p* **of** *next* **of** *p* **of** *p* **of** *P* ,   *etc.*

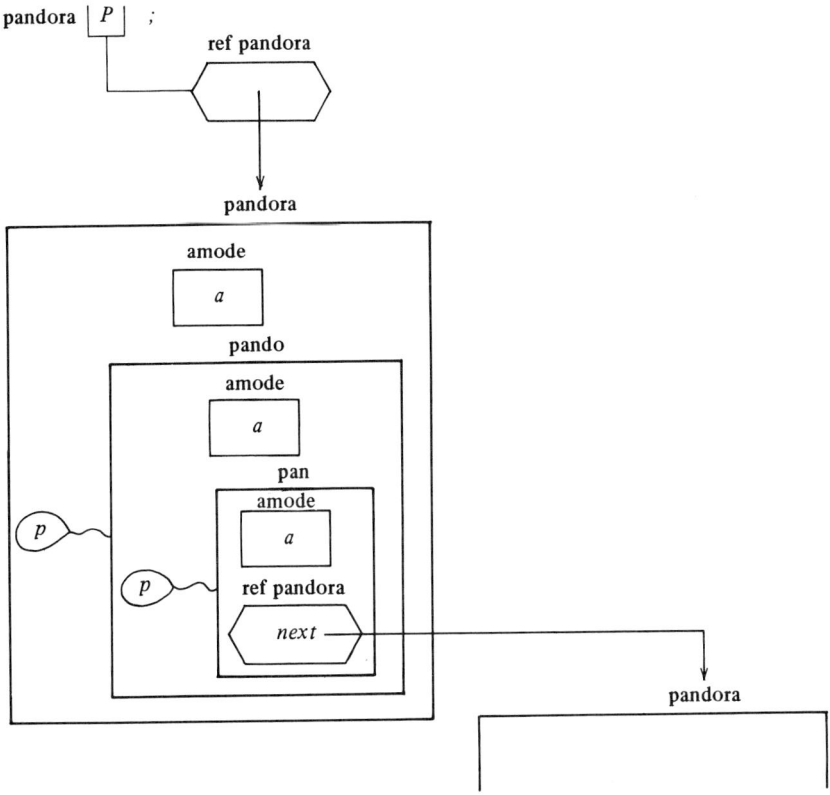

The declaration condition prohibits circular definitions like:

> **mode pandoravel** = **struct** (**amode** *a* , **pandoravel** *p*) ;

Here **pandoravel** is not shielded by a **ref**. The compiler cannot do anything sensible with this **pandoravel**. Obeying such a mode-declaration would result in an endless loop of development.

Observe that, as soon as a **ref** stands in front of some declarer, the only thing the compiler has to do is (to be prepared) to reserve a location for holding a name; that is why a declarer following a **ref** can be shielded.

Vertical readers, please turn to 2.4.

1.5. **Stowed values, multiples**

1.5.1. Multiple values and descriptors

A multiple value (or "multiple" for short) consists of:

1) zero, one or more values, all of the same mode.
   These values are the "elements" of the multiple. Each element is selected by a specific integer, its "index". In this section we use h, i, j, k, m, n, $m1$, $n1$, --- as units yielding an integral value.
2) a "descriptor".
   A descriptor describes how the elements of a multiple are "indexed" (numbered) and what degrees of freedom we have over the index bounds.

We find the descriptor in the actual-declarer of a row-of-MODE value. Syntactically, a descriptor consists of a sub-symbol "[", followed by a chain-of-row-of-rowers-separated-by-comma-symbols, followed by a bus-symbol "]". For a row-of-rower (in some other programming languages known as a "boundpair") we have the following possibilities:

	lower-bound	lower-state	upper-bound	upper-state
$m : n$	m	fixed	n	fixed
m **flex** $: n$	m	flexible	n	fixed
$m : n$ **flex**	m	fixed	n	flexible
m **flex** $: n$ **flex**	m	flexible	n	flexible

The lower-bound determines the lower-index and the upper-bound the upper index of a row. If the "state" of a bound is fixed, then this bound may not be changed; if it is flexible, then it may. If the upper-bound in a row-of-rower is lower than the lower-bound, then the multiple value consists of zero elements.

The actual-declarer (we give some examples below) consists of an actual descriptor, followed by a NONROW-declarer. That is to say, you are not allowed to write a descriptor in front of an **amode** which already specifies a row-of-MODE (see, however, 2.5.1). Examples of actual-row-of-MODE-declarers are:

[*m* : *n*] amode   [*m* : *n* **flex**] amode   [*m* **flex** : *n* **flex**] amode
[*k* : *k* , *m* : *n*] amode   [*h* : *k* **flex** , *m* : *n*] amode
[*m1* : *n1* , *m2* : *n2* , *m3* : *n3*] amode

In the descriptor of a formal-row-of-MODE-declarer, the lower- and upper-bounds may be omitted; if you do so and both its states are fixed (which is the normal case), then the up-to-symbol may be omitted also. Moreover, in a formal-row-of-MODE-declarer, it can also be expressed that a specific bound may be either fixed or flexible, for which purpose there is the either-symbol **either**. Examples of formal-row-of-MODE-declarers are:

[ ] amode   [,] amode   [, ,] amode   [, , ,] amode
[*h* : , *m* :] amode   [*h* : **flex**] amode   [*h* : **either**] amode
[*h* : *k* , *m* : *n*] amode   [**flex** : , : **either**] amode

In the sequel we shall in fact use the 'virtual-declarer' of a multiple value to indicate its mode. A virtual-declarer looks just like a formal one except that its row-of-rowers are always absent (see 2.5.1 and 2.5.2.3 for the details).

We shall bring multiple values into our pictures in the following way:

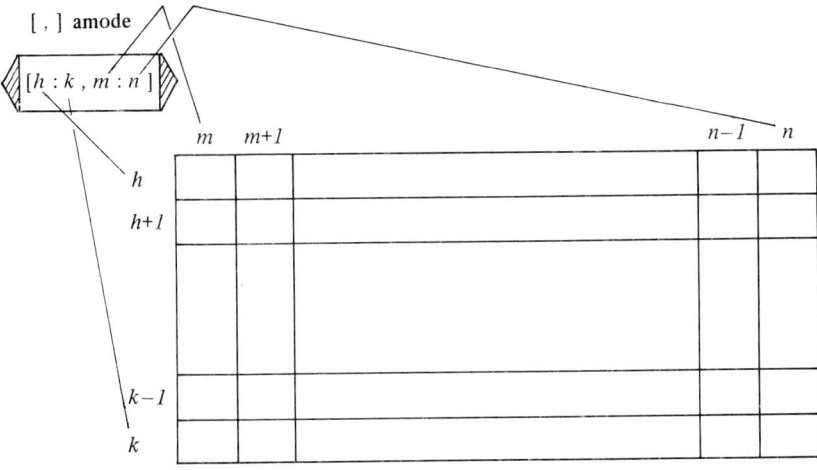

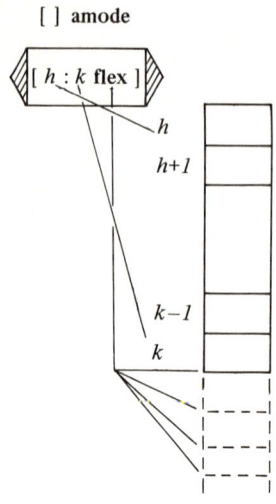

It is important to realize that the descriptor belongs to the multiple value. You even have a certain access to it (see 1.5.5).

The flexible bound feature may be an expensive luxury in some implementations. It presupposes a storage allocation regime in which multiples are allowed to "breathe".

1.5.2. Multiple values and indexers

1.5.2.1. Elements and subvalues

To select a "subvalue" of a given multiple (i.e. a value which is a subset of that given multiple value), we use 'indexers'. The smallest subvalue is one individual element of the multiple, which is obtained by "subscripting". All other subvalues can be obtained by "trimming"; the mode of a subvalue thus obtained is some row-of-MODE.

1.5.2.2. Indexers

An indexer consists of a sub-symbol "[", followed by one or more 'trimscripts' separated by comma-symbols followed by a bus-symbol "]" (see below). A trimscript is a trimmer-option (i.e. a 'trimmer' or EMPTY) or a 'subscript'. Examples:

[i] [i,j] [i,j,k] i, j and k are subscripts;
a subscript may be almost any unit yielding an integral value (see 5.5.1.3)

[i : j]	[h : j, i : k]	all is and hs are lower-bounds,
[i :]	[: j, i : k]	all js and ks are upper-bounds;
[: j]	[, i : k]	all such bounds must again yield
[ ]	[i : , : k]	integral values;
	[,]	$i:j, h:j, i:k$ etc. are trimmers

If a bound is omitted, then its value is that of the corresponding bound in the descriptor of the given multiple. As in the case of a formal-declarer, the up-to-symbol may be omitted also when both the bounds are omitted in a trimmer.

Examples in which we find trimscripts of both kinds in an indexer are:

[h, i : j]   [, k]   [, , k]
[h, i : j, k]   [: h, i, k :]

A special kind of a trimmer is a trimmer with a new-lower-bound:

[i : j at h]   the lower-bound of the multiple subvalue
                   trimmed by $i : j$ gets a new value which
or (in another notation)   is the value of h; a new-lower-bound
[i : j @ h]   must again yield an integral value.

Semantically, an indexer is pretty close to a descriptor. In fact, unless all its trimscripts are subscripts, it describes a multiple (sub)value in much the same way that a descriptor does. We give two examples:

1.5.2.3. Subscripting

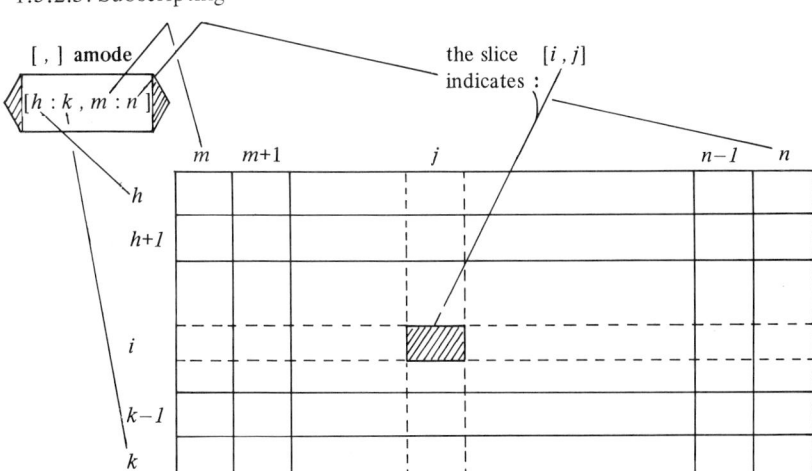

1.5.2.4. Trimming

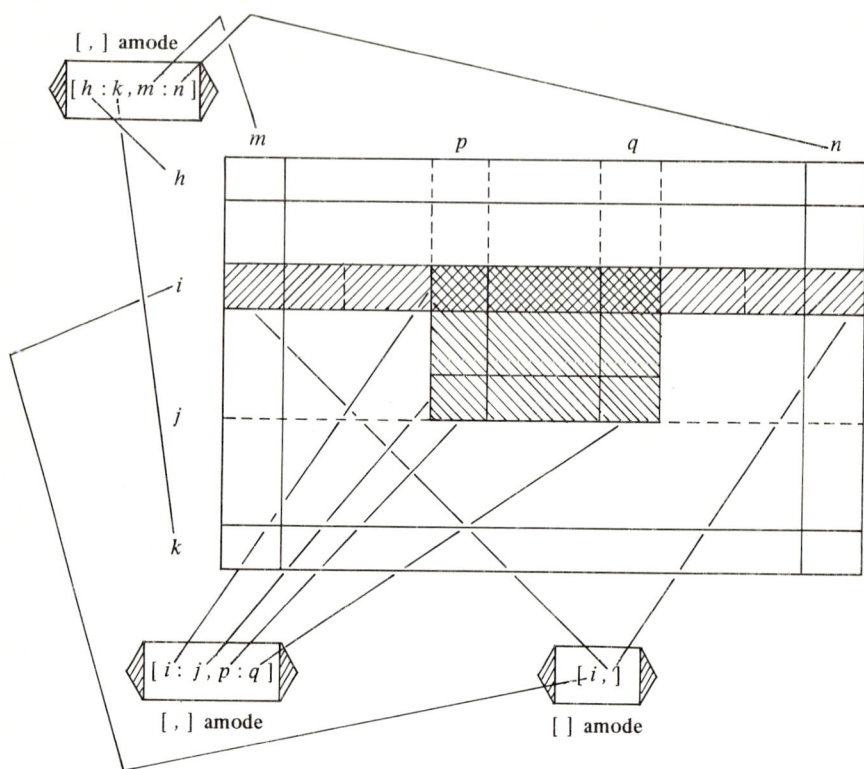

1.5.3. Identity declarations for multiples

We could discuss, systematically again, the three fundamental identity-declarations E1, E2 and E3 as elaborated for the general **amode** in Section 1.2, substituting now for **amode** all kinds of ROWS-of-NONROW, with and without **flex**s and **either**s in different positions. An exhaustive discussion would, however, be rather boring without giving substantially new information. We shall, therefore, confine ourselves to a brief survey of many possibilities and a few remarks on mixed matters.

(E3.1) **ref** [ ] **amode** *arow* = **loc** [$m : n$] **amode** ;
     ↑   ↑
  formal descriptor actual descriptor

or, as usual:

(E3.1*)   [m : n] amode *arow* ;

The identifier *arow* now possesses the name referring to a row of **amode**s, the descriptor of which is [m : n].

(E3.2)   ref [,] amode *arowrow* = loc [h : k , m : n] amode ;

or:

(E3.2*)   [h : k , m : n] amode *arowrow* ;

The identifier *arowrow* now possesses the name referring to a row of row of **amode**s, the descriptor of which is [h : k , m : n].

In both declarations E3.1 and E3.2 a new multiple value will be generated onto the stack; together with these multiple values, their descriptors will be made.

E3.2 elaborates into:

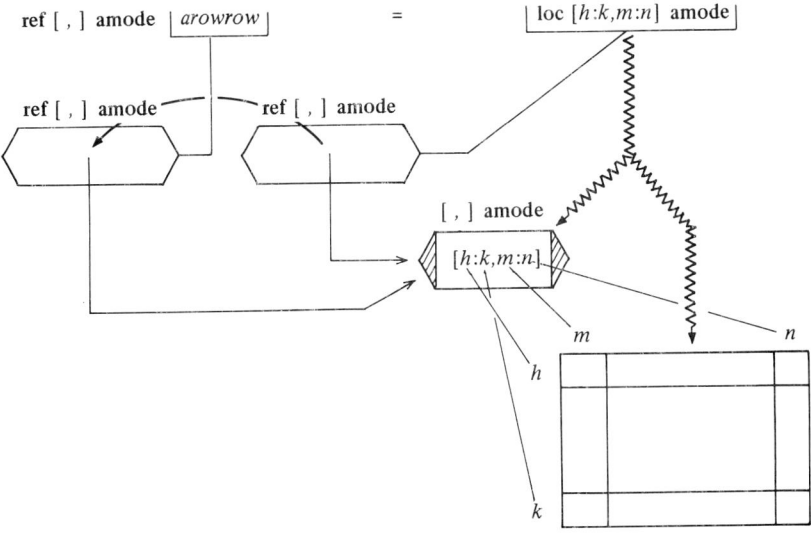

(E3.3)   ref [: flex] amode *arowflex* = loc [m : k flex] amode ;

or:

(E3.3*)   [m : k flex] amode *arowflex* ;

An example of an E1-type identity-declaration for multiples is:

(E1)   [,] **amode** *multipleconstant* = *arowrow* ;

in which the identifier *multipleconstant* is made to possess a new instance of the multiple value (and its descriptor) referred to by *arowrow*.

An example of an E2-type identity-declaration for multiples is:

(E2)   **ref** [ ] **amode** *namultiple* = *arow* ;

in which the identifier *namultiple* is made to possess a new instance of the name possessed by *arow* (and thus is made to refer to the multiple value referred to by *arow*).

By virtue of E1 you cannot assign to *multipleconstant* (being no name) and by virtue of E2 an assignation to *namultiple* results in assigning to *arow*.

All such identity-declarations imply some check that the actual-descriptor matches the formal-descriptor (see 2.5.2.1).

1.5.4. Slices

The external object which possesses or refers to a subvalue of a multiple is the 'slice'; it consists of an identifier (possessing or referring to a multiple value) followed by an indexer:

arow [*i*]	is an **amode** variable , *arow* is subscripted
arow [*i*:*j*]	is a [ ] **amode** variable , *arow* is trimmed
arowrow [*i*,*j*]	is an **amode** variable , *arowrow* is subscripted
arowrow [*i*,]	is a [ ] **amode** variable , *arowrow* is subscripted and trimmed
arowrow [*i*:*j*,*p*:*q*]	is a [,] **amode** variable , *arowrow* is trimmed

All these slices possess names (by virtue of E3.1 and E3.2) and you may assign to them.

In an assignation like:

   arow := *anotherrow*

the number of elements in *arow* and *anotherrow* must be equal. The same for assignations in which slices occur, such as:

   arow := *arowrow* [*i*,] ;
   arowrow [*i*:*j*,*p*:*q*] := *anotherrowrow* [*h*:*k*,*r*:*s*] ;
   arowrow [*i*,] := *arow* ;
   arow := *arowrow* [*j*,]

In an assignment like:

arowflex := *arow*

nothing can go wrong, because the upper-bound of *arowflex* is flexible, and both their lower-bounds *m* are already the same. See 5.5.4 for full details of such assignments.

Slices may also turn up in identity-declarations:

(E1.1)   [ ] **amode** *rowcopy* = *arowrow* [*i*,]

The identifier *rowcopy* now possesses a new instance of the *i*th row of the multiple value referred to by *arowrow* (this new instance of a subvalue has got its own descriptor, which is [*m*:*n*]).

(E1.2)   **ref** [ ] **amode** *arowname* = *arowrow* [*i*,]

The identifier *arowname* now possesses the name of the *i*th row of the multiple value referred to by *arowrow* (for which subvalue a new descriptor has been made). The element:

arowrow [*i,j*]

may now also be accessed by:

arowname [*j*]

Such identity-declarations are of the utmost importance in situations where you want to have an efficient access to a multiple subvalue. For applications see 8.5.3.

1.5.5. Interrogations

We already mentioned that its descriptor belongs to a multiple (sub)value and that you have a certain access to it. Flexible bounds, for example, can be changed by assignment (see 5.5.4.1).

In a formal-row-of-MODE-parameter the lower- and upper-bounds do not have to be specified, and the lower- and upper-state may be **either**. In that case, you cannot in general know the bounds and states that will appear in the actual-row-of-MODE-parameter. For example, if you are in a routine, then you cannot know the actual bounds and states if you explicitly left them free in the formal-parameter(s). For this purpose some standard operators, **lwb** , **upb** , **lws** and **ups** are provided:

1 **lwb** *arowrow*	or	**lwb** *arowrow*		yields the first lower-bound
2 **upb** *arowrow*				yields the second upper-bound
1 **ups** *arowrow*	or	**ups** *arowrow*		yields the first lower-state

For further details see 5.5.3 and 6.5.

1.6. Unions

1.6.1. United modes

A MODE may be MOOD or UNITED. Thus far we have considered MOODs. Every MOOD defines a certain class of values. A UNITED mode does not define a new class of values.

If we declare:

(E0)   **mode abcmode** = **union** *(* **amode** *,* **bmode** *,* **cmode** *) ;*

then an **abcmode** is either an **amode** value or a **bmode** value or a **cmode** value. There is no such thing as an **abcmode** value. Nevertheless we shall bring an **abcmode** into our pictures in the following way:

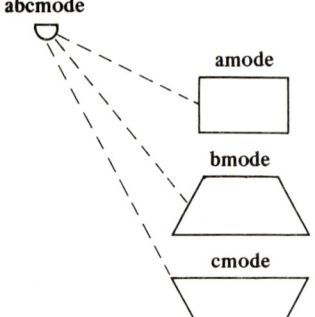

In any given situation, one of the dotted lines will be thick (i.e. one of the possible modes in a union will be in force).

Unions "commute" and "associate":

(E0.1)   **mode bacmode** = **union** *(* **bmode** *,* **amode** *,* **cmode** *) ;*

specifies the same united mode as **abcmode**.

(E0.2)   **mode abcmodedaemodeuv** = **union** *(* **amode** *,* **bmode** *,* **cmode** *,*
                                           union *(* **dmode** *,* **amode** *,* **emode** *,*
                                           union *(* **umode** *,* **vmode** *)*

Ch.1.6.1.1   BASIC CONCEPTS   131

specifies the same united mode as:

(E0.2*)   mode abcdeuvmode = union (amode , bmode , cmode ,
                                     dmode , emode ,
                                     umode , vmode) ;

Let there be declared:

   amode *maralyn* , bmode *marblyn* , cmode *marclyn* ;

1.6.1.1. United constants

Consider the identity-declaration:

(E1)   abcmode *marlyn* = *marblyn* ;

it elaborates into:

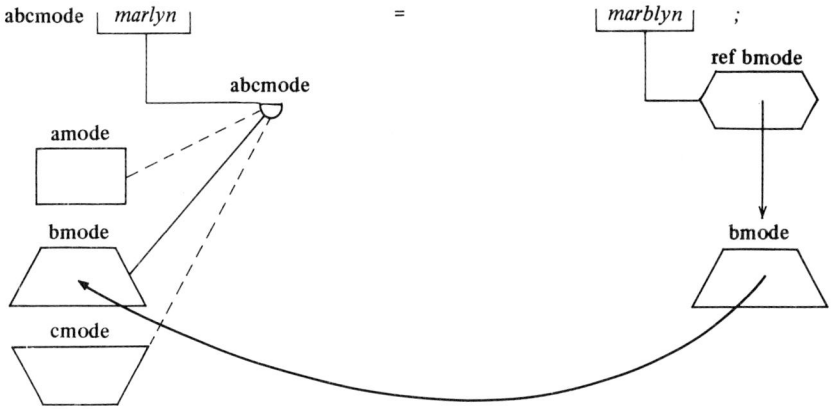

The identifier *marlyn* is made to possess a new instance of the **bmode** value referred to by *marblyn*. Observe that *marlyn* is still an **abcmode** identifier, but she now possesses a **bmode** value.

When we declare:

(E1.2)   abcmode *marlyn* = *maralyn* ;

then she is made to possess an **amode** value, and in:

(E1.3)   abcmode *marlyn* = *marclyn* ;

she is made to possess a **cmode** value.

In all these cases, *marlyn* is a constant. Strictly speaking *marlyn* is either an **amode** constant, or a **bmode** constant, or a **cmode** constant. So, recalling the fact that *marlyn* is declared to be of united mode, we might term *marlyn* a "united constant". United constants will be of little (if any) use when declared in this way, but these identity-declarations can easily arise when matching an actual-parameter to its formal counterpart in a routine-denotation (as in 2.6.2.E8, for example).

1.6.1.2. Equivalence of unions

Let *nylram* be a **ref abcmode**, i.e. *nylram* possesses the name of a **union** (amode , bmode , cmode). Although there is no such thing as an **abcmode** value, a **ref abcmode** is a well shaped internal object as are all names; it is simply a name referring to a union.

Consider the identity-declaration:

(E2)   **ref abcmode** *marlyn* = *nylram* ;

it elaborates into:

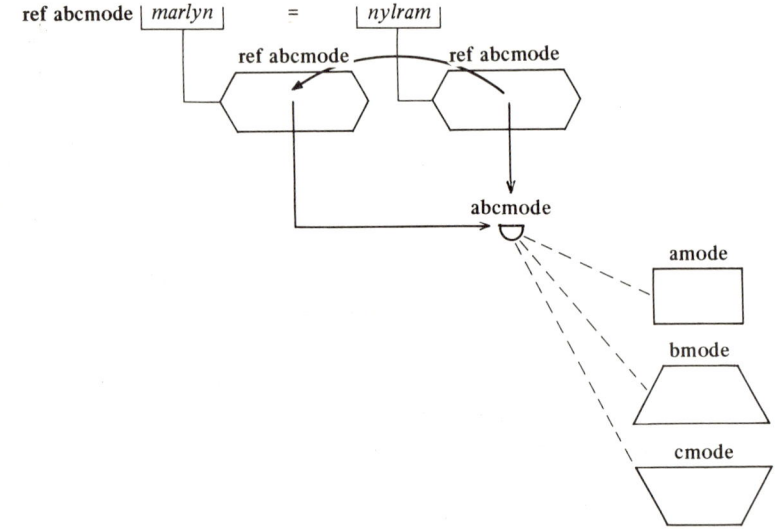

The identifier *marlyn* is made to possess a new instance of the name possessed by *nylram*, which refers to an **abcmode**. Now *marlyn* and *nylram* both possess names referring to the same union.

But what about the identity-declaration:

(???)   **ref abcmode** *marlyn* = *maralyn*   (???)

The actual-parameter refers to an **amode** value; the formal-parameter, however, requires a reference to a union. Although in this union there occurs an **amode**, this water is too wide. You can assign an **amode** value to a variable which is united from **amode**; you can never make a reference to such a union refer to a value which occurs in that union. Try drawing the picture, it cannot be done!

1.6.1.3. Local united generation

The happening:

(E3)   **ref abcmode** *marlyn* = **loc abcmode** ;

contracted into:

(E3*)   **abcmode** *marlyn* ;

can be depicted as follows:

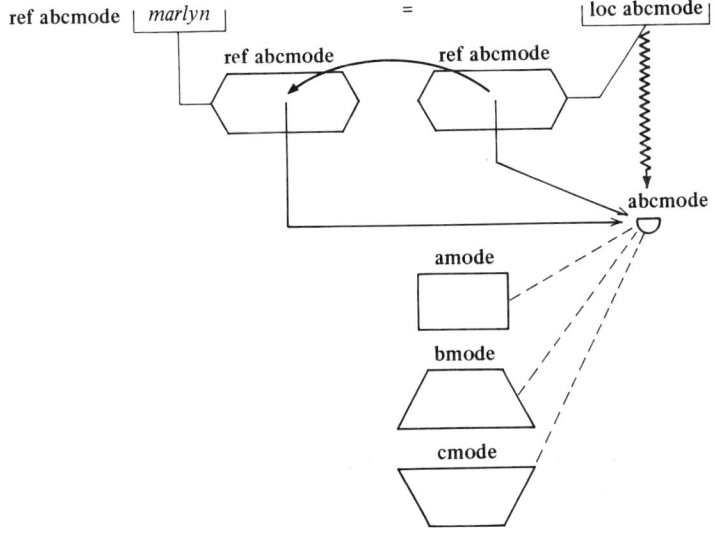

You might ask what value is now generated on the stack, because there is no such a thing as an **abcmode** value. You have to ask your implementor. His answer will be something pretty close to "I reserve sufficient location for an **amode**, or a **bmode**, or a **cmode** and, for use in conformity-relations (see 1.6.2), I also reserve space to record which of these is actually in residence".

1.6.2. Assignations and conformity relations

To an **abcmode** variable you may assign either an **amode** or a **bmode** or a **cmode** value. For example:

(E4)   *marlyn* := *marblyn*

elaborates into:

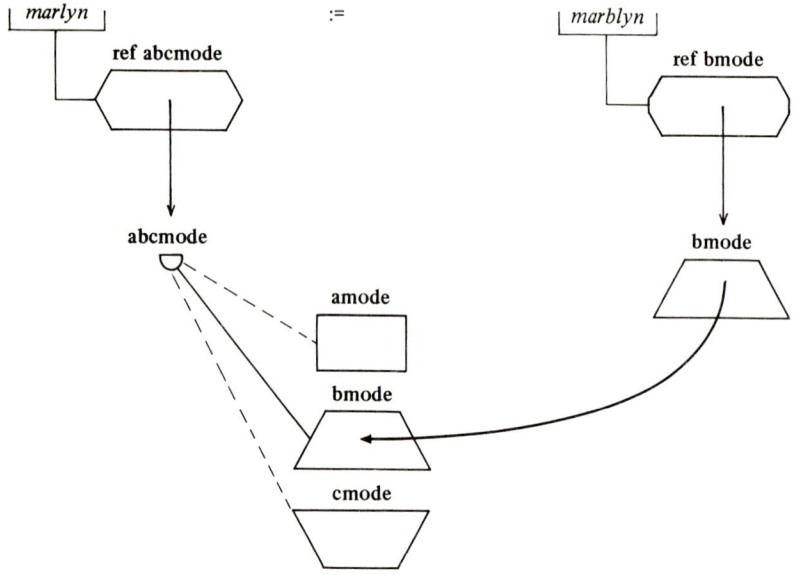

After this assignation the name possessed by *marlyn* now refers to a **bmode** value. In order to enable you to find out which is the mode in force in a union, we have the conformity-relators "::" (or **ct**) and "::=" (or **ctab**).

1.6.2.1. The conforms-to relator

After the assignation E4 the conformity-relation:

(E5.1)   *maralyn* :: *marlyn*   yields **false**
(E5.2)   *marblyn* :: *marlyn*   yields **true**
(E5.3)   *marclyn* :: *marlyn*   yields **false**

No values are compared here; their modes are compared. The fact that after E4 the values referred to by the names possessed by *maralyn* and *marlyn* (respectively) are the same is of no relevance. Even after the assignation:

$$marblyn := marb1lyn$$

the value yielded by

(E5.2)   *marblyn* :: *marlyn*   is still **true**

An important application of unions will be found in routines. Suppose you want to switch in a routine depending upon the mode of an actual-parameter when you declared the formal-parameter to be the union of several modes; then you most likely will want to find out (inside the routine) the mode of the parameter actually supplied, which you may even achieve by examining the **true**th of:

(E5.2*)   **bmode** :: *marlyn*

For full details of this, see 5.6.4.1.

1.6.2.2. The conforms-to-and-becomes relator

In many cases it will not suffice to find out the mode actually supplied, you may also want to know its value. Now you cannot assign:

$$marblyn := marlyn$$

not even when the modes conform (see 5.6.4.1). The proper tool in such cases is the conforms-to-and-becomes-symbol:

(E6)   *marblyn* ::= *marlyn*

which assigns the value of *marlyn* to *marblyn* and yields **true**, when their modes conform, but yields **false** without further action when the modes do not conform. For further details see 5.6.4.1 and 3.7.3.

After the assignment E4, the conformity-relation E6 elaborates into:

The value yielded by the
conformity-relation is **true** and
the **bmode** value in residence in the
union referred to by *marlyn* is assigned to *marblyn*.

The conformity-relation:

(E6*)   *maralyn* ::= *marlyn*

however, elaborates into:

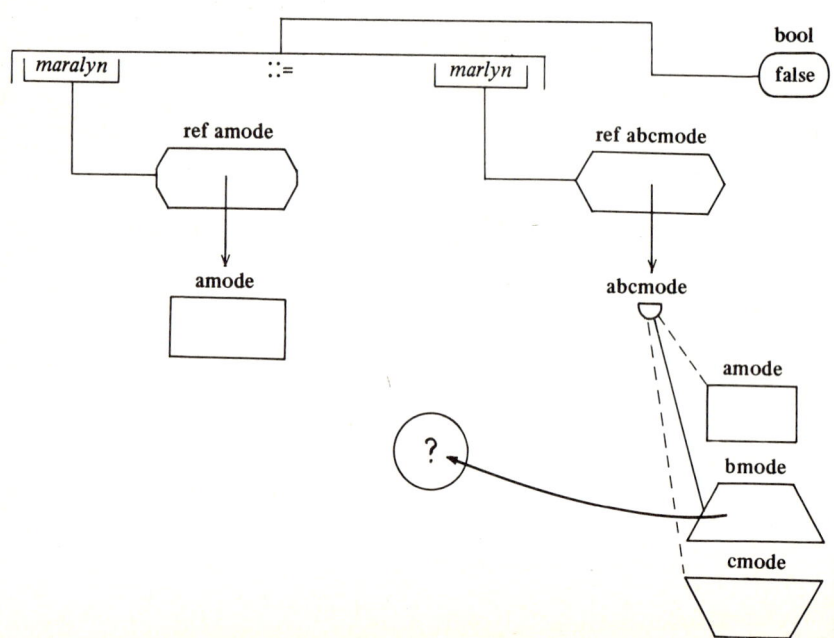

Ch.1.7 BASIC CONCEPTS 137

The modes do not conform: the **bmode** value in residence in the **union** referred to by *marlyn* cannot be assigned to *maralyn*; consequently, no assignation takes place and the value yielded by the conformity-relation is **false**.

1.7. Distinctive features

As we pointed out in 1.2.3, all modes in this language are derived from five PRIMITIVE modes with the assistance of the symbols **ref**, **proc**, **struct**, "[" and "]", **union** and **long**. Until now we have not discussed **long** and we have not discussed the identity-relation for **ref** modes (names); these are the subject matter of this section.

1.7.1. The **long** modes

Going down to the level of a concrete computer, the values of all PRIMITIVE modes (1.2.3) will be mapped into bit-patterns. A **bool** will most likely be a single bit, a **char** may be stored in at least six bits (more likely seven or eight, i.e. a "byte"), an **int** may occupy an entire machineword (a **bits**, see 2.7.1), a **real** one or two machinewords; the mapping of a **format** (see 7.6.2) into a bit-pattern is entirely a matter of implementation.

On most modern computers you will find provision for (if not in the hardware, then in the standard software) multilength arithmetic. That is to say, apart from an **int** occupying a single machineword, we may also be enabled to add, subtract, multiply and divide integers occupying, say, two machinewords, and maybe even larger ones (occupying three or more machinewords). The same may apply to **real**s and also to the primitive modes **bits** and **bytes** (discussed in 2.7.1).

To distinguish such different classes of INTEGRAL and REAL (and also BITS and BYTES) modes we have the long-symbol "**long**".

INTEGRAL	is the metanotion	LONGSETY-integral	,
REAL	is the metanotion	LONGSETY-real	,
BITS	is the metanotion	LONGSETY-bits	,
BYTES	is the metanotion	LONGSETY-bytes	, (see 1.2.3 and R 1.2.1)

The metanotion LONGSETY produces EMPTY, long, long-long, long-long-long, etc.

Thus we may distinguish an infinity of different modes

INTEGRAL:

   int , long int , long long int , long long long int , ---

and REAL:

   real , long real , long long real , long long long real , ---

and similarly for BITS and BYTES.

In a specific implementation, only a few of these will in fact be distinguishable as values of different length. The degree of discrimination is not necessarily the same for INTEGRAL, REAL, BITS and BYTES. It may be acquired from corresponding environment enquiries (see 6.7.1).

Modes of different **long**th derived from the same PRIMITIVE mode are different modes:

   int :: long int , long int :: long long int ,
   real :: long real , long real :: long long real

all yield **false**.

You may also unite from different **long**ths derived from the same (or different) PRIMITIVEs:

   mode integral = union (int , long int) ;
   mode number = union (real , long real , long long real) ;

1.7.2. Identity relations

As was pointed out in 1.2, a reference-to-MODE also possesses an internal object in the computer, i.e. a **ref** will also be mapped into a certain bit-pattern (the address of the value referred to). Consequently, names may also be operated upon and, in particular, compared. To compare names of the same mode we have the identity-relators :=: (or **is**) and :≠: (or **isnt**).

Consider the following picture:

Ch.1.7.2 BASIC CONCEPTS

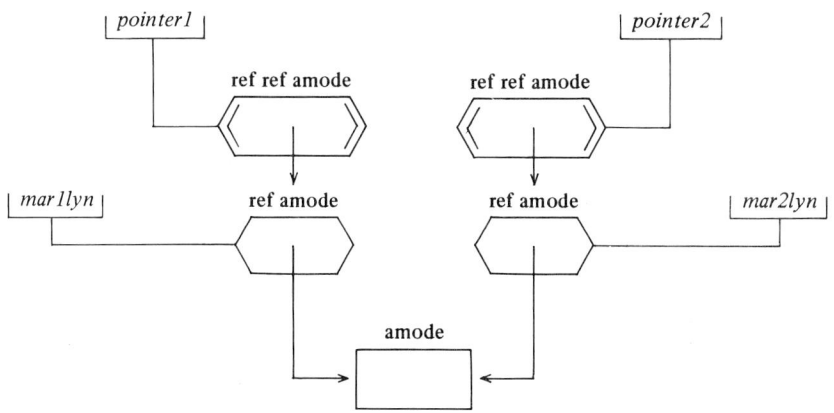

Apparently, the assignments:

pointer1 := *mar1lyn*

and

pointer2 := *mar2lyn*

have been made.
Now:

(E1) *pointer1* :≠: *pointer2*   because they refer to different internal objects

but:

(E2) *mar1lyn* :=: *mar2lyn*   because they refer to the same internal object.

We may also write:

(E3) *(* **ref amode**: *pointer1)* **is** *(* **ref amode**: *pointer2)*

which means the same thing.
We might write:

(E4) *pointer1* = *pointer2*

or:

(E5) *mar1lyn* = *mar2lyn*

or even:

(E6)   *pointer1* = *mar2lyn*

but, in all of these, the *pointer*s and the *marlyn*s would be dereferenced to yield the **amode**s ultimately referred to (assuming the operator "=" to have been declared for a pair of **amode**s), and it is these that would be compared. It would not then be possible to declare "=" between **ref amode**s or **ref ref amode**s (for otherwise E4–6 would become ambiguous). This is why ":=:" and ":≠:" had to be specially included in the language.

Vertical readers, please turn to 2.7.

2. DECLARATIONS

2.1. Primitive declarations

2.1.1. Primitives

In the previous chapter, we considered values of a hypothetical mode **amode**. In ALGOL 68 there is in principle an infinite number of possible modes which could be substituted for **amode**, and in the course of the present chapter we shall show you how to construct them all. They are, however, all derived from a small number of "primitive" modes (1.2.3). The primitives are as follows:

int   The values of this mode are the integers within some finite range dependant upon the implementation (e.g. from -2^{31} to $2^{31}-1$ for a 32 bit binary machine). See 6.2.1 for how to find the size of the range. Arithmetic performed upon **int** values will in general yield exact results, the same in every implementation.

real   The values of this mode will in general be held as floating point numbers by the implementation. Thus the range of numbers that can be held is much greater than for **int**, but one pays for this by a restricted precision (again see 6.2.1 for details).

bool   There are only two values of this mode, **true** and **false**.

char   The values of mode **char** are characters — i.e. internal representations of certain graphic marks on external media. These graphic marks will include at least the letters *a* to *z*, the digits *0* to *9*, **1** and **0** (pronounced "flip" and "flop" and used as external representations of **true** and **false**), **i** (plus i times), *(*, *)*, comma and space. Most implementations will add others to this list, and we shall assume, in our examples, that this has been done (and in particular we shall use *A* to *Z* quite freely).

format   This is a very strange beast, which you had best forget about until 7.6.2.

2.1.2. Simple declarations

Whenever we wish to have, at our disposal, a variable value of some mode, we must declare it, and provide an identifier to possess its name (1.1.1):

(E1) real *x;* int *i;* bool *p;* char *c;*

If we have to declare several values of the same mode, we have three methods:

(E2) real *x;* real *y;* real *z;* int *i;* int *j;*
(E3) real *x,* real *y,* real *z,* int *i,* int *j;*
(E4) real *x, y, z,* int *i, j;*

E3 and E4 in fact mean exactly the same thing, but E4 is more convenient to write. The difference between E2 (with ";"s) and E3 (with ","s) is that the declarations take place serially in the first case and collaterally in the second. The difference between them is quite academic in the case of these simple primitives, but could be of crucial importance in more complex situations, such as we shall meet in 2.5. Declarations are always separated from each other, and from other clauses, by go-on-symbols (i.e. ";"s), and for this purpose a collateral declaration such as E4 counts as one declaration:

(E5) bool *p,* real *x, y, z,* int *i, j;* char *c;*

Now that we have declared these variables, we are free to use them:

(E6) *x := 3.142;*
      y := x;
      i := 3

2.1.3. Sample declarations

In the chapters that follow, we shall give many examples using identifiers such as *x, y, i, j,* etc. To save confusing you, we shall not declare them each time we use them, and so whenever you see such an example, please assume the declarations listed in Appendix 2 to have been already made. You have already met most of them in Chapter 0 (where they were conspicuously marked with a "D"), and the Report itself also uses most of them in the same way [R 1.3].

Vertical readers, please turn to 3.1.

2.2. Identity declarations

2.2.1. Identity declarations

An identity-declaration serves to introduce a new identifier, to specify the mode of the internal object (value) that it is to possess, and to fix that

Ch.2.2.1 DECLARATIONS 143

value. Thereafter, until the end of the range (3.2.1) in which that identity-declaration occurs, all other occurrences of that identifier are deemed to possess that same value (see 3.2.3 for the precise mechanism of this).

An identity-declaration [R 7.4.1] has two sides — its left hand side, or 'formal parameter', and its right hand side, or 'actual parameter'. Consider:

(E1) **real** e = *2.718281828;*

An identity-declaration is constructed as follows:
Its LHS (the formal-parameter) (**real** e in the example) consists of:
   a) a 'formal declarer' (**real**) which simply specifies the mode of the internal object. For every mode which can be constructed in the language, a formal-declarer can be written. For example, **real, ref real, ref ref real, int, ref char, bool**, etc are all perfectly good formal-declarers, and the mode that each specifies is obvious.
   b) an identifier (e) which is thereby made to possess the object.
Its RHS (the actual-parameter) (*2.718281828* in the example) consists of:
   a unitary-clause (or unit) whose context is strong, and which yields a value whose mode (after coercion if necessary) is the same as that specified by the formal-parameter, and which now becomes the value possessed by the identifier.

The whole of Chapter 5 is devoted to describing what can and cannot stand as a unitary-clause, and to explaining all about the strength of contexts and coercion, so that it would be inappropriate here to do more than give a few examples that are particularly important. If you have already read 5.1.4.1, you will have noticed the similarity between the rule just given for an actual-parameter and that appropriate to the RHS of an assignation.

An identity-declaration is therefore a very simple concept, with a simple syntax and simple rules (a few additional rules will appear in 2.5.2 when we come to consider "rowed" modes). Do not therefore be afraid when you come across a particular example which seems to go on for page after page. It is simply because a long and complicated formal-declarer has been used to specify a long and complicated mode, or because the unit on the RHS happens to be rather a long one. The effect is just the same. We associate together a particular mode, a particular identifier, and a particular value of that mode.

Note, however, that once the identifier has been made to possess a value, this value cannot be changed (it is a constant (see 1.2.2.2.1)), and the compiler should be able to take advantage of this. After E1:

(E2) $x := e$

should compile into exactly the same code as:

(E3) $x := 2.718281828$

Things are slightly more complicated with examples like:

(E4)   **real** $xy = x \times y$

Here, the value to be possessed by xy is to be calculated ($x \times y$) at the time when this declaration is encountered during the elaboration of the program, and if it is encountered several times the values will presumably be different on each occasion. Nevertheless, although the compiler will now, presumably, have to reserve a word of store to hold this value, it should still be able to gain some benefit from knowing that it cannot change until the next time.

If we want to construct a **real** variable (1.2.2.4.1), then we have to work a little harder. The object to be possessed by its identifier must be of mode **ref real**, and so we expect to have an identity-declaration like:

ref real x = "something"

In this example, "something" must obviously be a unit that yields a constant value (a name) of mode **ref real**, but it must also have the property that it reserves a space in the store where a **real** value may be put, and it is the name referring to this space that it must yield. If you search through Chapter 5 looking for such a unit, you will find that it is known as a 'generator' and is not described until 5.7.2. This is because the use of generators other than in identity-declarations is rather specialised. There are two kinds of generator, and we recommend the **loc** one for the present purpose (as we have already explained in 1.2.2.3)::

(E5)   **ref real** x = **loc real**;

loc real is the generator, and the mode it yields is **ref real** in spite of its appearance to the contrary. The **loc** signifies that the **real** value thus created is local to the current range, as will be explained in 3.2.2. **real** is an 'actual declarer', and as far as you need be concerned at the present, actual-declarers look just like formal ones.

If you feel like trying a **heap** generator, then you should read 2.7.3 first.

2.2.2. Extended identity declarations

Declarations such as E5 are so common (and they are clearly redundant in their present form) that they are usually abbreviated [R 9.2.a]. The extension goes like this:

Ch.2.2.3   DECLARATIONS   145

(E6)   **ref real** *x* = **loc real**;

(E7)   **real** *x*;

Of course, we have already met this before in 1.2.2.3 — E7 means exactly the same as E6. But please note that the **real** in E7 is the actual-declarer from the generator of E6, and NOT just a part of the formal-declarer **ref real**. This distinction may not seem important just now, but you will forget it at your peril when you come to 2.5.2 and even in 2.2.3 it will be relevant.

E6 and E7 are examples of 'unitary declarations'. Several unitary-declarations may now be combined into a 'collateral declaration' [R 6.2.1.a] :

(E8)   **ref real** *x* = **loc real**, **ref real** *y* = **loc real**,
            ref real *z* = **loc real**;

or, by using our extension:

(E9)   **real** *x*, **real** *y*, **real** *z*;

Now we can shorten this even more by another extension [R 9.2.c] into:

(E10)   **real** *x, y, z*;

which brings us back to the point we had reached (a little prematurely as it turns out) in 2.1.2.E4.

2.2.3. Initialised declarations

We explained in 1.2.2.4 how you could write:

(E11)   **ref real** *ee* = **loc real** := *2.718281828*;

which, by our first extension, can become:

(E12)   **real** *ee* := *2.718281828*;

which has created a **real** variable and assigned an initial value to it all in one go. But beware! E12 (at least in this representation) looks deceptively like E1 — the difference is just one ":". We can subsequently assign a different value to *ee* (E12), but never to *e* (E1).

Now, if we have the collateral-declaration:

(E13)   **real** *x* := *1.0*, **real** *y* := *2.0*;

we may apply our second extension to obtain:

(E14)   real *x := 1.0, y := 2.0;*

Likewise, if we had had:

(E15)   real *x = 1.0,* real *y = 2.0;*

we could have obtained:

(E16)   real *x = 1.0, y = 2.0;*

which simply goes to show that formal-declarers (the **real**s in E15) may be gathered together in just the same way as actual ones (the **real**s in E13). But:

(E17)   real *x = 1.0,* real *y := 2.0;*

which is a perfectly good collateral-declaration, creating a **real** object *x* and a **ref real** object *y*, cannot be extended to:

real *x = 1.0, y := 2.0;*

for here we would be gathering together one formal-declarer and one actual one, and moreover it would be too confusing to have the one declarer **real** being used to create two objects of different modes.

Vertical readers, please turn to 3.2.

2.3. Mode declarations

2.3.1. Mode declarations

We introduced 'mode declarations' to you in 1.3.3.1. Consider:

(E1)   **mode myproc = proc**/**real, int, ref char**/ **bool**;

This is a 'mode declaration'. On the LHS we have introduced the indicant (1.3.2) **myproc** as a 'mode indication'. On the RHS we have an actual-declarer specifying the required mode. Henceforth, (or at least within this range) **myproc** and **proc** /**real, int, ref char**/ **bool** may be used interchangeably. You may have declarations such as:

(E2)   **myproc** *proc;*
         ref myproc *refproc;*

and you may now embark upon the construction of even more elaborate modes such as:

(E3)   **proc** /**myproc**/

See 2.5.2.2 for mode-declarations of row-of modes where bounds must be specified.

2.3.2. Extended mode declarations

A mode-declaration is a unitary-declaration (2.2.2) and it may therefore be combined with other unitary-declarations (whether they be other mode-declarations, or even identity-, priority-(4.3.1) or operator-(4.3.2) declarations) into a collateral-declaration:

(E4)   mode rl = real, mode it = int , mode bo = bool , real x;

to which we may now apply our second extension (2.2.2) [R 9.2.c] , collecting together all the **modes**:

(E5)   mode rl = real, it = int , bo = bool , real x;

2.3.3. The declaration condition

The declaration condition is one of the context conditions (1.2.1) intended to forbid circular mode declarations (as we explained in 1.3.3.1). The rule is precise but complex, and is to be found in R 4.4.4, to which you are referred if you really wish to pursue the matter in detail.

Vertical readers, please turn to 3.3.

2.4. Declarations of structures

2.4.1. struct declarers

The concept of a "structure" was introduced in 1.4.0. Each structured value is of some mode, and for each such mode we can write a declarer (and up to this point, formal- and actual-declarers are still looking the same):

(E1)   struct *(*real *first,* int *second,* ref char *third)*

This is the way you would write a **struct** declarer [R 7.1.1.e] ; but should you wish to declaim it in public you would take a deep breath and say *:

---

* If some pedant should notice that even this verbosity is not the full story, let him please keep the secret to himself. FUCK YOU * Mr. Author

"structured-with-(a-)real-field-first-and-(an-)integral-
field-second-and-(a-)reference-to-character-field-third"

This is the way in which the Report would specify this mode [R 1.2.1], but in this Introduction we shall stick to the corresponding declarers — they are much cleaner.

first, *second*, and *third* in E1 are 'selectors', not identifiers, and they are a part of the declarer, which identifiers could never be. Thus:

(E2)   **struct** *(* **real** *fourth,* **int** *fifth,* **ref char** *sixth)*

specifies a different mode from that specified by E1. A value of one could not be assigned to a name referring to a value of the other, and if you were to ask, in a conformity-relation (5.6.4.1) whether they were the same, you would be told that they were not.

The fields inside a structure can be of any mode whatsoever, including of course other **struct**s:

(E3)   **struct** *(* **proc** *(* **real, int, ref char** *)* **bool** *pr,*
         struct *(* **real** *first,* **int** *second,* **ref char** *third)* *group)*

The only limitation is that a **struct** cannot contain itself [R 4.4.4], although it can contain a reference to itself. To achieve this, however, we must use a mode-declaration (2.3.1):

(E4)   **mode sequence** = **struct** *(* **int** *object,* **ref sequence** *next);*

Modes such as this are particularly useful in conjunction with **heap** generators (5.7.2.2), and for a substantial example of their use you are referred to 8.7.1.

2.4.2. struct declarations

Now we can use **struct** declarers in the formal-parameters of identity-declarations, or as the actual-declarers in **loc** generators:

(E5)   **ref struct** *(* **real** *x,* **int** *i) ss* = **loc struct** *(* **real** *x,* **int** *i);*

or by extension:

(E6)   **struct** *(* **real** *x,* **int** *i) ss;*

in which a variable *ss* is created. *ss* can now be assigned to other variables of the same mode, or its individual fields may be accessed using their selectors:

(E7)   *x* := *x* **of** *ss*

Ch.2.4.3 DECLARATIONS 149

This subject will be treated more fully in 5.4.2.

2.4.3. Extended **struct** declarations

There are several extensions that we can perform. Firstly, if the same declarer occurs in several fields of a **struct** declarer:

(E8) **struct** *(***real** *re,* **real** *im)*

we can gather them together [R 9.2.c] :

(E9) **struct** *(***real** *re, im)*

and likewise:

(E10) **struct** *(***struct** *(***real** *re, im) aa,*
 struct *(***int** *one, two) bb)*

becomes:

(E11) **struct** *(***struct** *(***real** *re, im) aa,* *(***int** *one, two) bb)*

The mode-declaration for **sequence** in E4 can be extended [R 9.2.b] into:

(E12) **struct sequence** = *(***int** *object,* **ref sequence** *next);*

and if we have several such modes to declare collaterally, we can write:

(E13) **struct sequence** = *(***int** *object,* **ref sequence** *next),*
 realseq = *(***real** *object,* **ref realseq** *next);*

which is very similar to what we did between E4 and E5 of 2.3.2.

In addition to the extensions to identity-declarations discussed in 2.2.2, which of course still apply, you can produce:

(E14) **struct** *(***real** *re, im) c,*
 *(***int** *one, two) d;*

in which two **struct** variables are created.

2.4.4. The mode **compl**

The mode **compl** (for complex) is not a primitive in the language, although you would not come to much harm if you were to regard it as such, since it is provided with a complete set of operators and other useful facilities (5.4.0 and 5.4.3). It is, in fact, a **struct**, being declared in the standard prelude (1.1)

[R 10.2.7.a] by:

(E15)   **struct compl** = *(* **real** *re, im);*

Vertical readers, please turn to 3.4.

2.5. Declarations of multiples

2.5.1. Row declarers

The concept of a "multiple value" was introduced in 1.5.1. Each multiple value is of some mode, and for each such mode we can write declarers. Now, however, we are at the point where formal- and actual-declarers begin to look different and so, to add to your confusion, we shall start with 'virtual declarers':

(E1)   [, ,] **ref real**

which is pronounced:

"row-of-row-of-row-of-reference-to-real"

This specifies the mode of a multiple value which has three dimensions (because there are two ","s between the "[" and the "]"), and whose elements are names of mode **ref real**.

Here is an example of a virtual-declarer whose interest lies in its complexity, rather than in any use it might have:

(E2)   [ ] **struct** *(* **proc** *(* **int**, **ref** [ ] **real** *)* [ ] **real** *p*,
          [,] **ref compl** *q)*

The pronunciation of this one is left to the proverbial student as his proverbial exercise. You have enough information to do it, but have you the stamina? However, this example does show that we may have rows of **structs**, **structs** containing rows, and **procs** that use and yield rowed modes.

The elements of a multiple value can be of any mode whatsoever except another row-of mode (this being specifically excluded by the Report). However, many implementations will be somewhat kinder, and will accept declarers such as [ ] [ ] **real** (or [ ] **string** (see 2.5.3)).

2.5.2. Row declarations

In an identity-declaration involving a row-of mode (or a reference-to-row-of

Ch.2.5.2.1 DECLARATIONS 151

mode) we encounter a problem that did not arise before. A multiple value consists (1.5.1) of a descriptor and a set of elements, and whenever we create such a value, not only must it be of the required mode, but its descriptor must fit our requirements as well. It is the responsibility of the formal-declarer in the formal-parameter (2.2.1) to ensure that both these requirements are met.

2.5.2.1. Formal row-of declarers

Suppose that *rowvar* is an identifier which possesses the name of a flexible (1.5.1) [ ] **real** (i.e. it yields a one-dimensional multiple value of a size which may vary at run time). You will see presently that *rowvar* could have been declared as follows:

$$[1\ \textbf{flex} : 0\ \textbf{flex}]\ \textbf{real}\ rowvar := \textbf{skip};$$

where the **skip** is to signify that we do not at the moment have the slightest idea what size it is, or what are the values of its elements.

Here now is an identity-declaration:

(E3) $\qquad [2 : i + j]\ \textbf{real}\ xl = rowvar;$

Observe that the formal-declarer now contains bounds (*2* and $i + j$) which have to be elaborated to yield two **int** values. A bound can be any strong **int** tertiary, and you will see in Chapter 5 that "tertiary" covers a large number of possibilities. Now that a formal-parameter can contain objects which require elaboration, we must state that they are all elaborated collaterally with each other and with the actual-parameter on the RHS, each time that the identity-declaration is encountered [R 7.4.2].

Suppose, in this case, that the elaboration of $i + j$ yields the value *5*. Then the formal-declarer is telling us that a [ ] **real** with bounds [*2 : 5*] is expected, and your compiler should insert a run time check into your program to check that, on this occasion, those are indeed the bounds in the descriptor of the value yielded by *rowvar*.

Here is another identity-declaration:

(E4) $\qquad$ **ref** [**either** : **flex**] **real** $xlm = rowvar;$

This time, there happen to be no bounds in the formal-declarer, so the check is not needed. Any bounds will be accepted in the descriptor yielded by *rowvar*. However, we have specified that the upper-bound of any value to be referred to by *xlm* must be **flexible** (the lower-bound can be **either** flexible or fixed). In this case we know that *rowvar* refers to a value with both bounds flexible, and the compiler knows it too, so that no run time check is required. However, this might not always be the case.

Note that this check was not needed in the case of E3 because, there, *xl* was being made to possess a [ ] **real** and the question of whether this had flexible bounds or not was of no consequence since there was no question of changing them later. *xlm* on the other hand was, in E4, being made to possess the name of a space in the store (actually, the same space as that possessed by *rowvar*), and the compiler is entitled to know, when it encounters another occurrence of *xlm* (an "applied" occurrence (3.2.3)) what assumptions, if any, it can make about this space (whether or not it is on the heap, for example).

If we carry this one stage further and try to declare ourselves an *xlmn* to possess a **ref ref** [ ] **real**:

(E5)   **ref ref** [ ] **real** *xlmn* = *refrowvar;*

where *refrowvar* possesses something suitable, then there are no checks to be done at all, since it is assumed that a space that will hold a **ref** [ ] **real** (such as *xlmn* could refer to) is equally happy to hold a **ref** to a **flexible** [ ] **real** as to a fixed one, and moreover that it can **refer** to a [ ] **real** of any size [R 7.1.1.n]. Therefore no bounds are needed in the formal-declarer, and in fact any formal-declarer containing a **ref** (not counting one right at the beginning) becomes virtual from that point on. So now you know what a virtual-declarer is for. It is a part of a formal-(or actual-) declarer in which all the bounds are required to be empty.

Now we shall list all the things that you may put inside a bound of a formal-declarer. We shall illustrate them with the lower-bound of a **ref** [ ] **real**, but of course an upper-bound has exactly the same freedom. Note that *I* stands for any strong **int** tertiary (such as the *2* and the *i + j* in E3).

declarer	bound required	state required
ref [*I* **either** :] **real**	*I*	any
ref [*I* **flex** :] **real**	any	flexible
ref [*I* :] **real**	*I*	fixed
ref [**either** :] **real**	any	any
ref [**flex** :] **real**	any	flexible
ref [:] **real**	any	fixed

Note that the last example, in which both bounds are empty, may by extension [R 9.2.f] be contracted to:

(E6)   **ref** [ ] **real**

Ch.2.5.2.2   DECLARATIONS   153

For declarers without a **ref** at the beginning, the possibilities are the same, except that the state is never checked, whatever the bound may contain.

The more 'row-of's there are in your mode, the more pairs of bounds you are able to control by your formal-declarer, as is illustrated by the following three-dimensional one:

(E7)   [*1* : **flex**, *i* + *j* **flex** : *99* **either**,   ] **real**

Of course, formal-bounds can occur inside a formal **struct** declarer (2.4.1) if one of its fields has a row-of mode:

(E8)   **struct** (**ref** [ ] **real** *a*, [*1* : **flex**] **ref** [ ] **real** *b*)

Note where the bounds start to become virtual.

2.5.2.2. Actual row-of declarers

As usual, most row-of identity-declarations will have a **loc** generator on the RHS, and this will contain an actual row-of declarer. Such a **loc** generator will have to reserve a substantial region of store, and so it must know how much store to reserve, and whether it is likely to be changed later (through being flexible). This information is provided by bounds in the actual-declarer:

(E9)   **ref** [*1* : **either**] **real** *xlm* = **loc** [*1* : *99* **flex**] **real**;

The usual checks will show that the actual [*1* : *99* **flex**] is consistent with the formal [*1* : **either**], and so space for *99* **real**s is reserved [R 7.1.2.d], with the option of altering it later, and arrangements are made to release the space again when the current range is left.

Since an actual-declarer occurring in an actual-parameter is actually going to reserve some actual store, of some actual size, it follows that both the bounds must be actually present. If the upper-bound is less than the lower-bound, then the number of elements in the multiple is taken as zero (the bounds [*1* : *0* **flex**] are frequently used when an initially empty multiple is to be created, as in 2.5.E16 below). Clearly, **either** would be meaningless in an actual-declarer, and so the number of possibilities is less than in the formal case [R 7.1.1.t]. We shall illustrate them all with the aid of the upper-bounds in the following examples, all of mode [ ] **real**. As before, *I* stands for any strong **int** tertiary.

declarer	bound yielded	state yielded
[*1* : *I* **flex**] **real**	*I*	flexible
[*1* : *I*] **real**	*I*	strict

As with formal-declarers, actual ones go virtual after a certain point, the difference being that any one **ref** is sufficient to cause it to happen:

(E10)   **ref ref [ ] real** *xlmn* = **loc ref [ ] real**;

When the RHS of an identity-declaration is a generator specifying actual-bounds, there is little point in doing any checks — it would be like asking questions to which you already knew the answer. Therefore E9 might just as well be written as:

(E11)   **ref [either : either] real** *xlm* = **loc**[*1* : *99* **flex**] **real**;

Note that there is now nothing to be elaborated inside the formal-declarer. It is to this form that the usual extension may now be made [R 9.2.a], yielding:

(E12)   [*1* : *99* **flex**] **real** *xlm*;

But please do note that the [*1* : *99* **flex**] **real** in E12 is an actual-declarer, and must be constructed accordingly. Likewise, E10, where the bounds are virtual anyway, may be extended to:

(E13)   **ref [ ] real** *xlmn*;

Next you might like to reflect upon the fact that the RHS of a mode-declaration (2.3.1) is an actual-declarer, so that not only may an indicant be made to specify a mode, but it may also (indeed must where possible) specify the bounds as well. A splendid example of this is the mode **string** declared in 2.5.3. If such an indicant now appears as or in a formal-declarer, no harm is done, the actual-bounds associated with it now being treated as if they had been formal.

However, if the bounds of a mode-declaration require elaboration, as n in:

(E14)   **mode a** = [1 : *n*] **real** ;

then they are not elaborated at the time this mode-declaration is encountered. Instead, it is the value of n in force at the time **a** is applied that matters:

(E15)   *n* := *1*;
         a *a*;   ¢ i.e. [*1* : *1*] **real** *a*; ¢
         n := *2*;
         a *b*;   ¢ i.e. [*1* : *2*] **real** *b*; ¢

Finally, although we have this elaborate mechanism for checking bounds and states in identity-declarations, we must point out that it is seldom used in this form, since the bulk of row-of identity-declarations are extended forms

Ch.2.5.2.3   DECLARATIONS   155

of things like E11. However, formal-parameters also occur in routine-denotations (4.2.2.2), and it is when routines are called that this mechanism really comes into its own. All this will be explained in 4.5.1.

2.5.2.3. Virtual row-of declarers

For the sake of completeness, we shall now give the complete list of places in which a virtual-declarer can occur:
1) The declarer in a cast (5.1.4.2) is virtual right from the start [R 8.3.4.1].
2) The inside of a **union** is always virtual (2.6.1) [R 7.1.1.jj].
3) The declarers specifying the parameters in a **proc** declarer (4.2.1) (note that we did NOT say "in a routine-denotation (4.2.2.2)") are always virtual [R 7.1.1.x].
4) The declarer specifying the mode delivered in a **proc** declarer, or in a routine-denotation, is always virtual [R 7.1.1.x].
5) Declarers which start off as formal or actual may become virtual after some point, after which they remain virtual to the end [R 7.1.1] (or at least as far as the end of the current field, as in the case of the field *a* in E8).
6) An actual-declarer becomes virtual as soon as a **ref** is encountered.
7) A formal-declarer also becomes virtual as soon as one **ref** is encountered, except that a **ref** right at the beginning does not count for this purpose.

2.5.3. The mode **string**

The mode **string** is not a primitive in the language, although you would not come to much harm if you were to regard it as such, since it is provided with a complete set of operators and other useful facilities (5.5.1.1, 5.7.0.2, 6.1). It is, in fact, a [ ] **char**, being defined in the standard prelude (1.1) [R 10.2.10.aa] by:

(E16)   mode string = [*1 : 0* **flex**] char;

An interesting consequence of this is that if we declare:

(E17)   string *t;*

we have not created an object with an undefined value as we would have done in:

real *x;*

Instead, *t* has been made to refer to an empty **string**, which is a very definite (and useful) entity, and the only thing undefined about it is the value of the elements which it hasn't got.

Note that [ ] **char**s which are not **strings** can exist (see 7.1.2 for an interesting consequence of this). Also that [ ] **string** is not a legitimate mode, unless your implementation is particularly kind to you, because the elements of a multiple value cannot be of row-of modes (2.5.1).

Vertical readers, please turn to 3.5.

2.6. Union declarations

2.6.1. union declarers

We introduced you to **union**s in 1.6.1. Although we cannot create values of united modes, we can talk about such modes, and to do this we need declarers:

(E1)   **union** *(* [ ] **real**, [ ] **int***)*

Note how the inside of a **union** is always virtual (2.5.2.3), so that there is no difference in appearance between formal, actual and virtual **union** declarers [R 7.1.1.jj].

You will remember that (1.6.1) the order in which the modes are specified inside a **union** is quite immaterial [R 7.1.1.cc, R 4.4.3.d], so that:

(E2)   **union** *(* [ ] **int**, [ ] **real***)*

specifies exactly the same mode as that specified by E1. Moreover:

(E3)   **union** *(* **int**, **string**, **union** *(* **real**, **union** *(* [ ] **char**, **int***)))*

could equally well (and with less ink) have been:

(E4)   **union** *(* **int**, **real**, [ ] **char***)*

Even a conformity relation could not tell the difference (5.6.4.1).
    However:

           union *(* **int**, **ref int***)*

is not allowed because, if this mode were required (a posteriori) in a firm context (e.g. as the operand in a formula), and a **ref int** were available (a priori), we should not know whether to dereference it and then unite it (5.6.0), or whether to unite it straight away. There is therefore a context condition (1.2.1) forbidding the uniting of two "related" modes. Two modes are related if there exists a firm coercion (5.1.0) that will turn one into the other (or indeed there exists a common mode from which they could both be coerced). Thus:

   union *(*real, proc ref real*)*

would not do either, because the two halves of it can be coerced from **ref real** (by dereferencing and proceduring respectively).

2.6.2. union declarations

Now we can use **union** declarers in the formal-parameters of identity-declarations, or as the actual-declarers in **loc** generators:

(E5)   **ref union** *(*real, int*) ri* = **loc union** *(*real, int*)*;

or by extension:

(E6)   **union** *(*real, int*) ri;*

in which a variable *ri* is created, to which either a **real** or an **int** may subsequently be assigned (5.6.0). At the moment, it is not defined whether *ri* refers to a **real** or an **int**, but it will certainly be one of them [R 7.1.2.d].

Since there is no such thing as a value of a united mode, there are some declarations which, whilst being legal, are not at all useful:

(E7)   **union** *(*bool, real*) br = 3.142;*

br will now, in fact, always possess a **real** value, but wherever it is used allowance for both possibilities will nevertheless be made (and, for example, *x := br* will not be allowed). This declaration could, however, very reasonably arise when matching the actual-parameter of a call to the formal-parameter of a routine-denotation (4.2.2.2):

(E8)   **proc** *pbr =* **(union** *(*bool, real*) br)* : XXXXX;
        pbr (3.142)

Here, *pbr* possesses a routine which is prepared to accept either a **bool** or a **real** as its actual-parameter (and occurrences of *br* within XXXXX will be treated accordingly).

2.6.3. Extended union declarations

The extensions possible with **union**s are similar to those possible with structs (2.4.3). Firstly, occurrences of **union** can be gathered together [R 9.2.c] :

(E9)   **struct** *(***union** *(*real, int*)* aa, **union** *(*bool, char*)* bb*)*

May become:

(E10)   **struct** *(***union** *(*real, int*)* aa, *(*bool, char*)* bb*)*

The mode-declaration:

(E11)   **mode realint** = **union** *(*real, int*)*;

may become [R 9.2.b] :

(E12)   **union realint** = *(*real, int*)*;

and if we have several such modes to declare collaterally, we can write:

(E13)   **union realint** = *(*real, int*)* ,
         boolchar = *(*bool, char*)* ;

In addition to the extensions to identity-declarations discussed in 2.2.2, which of course still apply, you can produce:

(E14)   **union** *(*real, int*)* c,
         *(*bool, char*)* d;

in which two **union** variables are created.

Vertical readers, please turn to 5.6.

2.7. bits, bytes and longs

2.7.1. bits and bytes

bits and **bytes** [R 10.2.8,9] are two primitive modes * which are intended to give you access to the actual words in you computer, so that you may achive greater efficiency. **bits** is similar to [ ] **bool** and **bytes** to [ ] **char** (or **string**), except that the number of **bools** or **chars** respectively is limited to exactly that number which can be fitted into one computer word. Thus in-

---

* Pedantically speaking, they are not quite so primitive as **real** and **int**, because you can redefine them in a mode-declaration (**mode bits** = something else) whereas you are not allowed to say **mode real** = anything. In fact, the Report regards them as structures [R 10.2.8.a, R 10.2.9.a], using the mysterious 'letter aleph symbol', of which we gave you a slight smell in 0.9.2.

Ch.2.7.2　　　　　　　　DECLARATIONS　　　　　　　　　　159

dividual **bits** or **bytes** values can be passed around inside your program with great efficiency, at the expense of some additional effort (by widening (5.7.0.2) or the operators **btb** and **ctb** (6.1.1) and **elem** (6.1.2)) whenever you want to get at the individual **bools** or **chars** within them. Environment enquires are provided (6.2.1) to tell you how much you can get into a single **bits** or **bytes** in your implementation.

bits and **bytes** are, of course, easily declared:

(E1)　　　　**bits** *bits;* **bytes** *bytes;*

Note that [ ] **bits** and [ ] **bytes** may be declared (as opposed to [ ] [ ] **bool** and [ ] **string** which may not). Likewise, **bits** and **bytes** may appear inside **struct**, **union** and **proc** modes.

2.7.2. **long** modes

Double, triple, etc. length working is used in computers in order to obtain greater accuracy, or to distinguish between a greater number of possible values of some mode, or to pack more information into one value. The ALGOL 68 modes where this facility would be useful are:

　　　　int, real, compl, bits and **bytes**

Indeed, it is possible to prefix all of these modes by "**long**" in order to obtain new modes of approximately double the precision, by "**long long**" for triple precision, and so on. A given implementation does not have to carry this on indefinitely, however. After some number of **long**s (perhaps only one) it will treat values of **long**er modes as being of the same precision. Various environment enquiries are provided to tell you how many **long**s are effective, and how precise they are (6.7.1), and a full set of operators (6.7.3) and procedures (6.7.2) is provided for them.

long modes are, of course, easily declared:

(E2)　　　　**long real** *reaeal;* **long long int** *iiiiiint;*
　　　　　　proc *(***long int**, **int***)* **long long int** *power;*

2.7.3. **heap** declarations

Just as:

(E3)　　　　**real** *x;*

is an extension (2.2.2) of:

(E4)   **ref real** x = **loc real**;

so:

(E5)   **heap real** x;

is an extension of:

(E6)   **ref real** x = **heap real**;

in which the **heap real** is a **heap** generator. The effect of E5 is to reserve a space in the store for the variable x which will not disappear when the current range is left. (It will not, of course, then be accessible via the identifier x, but its name may in the meantime have been assigned to a **ref real** variable with a larger scope).

This and other uses of **heap** generators will be described more fully in 5.7.2.1.

Vertical readers, please turn to 3.7.

3. CLAUSES

3.1. Serial clauses

A particular-program (1.1.1) [R 2.1.d] consists of a CLOSED-clause (3.2.4), which is usually a 'serial clause' closed by embedding between **begin** and **end** (or, if you prefer, between "(" and ")", which can be used as alternatives wherever **begin** and **end** may occur).

The bricks out of which a serial-clause is constructed are called 'declarations', 'statements' and 'expressions'. Declarations we have already met (1.1.3 and 2). 'Statements' and 'expressions' [R 6.0.1.b, c] are alternative names for 'unitary void clauses' and 'unitary MODE clauses' respectively, and unitary-clauses in general will be discussed in Chapter 5. In the meantime, it will suffice to say that:

$x := a+b$

is a statement (usually) and:

$a+b$

is an expression (likewise).

We shall also need 'go on symbols' (better known as semicolons) which constitute the mortar which bind the bricks together, and 'labels' which enable us to find our way around.

3.1.1. Declaration preludes

The building rules are really quite simple [R 6.1.1]. The foundations, which come first, consist of declarations (as many as you like) with mortar in between:

(E1)   **begin**   ¢ the **begin** is not part of the serial clause proper; it is
         real a;   the earth in which the foundations are embedded ¢
         int i;
         char c,d,e;

(The last one is a collateral-declaration (see 1.1.3) which stands for:

(E2)   **char** c, **char** d, **char** e;

however, it all counts as one brick for our present purpose.

Statements are also allowed within the foundations, but labels are not. This is particularly useful when you are declaring multiple values (as described in 2.5.2) in which the bounds are first to be calculated:

(E3) **begin**
      int *i;*
      read (i);   ¢ (7.1.2) ¢
      [*1* : *i*] **real** *x1;* ¢ declares a multiple with bounds *1* to *i* ¢

The official name for the foundations is 'declaration preludes'. Note that it is perfectly possible for there to be no declaration-preludes at all, the building starting straight away with the walls. This would be rather unusual for a serial-clause which constituted the body of a particular-program, but there are plenty of other places where such serial-clauses could occur.

3.1.2. Statement interludes

The walls (officially the 'statement interlude') come next, and these too may be entirely absent. They consist of statements and semicolons, with labels attached where required (a label always comes before a statement (or before an expression) and consists of an identifier (1.1.2) followed by a colon).

(E4) **begin**
      int *i;* **real** *x, y, z;*
      comment those were the foundations: now for the walls ¢
      $z := 1 - 3 \times sqrt\ (small\ real);$ ¢ for *small real* see 6.2 ¢
labl: *read (i);*
      $x := i;$
lobl:
lubl: $y := i/x\uparrow 2;$
      $x := (2 \times x + y)/3;$
      if $y/x < z$ **then go to** *lobl* **fi**;
      print (x); ¢(7.1.1) ¢
      go to *labl;*

This will compute and print the cube roots of the (nonzero) integers read in. The conditional statement (**if** ...... **fi**) does what you would expect it to do (see 3.2.4.2 for details).

We now observe (as you have doubtless guessed already) that when a statement is followed by a ";" the completion of the elaboration of that statement is followed by the initiation of the elaboration of the following statement [R 6.1.2.b] . Only when we come to a **go to** statement (consisting of **go to** followed by a label-identifier, or alternatively of just the label-identifier) is this sequence broken. Note that several labels can precede one statement (as *lobl*: and *lubl*: in E4).

3.1.3. The value of a serial clause

Finally, we come to the roof (no special name, unless you would like to call it a 'unitary MOID clause'). This consists of just one statement (unitary-void-clause) or one expression (unitary-MODE-clause) (and there may be some labels before it).

(E5)   **begin**
       int *i; read (i);* **real** *x, y, z;*
           ¢ those were the foundations ¢
       z := 1 − 3 × sqrt (small real); x := i;
       lobl: y := i/x↑2; x := (2 × x + y)/3;
           if *y/x < z* **then go to** *lobl* **fi**;
           ¢ those were the walls ¢
       print (x)
       end   ¢ the **end** is part of the embedding, too ¢

In this case the roof (*print (x)*) was a statement − it was, in fact, just the last statement of the clause, and if there had been any more following it would have been quite content to be part of the walls.

Note that, in accordance with the best building practice, there is no mortar underneath the foundations, and there is none on top of the roof. Also, there is exactly one ";" between each brick. Contrast this with ALGOL 60 where extra ";"s mostly did no harm.

Now, if the roof is an expression, then it must yield a value. What happens to this value?

(E6)   *a := b +* (**real** *x, y, z; z := 1 − 3 × sqrt (small real); x := i;*
           lobl: y := i/x↑2; x := (2 × x + y)/3;
               if *y/x < z* **then go to** *lobl* **fi**;
           x)

Here, the piece between the "(" and the ")" is indeed a serial-clause and it occurs in a place where it is expected to yield a value (it is in fact a 'serial real clause'). *x* is its roof and is an expression which (after a little dereferencing which you had best ignore until you have read 5.2.0.1) yields a **real** value. This value now becomes the value of the serial-clause as a whole, and in due course it gets added to *b*, and the result is put into *a*.

3.1.4. Completers

We will now consider buildings with several roofs. Suppose, in the example E6, we only wanted the cube root of *i* if *i* was positive or the cube root was less than *10.0* (actually, it was rather a poor way of finding cube roots for largish numbers anyway). In the other cases, we wanted to print a message and to yield the result *10.0* regardless. Then we could build a house like this:

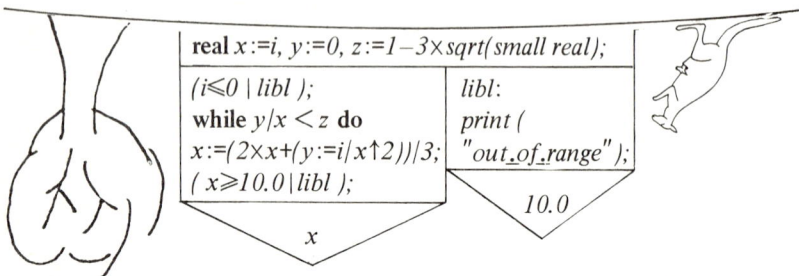

We have to make it an Australian house, so that you can read the program from the top downwards. We also included one or two short cuts in the program, which you might be able to follow.

Observe that the declaration-preludes (the foundations) are common to both roofs. The complete statement containing the two-roofed serial-clause (and without the short cuts) will now look like this:

(E7)   *a* := *b* + *(*real *x, y, z; z* := *1* − *3* × *sqrt(small real); x* := *i;*
         if *x* ⩽ *0* then go to *libl* fi;
lobl: *y* := *i/x*↑*2; x* := *(2* × *x* + *y)/3;*
         if *y/x* < *z* then go to *lobl* fi;
         if *x* ⩾ *10.0* then go to *libl* fi;
         x exit
libl: print *(" out.of.range");*
         10.0)

exit means that we have come to the first roof, and if this point is reached during the elaboration, then *x* is the value of the serial-clause. Otherwise (there being no more exits in this particular clause) *10.0* is the roof and provides the value. Inevitably, the exit must be followed by a label (for how else could the following statement be reached), and so the exit with its label attached constitute what is known as a 'completer' and the process of leaving a serial-clause through the roof (i.e. via either the *x* or the *10.0* in the E7 example) is known as "completing". Contrariwise, if you jump out of the middle of a serial-clause by means of a go to (out of the window perhaps) then that is to "terminate" it, and in this case no value is yielded. The mode of the value yielded on completing may be coerced and balanced (5.2.0.1) according to the context in which the serial clause as a whole appears.

You can try imagining how E7 could have been written without the **exit** facility. It would have been necessary to re-arrange it so that the x to be yielded came right at the end. After *libl*, it would have been necessary to assign 10.0 to x, and then to **go to** another label just before the final x.

Note that, syntactically, a completer is a special type of mortar, so one does not expect to see any ";"s either before or after it. It might be tempting to regard it as a statement meaning "and now **go to** the end of the clause" but this would be dangerous. This will become more apparent when it is pointed out that an alternative to **exit** is simply a "." (Appendix 1) (again followed by a label, of course). This now looks more like mortar, but we did not use it in the example because it does tend to look a little inconspicuous. (Students of ambiguities might also like to consider the consequences of not insisting that such a "." is followed by a label!)

Please do not confuse **exit** with *exit*, which is a label permanently fixed to the end of your program (see 6.1).

Vertical readers, please turn to 4.1.

3.1.5. Delimiters

In all the examples given above, the serial-clause itself was the part between the **begin** and the **end** (or "(" and ")"). However, serial-clauses can occur in a variety of contexts, and the complete list of delimiter pairs applicable is as follows:

between		and		
	begin	and	**end**	(in particular-programs or closed-clauses)
	(	and	**)**	,,
	if / **thef**	and	**then** / **thef**	(in conditional-clauses)
	then	and	**fi** / **else** / **elsf**	,,
	elsf	and	**then** / **thef**	,,
	else	and	**fi**	,,
	out	and	**esac**	(in case-clauses)
	while	and	**do**	(in repetitive statements – see 3.5.2)

Closed- conditional- and case-clauses will be discussed in 3.2.

3.2. Closed clauses

3.2.1. Ranges and reaches

A 'range' [R 4.1.1.e] is a piece of source text which constitutes a serial-clause (or one which constitutes a routine-denotation (see 4.2.2.2) or certain unitary-clauses (see 5.7.2.1)). A range can "contain" further ranges within itself, and so on recursively. Here is a (not very sensible) particular-program, with all its ranges marked and numbered:

(E1)
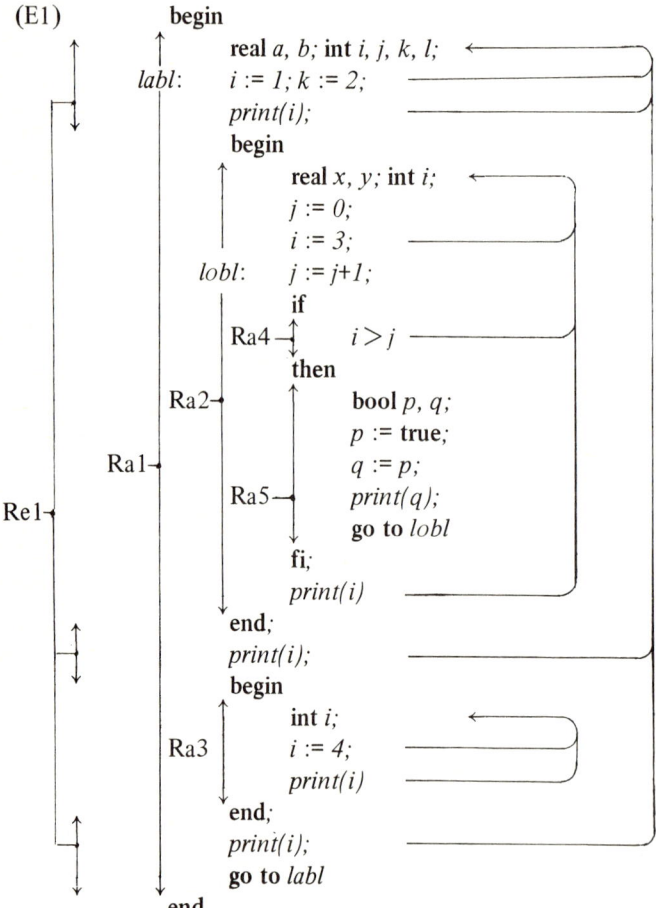

A "reach" [R 4.4.2.a] is a range, with the exclusion of all the ranges contained within it. Thus Re1 in the above example is a reach.

Note how all the ranges in E1 are in fact serial-clauses, and how they are all contained between the delimiters listed in 3.1.5.

3.2.2. Scopes of names

Consider the declaration **real** x at the head of Ra2 which, as usual, stands for:

(E2)   **ref real** x = **loc real**

When this is reached during elaboration of the program (i.e. just after the beginning of Ra2), a name is created (a location in the store is reserved) and the identifier x is made to possess it [R 7.1.2.d, 8.5.1.2.b]. The **loc** in E2 means the the "scope" of this name is restricted to the range Ra2 (in whose declaration-preludes it occurs). Therefore, as soon as we cease elaborating statements within Ra2 (when we reach the delimiter **end** which terminates it in this instance), the name (to all intents and purposes) ceases to exist (the location in store is relinquished).

Thus, anything that you declare at the head of a range is only available to you inside that range (this is of course exactly the same as in ALGOL 60, except that there they are termed "blocks" instead of "ranges").

In an assignation (5.1.4.1) the scope of the RHS must be at least as great as that of the LHS, for otherwise the value referred to by the LHS would be undefined in some reach:

(E3)   **begin ref real** xx; **real** y;
　　　　begin real x;
　　　　$read(x)$; ¢ reads a plain value (2.0, perhaps) ¢
　　　　$y := x$; ¢ this is all right because the plain value is being assigned, and its scope is not limited ¢
　　　　$xx := x$ ¢ this one is going to cause trouble ¢
　　　　end;
　　$print(y)$; ¢ no complaints ¢
　　$y := xx$;
　　$print(y)$ ¢ now what? ¢
　　end

3.2.3. Identification

Identifiers may occur in declarations — these are called "defining occurrences". In all other places (in assignations to take the most obvious example) they are "applied occurrences". Consider the range Ra5 in E1. The identifier *p* is defined in:

(E4)   **bool** *p*

and is applied in:

(E5)   *p* := **true**   and in   *q* := *p*

Now it is up to the compiler to correlate each applied occurrence with a defining one, and when this has been done the former is said to "identify" the latter. The two occurrences of *p* in E5 thus identify the *p* in E4 (still in the context of the range Ra5, of course) and this means that all these *p* s possess the same name (they get hold of the same location in the store) and they are all of the same mode (**ref bool** in this case).

Now, what about the identifier *i*, which has defining occurrences at the head of Ra1, Ra2 and Ra3 in E1, and applied occurrences (notably as *print(i)*) all over the place? The rule is quite straightforward [R 4.1.2] :

Start at the applied occurrence in question (call it "A")
Look for a defining occurrence in the same reach as A (call it "B")
If none is found,
⟶ then look for a defining occurrence in the reach which is immediately outside the range which contains the reach which you have just been looking at (call it "B")

If none is found, ⟶

A then identifies B.

The arrows on the right hand side of example E1 show how all the applied occurrences of *i* are identified, and if you follow through the elaboration of this particular-program, you will find that what it prints out is:

1 <u>1</u> <u>1</u> 3 1 4 1 1 <u>1</u> <u>1</u> 3 1 4 1 1 <u>1</u> . . .

where <u>1</u> is printed for the value **true** (see 7.1.1).

Note that, each time a new defining occurrence of *i* is encountered, then *i* is made to possess a different name until further notice. This certainly does not mean that the old name possessed by *i* ceases to exist. It simply goes underground, and cannot be accessed (at least not via *i*) until after the end of the range in which *i* was redefined. It can, of course, be accessed if the programmer has made provision for some other object to possess or to refer to it).

Labels are identified just like any other identifiers, being defined as in:

   labl:

Ch.3.2.4 CLAUSES 169

and applied as in:

> **go to** *labl*

This means that the **go to** *lobl* at the end of Ra5 can be used to jump out of Ra5 (which is then terminated – 3.1.4) into Ra2, which contains it; but it would be quite impossible to jump into Ra2 at *lobl*: from anywhere in the reach Re1. The identification just would not work. Thus, a range can only be entered via its declaration preludes (which is just as well, if you think about it).

Finally, as you might expect, there is a context condition (1.2.1) which states that each applied occurrence must identify one, and only one, defining occurrence [R 4.4.2.b, R 4.4.1.b] . Thus all variables which you use must be declared (as in ALGOL 60, but not as in FORTRAN) and any given identifier may only be declared once within a reach. However, an applied occurrence need not necessarily come after its defining occurrence:

(E6)   **begin**
            proc real a = **real**: $b := c;$
            real $b := 1, c := 2;$
            $x := a$
       end

is perfectly legitimate (see 4.2.2.1 for further details of procedured casts, of which **real**: $b := c$ is one). However, some implementations may not allow this (see Appendix 4). On the other hand:

(E7)   **begin**
            real $b;$
            $b := c;$
            real $c;$
            $c := b$
       end

is syntactically correct, and the identification of c works, but the assignment $b := c$ will not work because the name (location) possessed by c has not been created at this point of the elaboration.

For the identification of modes see 3.3.1, and for operators see 4.3.3.

3.2.4. CLOSED clauses

A CLOSED-clause is either:

a closed-clause
a collateral-clause
a conditional-clause
or a case-clause

CLOSED-clauses occur primarily in primaries (5.1.0.1). This means, inter alia, that they can stand as statements or as expressions (yielding respectively either **void** or some mode).

Collateral-clauses will be deferred until 3.7.1. The others will be considered now.

3.2.4.1. Closed clauses

A closed-clause is a serial-clause enclosed between **begin** and **end**, or between "**(**" and "**)**" [R 6.3]. There are two chief reasons for using them. The first is to create some variables (strictly names) which are to be local to some range:

(E8)   **begin**
       real *pie;*
          begin
          real $w := 0$, **int** $i := 1;$ **real** $z = sqrt\ (small\ real/2);$
       loop: $w := w + 2/(i \times (i + 2));$
       $i := i + 4;$
       if $1/i > z$ **then go to** *loop* **fi**;
       pie $:= 4 \times w$
       end;
      print(pie)
    end

Here, the closed-clause was a statement, and it was created because w, i, z and *loop* were not needed outside it. Here is a similar example in which the closed-clause is an expression:

(E9)   **begin**
       print $(4 \times ($ **real** $w := 0$, **int** $i := 1;$ **real** $z = sqrt\ (small\ real/2);$
          loop: $w := w + 2/(i \times (i + 2));$ $i := i + 4;$
          if $1/i > z$ **then** *loop* **fi**;
          w))
    end

Indeed, 99% of an entire particular-program could be contained within one such expression. Note here the alternative form of the **go to** statement in which the "**go to**" is omitted.

The second reason why closed-clauses are used is to alter the priority of operators in formulas (5.1.3):

(E10) $y := x \times (a+b)$

In these cases, the serial-clause inside the closed-clause often contains just one unitary-clause (the building is nothing but a roof, using the metaphor of 3.1).

3.2.4.2. Conditional clauses

> **if**
>> some strong serial **bool** clause yields the value **true**
>
> **then**
>> let us elaborate a serial-clause (and yield a value if one is asked for)
>
> **else**
>> let us elaborate another serial-clause (and yield its value)
>
> **fi**

In general, therefore, a conditional-clause contains three serial-clauses, and any or all of them can contain declarations, statements, closed-clauses, completers, and all the rest of the paraphernalia [R 6.4]. At the other extreme, each of them can be as simple as a single unitary-clause:

(E11)   **if** p **then** r **else** s **fi**

where p would have to be a **bool** (or a **proc bool**), and r and s might be labels, or they might be **procs**. Either way, r and s would be statements and therefore the whole conditional-clause would be a statement, and would yield no value.

In order to save ink, there are alternative representations that may be used for **if**, **then**, **else** and **fi**:

(p | r | s)

It is quite in order to omit the **else** and its associated clause [R 9.4.a]:

(p | r)

If p is **true** the statement r is elaborated. Otherwise no statement is elaborated at all. However, this is not a sensible thing to do if the conditional-clause is expected to yield a value, for then the value yielded if p were **false** would be undefined.

$x := (i < j | a+b | a-b)$

That was a slightly more ambitious example. $i<j$ is a formula yielding a **bool** value (5.1.3 and 6.1.2). The conditional-clause as a whole is required to yield

real (in order that it may be assigned to *x*). Both *a+b* and *a−b* are formulas yielding **real**, and so all is well. As a matter of fact, it would have been sufficient for them to have been coerceable to **real**, and a phenomenon known as "balancing" could have been invoked to aid the process. However, we shall leave discussion of this (and indeed of the coercion of all CLOSED-clauses) to 5.2.0.1.

> **if**
>> some strong serial **bool** clause is **true**
>
>> **thef**
>>> some other strong serial **bool** clause is also **true**
>>
>>> **thef**
>>>> and a third one
>>
>>> **then**
>>>> let us elaborate some serial-clause
>>
>>> **else**
>>>> let us elaborate another one
>
> **fi**

This is a piece of syntactic sugar to save you from losing count of your **fis** [R 9.4.b]. Note that the **else** option is only exercised if the first two **bool** clauses yield **true** and the third one yields **false**. If either of the first two is **false** then nothing at all happens. An interesting consequence of this is that clauses with **thefs** in them are of no use where values are to be yielded. **thef** is sometimes useful as a substitute for the "∧" operator, where it is wished to avoid elaborating the things to the right of the "∧" when the things to the left have already yielded **false** (as is also done in the "McCarthy and" example in R 7.5.2). However, the effect is not exactly the same, on account of the different effect of the **else** part if an "∧" is used.

As before, there is an alternative representation for **thef**:

(E12)   *(p |: q | r | s)*

which means the same as:

(E13)   **if** *p* **then**   **if** *q* **then** *r* **else** *s* **fi**   **fi**

Here is some more sugar:

if
    some serial **bool** clause is true
then
    do this serial-clause
elsf
    some other **bool** clause is true
    then
        do this other serial-clause
    elsf
        this third **bool**
        then
            this third clause
        else
            this last resort
fi

This piece of sugar also has an alternative representation:

(E14) $(p \mid r \mid : q \mid s \mid t)$

meaning:

(E15)   **if** p **then** r **else**   **if** q **then** s **else** t **fi**   **fi**

If you are very clever, you can have **thef** and **elsf** in the same conditional clause:

(E16)   **if** p
        thef q
        then r ¢ i.e. if $p \wedge q$ ¢
        elsf $i < j$
            then s ¢ i.e. if $p \wedge \neg q \wedge i < j$ ¢
            else t ¢ i.e. if $p \wedge \neg q \wedge \neg(i < j)$ ¢
    fi

and if p is not **true** then none of them happens.

3.2.4.3. Case clauses

Case-clauses are of two types [R 9.4.c,d]. "Case conformities" are described in 3.7.3. The rest are described here.

> **case**
>> some strong unitary **int** clause yielding a value, say *i*
>
> **in**
>> a unitary-clause
>
> ,
>> a 2nd unitary-clause
>
> ,
>> a 3rd unitary-clause
>
> **out**
>> an alternative serial-clause
>
> **esac**

Some number, say *n*, of unitary-clauses are separated by ",".s. If the value of *i* is such that

$$i \leqslant 0 \text{ or } i > n$$

then the **out** clause is elaborated. Otherwise the *i*th unitary-clause is elaborated. If the case-clause as a whole is required to yield a value, then each unitary-clause must be capable of yielding a value of the required mode (but all legitimate coercions and balancings may be applied to this end (see 5.2.0.1)).

It is quite in order to omit the **out** and its associated unitary-clause. If the clause as a whole is a statement, this means that no action is taken. If it is an expression, however, the value yielded is undefined:

(E17)   **begin int** *days, month, year;*
             days := **case** *month* **in**
                 31, (year **mod** *4 = 0* ∧ *year* **mod** *100* ≠ *0* ∨ *year* **mod**
                     400 = 0 | 29 | 28),
                 31, 30, 31, 30, 31, 31, 30, 31, 30, 31 **esac**
         end

As usual, there are alternative representations for **case, in, out** and **esac**:

(E18)   print ((i | *"SUNDAY", "MONDAY", "TUESDAY", "WEDNESDAY",*
             "THURSDAY", "FRIDAY", "SATURDAY" | *"NODAY"*))

If you think it confusing that "(", ")", "|" and "|:" should be able to represent so many things, please accept our assurance that no syntactic ambiguity arises. They are quick and easy to write, although it might be kinder to use the longer versions in algorithms intended for publication.

Likewise, you may use **if** when you mean **case**, **then** when you mean **in**, **else** when you mean **out**, **fi** when you mean **esac** and vice versa. Your compiler will not object, but your colleagues may.

Ch.3.3 CLAUSES 175

Vertical readers, please turn to 4.2.

3.3. Indicants

Indicants are declared to possess modes or routines by means of mode-declarations (2.3.1) and operation-declarations (4.3.2). These declarations are valid for some range, and so the question of identification arises.

3.3.1. Identification of modes

The identification of identifiers was described in 3.2.3. The purpose and method of identification of indicants declared in mode-declarations are exactly the same [R 4.2.2]. Consider the identification of **r** in:

(E1)
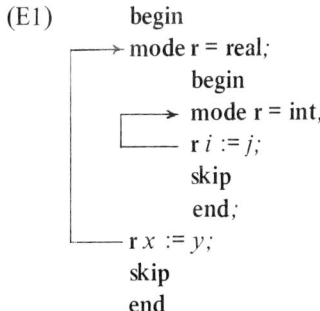
```
         begin
    ┌──→ mode r = real;
    │       begin
    │  ┌──→ mode r = int;
    │  └──  r i := j;
    │       skip
    │       end;
    └── r x := y;
        skip
        end
```

An explanation of the identification of indicants which are used as operators will be postponed until 4.3.3.

Vertical readers, please turn to 4.3.

3.4. Structure displays

Structure denotations as such do not exist in the language (except for the special case of **bits** discussed in 5.7.1.1). However, the required effect can be obtained by means of a particular form of CLOSED-clause known as a 'structure display'. These can stand in any strong position where a primary yielding a structure would be allowed (because the position is strong, it follows that the exact mode of the structure-display is always known). Thus, given the declarations involving the mode **vec** in Appendix 2, and the declaration:

(E1)   vec $v1, v2, v3;$

we can write:

(E2) $v1 := (1, 1, 1)$

but not:

(???) $v1 := v1 * (1, 1, 1)$

where the context would be firm (see 5.1.0 and 5.1.3).

A structure-display, then, is enclosed between "(" and ")" (or between **begin** and **end**) and contains one strong unit (5.1) for each field (of which there must be at least two) [R 6.0.1.g, R 6.2.1.f]. Because each field position is strong, widening is permitted (as indeed happened in the case of the $(1, 1, 1)$ in the E2 example above). Because a field position is also a unit, structure-displays are considerably more than a substitute for structure denotations, e.g.:

(E3) $v1 := (x + 2, 3.4, i-3)$

Note that the various fields are elaborated collaterally (1.1.2.2).

Vertical readers, please turn to 5.4.

3.5. Row displays and repetitions

3.5.1. Row displays

Multiple denotations as such do not exist in the language (except for the special case of **string** (5.5.1.1)). However, as in the case of structures (3.4), the required effect can be obtained by means of a particular form of CLOSED-clause known as a 'row display'. Thus:

(E1) $x1 := (1.2, 2.3, 3.4);$
(E2) $y1 := (x, y, a \times b + 1)$

A row-display, then, is enclosed between "(" and ")" (or between **begin** and **end**) and contains one unit (5.1) for each of its elements (of which there must be at least two) [R 6.0.1.h, R 6.2.1.c,d]. The strength of at least one of the element positions must be as weak as the context in which the whole display occurs, but the rest of the element positions are strong (see 5.2.0.1 for further discussion of such balancing). Thus, if the operator "+" has been declared to operate between pairs of [ ] **real** (but not [ ] **int**), we may not write:

(E3) $x1 := y1 + (1, 2, 3, 4, 5)$

but we may write:

(E4) $x1 := y1 + (1, 2, 3.0, 4, 5)$

i.e., because the *3.0* is present to indicate that the row-display as a whole (whose context is firm) is to be of mode [ ] **real**, it is permissable to widen the *1*, *2*, *4* and *5*. If the context had been strong, they could all have been widened, as in:

(E5) $x1 := (1, 2, 3, 4, 5)$

Note that the various elements are elaborated collaterally (1.1.2.2).

A row-display yields, of course, a multiple value, whose elements are yielded by its units [R 6.2.2.c]. The bounds of this multiple value are always fixed (see 1.5.1), the lower-bound is always *1*, and the upper-bound is the number of units in the row-display. Thus:

(1, 2, 3, 4, 5)

has fixed bounds [*1:5*], and:

((1, 2, 3), (4, 5, 6))

has fixed bounds [*1:2, 1:3*]. Note how the row-display here contains as many row-displays as there are rows, each of which contains as many elements as there are columns.

A row-display is not, as the Report stands at present, permitted to appear in a weak (or soft) context (5.1.0.2). The effect of this is that it cannot be sliced (5.5.1.3). The reason is that ambiguities could arise during weak coercion in certain cases. In fact, most implementations are likely to permit row-displays to be sliced in the safe cases — and these include all the ones you are ever likely to meet in practice.

3.5.2. Repetitive statements

[R 9.3]

for
    some **int** identifier, which is hereby declared   (I)
from
    some unitary **int** clause   (J)
by
    some other unitary **int** clause   (K)
to
    a third unitary **int** clause   (L)
while
    a serial **bool** clause   (P)
do
    a unitary statement   (S)

For example:

(E6)   **for** i **from** $k-2$ **by** 1 **to** m **while real** $lim = max\ real/a;\ x < lim$ **do**
      $x := x + a\uparrow i/i$

This sums a certain series from $k-2$ to m, or until x is getting too large, whichever happens first.

Now a repetitive statement consists of various parts labelled as I through S above. S is the statement which is to be repeated, and in most applications it will be CLOSED (3.2.4) in order that it may contain a substantial amount of program within itself:

(E7)   **for** i **from** j **by** k **to** l **while** p **do**
      begin
      $x := x + x1[i]\ ;$
      $p := x < max\ real/2$
      end

From inside S you may access I and you may do things which will alter the value of P, but you may not alter I because its mode is **int** and not **ref int** (this means that the compiler is at liberty to treat I specially, perhaps keeping it in some fast access register). You can do what you like to J, K and L, but it will make no difference to the number of times the loop is obeyed, which is determined once and for all (effects of P apart) at the beginning. The loop is obeyed until I $>$ L (or $<$ if K is negative). I.e. the number of times obeyed is

$$-\ \mathbf{entier}\ -((L-J)/K + 1)$$

or zero if this is negative. The loop will be obeyed zero times if P yields **false** upon entry.

More precisely, the interpretation of a repetitive statement is illustrated by the following piece of program, which is entirely equivalent to E7:

(E8)   **begin**
         int *from* := *j*, **int** *by* = *k*, *to* = *l*;
         ¢ *j*, *k* and *l* are elaborated (collaterally) and their values are
         remembered. The counting is going to be done in *from* ¢
  m: **if**   *by* > *0* ∧ *from* ≤ *to* ∨ *by* < *0* ∧ *from* ≥ *to* ∨ *by* = *0*
         ¢ i.e. **if** the count is not yet exhausted ¢
         then **int** *i* = *from*; ¢ the user's *i* is declared here, and is a copy
                            of the current value of *from* ¢
              if   *p*   ¢ the user's *p*, however complex it may be, is
                            elaborated here, each time the loop is about
                            to be obeyed ¢
              then ¢ now comes the user's statement, in this case a
                            closed-clause ¢
                        begin
                            x := *x* + *x1* [*i*] ; ¢ the user may access his *i* ¢
                            p := *x* < *max real*/2 ¢ the user may change his *p* ¢
                        end; ¢ of the user's statement ¢
                        from := *from* + *by*; ¢ the count is in(de)cremented ¢
                        go to *m*
              fi
         fi ¢ we are now outside the scope of *i*, so the question of its
                value upon exit does not arise ¢
         end

In fact, this is how the meaning of the **for** statement is defined (as an extension) in the Report [R 9.3].

You may omit those parts of a repetitive statement that you do not need:

if **for** I	is omitted, there is no I to be accessed	
if **from** J	is omitted, **from** *1*	is assumed
if **by** K	is omitted, **by** *1*	is assumed
if **to** L	is omitted, **to** ∞	is assumed
if **while** P	is omitted, **while true**	is assumed

In fact, the only part which has to be there at all times is the **do** E. If this does stand on its own, then the loop is executed indefinitely, unless you jump out of it.

(E9)　**ref int** $h = i$; ¢ so that h and i are interchangeable identifiers ¢
　　　　$i := -4$;　**for** i　**from** 3　**by** 2　**to** 3　**while** $i<0$　**do** $h:= h+1$; ¢ obeyed 0 time
　　　　$i := -4$;　　　　　**from** 3　**by** 2　**to** 3　**while** $i<0$　**do** $h:= h+1$; ¢ obeyed 1 time
　　　　$i := -4$;　　　　　　　　　　**by** 2　**to** 3　**while** $i<0$　**do** $h:= h+1$; ¢ obeyed 2 time
　　　　$i := -4$;　　　　　　　　　　　　　　**to** 3　**while** $i<0$　**do** $h:= h+1$; ¢ obeyed 3 time
　　　　$i := -4$;　　　　　　　　　　　　　　　　　　**while** $i<0$　**do** $h:= h+1$; ¢ obeyed 4 time
　　　　$i := -4$;　　　　　　　　　　　　　　　　　　　　　　　　**do** $h:= h+1$　¢ ad lib ¢

Vertical readers, please turn to 4.5.

3.7. Collaterality

3.7.1. Collateral clauses

Collateral-clauses [R 6.2] include such things as structure-displays (3.4) and row-displays (3.5.1), but the ones we are particularly interested in at the moment are collateral-void-clauses. These consist of a list of two or more unitary statements separated by commas, and enclosed between **begin** and **end**, or between "*(*" and "*)*":

(E1)　　　*(x:=1, y:=2, z:=3)*

These three statements are elaborated "collaterally". There is not likely to be much gain in using collateral-clauses in this way unless your hardware contains three central processors (so that they can do a statement each), or unless you have reason to believe that your compiler is sufficiently clever to discover that they can be done more efficiently in an order other than that in which they were written down. Alternatively, it might be the case that one of the statements was likely to get held up awaiting some event in real time (transput perhaps), in which case the others would be carrying on. This situation is more likely to arise when parallel-clauses are used (see next section). In the meantime we must consider exactly what "collateral" means.

Collateral elaboration occurs, inter alia, in the following situations:

　　collateral-declarations
　　collateral-clauses
　　structure-and row-displays
　　between the two sides of an assignation or an identity-relation
　　between the two operands of a dyadic-operator (but see 5.7.3)
　　actual-parameters of a procedure call (but see 4.5.2).

Suppose two phrases A and B (it could be more) are to be elaborated collaterally. Then the elaboration of A may be merged in time with that of B in a manner left quite undefined by the Report [R 2.2.5.b]. So long as the elaboration of A has no side effect upon that of B, and vice versa, then the manner of this merging has no effect on the result — otherwise, anything might happen. Normally, the two elaborations would proceed until both were completed (3.1.4), but if one were terminated by a **go to**, then the other would be stopped abruptly at whatever stage (if any) it had reached.

In practical compilers, it is probable that A would be elaborated first and then B, or vice versa, but one is not entitled to make any assumptions based on this. Consider the following:

(E2)   **begin int** *i;*
       proc int *side = (i := 1; i := 2; i);*
       proc *add = (* **int** *ii,* **int** *jj)* **int***: ii+jj;*
       print (add(side, side))
       end

The two calls on *side* are elaborated collaterally. If one were elaborated entirely before the other (in either order), each would yield the value 2, and 4 would be printed. In the corresponding ALGOL 60 program, this would be the guaranteed result. However, this ALGOL 68 program is perfectly entitled to print 3 as its answer, because *i* is global to *side* and the collateral elaboration of the two calls is quite entitled to be merged [R 2.2.5] in the following manner:

i := 1;		¢ on behalf of the first *side* ¢
i := 2;		¢ likewise ¢
	i := 1;	¢ this is the second *side* starting up ¢
i		¢ on behalf of the first *side*, which therefore yields the value *1*, as set by the second *side* ¢
	i := 2;	¢ the second *side* ¢
	i	¢ the second *side* yields 2 ¢

Here is another example:

(E3)   *i := 0;*
       x1[(i **plus** *1; j − 2)] := x2[(i* **plus** *1; j − 2)] ;*
       print (i)

The two subscripts are to be elaborated collaterally. Suppose their elaborations were merged as follows:

Take $i\ (=0)$
Add $1\ (=1)$

                    Take $i\ (=0)$
                    Add $1\ (=1)$
Store in $i\ (1)$ (because the operator **plus** in-
                    Store in $i\ (1)$ cludes assignation)
Take j

                    Take j
subtract 2

                    subtract 2
use to index $x1$

                    use to index $x2$

Thus 1 is printed, even though *i* **plus** *1* has been elaborated twice. In general it may be said that if two identical clauses are to be elaborated collaterally, then the implementation is quite entitled (but not of course bound) to perform the elaboration of only one of them and to assume that the other yields the same result. In other words, a compiler may detect common subexpressions (such as the *(i* **plus** *1; j − 2)* in E3), and optimise its code accordingly, and if a user has put side effects into these sub-expressions, he has no right to complain if they do not behave as he expected.

So the moral of this story, if you were thinking of use side effects and collaterality is involved, is "Don't".

3.7.2. Parallel clauses

These are like collateral-clauses, except that you are provided with some control over the synchronisation of the constituent statements. They consist [R 6.2.1.b] of **par** followed by a collateral-void-clause:

(E4)   **par**$(x:=1,\ y:=2,\ z:=3)$

However this example, although legitimate, does not take advantage of the synchronisation facilities provided. To take a more realistic example, suppose we have a procedure which generates lines of output at random intervals:

(E5)   **proc item** *generate* = *(* **c** *computes the next* **item** *of output,*
                        taking a random length of time to do so **c***);*
      struct item = *(* **c** *a collection of values intended to be printed* **c** *);*

We wish to print these **item**s of output on a lineprinter which operates in real time (i.e. not disguised by an operating system), and at some fixed number

Ch.3.7.2   CLAUSES   183

of lines per minute. In order to smooth out the irregular periods between the generation of **items** (so as, hopefully, to keep both the printer and the central processor busy at all times), we shall put the **items** into a buffer as they are generated, and take them out at a rate suited to the printer. First let us declare our buffer:

(E6)   **int** *nmb buffers* = c *the number of* **items** *the buffer can hold* c;
         [*1* : *nmb buffers*] **item** *buffer;*
         int *index*:=0, *exdex*:=0; ¢ *pointers to* **items** *within the buffer* ¢
         bool *work to be done* := **true**, *printing to be done* := **true**;
                  ¢ *we shall need these in order to know when to stop* ¢

Now we must set up some semaphores so that the generating department and the printing department can communicate with each other. There is a special mode provided for this purpose:

(E7)   **sema** *free slots, full slots;*

A **sema** has a reference to an **int** hidden inside it, but you are only allowed to get at it by means of the special monadic operators "/" (or **its**), **up** and **down** [R 10.4] :

operator	priority	mode of *a*	mode of result	meaning
/ **its**	10	**int**	**sema**	yields a **sema** referring to a to a copy of the **int** *a*
down ↓	10	**sema**	**void**	if the **int** referred to is zero, then the elaboration of this part of the parallel clause is "halted", otherwise the **int** is reduced by *1*
up ** ↑ ^	10	**sema**	**void**	the **int** referred to is increased by *1* and all elaborations previously halted by the operation of **down** on this particular **sema** are "resumed" by repeating the tests for zero in their **downs**

The **its** operator (it stands for "**int** to **sema**"), although not specified as an alternative for "/" by the Report, is likely to be required by most implementations which provide the parallel-clause feature. This is because, if "/" is permitted to be a monadic-operator, difficulties arise in the parsing phase of the compiler. **down** and **up** are meaningless unless they occur inside a parallel-clause.

We shall now initialise our semaphores:

(E8)   *free slots* := /¢ or **its** ¢ *nmb buffers;* ¢ *because we have not generated any items yet* ¢

   full slots := /¢ or **its** ¢ *0*   ¢ *because there are no items waiting for printing* ¢

Now we come to our parallel-clause:

(E9)   **par begin**
            ¢ *the generating department* ¢
            while *work to be done* **do**
            begin
            down *free slots;* ¢ *halts this department if all the slots are full. Initially, there are plenty* ¢
            index **modb** *nmb buffers* **plus** *1;* ¢ *increment index modulo nmb buffers* ¢
            buffer [index] := *generate;*
            if c *there are no more items to generate* c
               then *work to be done* := **false fi;**
            up *full slots* ¢ *to enable the other department to get going* ¢
            end
       , ¢ *comma to separate the two statements.* ¢
            ¢ *the printing department* ¢
            while *printing to be done* **do**
            begin
            down *full slots;* ¢ *halts this department if there is nothing to print (as initially)* ¢
            exdex **modb** *nmb buffers* **plus** *1;*
            print (buffer [exdex]);
            printing to be done := *work to be done* ∨ *index≠exdex;*
            up *free slots* ¢ *if the other department was halted, it may now be resumed* ¢
            end
   end

For a more ambitious example of parallel-clauses see R 11.13. For a general discussion of the use of these semaphores see:

> E.W. Dijkstra, Cooperating Sequential Processes, contained in "Programming Languages", Ed. F. Genuys, Academic Press.
> and E.W. Dijkstra, Comm ACM 11 5 May 1968 p 341.

3.7.3. Case conformities

You are recommended to postpone reading this section if you have not yet studied 5.6.4.1. (conformity-relations).
[R 9.4.e,f,g]

> **case**
>   a soft **ref amode** tertiary
> ,
>   a soft **ref bmode** tertiary
> ,
>   a soft **ref cmode** tertiary
> :: (or ::=)
>   an unknown tertiary (usually of mode **union** (....))
> **in**
>   a unitary-clause
> ,
>   a 2nd unitary-clause
> ,
>   a 3rd unitary-clause
> **out**
>   an alternative serial-clause
> **esac**

If the **ref amode** tertiary conforms to (i.e. refers to the same mode as that of the current value of) the unknown tertiary, then the 1st unitary-clause is elaborated; if the **ref bmode** tertiary conforms, then the 2nd unitary-clause; and so on. The implied conformity-relations:

> **ref amode** tertiary :: copy of unknown tertiary
> **ref bmode** tertiary :: copy of unknown tertiary
> **ref cmode** tertiary :: copy of unknown tertiary

are all elaborated collaterally, so that if more than one of them matches it is not defined which one of them is taken (if none matches, there is of course the **out** alternative). The left hand sides are not elaborated at all (except for the chosen one where the "::=" alternative is used), and the unknown tertiary is elaborated only once (because a copy of it is used).

Here is an example of a case conformity yielding a **bool**:

(E10)   **union** *(***char, bool, int, real***)* *cbira;*
        if   **bool** *b*, **int** *i*, **real** *r;*
            case *b, i, r* ::= *cbira* **in** *b, i>0, r>0* **out false esac**
        then ¢ we get here if *cbira* was not a **char** and was otherwise
              true or *>0*, as the case may be ¢ **skip**
        fi

As in ordinary case-clauses (3.2.4.3), you may omit the **out** and substitute the usual alternatives for **case** etc:

(E11)   *(***char, bool, int, real** :: *cbira* | **go to** *lc, lb, li, lr)*

where *lc, lb, li* and *lr* are labels. Note the use of generators as the left hand sides of the implied conformity relations, as discussed more fully in 5.6.4.1.

Vertical readers, please turn to 5.7.

4. ROUTINES

4.1. Procedures and operators

In ALGOL 68, procedures arise out of the structure of the language in a very natural way. Thus routines are values, which therefore possess modes and denotations. They become attached to identifiers or operators by the elaboration of declarations, and they are called in the course of a variety of unitary-clauses.

Therefore, there is hardly a topic in this area which could not have been fitted in elsewhere in our orthogonal plan (which is, indeed, why the Report itself contains no chapter on the subject). However, the chapter which you are about to read is not entirely redundant, since we thought it proper in view of their central importance to gather all the information about routines, procedures and operators into one place.

The necessary concepts were introduced in 1.1.4, which indicated how to declare a procedure:

(E1) **proc** *reciprocal* = *(* **real** *a)* **real** : *1/a;*

and how to call it:

(E2) **real** *x;*
      x := reciprocal (3.14)

Also how to declare an operator:

(E3) **op** *oneover* = *(* **real** *a)* **real** : *1/a;*

and how to use it in a formula:

(E4) **real** *x;*
      x := **oneover** *3.14*

All these matters will be described at greater length in 4.2 in the case of procedures, and 4.3 in the case of operators. In particular, note how the right hand side of E1 is the same as that of E3. This is the part which defines precisely what the routine, which is being created in either case, is to do, and is known as a 'routine denotation' (4.2.2.2).

4.1.1. Standard prelude routines

However, a large proportion of the operators and procedures which you will call in the course of your programs will not have been declared by you in this way, because they will be already built in to your program by means of the 'standard prelude' (1.1). Amongst these you will find procedures for all the usual mathematical functions (sine, cosine, square root, etc. — the full list is given in 6.2.2), and operators for all the usual mathematical operations (+, −, ×, ÷, etc., and a lot of not-so-obvious ones — all listed in 6.1, 6.3, 6.5 and 6.7).

Although the procedures declared in the standard-prelude will be just that — when you call them, certain built-in routines will be entered — this may not be so for the operators. For example, the operator "+", used to add two **int**s together, is defined in the Report [R 10.2.3.i] by the following operation-declaration:

(E5)   **op** + = *(* **int** *a, b)* **int** : *a* − − *b;*

If you had used this in your own program, it would have compiled a routine to do *(a* − − *b)*, and called it in whenever such a "+" was encountered in a formula. This is not the intention for the standard-prelude operators. When this "+" appears in a formula, your compiler should produce, on the spot, the most efficient possible code to do the same job.

Therefore you need hardly be aware, when using these operators, of the strange way in which they were introduced into the language, and any such lack of awareness should be no bar to a full understanding of 5.1.3 where the use of operators in formulas is fully discussed.

Vertical readers, please turn to 5.1.

4.2. Procedure declarations

4.2.1. **proc** declarers

The concept of a "routine" was introduced in 1.1.4. Each routine is of some mode, and for each such mode we can write declarers. There are four classes of routine, categorised according to whether they require parameters or not, and whether they deliver a value or **void**.

(E1)   **proc**   ¢ no parameters, delivers **void** ¢
(E2)   **proc int**   ¢ no parameters, delivers **int** ¢
(E3)   **proc** *(* **real, int, ref char** *)*   ¢ 3 parameters, delivers **void** ¢
(E4)   **proc** *(* **real, int, ref char** *)* **bool**   ¢ 3 parameters, delivers **bool** ¢

This last one would be pronounced in public as:

"procedure-with-(a-)real-parameter-and-(an-)integral-parameter-and-(a-)reference-to-character-parameter-(delivering-a-)boolean"

To say that a routine delivers "**void**" is to say that it delivers no value at all. Some implementations (see Appendix 4) emphasise this point of view by allowing you to write, in place of E1 and E3:

> **proc void**
> and **proc (real, int, ref char) void**

This we shall not do in our examples, since we are adhering strictly to the Report. However, we shall, from time to time, slip in a ¢ **void** ¢ to make our meaning clear. This is just a comment (see 1.3.2), and is therefore quite in order.

Formal **proc** declarers and actual **proc** declarers look exactly the same [R 7.1.1.w]. (Note also that the declarers specifying the modes of the parameters and of the value delivered are virtual — the significance of this is explained in 2.5.2.1.)

The parameters and delivered value of a routine can be of any mode whatsoever, including another **proc** mode:

(E5)   **proc (real, proc (real, int)) proc (int) real**

A 'procedure' [R 6.0.1.f] is an external object which possesses (or upon elaboration yields) a routine:

(E6)   **proc** *proca;*

declares a **ref proc** *proca*, by means of the usual extension (2.2.2) of:

(E7)   **ref proc** *proca* = **loc proc;**

The value referred to by *proca* is at present undefined, since we have not yet provided a routine for it. However, if it had referred to some routine, then:

(E8)   **proc** *procb* := *proca;*

would have created *procb*, making it refer to the same routine (initially). Which all goes to show that routines may be assigned and otherwise handled just like values of any other mode.

4.2.2. Routines

What, then, is a routine? It is a piece of code somewhere within your program, compiled there as a result of some statements written by you (or maybe it was put there by the standard-prelude (6.2.2)). When a routine is assigned, as in E8 above, there is of course no question of moving pieces of code around inside the computer – it is a pointer to the piece of code that is handled during these operations, but the effect is just the same. Note that there are no operations operating on routines defined within the standard-prelude (with a little ingenuity, you might construct some of your own, but they would probably not be particularly useful).

There are, therefore, two questions that we have to answer:
1) How do we introduce routines into a program, and cause them to be yielded by procedures?
2) How do we "call" them – i.e. cause them to be obeyed?

Major discussion of the second question will be deferred until 5.2.1. The answer to the first falls into two parts, according to whether the routine has parameters or not. The latter case, being simpler, will be considered first.

4.2.2.1. Proceduring

	proc real *p;*
(E9)	*y := x := 3.14;*
(E10)	*p := x := 3.14*

The difference between E9 and E10 is an excellent illustration of what coercion is all about (1.1.6). In E9, we have the assignment *x := 3.14*, which is elaborated by assigning the value *3.14* to *x* (*x* gets changed). The value of *x := 3.14* as a whole is of mode **ref real** (see 1.1.3), but this can be dereferenced (5.1.0.3 or 1.1.6) to the mode **real**, so that it yields the value *3.14*. It is now perfectly in order to assign this to *y* (*y* gets changed), because *y* is of a suitable mode (**ref real**) to receive it.

The same is not true at all in the case of E10. *p* is of mode **ref proc real**, which means that only a **proc real** may be assigned to it. *3.14* is not a **proc real**, neither is *x*. Perhaps, however, *x := 3.14* might be, in which case the whole interpretation would be quite different. *x := 3.14* would not be elaborated at this stage (*x* would not get changed), but would instead become a routine (one which assigned *3.14* to *x* and then yielded *3.14* as its **real** result) and as such be assigned to *p* (*p* gets changed).

Indeed, this is what happens, and the process of taking *x := 3.14* and turning its mode into **proc real** (at the same time turning it into a routine instead of elaborating it on the spot) is a coercion known as "proceduring" [R 8.2.3], which may be used in any context which is at least firm (see 5.1.0 for a more detailed discussion of coercions and the contexts in which they may be used, and note there in particular that proceduring cannot follow deproceduring).

Now let us try to do the same thing for a **proc ¢ void ¢**:

>   **proc ¢ void ¢** *q;*
>   *q := x := 3.14*

Unfortunately, this does not work (to understand why, you will have to read 5.7.0.1 and then try to work this example through the coercion chart in 5.1.0.2). Indeed, you might like to spend some time trying to see just what objects can be procedured to **proc ¢ void ¢**. You will find that the only common ones are the void-cast-pack (5.1.4.2) and the jump (5.7.0.1). Therefore we must write:

(E11)   **proc** *q;*
        q := (¢ **void** *¢ : x := 3.14)*

just as we could have written:

(E10*) *p :⁻* **real** *: x :⁻ 3.14*

instead of E10, but that would have been a needless complication. The RHS of E10* is a **real** cast (1.2.2.5).

It is more usual to declare an identifier to possess a **proc** by means of an identity-declaration, since it is not all that common to assign routines to **ref procs** as was done in E10 and E11:

(E12)   **proc real** *pp = x := 3.14;*
        proc *qq = : x := 3.14;*

A special dispensation [R 9.2.d] allows us to unpack the void-cast when it stands as an actual-parameter (2.2.1).

It is possible to make the routine which is to be assigned or possessed dependant upon some condition:

(E13)   **proc real** *pq = (i<0 | x := 3.14 | y := 2.718);*

Here we have two routines available, made by procedering *x := 3.14* and *y := 2.718*. Which of the two becomes possessed by *pq* will depend on the value of *i* at the time E13 is encountered. Likewise:

(E14)   **proc** *qp = (i<0 | (: x := 3.14) | (: y := 2.718));*

Suppose, however, that the RHS of E13 were to be contained within a **real** cast:

(E15)   **proc real** *rpq =* **real**: *(i<0 | x := 3.14 | y := 2.718);*

Now the object which is to be procedured into a **proc real** is the whole of

real: *(i<0 | x := 3.14 | y := 2.718)*. There is only one routine, which tests *i* whenever it is called, assigns to *x* or to *y*, and yields *3.14* or *2.718* accordingly. A cast such as this is in fact the only way of making the whole of some CLOSED-clause (3.2.4) into a routine. You might be tempted to extend E15 into:

proc *rpq* = **real**: *(i<0 | x := 3.14 | y := 2.718);*

(cf. 4.2.2.2 E20). Indeed, your implementation would probably understand what you meant but, strictly speaking, the Report does not allow it, since the extension involved [R 9.2.e] applies to routine-denotations but not to casts.

If no value is to be delivered, a void-cast may be used:

(E16)   **proc** *rqp* = ¢ **void** ¢ : *(i<0 | x := 3.14 | y := 2.718);*

If you get the impression that casts, as used here, look suspiciously like cut down versions of the routine-denotations which you are about to encounter, then please be assured that the similarity is quite intentional.

A routine which has been created by proceduring is called by means of another coercion known as deproceduring. This is described fully in 5.2.1, but here is a brief example:

(E17)   **begin**
        real *x;*
        proc *pp* = ¢ **void** ¢ : *x := 3.14 ;*
            begin
            real *x := 0;*
            pp;   ¢ *pp* is called ¢
            print (x) ¢ prints 0.0 ¢
            end*;*
        print (x) ¢ prints 3.14 ¢
        end

When *pp* is called, the routine compiled from : *x := 3.14* is entered. Note, however, that the name *x* assigned to by this routine is (as we hope you would expect) the one declared in the outer range, and not the one declared just before the call [R 6.1.2.a] .

4.2.2.2. Routine denotations

A 'routine denotation' [R 5.4.1] is used to create a routine that has parameters. It may stand, inter alia, as the actual-parameter of an identity-declaration, or of a call (see E25 below), or as the RHS of an assignment. Here is a routine-denotation yielding a routine of mode **proc** *(* **real**, **real** *)* **real**:

(E18)   (real *a*, real *b*) real: *a+b*

Please note that *(real a, real b)* real is not a declarer such as proc *(real, real)* real is (declarers do not contain identifiers). The real *a* and the real *b* occurring in E18 are formal-parameters, such as you would expect to find on the LHS of an identity-declaration (2.2.1), and the two reals in these formal-parameters are therefore formal-declarers (but the third real in E18 is virtual (2.5.2.3)). In this example, the two formal-parameters were separated by a ",", but for special purposes (4.5.2) a ";" can be used.

Now we may use E18 in an identity-declaration, to declare a proc *(* real, real *)* real:

(E19)   proc *(* real, real *)* real *sum* = *(* real *a*, real *b* *)* real: *a+b;*

Rather a cumbersome way of adding two reals together, and rather a cumbersome way of declaring it, too. There are two extensions we can use to shorten it. Firstly, the reals in the two formal-parameters of the routine-denotation may be gathered together in the familiar (2.2.2) fashion (i.e. *(real a, b)*) [R 9.2.c]. Then, there still being considerable redundancy, all of the formal-declarer after the proc may be omitted [R 9.2.e], leaving:

(E20)   proc *sum* = *(*real *a, b)* real: *a+b;*

which really is about as short as you could expect. Likewise:

proc *refsum* ¢ of mode ref proc etc ¢ := *(*real *a, b)* real: *a+b*

However, see 4.2.2.1 for when this extension may not be used.

The part after the ":" in a routine-denotation can be any strong unit (Chapter 5) yielding the required mode. Most often it will be some form of CLOSED-clause (3.2.4), as in the following example in which we also illustrate a routine-denotation yielding void:

(E21)   proc *pqrs* = *(*ref real *a, b)* ¢ void ¢ : *(i<0 | a := 3.14 | b := 3.14);*

A routine-denotation is a confrontation *, and therefore a quaternary (5.1.0.1), and this determines where it may be used (thus if it was needed as the operand of a formula (5.1.3) it would need to be enclosed between "*(*" and "*)*"). Since all other denotations are bases (5.1.1) it might be argued that 'routine denotation' is not really a very good term for it.

---

* Actually, it is not as simple as this. According to the Report [R 5.4.1.b and R 9.2.d], a routine-denotation must also be packed should it occur in a row- or structure-display, or in a cast, or at the end of a serial-clause. Hopefully, your implementation will not be too insistent upon this point.

A routine created from a routine-denotation can be called by providing it with actual-parameters to match its formal ones. Within the context of E20 we could put:

(E22) $a := sum\ (x, y)$

x and y are the actual-parameters of this call, and are just such as you would expect to find on the RHS of an identity-declaration (2.2.1). In fact what happens next is as if the identity-declaration matching each formal-parameter with its actual counterpart had been constructed and elaborated [R 8.6.2.2], which in this case would have lead to the following:

> **begin**
> **real** $a = x$, **real** $b = y;$

after which the body of the routine is entered:

> $a+b$
> **end**

Observe how the **begin** and the **end** demarcate a new range, so that the formal-parameters a and b, which are now declared to possess **real** values for the duration of this call, may not be confused with any occurrences of a and b elsewhere.

In this example, the formal-parameters a and b were made to possess **real** values, and so it would have been illegal to try to assign to them from within the routine. In ALGOL 60, this would have been known as "call by value". If we do wish to alter the value referred to by a formal-parameter, then that parameter must be of a mode that refers to something, as in E21 which permits the following call:

(E23) $pqrs\ (x, y)$

which will assign 3.14 to either x or y, according to the value of i at the time. We term this "call by reference". In ALGOL 60, you would have had to use (or misuse) "call by name" for that one.

To get some other effects of the ALGOL 60 call by name, however, you must declare your procedure with **proc** mode parameters:

(E24)   **proc** $series$ = **(int** k, **proc (int)** **real** $term$**) real**:
              begin real $sum := 0;$
              for j **to** k **do** sum **plus** $term\ (j)$;
              sum
              end;

ROUTINES

This sums the terms of some series from *1* to *k*. When it is called, the actual-parameter provided for the term can be any unit that yields a **proc** *(int)* **real**, and very commonly this will be a routine-denotation:

(E25)   *x := series (100, (* **int** *i)* **real** *: 1/i)*

During a call of this routine, the procedure possessed by *term* (in this case the routine-denotation) is called once each time round the **for** loop. This is how, in ALGOL 68, we achieve the effect of Jensen's device. 0.8.4. E34 showed you how, if the formal-parameter had been a procedure without parameters, a suitable actual-parameter could have been provided using proceduring.

See 5.2.1 also for other examples and further discussion of calls.

4.2.2.3. Recursion

Suppose, now, that a routine happens to contain a call on itself (either directly, or via a chain of calls on other routines which eventually calls the same one again). Are there any problems? In some programming languages there may be, but not in this one. It all works out normally, just like you would expect. You will find several examples of such recursion in this book, notably in 8.7.1. Here is another one:

(E26)   **begin**
         proc *blocked = (* **int** *x, y)* **bool**: c *A description of a maze, centred*
                                              at (0, 0) with entrance at (0,100).
                                              Yields **true** *if the point (x, y) is*
                                              inaccessible (part of the walls). The
                                              maze is presumed to contain no
                                              cycles. c;
         int *x := 0, y := 100, d := 0;* ¢ *starting coordinates and direction* ¢
         proc bool *maze =* **bool** :
                  if   *blocked (x, y)* **then false**
                  elsf *x = 0 ∧ y = 0* **then true**
                  else **int** *presx := x, presy := y, presd := d, i := 0;*
         loop: i := i + 1;
                  x := presx + ((d := (presd + 2 + i) **mod** *4) + 1 | 0, −1, 0, +1);*
                  y := presy + (d + 1 | −1, 0, +1, 0);
                  if *maze* **then true else** *(i < 3 |* **go to** *loop);* **false fi**
                  fi;
         print (**if** *maze* **then** *"Maze is solved"* **else** *"No route to centre "* **fi** *)*
         end

Clearly, *maze* can call itself recursively to a considerable depth. Now *maze* contains declarations for the variables *presx*, *presy*, *presd* and *i*, which must be elaborated whenever it is called (two trivial cases apart). This means that four locations must be reserved on the stack (1.2.2.3). Next, *maze* calls itself recursively, and we meet these declarations again. Do we get the same four locations? Of course not! We reserve another four on the stack, and the first four become inaccessible [R 8.2.2.2, R 6.1.2.a] until such time as we return to the particular call of *maze* in which they were created. Then we will find that their values have not been touched since we left them.

So, by the time *maze* has called itself to a depth of 20, there are 20 instances of these four variables on the stack, and their values form a complete record of how we got from the entrance to where we are. So, if we replace the last line but one of *maze* by:

    if *maze* **then** *print ((presx, presy, newline));* **true else** *(i < 3 | . . .*

then we shall get printed a complete set of directions showing how to get out again.

4.2.3. Scopes of routines

The following example should be compared carefully with 3.2.2. E3:

(E27)   **begin proc** *pp;* **real** *y;*
        begin real *x;* **proc** *p =* ¢ **void** ¢ *: y := x;*
        x := 2.0;
        p;   ¢ this is all right. *2.0* is assigned to *y* ¢
        pp := p ¢ this one is going to cause trouble ¢
        end;
    print (y); ¢ no complaints ¢
    pp;   ¢ tries to assign *x* to *y*, but who is *x*? ¢
    print (y) ¢ now what? ¢
    end

In an assignment, the scope of the RHS must be at least as great as that of the LHS, and in the case of *pp := p* above, it was obviously the scope of the routine possessed by *p* (the one procedured from: *y := x*) that was too small.

In fact, the scope of a routine is the smallest range containing a declaration of an identifier or an indicant (2.3.1 or 4.3.2) which is used inside that routine [R 2.2.4.2.b] (i.e. the inner range in the above example because the routine contained an *x*).

In both this example, and in 3.2.2. E3, the trouble could have been caught by a check at compile time, but in the following example a run time check would be necessary, and we doubt whether most compilers will bother to put it in:

(E28)   **begin ref real** *xx*, **proc** *copy* = *(* **ref real** *a)* **ref real**: *a;*
        begin
        real *x* := *2.0;*
        xx := *copy (x)*
        end;
    print (xx)
    end

Vertical readers, please turn to 5.2.

4.3. Operation declarations

The operators used in formulas (5.1.3) are either symbols built in to the language for the purpose, or indicants (1.3.2) invented by the user. (Note that an indicant used in a mode-declaration (2.3.1) may not, in the same program, be used for a monadic-operator, although it may be used for a dyadic one [R 1.1.5.b]). (Note also that the built in symbols may all be used for either monadic- or dyadic-operators, except for the equals-symbol (=) and the times-symbol ($\times$ or $*$) which may not be monadic [R 4.2.1.f].)

In order to be used, an operator must possess a routine, and if it is to be used as a dyadic-operator it must have a priority too. Now a given symbol (or indicant) may in fact possess several routines at one and the same time (subject to a restriction that will be discussed below in 4.3.3), but it may only have one priority. Therefore, before a symbol can be used as a dyadic-operator, it must be given a priority (unless it has already acquired one in the standard-prelude [R 10.2.0]).

4.3.1. Priority declarations

There are 9 available priority levels for symbols to be used as dyadic-operators (for convenience, we classify monadic-operators as having priority 10 in Chapter 6, but this is purely our own convention). We associate a priority with a symbol (for the duration of some range) thus [R 7.3.1] :

(E1)   **priority** min = *9;*

Priority-declarations, being unitary-declarations, may be incorporated into collateral-declarations:

(E2)   **priority min** = 9, **priority max** = 9;

and, by extension [R 9.2.c], this may be made into:

(E3)   **priority min** = 9, **max** = 9;

4.3.2. Operation declarations

An operation-declaration looks rather like an identity-declaration:

(E4)   **op** *(***real**, **real***)* **real min** = *(***real** *a, b)* **real**: *(a* < *b | a | b)*;

The RHS of this one is a routine-denotation (4.2.2.2), but in general it is an actual-parameter (2.2.1) — so if you were trying to be very posh you might try to organise yourself some other unit which (after suitable coercion, of course) would yield a **proc** *(***real**, **real***)* **real**. Normally, however, a routine-denotation is as far as you will ever need to go, in which case you may then immediately extend [R 9.2.e] to:

(E5)   **op min** = *(***real** *a, b)* **real**: *(a* < *b | a | b)*;

The operator **min** now works for pairs of **reals**. However, we may wish it to work for other combinations:

(E6)   **op min** = *(***int** *a, b)* **int** : *(a* < *b | a | b)*,
(E7)   **min** = *(***int** *a,* **real** *b)* **real**: *(a* < *b | a | b)*,
(E8)   **min** = *(***real** *a,* **int** *b)* **real**: *a* **min** *(***real**: *b)*;

E8 was trying to be clever by using the version of **min** already declared in E5. It is an interesting example of the use of a cast (5.1.4.2) but not an efficient way of doing a job, as E6 was. Note the extension [R 9.2.c] whereby the **ops** have been gathered together.

Now **min** possesses four routines, but this is only the start of it. Now there are all the combinations of **long reals** and **long ints** (2.7.2), and no doubt sensible meanings could be found for **min** when operating upon **chars**, **strings** and all sorts of things.

min is a dyadic-operator (so far), and as such possesses routines which have two formal-parameters. Monadic-operators, of course, possess routines with one formal-parameter:

(E9)   op min = $([1 :]$ real $a1)$ real:
        begin real $x := $ max real ¢ 6.2.1 ¢;
        for i to upb $a1$ do $(a1$ $[i]$ $< x$ $| x := a1$ $[i]$ $);$
        x end;

Routines possessed by operators are entered when those operators are encountered in the elaboration of formulas [R 8.4.2]. For a full understanding of formulas, you should consult 5.1.3. It will suffice here to show how the operands of the formula are matched up to the formal-parameters of the possessed routine (having selected the right routine to match the modes of the operands, of course). This process is identical to that used when procedures with parameters are called (4.2.2.2). So, if we have the formula:

(E10) i min x

we first select the E7 version of **min**, and then construct the following collateral-declaration:

int $a = i$, real $b = x;$

In the context of this declaration, $(a < b$ $| a | b)$ is elaborated, and the **real** result becomes the value yielded by the formula.

4.3.3. Identification of operators

The identification of identifiers was described in 3.2.3, and the purpose and method of identification of operators are essentially similar. Consider the identification of **min** in:

(E11)   begin
         priority min = $9;$
         op min = $($real $a, b)$ real: $(a < b | a | b),$
         min = $($int $a, b)$ int: $(a < b | a | b);$
         $a := x$ min $y;$
             begin
             priority min = $8;$
             op min = $($ref real $a, b)$ ref real: $(a < b | a | b);$
             $xx := x$ min y
             end;
         $k := i$ min j
         end

The first task is to identify all the applied occurrences of **min** in the operation-declarations with their defining occurrences in the priority-declarations. The rule for this is exactly that given in 3.2.3 [R 4.2.2], and it results in the thick lines on the left of example E11.

Secondly, you must identify all the applied occurrences of **min** in the formulas with the same defining occurrences in the priority-declarations. This adds the dotted lines to the left hand side of E11.

Thirdly, you must now regard the occurrences of **min** in the operation-declarations as defining occurrences, and try to identify the applied occurrences in the formulas with them. The rule here is again the same except that you must only accept, in your search, a defining occurrence the modes of whose formal-parameters can be firmly coerced from the modes of the operands of the formula [R 4.3.2]. This results in the lines on the right of E11.

Fourthly, you must check that the two routes you now have from the **min** in each formula to some **min** in a priority-declaration (one route going indirectly via an operation-declaration) do in fact lead to the same priority-declaration (if not, then you have not written a proper program [R 4.4.1.c]).

However, let us now try to declare another version of **min**:

(E12)   op min = *(*ref real *a, b)* ref real : *(a < b | a | b)*;

The purpose of this one is to determine which of two names (of mode **ref real**) refers to the smaller value. Let us use it in a formula:

(E13)   *x* min *y*

But Oh dear! Doesn't this also identify the version of **min** declared in E5 (in a formula, the operands are firm, and so *x* and *y* can be dereferenced in this example (5.1.0))?

Clearly, there must be a context condition (1.2.1) which forbids E13 from occurring in the context of both E5 and E12. The trouble is liable to arise whenever the modes in the formal-parameters of two operators are related (see 2.6.1) [R 4.4.2.c]. However, this is not the whole story. Let us attempt yet another version of **min**:

(E14)   op min = *([1 :]* ref real *a1)* real: XXXXX;

and let us try to call it:

(E15)   min *(x, y)*

(x, y) might be a row-display of mode [ ] **ref real** to suit E14, but because it occurs in a firm context, *x* and *y* can be dereferenced (see 5.2.0.1 for the coercion of CLOSED-clauses), so that its mode becomes [ ] **real** to suit E9, even though the modes involved ([ ] **ref real** and [ ] **real**) are not related.

In fact, it is very difficult to predict whether a given pair of operators is going to cause trouble. The proof of the pudding must be in the eating – if there exists a formula, and two operation-declarations which it could identify, then the program is improper and must be rejected.

Vertical readers, please turn to 6.3.

4.5. Routines and multiples

4.5.1. Procedures with row-of parameters

Consider routines of mode **proc** *(* [ ] **real***)*. Depending upon the application, such a routine might be intended to accept a [ ] **real** with any bounds whatsoever, or it might be restricted to a particular pair of bounds, peculiar to the application, or, and this will probably be the commonest case, its lower bound will be restricted to *1*, its upper bound being unlimited:

(E1) **proc** *a1* = *(* [ ] **real** *b1)*: XXXXX;
(E2) **proc** *a2* = *(* [*0 : 99*] **real** *b1)*: XXXXX;
(E3) **proc** *a3* = *(* [*1 :*] **real** *b1)*: XXXXX;

In each case, a valid formal-declarer (2.5.2.1) has been provided, and when such a routine is called and the identity-declaration matching each formal-parameter to its actual counterpart has been "constructed" (4.2.2.2), then the checks described in 2.5.2.1 can be applied. In the case of *a3*, for example, if we provide as actual-parameter a row-display with bounds [*1*: *4*] (3.5.1):

(E4)   *a3 ((1.1, 2.2, 3.3, 4.4))*

then the elaboration of the call may proceed because the lower-bound of the formal-parameter (which is elaborated at this time, and of course yields *1*) matches the lower-bound of the row-display, and because the upper-bound does not need checking, because it is empty.

It should be remembered, however, that if a [ ] **real** is called by value in this way, the compiler is obliged to take a copy of the value of the actual-parameter – in general a time consuming operation – just in case the body of the routine should contrive in some way to alter the original:

(E5)   [*0 : 99*] **real** *x1*;
       proc *a2* = *(* [*0 : 99*] **real** *b1)*: **for** *i* **to** *99* **do** *x1*[*i*] := *b1*[*i−1*];
       a2 (x1)

The intention and effect of this example is not to make every element of *x1* a copy of $x1[0]$, which is what would have happened if $b1$ had not possessed a copy of the value of $x1$ at the start of the call.

However, cases such as this are rare. Usually, you will know perfectly well that this is not going to happen, and so you will avoid the time wasted by the copying operation by declaring your formal-parameter as a **ref** [ ] **real**. Then, at call, it is only a name which has to be passed to the routine, which uses it to access the original multiple value that it refers to. However, if a routine is provided with a name, it is entitled to be told whether the multiple value referred to may be assumed to be fixed or **flexible**, or whether it must be prepared to cope with **either**:

(E6)   **proc** $a4$ = (**ref** [either : either] **real** $b1$): XXXXX;
                 proc $a5$ = (**ref** [0 : 99] **real** $b1$): XXXXX;
                 proc $a6$ = (**ref** [1 : **flex**] **real** $b1$): XXXXX;

The full range of possibilities was listed in 2.5.2.1.

Now suppose that we call $a6$:

(E7)   [1 : 0 **flex**] **real** *array* := (1.1, 2.2, 3.3, 4.4);
                ¢ so that *array* refers to a value with descriptor [1:4 **flex**] ¢
                $a6$ (*array*)

The identity-declaration that is effectively elaborated at the time of call is:

                ref [1 : **flex**] **real** $b1$ = *array*;

and, if you follow this case through the rules given in 2.5.2.1, you will find that it:

                Checks that the lower-bound on each side is *1*;
                Checks that the lower-state on each side is fixed;
                Checks that the upper-state on each side is flexible.

Note that the checking of states only arises when the mode specified by the formal-declarer is **ref** [ ] **amode** (e.g. it did not arise in E4).

4.5.2. Order of elaboration of actual parameters

If a routine has several formal-parameters:

(E8)   **proc** $a7$ = ([1:*m*] **real** $b1$, [1:*n*] **int** $c1$): XXXXX;
                $a7$ (*x1*, *i1*)

then a collateral-declaration is effectively constructed:

[1:m] real b1 = x1, [1:n] int c1 = i1;

which means in particular that m and n are elaborated collaterally.

However, it is permissable to have ";"s instead of ","s between the formal-parameters of a routine-denotation [R 5.4.1.c] , and this facility is particularly useful if you want to write a routine which will only accept two multiples of the same size. In the interests of efficiency we shall call them by their names:

(E9)   proc a8 = (ref [1 :] real b1;
                      ref [1 : upb b1] real b2): XXXXX;
            a8 (x1, y1)

(upb is an operator yielding the upper-bound of its operand (5.5.3)). At call time, this effectively creates two separate identity-declarations separated by a ";":

    ref [1 :] real b1 = x1 ;
    ref [1 : upb b1] real b2 = y1;

These are no longer elaborated collaterally, so that by the time the **upb** is encountered, all the information about b1 is fully available. Thus it will check that the upper bound of y1 is the same as that of b1, and b1 has just been made to refer to the same value (including bounds) as x1. For an application of this device, see 8.5.2.

By a strange quirk of the language [R 7.4.2] , there would have been no check carried out if the formal-declarer preceding b2 had been:

    ref [1: upb b1 flex] real

this check only being available if the formal-declarer specifies fixed or either. This is unfortunate, but would have led to some even stranger quirks when indicants in mode-declarations were used in formal-parameters, had it been otherwise.

See 5.7.3 for a discussion of the effects of ";"s in routine-denotations appearing in operation-declarations.

4.5.3. Procedures delivering row-of values

In contrast to all the checks discussed above for row-of formal-parameters, the value delivered by a routine is quite unfettered. Its mode is always specified by a virtual-declarer (2.5.2.3), and when delivered will contain some states and bounds. If the object receiving this value is particular about what states and bounds it receives (if it is a formal-parameter, for example), then it will have to institute a run time check for the purpose.

Vertical readers, please turn to 5.5.

5. UNITARY CLAUSES

5.1. Simple units

Unitary-clauses (often abbreviated to 'units') are the entities in the language which actually get things done. The simplest example of a unit is the simple type of assignation (e.g. $x := y + 2.4$) which we have used many times already. However, examples much more complex than this can be constructed in accordance with a set of rules which it is the purpose of this chapter to describe. (The corresponding definitions are mostly to be found in R 8.)

5.1.0. Coercion

5.1.0.1. Coercends

The basic building blocks out of which units are made are known as 'coercends', of which there are 4 types

confrontations	(e.g. $x := y + re$ of z)
formulas	(e.g. $y + re$ of z)
cohesions	(e.g. re of z)
and bases	(e.g. x, y, z).

They are arranged in a hierarchy, as follows:

```
confrontations  ⎫
formulas        ⎪ ⎫
cohesions       ⎬primaries ⎫ ⎫
bases           ⎪ ⎬secondaries ⎬tertiaries ⎬quaternaries
CLOSED-clauses  ⎭ ⎭           ⎭            ⎭(or units)
```

A unitary-clause can be any quaternary. Right at the bottom are CLOSED-clauses (as *(a+b)* in $x := y \times (a+b)$) which are themselves made up of further unitary-clauses (as described in 3.2.4), so that the definition of the whole setup is recursive.

Now the elaboration of a unit (i.e. of a coercend or of a CLOSED-clause) has two effects.

Firstly, it must yield a value, or it may yield **void** (e.g. the value of the formula *2+3* is *5*). If it yields **void** then it is a statement. If it yields a value (i.e. it is an expression) then this value will be of some mode (uniquely determinable at compile time). Secondly, some other actions (independent of what is yielded) may take place (e.g. in $x := 2.4$, the value 2.4 is assigned to x).

5.1.0.2. Coercion

Now the a priori mode of a coercend may have to be coerced (see 1.1.6) into the mode that is required by the "context" in which that coercend appears [R 8.2]. Thus, the a priori mode of the base 2 is **int**. If 2 occurs in the context $x := 2$, then the expected mode (after the $x :=$) is **real**. When this assignation is elaborated, then, the integral value 2 must be coerced into the real value 2.0 before the assignation can proceed. Fortunately this particular coercion (which is known as "widening") is permitted in this particular context and this assignation is therefore legitimate. The question as to whether any one of the 8 permissible coercions may be applied in a particular case depends upon the context. For this purpose, contexts are divided into 5 classes:

>strong
>firm
>weak
>soft
>and empty.

All 8 coercions may be applied in strong positions, and none at all in empty ones. During the rest of this chapter, as we describe each form of unit, we shall indicate the strength of the contexts occurring in it. Here, in the meantime, is a summary:

>strong contexts The RHS of assignations (5.1.4.1)
> The RHS of casts (5.1.4.2)
> Actual-parameters, in calls (5.2.1) and in
>   identity-declarations (2.2.1)
> Trimscripts (must yield **int**) (5.5.1.3)
> Conditions (must yield **bool**) (3.2.4.2)
> Cases (must yield **int**) (3.2.4.3)
> Statements (must yield **void**) (5.7.0.1)
> All constituents but one of a balanced clause (5.2.0.1)
> One side of an identity-relation (5.7.4) ← — — — — — —
>
>firm contexts Operands of formulas (5.1.3)
> In effect, the actual-parameters of transput
>   calls (7.1.1)
> Primaries of calls (e.g. *sin* in *sin (x)*) (5.2.1)

weak contexts	Primaries of slices (e.g. *x* in *x*[*i*]) (5.5.1.3)
	Secondaries of selections (e.g. *z* in *re* **of** *z*) (5.4.2)
soft contexts	The LHS of assignations (5.1.4.1)
	The LHS of conformity-relations (5.6.4.1)
	The known tertiaries of a case conformity (3.7.3)
	→The other side of an identity-relation (5.7.4)
empty contexts	The RHS of conformity-relations (5.6.4.1)
	The unknown tertiary of a case conformity (3.7.3)

A complete chart of all the coercions is given below. The way to use this chart is as follows. Consider first the mode (a priori) of the available coercend and secondly the mode (a posteriori) required by the context. Then you must find a route following the arrows on the chart that will, through a sequence of intermediate modes, take you from the first to the second. If the coercion is possible, then there will be such a route (if there are several routes, they will always be found to be equivalent).

Suppose, for example, that in a strong context you have (a priori) a coercend of mode **proc ref bool** and what you really need (a posteriori) is a value of mode **proc [ ] union** *(real,* **proc union** *(int,* **bool***))*. Then there is indeed a route between them, but the simplest way of describing it to you will be to introduce a fictitious operator to represent each coercion on the way, as suggested in 1.1.6 (of course these operators are not really part of ALGOL 68). Thus the required value is obtained by the following operations on the coercend:

PROCEDURE *(* **ROW** *(* **UNITE** *(* **PROCEDURE** *(* **UNITE**
  ı (**DEREFERENCE** *(* **DEPROCEDURE** *(*coercend*)))))))*

and you will encounter these operations (from the innermost to the outermost) as you follow the route. Doubtless you will be relieved to hear that coercions do not invariably get so complex.

The change of mode brought about by each of these fictitious operators is given in the chart. Their effect upon the elaboration of the program will be found at appropriate points in this introduction, as follows:

hipping	5.7.0.1
voiding	5.7.0.1
rowing	5.5.0
widening	5.1.0.4, 5.4.0, 5.7.0.2
uniting	5.6.0
proceduring	4.2.2.1, 5.2.0.2
dereferencing	5.1.0.3, 5.4.2
deproceduring	4.2.2.1, 5.2.0.3, 5.2.1

COERCION CHART

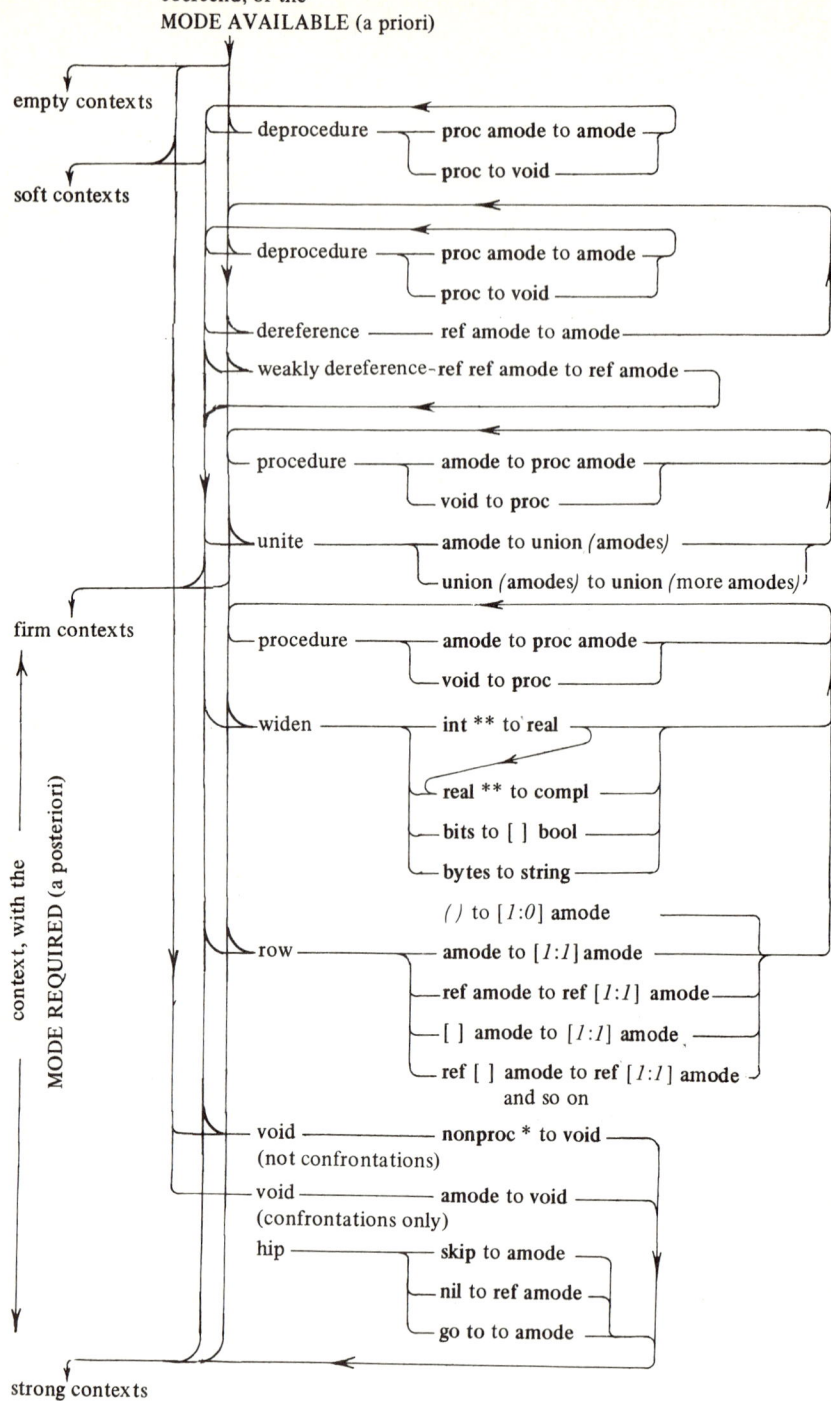

* **nonproc** is all modes except **proc** moid, **refs proc** moid or **[,s] proc** moid where **moid** stands for **amode** or **void**.
** The corresponding **longs** versions can also be widened.

If you cannot find a suitable route through the maze simply because your context is not strong enough, then all is not lost. A device known as a 'cast' has been provided wherein you first state the mode you would like to have (a posteriori), and then strongly coerce yourself into it regardless. Casts are described in 5.1.4.2 below. They are particularly useful for dereferencing in soft contexts and for widening in firm ones.

5.1.0.3. Dereferencing

We have already explained in 1.1.2.1 how a declaration such as **real** x; causes a location in the memory to be reserved (or "generated") for a **real** value, and the identifier x is made to possess the name which refers to that value. Thus, the value yielded by x is a name of a priori mode **ref real**.

Now, very frequently, what we want is the **real** value stored in the location referred to (as x in the assignation $y := x$) and what we have got is its name. We must therefore have resort to the coercion known as "dereferencing".

Dereferencing [R 8.2.1] is permitted in any context that is strong, firm, or weak (which is almost everywhere). (A slight restriction in the case of weak positions will be discussed in 5.4.2). The effect is to remove one **ref** from the a priori mode, and to yield the value of the thing that was named. If this value is in turn another name, then further dereferencing may be required.

Thus if the **ref real** identifier x stands as a base in a context that is strong, firm or weak, and if the expected mode is **real**, then the value yielded is the **real** value that x refers to.

5.1.0.4. Widening

Consider:

(E1) $x := i$

Widening [R 8.2.5] is used to turn an **int** value into a **real** value (also a **real** value into a **compl** value (see 5.4.0) and some further cases in 5.7.0.2). In this example, therefore, the **ref int** i is first dereferenced to yield an **int** value, which is then widened to yield the corresponding **real** value, which can then be assigned to the name x.

We shall now consider the simpler forms of coercend, starting with the most basic ones:

5.1.1. Bases

We shall consider three forms of base here — denotations, identifiers, and **skip**.

5.1.1.1. Denotations

Denotations are those entities which, in earlier languages, would have been known as "literals" or "constants". The following examples show some legitimate denotations, together with the a priori modes of the values that they yield [R 5.1].

Yielding **int** $\quad$ *2 ; 1024 ; 123 ; 0123*
Yielding **real** $\quad$ *12.3 ; 1.23$_{10}$1 ; .123$_{10}$+1 ; 0.123e+1 ; 1230e−1*
$\qquad\qquad\qquad$ *0.00123 ; .00123 ; 123.0* ; but not *123*.
Yielding **bool** $\quad$ **true** ; **false**
Yielding **char** $\quad$ *"a" ;"B" ;"1" ;"," ; "˷"* for a space symbol;
$\qquad\qquad\qquad$ *" "" "* for a (single) quote symbol

From a study of these examples, you should be able to construct any other denotation that you might require.

For **format** denotations see Section 7.6.1, for **string** denotations see 5.5.1.1 and for **bits** and **long** denotations see 5.7.1.

5.1.1.2. Identifiers

An identifier standing as a base constitutes an applied occurrence (1.1.5) of that identifier. Somewhere, that same identifier will have been declared (at its defining occurrence). These two occurrences must be correlated since the a priori mode of the value yielded when it stands as a base is the same as the mode with which it was declared. The exact method of correlation is considered in 3.2.3.

5.1.1.3. skip

skip is a special form of base (see also 5.7.0). As a statement, it is a dummy. In other strong contexts, it yields an undefined value of the mode demanded.

5.1.2. Cohesions

Discussion of cohesions will be postponed until Section 5.4.2.

5.1.3. Formulas

(The reason why we sometimes prefer to talk of formulas rather than formulae is to be found in the Report at 1.1.6.c, but we would not recommend that you should read that just yet.)

Ch.5.1.3   UNITARY CLAUSES   211

The following are examples of 'formulas':

(E2) $x - 2$; $x \Diamond y \notin$ if a meaning for $\Diamond$ has been declared $\notin$;
          $x \times a + b$; $x \times (a + b)$; -2

It will be seen that the essential feature of formulas is that they contain operators which operate upon operands [R 8.4].

If a formula contains more than one operator, then there is an implied bracketing which ensures that each dyadic-operator has two clearly defined operands, and each monadic has one. In order to assist with the implied bracketing, each dyadic-operator has an associated priority in the range of *1* through *9*, all monadic-operators effectively having priority 10. For example, "↑" has priority *8*, "×" and "/" have *7*, and "+" and "−" have *6*. The rule is that the operators with the highest priority are always considered first. Thus:

(E3) $x \times a + b$ means $(x \times a) + b$
(E4) $-a + b$ means $(-a) + b$ (because the "−" here is monadic)
(E5) $+4 - 2 \uparrow 2$ means $(+4) - (2 \uparrow 2)$ (and yields *0*)
(E6) $-2 \uparrow 2 + 4$ means $((-2) \uparrow 2) + 4$ (and yields *8*)
(E7) $4 + -2 \uparrow 2$ means $4 + ((-2) \uparrow 2)$ (and yields *8*) .

We agree that E5 and E6 are confusing, but it was thought that to have some dyadic-operators of priority higher than the monadics would have been even more so. The operator "↑", as in $a \uparrow b$, should not be thought of as equivalent to the usual mathematical notation for "to the power" as in a^b, which is itself a notation for a function such as $pw\,(a, b)$.

Where several operators of the same priority occur together, an additional rule is needed. Thus for dyadic-operators:

(E8) $i - j + k - m + n$

means

(E9) $(((i - j) + k) - m) + n$

Likewise for monadic-operators:

(E10)   + abs entier $- x$

means

(E11) $+(abs\,(entier\,(-x)))$

The priority and meaning of each operator are either built into the standard-prelude (6) or library-prelude (1.1) or are defined by the user (1.3.3.2 and 4.3).

The mode(s) of the operand(s) in a formula must match the mode(s) for which its operator has been defined. For example, the dyadic-operator "+" is defined (6.1.2) to do a variety of things, amongst which is a definition which states that if its first operand is **real** and its second operand is **real**, then it yields a **real** value which is to be the sum of its two operands (within the accuracy permitted by the implementation). A separate definition states that if its first operand is **int** and its second is **int**, then it yields an **int** value, and there are ten other similar definitions, not to mention three more for its monadic counterpart (6.1.1).

An operand can be any tertiary, provided it is of the required mode. This means that it can be another formula (as in the implied bracketing examples above), a cohesion, a base, or a CLOSED-clause, but it cannot be a confrontation — thus if you wanted to operate upon a confrontation, you would have to make it into a closed-clause thus:

(E12) $x + (b := a \times y)$

The tertiary which constitutes an operand is in fact firm, and the permitted coercions therefore include dereferencing, but not widening. Thus in:

(E13) $x + y$

the names x and y are first dereferenced to yield two **real** values, which are then added to yield the **real** value of the formula.

Consider also:

(E14) $x := i + j$

i and j cannot be widened because of the firm context, but the version of "+" to add two **ints** can be used. Then the value of the whole formula $i+j$, being of mode **int**, can be widened to **real**.

(E15) $x := i + y$

Here again, i cannot be widened in order to be added to y. The formula $i+y$ is only valid by virtue of the fact that the operator "+" is also defined (6.1.2) for the case of an **int** plus a **real** yielding a **real**.

5.1.4. Confrontations

5.1.4.1. Assignations

An 'assignation' [R 8.3.1] is the commonest form of confrontation. It consists of two parts — a left hand side (its 'destination') and a right hand side

Ch.5.1.4.1 UNITARY CLAUSES 213

(its 'source'). Consider the following example:

(E16) $x := y + 3.14$

The LHS (x in this example) is subject to the following restrictions:
   a) It must yield a name (i.e. its mode must be **ref amode**; in the example above x was **ref real**).
   b) It must be a tertiary (in the example x was a base; a formula is also possible but in fact few operators yield names (but see 6.3))
   c) Its context is soft, which means in particular that no dereferencing is allowed (unless you use a cast).

Application of these rules completely determines the mode of the value referred to by the name yielded.

The RHS ($y + 3.14$ in the example) therefore has considerable freedom, the rules being the following:
   a) It must yield a value whose mode is the same as that of the value referred to by the left hand side (in the example a **real** value is yielded, which is in agreement with the **ref real** mode of the left hand side).
   b) It can be any quaternary, which means it can be any coercend or any CLOSED-clause, provided a suitable mode is yielded (in the example it was a formula).
   c) Its context is strong, which means that any known coercion can be applied in order to obtain the required mode (in particular, both widening and dereferencing can be used).
   d) It has a scope restriction, but this is described in 3.2.2.
   Consider:

(E17) $x := y$

Both x and y are, a priori, names (of mode **ref real**). y must be dereferenced to yield a **real** value. The value formerly referred to by x is then superseded by this **real** value.

$$x := a + b$$

In this case the RHS is the formula $a + b$, which already yields a **real** value. No dereferencing is therefore needed (note, however, that a and b were in fact dereferenced during the elaboration of the formula itself).

Since any quaternary can stand for the RHS of an assignation, it follows in particular that another assignation can so stand. It is therefore necessary to specify what value (and of what mode) is to be yielded. In fact, the value yielded by an assignation is the value yielded by its LHS, which is always of mode **ref amode**. Consider the following:

(E18) $a := b := x := 2.4$

Let us first insert the implied bracketing (which, as you will observe, is not that of a dyadic-operator (see 5.1.3. E9)):

(E19) $a := (b := (x := 2.4))$

First of all, the **real** value *2.4* is assigned to *x*. The value of $x := 2.4$ as a whole is the name *x* which, being of mode **ref real**, must be dereferenced before the value to which it refers (which is now *2.4*, of course) can be assigned to *b*. The value of this assignment is the name *b*, the value referred to by which (*2.4* again) can now be assigned to *a*. Thus, everybody lands up by referring to his private instance of *2.4*. The formula $x + (b := a \times y)$ given in example E12 causes the product $a \times y$ to be assigned to *b*. *x* and the new value now referred to by *b* are then added together.

5.1.4.2. Casts

Suppose the operator ◊ had been defined for pairs of **real**s, but not for **int**s, and suppose you wanted the formula:

(E20) $x \diamond i$

which would not then be allowed. *i* cannot be widened because its context is only firm. If only it were strong. Let us therefore make a mould the shape of a **real**, and melt up our **int**, and cast it into the required shape:

(E21) $x \diamond (\textbf{real}: i)$

This is all right. **real**: *i* is a 'cast' [R 8.3.4]. The virtual-declarer **real** before the colon specifies that it shall yield a **real**, which suits the ◊ operator. Immediately after the colon the context is strong, and a unit is expected. Thus the **int** *i* may be widened to **real** and everyone is happy.

A cast is actually a confrontation, which makes it a quaternary. This is why it had to be enclosed in parentheses ("packed") in E21 (the operand of a formula being only a tertiary). In fact, casts are nearly always so packed because most of the places where quaternaries might be used (without packing) are already strong anyway.

Other examples of the use of casts will be given in 5.2.4. Ingenious users will find many other applications. For example, in transput (see 7.1), given $i = 1234$:

(E22)   *print(i);*   ¢ will print $+1234$ ¢
           print(**real**: *i)* ¢ will print $+1.234_{10}+3$ ¢

Ch.5.2   UNITARY CLAUSES   215

A further important application of casts is to specify the routine that is to be possessed or referred to by a procedure that has no parameters. In this respect, it does instead of a routine-denotation, as described in 4.2.2.1. The coercion "proceduring" which is also involved in this process is also described there. For the benefit of procedures that do not yield a value, it is possible to have a 'void cast'. This may occur as the actual-parameter of an identity-declaration (4.2.2.1) or of a call (4.2.2.2). Anywhere else where it may occur it must be packed, to avoid certain ambiguities, and it is then called a 'void cast pack' [R 8.6.0.1] and is a base rather than a confrontation:

(E23)   **proc** $p := ($: **begin** $i := i + 1; j := j + 1$ **end** $)$

shows a legitimate use of such a void-cast-pack. Observe that, without the packing, this would have been an identity-relation (see 5.7.4). To emphasize that this is a cast, which just happens to yield **void** (i.e. no value at all), you might prefer to insert a comment (1.3.2) into this:

proc $p := ($ ¢ **void** ¢ : **begin** $i := i + 1; j := j + 1$ **end** $)$

Indeed, some implementations (see Appendix 4) will permit an explicit "**void**" here, in which case the packing is no longer necessary.

Vertical readers, please turn to 6.1.

5.2. Balance and call

In this section we consider balancing, procedure calls, and also some further examples of coercends involving names.

5.2.0. Coercion

5.2.0.1. CLOSED clauses and balancing

Any form of CLOSED-clause (3.2.4) may stand as a primary. Often, the effect is straightforward:

(E1) $y := x \times (a+b)$

However, let us consider again the example E9 from 3.2.4.1:

(E2)   **begin**
         print (4 × *(* **real** *w := 0,* **int** *i := 1;* **real** *z = sqrt (small real/2);*
         loop: w := w + 2/(i × *(i + 2)); i := i + 4;*
         if *1/i > z* **then** *loop* **fi**;
         w))
         end

In this example, the value of the serial-clause within the parentheses is, a priori, the name *w* (of mode **ref real**) which will have vanished by the time we are outside the clause. Fortunately it is also clear that, if the value of this serial-clause is a name, it ought to have been dereferenced (because the operator "×" is expecting a **real**). However, the rules provide that a CLOSED-clause cannot be dereferenced (it is not a coercend). Instead, the required mode and the strength of the context are passed on to the unit which is to be yielded, which in this case is the base *w*. Therefore, it is *w* that gets dereferenced, right at the last moment before it disappears, and the resultant **real** value is passed on. The following piece of syntax (which is not the complete syntax for a serial-clause) may make this clearer to those who have some familiarity with the Report [R 6.1.1].

> SORTETY: strong; firm; weak; soft; EMPTY.
> SORTETY serial MODE clause:
>   declaration prelude sequence option, statement
>   interlude option, SORTETY unitary MODE clause.

The CLOSED-clause might well be a conditional-clause:

(E3)   *x := (i<0 | −i | i)*

or it might be a case-clause:

(E4)   *x := (i | j, k, m, n)*

In these cases as well, any coercion that might appear to be needed on the CLOSED-clause as a whole is instead performed on the unit(s) inside, as the context may permit. Indeed, different coercions may be applied to different internal units:

(E5)   *x :=* **case** *i* **in** *j, k, x, y* **esac**

The first two alternatives in E5 would have to be widened − the last two are already **real**. Widening is possible because the case-clause occurs in a strong context. However, even if the context had been firm, widening would have been permitted provided that at least one of the alternatives had been **real**, e.g.:

(E6) $a := x \times (i < 0 \mid j \mid y)$

The fact that y is **real** shows that the version of the operator "×" requiring a **real** is intended, and therefore the context of j can be promoted to strong. The same holds for

(E7) $a := x \times (i < 0 \mid y \mid j)$

This principle is known as "balancing". However:

(E8) $a := x \times (i < 0 \mid j \mid k)$

involves the multiplication of a **real** with an **int**, and is not balanced.

Balancing is permitted between:
a) The completion points of a serial-clause [R 6.1.1] (i.e. the **exits** and the final unit (3.1.4)), e.g.

(E9) $a := b + ($**real** $x, y, z; z := 1 - 3 \times sqrt(small\ real); x := i;$
         if $x \leq 0$ **then go to** *libl* **fi**;
   lobl: $y := i/x \uparrow 2; x := (2 \times x + y)/3;$
         if $y/x < z$ **then go to** *lobl* **fi**;
         if $x \geq 10.0$ **then go to** *libl* **fi**;
         x **exit**
   libl: *print* $("out\_of\_range");$
         $10)$

Please compare that carefully with 3.1.4. E7.
b) The elements of a row-display (3.5.1. E4) [R 6.2.1]. Remember, however, that row-displays cannot occur in weak or soft contexts (3.5.1).
c) The alternatives of a conditional-clause [R 6.4.1], following **then, else** or **elsf** (3.2.4.2 and examples E6 and E7 above).
d) The alternatives of a case-clause, including the **out** option (3.2.4.3 and 3.7.3), e.g.:

(E10) $a := y \times (i \mid j, k, x, y)$

e) The LHS and RHS of an identity-relation (5.7.4). Experienced readers might like to consider the rather delicate example 5.7.4. E33.

5.2.0.2. Proceduring.

Proceduring is a method of creating routines not having parameters, and has already been discussed in 4.2.2.1.

5.2.0.3. Deproceduring

Deproceduring is a method of calling routines not having parameters, and has already been introduced in 4.2.2.1. We think it best, however, to consider it alongside calls of routines which do have parameters, which brings us to:

5.2.1. Bases – procedure calls

It will have been seen (1.2.3.1 and 4.2) that procedures are declared in much the same way as other objects, and that they possess values (i.e. their routines). Thus **proc**, **proc real**, **ref proc** *(* **int**, **real** *)* are perfectly valid modes. The consequence of which is that if *random* (which is declared to be of mode **proc real** (see 6.2.2)) appears as a coercend, it is not immediately apparent whether its value (i.e. its routine, which is of mode **proc real**) is to be yielded, or whether the intention is to elaborate the routine and to yield its **real** result (although the latter may well be intended 99% of the time, the former facility is needed whenever a procedure is to be assigned, or operated upon in a formula, or yielded by another procedure – all of these things being quite allowable).

The distinction between these two interpretations can only be made by context. There are two cases:
a) Calls [R 8.6.2]

(E11)   **proc** *(* **proc** *)* *p;* **proc** *(* **proc** *)* *go to* = *(* **proc** *x)*: *x;*
         l: go to (1); ¢ the actual-parameter *l* being short for **go to** *l*,
         which can be procedured into a routine (5.7.0.1) ¢
(E12)   *p := go to*

go to has been declared to be a procedure requiring a parameter. Therefore, in E11 where an actual-parameter is indeed present, the intention is clearly that the procedure should be called (and we have a loop stop). If there are no parameters, as in E12, then its body must be yielded. Thus the problem does not arise.
b) Deproceduring [R 8.2.2]

         proc *q;* **proc** *go to l* = *¢* **void** *¢* : **go to** *l;*
(E13)   *l: go to l;*
(E14)   *q := go to l*

go to l does not require parameters. Therefore, we must see which mode is required by the context. In E13, **void** is required, which is what the routine possessed by *go to l* yields. Therefore we must employ the coercion known as "deproceduring".

The effect of deproceduring is always to convert the mode of a coercend of **proc amode** into **amode** (or **proc** into **void**), at the same time calling the value (i.e. the routine) that the coercend yields.

In E14, on the other hand, the mode required is **proc** and so the routine obtained by proceduring (as in 5.7.0.1) : **go to** *l*, which is of this mode, is • assigned without any coercion.

Deproceduring can be used in any soft context, which means almost anywhere – including the LHS of an assignation. There is a further rule [R 8.2.8.1.b] which states that, when in doubt, the procedure should be called (this resolves one or two ambiguities).

In elaborating a call of either sort, it is first necessary to establish what is to be called. In case (a) this is specified by a firm primary yielding the required routine, and the primary is followed by the actual-parameters. The interpretation of these has already been described in 4.2.2.2. Usually, the primary will be a base, as *ncos* (see Appendix 2) in:

(E15) $x := ncos\,(i)$

However, it could be a CLOSED- (e.g. conditional-(3.2.4.2)) clause, as in:

(E16) $x := (p \mid ncos \mid nsin)\,(i)$

In case (b), where deproceduring is to be used, the required routine must be yielded by a suitable base, cohesion, or formula (but not a confrontation). Again, usually, it will be a base as in:

$x := random$

It cannot, however, be a CLOSED-clause (which is not a coercend). If *proca* and *procb* are both of mode **proc real**, then:

(E17) $x := (p \mid proca \mid procb)$

is legitimate, but the deproceduring of *proca* and *procb* takes place in situ, as you have already seen in 5.2.0.1, and the conditional-clause as a whole yields **real** without further coercion.

The corresponding situation in the case of calls with actual-parameters arises in:

(E18) $x := (p \mid ncos(i) \mid nsin(i))$

which should be compared with example E16 in which the actual-parameter (i) appeared only once.

220   UNITARY CLAUSES   Ch.5.2.4

The mode yielded by the actual-parameters in a call must, of course, match those of the formal-parameters (4.2.2.2) of the routine. However, the context of an actual-parameter is strong, so that all the coercions are available. See 4.5.2 for the order in which the actual-parameters are elaborated.

5.2.4. Confrontations — assignments involving names

Here are some examples of assignments involving names. Remember that *xx* and *yy* are of mode **ref ref real** and that *a*, *x* and *y* are merely **ref real**:

(E19)   *xx* := **if** *i<0* **then** *x* **else** *y* **fi**;

The value of *xx* is therefore the name *x* or the name *y*.

(E20)   *yy* := *xx*;

and so is the value of *yy*.

(E21)   *a* := *xx*;

The value currently referred to by *x* or *y* (whichever was assigned to *xx*) is assigned to *a*. Note that *xx* is dereferenced twice in this example.

(E22)   *(* **ref real**: *xx)* := *a*;

The value referred to by *a* is assigned to *x* or to *y*. *xx* is here put in a cast, so that it may be dereferenced. There is normally little point in using a cast as the RHS of an assignation, since:

(E23)   *y* := **real**: *x*;

means the same as:

(E24)   *y* := *x*;

(E25)   *a* := *xx* := *x*;

means the same as *a* := **real**: *(xx* := *x)*, in which the name *x* is assigned to *xx*, the value referred to by the value referred to by which (i.e. it is dereferenced twice) being then assigned to *a*. On the other hand:

(E26)   *xx* := *a* := *x*;

means the same as *xx* := *(a* := *x)*, in which the value referred to by *x* is first assigned to *a*, and the name *a* is then assigned to *xx* (but the resultant value of *xx* is in no way dependent upon *x*, so that one might just as well have written *a* := *x*; *xx* := *a*;).

Ch.5.4.0 UNITARY CLAUSES 221

(E27) $xx := \mathbf{nil}$

means that xx no longer refers to any name. **nil** is a special base of mode **ref amode** which yields a name which does not refer to any value. **nil** is in fact an example of a coercion known as hipping, which will be described in 5.7.0.

Vertical readers, please turn to 6.2.

5.4. Unitary clauses and structures

5.4.0. Coercion — complex widening

The widening of **ints** into **reals** was introduced in 5.1.0.4. In a similar fashion, it is possible to widen a **real** into a **compl**, provided the context is strong. Thus:

(E1) $z := x$

x is first dereferenced into a **real** and then widened.

(E2) $z := 2$

Here the **int** 2 is first widened into a **real**, and then widened again into **compl**.

Even an implementation (of a sublanguage) which does not include the **compl** operators in its standard-prelude ought to implement this particular widening (i.e. of a **struct** *(real re, im)*), in order that a user may then declare these operators himself, and use them in the normal fashion.

5.4.1. Bases — identifiers

Clearly, once an identifier has been declared to possess a **struct** (or a **ref struct**, etc.) then that identifier can stand as a base, and the value yielded is the whole of some structure (however complicated) of the appropriate mode (or the name of such a structure). For example, in:

(E3) $v1 := v2$

$v2$, which is of mode **ref struct** *(real xcoord, ycoord, zcoord)* (see Appendix 2) is dereferenced to yield a value (consisting of three **real** quantities) which is of mode **struct** *(real xcoord, ycoord, zcoord)*. Such bases can occur in assignations (as above), or in formulas, as in:

(E4) $v1 := v2 + v3$

or in selections, as will now be discussed.

5.4.2. Cohesions — selections

A 'selection' is a form of cohesion which can be used to obtain an individual field out of a structure, thus:

(E5)   *xcoord* **of** *v1; re* **of** *z*

Here, *xcoord* and *re* are selectors (see 2.4.1) and *v1* and *z* are bases. More specifically, any weak secondary can be selected from, and this has various consequences as follows:

a) Because it is weak, the secondary can be dereferenced, but a special provision attaches to weak dereferencing. Since we require to obtain only a part (a field) of the whole structure, the dereferencing of the secondary must yield the name of the structure, and never the structure itself. Therefore, in weak dereferencing, succeeding **ref**s may be removed from the mode of the secondary until one remains, but this last one cannot go.

A special rule now provides that where the secondary thus yields the name of a structure, the selection as a whole yields the name of the selected field (but if the secondary (being of a non-**ref** mode) yields the structure itself, then the selection yields the field itself). For example in:

(E6)   *xcoord* **of** *v1*

v1 is of mode **ref struct** *(real xcoord, ycoord, zcoord)* and hence the example as a whole yields a name of mode **ref real**. This selection as a whole may now be dereferenced if its context is strong or firm, as happens in:

(E7)   *x := y + xcoord* **of** *v1*

However, if we declare:

(E8)   **vec** *w1 = (1, 2, 3);*

in which *w1* is of mode **vec**, then:

(E9)   *xcoord* **of** *w1*

is of mode **real**. Thus both *v1* and *xcoord* **of** *v1* are acceptable on the LHS of an assignation, but *w1* and *xcoord* **of** *w1* are not.

For another viewpoint over this whole matter, you are invited to re-read 1.4.3.

b) Because it is a secondary from which the selection is made, and because

Ch.5.4.3   UNITARY CLAUSES   223

a selection is a cohesion, it follows that selections can be selected from. If we declare:

(E10)   **mode tens = struct** *(***vec** *xlevel, ylevel, zlevel); ***tens** *u1;*

then we may call upon:

(E11)   *xcoord* **of** *ylevel* **of** *u1*

and the result is of mode **ref real**. Moreover, if we declare:

(E12)   **mode man = struct** *(***int** *age,* **ref man** *father);* **man** *jones;*

then we may call upon:

(E13)   *age* **of** *father* **of** *father* **of** *father* **of** *father* **of** *father* **of** *jones*

and the result is of mode **ref int**. Each time we select a *father* in this example, we obtain a **ref ref man** which, since it occurs in a weak position, can be dereferenced as far as **ref man** which is just what we need in order to be able to select another **ref ref man** from it.

5.4.3. Formulas — complex operators

It will be recalled (2.4.4) that **compl** is really a structure of mode **struct** *(***real** *re, im)*. Five special operators are provided for use with **compl**s. They are **re, im, abs, conj** and **i**. The first three operate on **compl** and yield **real**. Thus:

(E14)   **re** *z* means the same as *(***real**: *re* **of** *z)*

(E15)   **re** *(w + z)* means the same as *re* **of** *(w + z)*

(E16)   **abs** *z* means the same as *sqrt (***re** *z↑2 +* **im** *z↑2)*

Contrariwise:

(E17)   **re** *w := x*

is not permitted, although:

(E18)   *re* **of** *w := x*

is.

(E19)   **conj** *z* means the same as **re** *z* **i** *−* **im** *z*

i is a dyadic operator which produces a **compl** out of two **real**s or **int**s. Thus:

(E20) $z := x \mathbin{\mathbf{i}} y$ means the same as $z := (x, y)$

However:

$$z := w + (x, y)$$

is not legitimate because the context of (x, y) is not strong.

(E21) $z := w + x \mathbin{\mathbf{i}} y$

is all right because **i** is of higher priority than "+".

N.B. Those still unhappy with the interpretation of $-x{\uparrow}2$ should pay some attention to **re** $z{\uparrow}2$, in E16 above.

Vertical readers, please turn to 7.4.

5.5. Unitary clauses and multiples

5.5.0. Coercion — rowing

The restriction that a row-display (3.5.1) should contain at least two units is necessary in order to avoid ambiguity. However, a multiple value is perfectly entitled to contain only one, or even zero elements, and in order to be able to assign values to such multiples a coercion known as "rowing" is provided. This may be used in any strong context. Thus, given:

(E1)   [*1* : *2* **flex**] **real** *w1;*

then

(E2) $w1 := 2.4;$

causes a multiple (with bounds [*1* : *1*]) of one element (i.e. *2.4*) to be assigned to *w1*. Likewise:

(E3) $w1 := ;$

causes a multiple of zero elements (i.e. with fixed bounds [*1:0*] to be assigned. The empty space that seems to be being assigned to *w1* is called a "vacuum", and it is so inconspicuous that we strongly recommend you to enclose it in a closed-clause (3.2.4.1) to make your programs easier to follow:

(E3*) $w1 := ( );$

We certainly intend to follow our own advice in the remainder of this book. Also:

Ch.5.5.1 UNITARY CLAUSES

(E4) $w1 := (1, 2, 3)$;
       $[1 : 2$ **flex**, $1 : 3]$ **real** $w2 := w1$;

given $w2$ the bounds $[1 : 1$ **flex**, $1 : 3]$.

Thus, rowing consists of adding one row-of to the mode of a value, at the same time providing bounds $[1 : 1]$ or $[1 : 0]$ (several row-ofs may be added by repeated rowing). See also 5.5.1.3. E20 for how to produce names by rowing.

5.5.1. Bases

5.5.1.1. String denotations

A **string** is of course of mode $[1:0$ **flex**$]$ **char**, and therefore a literal string could be provided by means of a row-display:

(E5) $s := ("T", "H", "E", "\underline{\;}", "Q", "U", "I", "C", "K")$

However, a more compact denotation is provided:

(E6) $s := "THE\underline{\;}QUICK\underline{\;}BROWN\underline{\;}FOX\underline{\;}JUMPS\underline{\;}OVER\underline{\;}THE\underline{\;}LAZY\underline{\;}DOG"$

The value of the RHS here is a multiple value of mode **string**, and with bounds $[1:43]$. Note the denotation "$\underline{\;}$" for the space character.

If the quote-symbol itself is required to appear in the string, it must be represented by two quote-symbols (i.e. $""$), thus:

(E7) $s := "He\underline{\;}said\underline{\;}""she\underline{\;}said\underline{\;}""he\underline{\;}is\underline{\;}a\underline{\;}liar"".""\underline{\;}."$

An empty string can also be assigned:

(E8), $s := ""$

There is no denotation for a string of one character only. However, in strong positions the same result can be obtained by taking a character-denotation (5.1.1.1) and rowing it (5.5.0):

(E9) $s := "A"$;
       $s := """"$ "

Note that a comment may not appear inside a string- (or character-) denotation, and thus the comment symbol (¢) may safely appear, and stand for itself [R 9.b].

5.5.1.2. Identifiers

Clearly, once an identifier has been declared to possess a multiple (or a **ref** to a multiple, etc.) then that identifier can stand as a base, and the value yielded is the whole of some multiple value of the appropriate mode (or the name of such a value). Note that the value so yielded includes a descriptor, the bounds specified by which may turn out to be flexible (compare this with the values yielded by slices (see 5.5.1.3 below)). For example:

(E10)   *x1* := *y1*

(in which *y1* has to be dereferenced before a multiple value is obtained).

5.5.1.3. Slices

Slices are used in order to dissect multiple values. They consist of a weak primary, which yields a multiple value, followed by an 'indexer' containing a series of 'trimscripts' which specify which parts of that multiple value are required. Trimscripts may be either 'subscripts' or 'trimmers'.

Let us declare:

(E11) $[0:l-1, 0:m-1, 0:n-1]$ **real** *x3* = **(c** *some row-display* **c)**;

which is of mode [, ,] **real**. It can be represented thus:

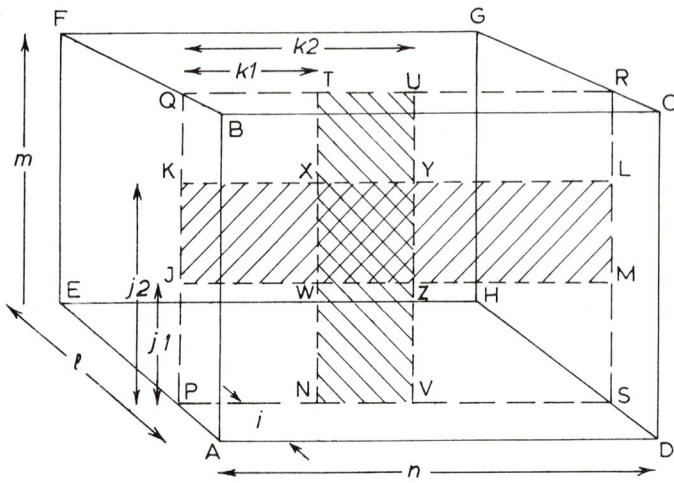

ABCDEFGH represents the whole value, *x3*. From this, we may select the plane PQRS by writing:

(E12)   *x3* [*i*]

which yields a value of mode [,] **real**. This could now be assigned to any 2-dimensional variable which it happened to fit. Here, [*i*] is a subscript. Further

Ch.5.5.1.3   UNITARY CLAUSES   227

subscripts can be used to yield the row JM (of mode [ ] **real**) and the element W (of mode **real**):

(E13) $x3\ [i, j1]\ ; x3[i, j1, k1]$

To obtain the column TN (of mode [ ] **real**) we write:

(E14) $x3\ [i, , k1]$

Trimmers are used to obtain a part (a "subvalue") of a row, column, etc. The required lower- and upper-bounds (both inclusive) are given, separated by a colon. Additionally, the 'new lower bound' from which the yielded bounds are to run is also specified following an @ (effectively, the subvalue between the specified lower- and upper-bounds is extracted, and its bounds are then "slid down" until the new-lower-bound is reached). If no new-lower-bound is specified, @ *1* is assumed. The following examples should make this clear:

	slice	value yielded	mode yielded	bounds yielded
(E15)	$x3[i, j1:j2\ @j1]$	JKLM	[,] **real**	$[j1:j2,\ 0:n-1]$
	$x3[i, j1:j2]$	JKLM	[,] **real**	$[1:j2-j1+1,\ 0:n-1]$
	$x3[i, :j1]$	PJMS	[,] **real**	$[1:j1+1,\ 0:n-1]$
	$x3[i, j2:\ @j2]$	KQRL	[,] **real**	$[j2:m-1,\ 0:n-1]$
	$x3[i, , k1:k2]$	NTUV	[,] **real**	$[0:m-1,\ 1:k2-k1+1]$
	$x3[i, j1:j2@j1, k1:k2@k1]$	WXYZ	[,] **real**	$[j1:j2,\ k1:k2]$
	$x3[i, j1, k1:k2]$	WZ	[ ] **real**	$[1:k2-k1+1]$
	$x3[i, j1:j2, k1]$	WX	[ ] **real**	$[1:j2-j1+1]$
	$x3[i, j1, k1]$	W	**real**	—
	$x3[, ,]$	ABCDEFGH	[,,] **real**	$[0:l-1,\ 0:m-1,\ 0:n-1]$
	$x3[,]$	ABCDEFGH	[,,] **real**	$[0:l-1,\ 0:m-1,\ 0:n-1]$
	$x3[\ ]$	ABCDEFGH	[,,] **real**	$[0:l-1,\ 0:m-1,\ 0:n-1]$
	$x3$	ABCDEFGH	[,,] **real**	$[0:l-1,\ 0:m-1,\ 0:n-1]$

(The last line is not strictly a slice at all).

Note that, if a bound is omitted from a trimmer, the bound currently existing in that multiple is implied. Moreover, if both bounds are omitted, the existing lower-bound is assumed (i.e. there is no sliding) and the colon may be omitted also. Trimscripts may be omitted entirely, starting at the right hand end, as illustrated in the last four examples.

The bounds yielded by a slice are always fixed (see 1.5.1).

Subscripts, and bounds occurring in trimmers, are strong **int** tertiaries, and therefore expressions of considerable complexity can be used, including any coercion that is able to yield **int**. However, an assignation or a cast would not do (they are quaternaries — try for yourself the ambiguities of allowing a cast). To get around this, they must be turned into primaries:

(E16) $x3[(j:=i)]$

A slice consists of a weak primary, followed by an indexer. The weak primary leads to the following consequences:

a) Because it is weak, it can be dereferenced, but only until one **ref** is left (see 5.4.2 for the corresponding phenomenon in connection with selections). Thus dereferencing can never yield the multiple value itself — basically this is because the purpose of a slice is to obtain only a part of it.

A special rule now provides that where the primary thus yields the name of a multiple value, the slice yields another name which refers to the element or subvalue that has been sliced (but if the primary already yields a multiple value — as $x3$ in the examples above — then the slice yields a multiple value also). The similarity between this and the corresponding provisions for selections (5.4.2) should be noted. For example, in:

(E17) $x1[i]$

$x1$ is of mode **ref**[ ] **real**, and hence the example as a whole yields a name of mode **ref real**, which may itself now be dereferenced if its context is strong or firm, as happens in:

(E18) $x := y + x1[i]$

whereas in:

(E19) $xx := x1[i]$

we have obtained, in xx, a pointer to a **real** value, which just happens to be a particular element of a [ ] **real**.

(The converse operation, in which a pointer intended for a multiple value can instead point to a single value is also possible:

(E20)   **ref** [ ] **real** $xx1 := x;$

This involves rowing (5.5.0), and the bounds, when the **real** value referred to is accessed via $xx1$, are $[1 : 1]$). A pointer to a subvalue can also be obtained:

(E21)   **ref** [ ] **real** $xx1 := x2[2 : 4, i]$;

in which $xx1$ is made to point to part of the ith column of $x2$.

b) Because it is a primary, it follows that any suitable CLOSED-clause can be used, thus:

(E22)   **if** $i < j$ **then** $x1$ **else** $y1$ **fi** $[2 : n-1]$

Even a **string** denotation can be trimscripted:

(E23) $"abcd"[2]$

yields $"b"$. However, a row-display should not be used (see 3.5.1) unless your implementation specifically permits it.

c) Because a selection is a cohesion, and therefore a secondary, parentheses may be needed when slices and selections are to be combined:

(E24) p of $q[i]$

is only meaningful if q is of some mode such as [ ] **struct** *(amode p, ...)*, in which case the ith structure is to be sliced from the multiple, and then the field p is to be selected from it.

(E25)   *(p* of *q)* [i]

is only meaningful if q is of some mode such as **struct** *(* [ ] **amode** *p, ...)*, in which case the field p (which is a multiple) is to be selected from the structure q, and the ith element is to be sliced from it. See 1.4. E13 for a similar case concerning a selection which yields a procedure.

5.5.3. Formulas – bound and state interrogations

It is useful to be able to discover the actual value of the bounds of a multiple which is on hand, particularly so when it is a formal-parameter of a routine, and the bounds of the actual-parameter are needed inside the routine. Two special operators are provided for this purpose:

(E26) n **lwb** $x3$;
          n **upb** $x3$

These two formulas yield, respectively, the lower- and upper-bounds of the nth row-of-rower (or boundpair (see 1.5.0)) of the multiple $x3$. (For example, with $x3$ declared as in E11, *3* **upb** *x3* would yield the value $n - 1$).

It may also be useful to discover whether a given bound is flexible or fixed, and there are two special operators for this:

(E27) n **lws** $x3$;
          n **ups** $x3$

These formulas yield **true** if the corresponding bound is fixed (see 1.5.1), and **false** if it is flexible.

For getting at the first (or only) dimension, monadic versions or **lwb**, **upb**, **lws** and **ups** are provided. Thus:

(E28)   **upb** $x1$

means the same as

(E29) 1 **upb** $x1$

All these operators are introduced formally in 6.5.

5.5.4. Confrontations — assignments

There are three questions to be answered:
1) What happens when one of the bounds of the multiple referred to by the LHS is flexible?
2) What happens when the LHS is a slice?
(Note that these two questions can never arise together, because the bounds of a slice are always fixed).
3) What happens when the LHS and the RHS involve the same multiple value?

5.5.4.1. Flexible assignments

In the first place, it must be stated that the bounds on the two sides of an assignment must match exactly. Thus:

(E30) $[1:3]$ **real** $xa, [2:4]$ **real** xb ; $xa := xb$

can never be legitimate under any circumstances.

However, if a bound on the LHS is flexible (and this can only occur when the whole of some multiple is being assigned to), then the corresponding bound from the RHS is copied across. This means that a flexible multiple may well change its size when the whole of it is assigned to. Given the declaration:

(E31) $[1$ **flex**: 0 **flex**$]$ **real** $a1$, $[0:n-1]$ **real** $b1$;

(E32) $a1 := b1$

causes $a1$ to acquire the bounds $[0:n-1]$, whereas:

(E33) $a1 := b1[2:n-2]$

causes $a1$ to acquire the bounds $[1:n-3]$.

Now it is possible to assign the name of a slice (i.e. a name referring to a subvalue) to a suitable destination. E.g.:

(E34)   **ref** $[\ ]$ **real** $xx1$; $xx1 := x1[1:4]$

xx1 now points to a part of the multiple named *x1*. However, if one were to attempt to point to a part of a flexible multiple, which subsequently changed its bounds and its size, then the pointer could hardly be expected to point at anything very sensible (moreover the implementation could hardly be expected to keep it pointing into that multiple at all). Therefore, the result of assigning the name which refers to an element or a subvalue of a flexible multiple is undefined [R 8.3.1.2.c Step 1].

5.5.4.2. Assignation to slices

When the LHS of an assignation is a slice, then of course only the sliced part of the multiple referred to is assigned to. First, however, the bounds of the slice are elaborated, and slid down according to any @s that may be present. These bounds are then compared with those on the RHS to see whether the assignation is legitimate. If it is, the value of the RHS is assigned to the slice on the left (but as selected by the un-slid bounds, of course). Thus, given the declarations:

(E35)   [1:3] real *xa*, [2:4] real *xb*, [1:2] real *xc*, [2:3] real *xd;*

the following statements are all legitimate:

(E36)   *xa* [2:3] := *xc;*
         xa [2:3 @ 2] := *xd;*
         xa [2:3] := *xd*[@ 1];
         xa[@ 1] := *xb* [@ 1]

In these examples the bounds used for comparison pruposes are [1:2], [2:3], [1:2] and [1:3] respectively, but in all of the first three cases it is [2:3] of *xa* that get altered. The fourth case shows how the presumably intended effect of *xa* := *xb* (which is not legitimate) can be achieved.

5.5.4.3. Overlapping slices

Suppose we wish to effect a cyclic permutation of the elements of *x1*. Then we may write (cf. R 8.6.1.2):

(E37)   *y1*[2 : *n*] := *x1*[1 : *n*−1];
         y1[1] := *x1*[*n*];
         x1 := *y1*

However, we might consider the effect of:

(E38) $x := x1[n];$
       $x1[2:n] := x1[1:n-1];$
       $x1[1] := x$

Consider the second line of this:

$$x1[2:n] := x1[1:n-1];$$

in which the slice being assigned from overlaps the slice being assigned to. Does this work, or is it equivalent to:

for i **from** 2 **to** n **do** $x1[i] := x1[i-1];$

(which has rather a disastrous effect)? Fortunately, the overlapping slices of E38 do work correctly, and it is up to the implementation to ensure that it starts the copying operation at the correct end.

Vertical readers, please turn to 6.5.

5.6. Units and unions

(E1)   **union** *(***int**, **real***) ira, irb;*

ira and *irb* may refer to values of mode either **int** or **real**. However, this raises no problem when one is assigned to the other:

(E2)   *ira := irb;*

since *ira* now refers to whichever mode *irb* referred to before. The modes on the two sides of E2 are both **ref union** *(***int**, **real***)*, and the RHS is dereferenced as usual.

The problems do not begin to arise until we want to set the mode of *irb* in the first place (by assigning an **int** to it, for example) or until we want to get an **int** out of it again (always assuming that it happens to refer to an **int** at the time in question). The first of these problems is dealt with by a new coercion known as "uniting", and the second by means of a new confrontation known as a 'conformity relation'.

5.6.0. Coercion — uniting

It should be emphasised that there are no built-in operators for operating on **unions** so that *ira + irb* is not a valid formula unless you have suitably defined "+" for yourself. This is reasonable because your compiler could not tell whether you were trying to add a **real** to an **int** or an **int** to an **int** or whatever. Therefore, all arithmetic must be done on ununited operands. Once you have a value of some definite mode, however, (and if your context is at least firm) then you may unite it to yield any **union** containing that mode which may be demanded by the context:

(E3)   *ira* := *i*+2;

Here, *i*+2 is of mode **int**. The mode required is **union** *(***int***, ***real***)* and the context is strong (being the RHS of an assignation). Therefore *i*+2 is united to be of mode **union** *(***int***, ***real***)* and as such it can now be assigned to *ira*. Because the uniting was from an **int**, *ira* now refers to an **int** value. You might be tempted to think that this example is ambiguous, because the *i*+2 might also be widened to **real** and then united. However, if you try to follow through this possibility on the coercion chart given in 5.1.0.2, then you will find that it has been carefully excluded.

(E4)   **union** *(***bool***, ***int***, ***real***)* *bira;*
        bira := *ira*

Here, *ira* is united from **union** *(***int***, ***real***)* into **union** *(***bool***, ***int***, ***real***)*. This is quite in order because all the constituent modes of the former are also constituents of the latter.

5.6.4. Confrontations

5.6.4.1. Conformity relations

Suppose we have an *ira* on hand, as declared in the last section, and suppose it is thought to refer to an **int** (for the nonce). We want to assign it to *i*, say, which is a **ref int**. The first thing to establish is that it does indeed refer to an **int**, for ALGOL 68 goes to great lengths to ensure that you never assign from a **union** until you are quite sure that its current mode will fit the proposed destination. (By defining your own operators and dabbling in machine code you might get around this, but that would be at your own risk).

(Here we must observe that every value referred to by a **ref union** must include within itself an indication to show of which of its permitted modes it currently is. Therefore a **union** *(***int***, ***real***)*, whilst being a very convenient example with which to illustrate the point, is likely to occupy two words of storage — one for the **int** or the **real**, and one to say which it is. Thus there is no practical benefit in using this mode if the intention is to save storage space.

A real saving would occur in the following case:

   union *(* [ ] int, [ ] real*)* *ir1;*

because the elements in these multiples are all **int** or all **real**, and only one additional word is needed to indicate the mode of the whole lot.)

Returning now to our *ira*, and whether it is an **int** or not, we can write:

(E5)   if int ∷ *ira* then . . . . . . fi

int ∷ *ira* is a 'conformity relation' [R 8.3.2], and yields **true** so long as its RHS is in a fit state (modewise) to be assigned to its LHS. Thus:

(E6)   *ira* ∷ *bira*

would be **true** so long as *bira* did not currently refer to a **bool**. (Note that in considering whether the RHS could be assigned to the LHS, the only coercions which may be tried are dereferencing and uniting.)

The rules governing the use of a conformity-relation are the following: For its LHS:
  a) It must yield a name (presumably of a mode to which the RHS could possibly be assigned). A **ref union** will do (as in E6) and then any of its constituent modes on the RHS will be acceptable. The LHS of E5 is actually a generator (see 5.7.2) and it does in fact yield a **ref int**, even though it does not look like it.
  b) It must be a tertiary.
  c) Its context is soft (so that a **proc** yielding a suitable name would do instead).
  d) It is not elaborated (not at this stage, anyway) because all we are interested in is the mode that it refers to, and this can be deduced at compile time. In particular, if the LHS is a generator (as in E5), this means that no storage space on the heap is reserved (5.7.2.2). A generator on the LHS is therefore both convenient and safe.

For its RHS:
  a) It must be a tertiary.
  b) Its context is empty (i.e. no coercion is possible).
  c) It is elaborated, and its current mode is found. If this mode does not fit the LHS it may be dereferenced (as in E5 and E6) until it does (or until no further dereferencing is possible, in which case the conformity-relation as a whole yields **false**).

Note that the RHS does not have to be a **union**, but the mode yielded would be evident at compile time if it were not. Thus:

(E7) **real** :: *i*

is legitimate, but will always yield **false**.

An alternative way to find out the current mode of *ira*, and to act accordingly, would be to use a case conformity (see 3.7.3).

So far we have discovered whether *ira* refers to an **int**. If it does, we may assign it as follows:

(E8) *i* ::= *ira*

You might like to call this a 'conforms-to-and-becomes-ity-relation'. First of all it is treated just like:

$i :: ira$

and if this yields **true**, then its LHS is elaborated and the value obtained from its RHS is assigned to it. If it yields **false**, then nothing further happens. E8 looks rather like an assignation, and indeed it behaves like one if the mode happens to fit. There is, however, one difference. The value yielded by an assignation is that yielded by its LHS (which is always a name). The value yielded by a conformity relation is always **true** or **false**, according to whether the mode fitted or not. Thus you may write:

(E9) **if** *i* ::= *ira* **then** ¢ you will only get in here if and when *ira* has been assigned to *i* ¢ . . . . . **fi**

and:

(E10) $i := j := k$

but not:

$i := j ::= ira$

5.6.4.2. Assignations of unions of rows

Multiple values inside **union**s are always declared with virtual bounds (2.5.2.3) [R 7.1.1.jj] :

(E11) **union** /[ ] **int**, [ ] **real**, **bool**/ *irla;*

The effect is much as if the bounds had been flexible, insofar as a multiple value of any size (and suitable mode) may be assigned thereto:

(E12) $irla := y1;$
       $irla := i1[17:23];$
       $irla := i1$

In all these examples, the RHS is united before being assigned. The whole of the multiple value on the RHS (bounds, states and all) is copied across regardless [R 8.3.1.2.c]. There is no question of checking the existing bounds or states of the LHS (for if *ir1a* had previously referred to a **bool**, there would have been none).

A **union** containing multiples cannot be sliced (5.5.1.3), so there is no question of assigning to only a part of it. Moreover, to get at a part of its existing value is quite hard work. The following method is recommended:

(E13)   *i1*[*17:23*] := *(* [*1* **flex**: *0* **flex**] **int** *ij1; ij1* ::= *ir1a; ij1) [17:23]*

This will not be at all efficient, since the whole of the multiple inside *ir1a* must first be copied to the specially declared *ij1*. Only then can the required slice be trimmed out. Note that if *ir1a* did not refer to a [ ] **int** at this time, the result of E13 would be undefined, since nothing at all would be assigned to *ij1*.

It is, however, possible to discover the bounds and states of the multiple within a **union** without all this bother, provided the **union** consists of multiples and nothing else [R 10.2.1.a]. Thus *ir1a* as declared in E11 would not do, but if we declare:

(E14)   **union** *(* [ ] **int**, [,] **real***) ir1b;*

then we can say:

(E15)   *i* := **lwb** *ir1b;* ¢ yields the lower-bound of the first or only row-of-rower ¢

p := 2 **ups** *ir1b*¢ yields the second upper-state, so that it is undefined unless *ir1b* is currently exercising its [,] **real** option ¢

Vertical readers, please turn to 7.6.

5.7. Hop, skip and jump

5.7.0. Coercion

5.7.0.1. Hipping and voiding

We have two coercions left to consider, although we have in fact been using them informally all along. Formally, they are necessary in order to satisfy the general syntactic rule that the mode of each external object must, a posteriori, be that required by its context. But what on earth is the mode of **skip**, or of **go to** *label*, or of **nil**?

These three cases are covered by means of "hipping" [R 8.2.7] :

(E1) $i :=$ **skip**;   ¢ **skip** is hipped to **int** ¢
        $x :=$ **skip**;   ¢ **skip** is hipped to **real** ¢
        ref real $zz :=$ **nil**;   ¢ **nil** is hipped to **ref real** (**nil** is always
                                     hipped to **ref** something) ¢
        $x :=$ **if** p **then** y **else go to** *exit* **fi**
                ¢ **go to** *exit* is hipped to **real** ¢

In all these cases, it was quite apparent which mode was required, because the contexts were strong. The coercion chart in 5.1.0.2 shows exactly where hipping may be used. In particular, if it occurs at all, then it must be the only coercion present.

A special case arises, however, if the context expects a procedure:

(E2)   **proc** *ppp*;
        ppp := **go to** *exit*

In this case, the jump is not followed at the time of this assignation. Instead it is, in effect, procedured (4.2.2.1) and a routine consisting of this jump is assigned to *ppp*. We could just as well have written:

(E3)   *ppp* := (: **go to** *exit*)

An interesting application of this principle can be used to realise the equivalent of the ALGOL 60 **switch** facility:

(E4)   [ ] **proc** *switch* = (*e1, e2, e3*);   ¢ a multiple of **procs**. *e1, e2*
                                              and *e3* are labels ¢
        switch [*i*]   ¢ jumps to the label selected by i ¢

The bulk of any ALGOL 68 program will consist of unitary-statements forming the bodies of serial-clauses (3.1.2). Statements are, of course, void-clauses, but in practice most of them will be assignments which yield a value (the name yielded by the LHS). This value is thrown away by "voiding" [R 8.2.8] :

(E5)   **begin** $x := 1; y := 2; z := 3$ **end**

The first two assignations in this will certainly be voided. Whether the third one is or not depends upon whether the context in which the whole closed-clause occurs expects a mode.

Voiding can occur in strong contexts (but all contexts where **void** is required are strong anyway) and may in most cases be preceded by deproceduring (see coercion chart in 5.1.0.2)):

(E6)   ....; *x or y*; ¢ see Appendix 2. *x or y* is deprocedured and the next random number is taken but (the context requiring **void**) its **real** result is then thrown away by voiding ¢

However, a confrontation must never be deprocedured and then voided, for otherwise in:

(E7)   **proc** *ppp*; *ppp* := *stop*;

we should have to assign *stop* to *ppp* and then call the routine now referred to by *ppp* (i.e. *stop*). It is therefore voided straight away.

It is useful to note that the context immediately preceding a ";" is always **void** (and strong).

5.7.0.2. bits and bytes widening

In strong contexts, **bits** values can be widened to [ ] **bool** and **bytes** values to **string**. The bounds of the [ ] **bool** will always be [*1* : *bits width*] (see 6.2.1) and the **string** will always contain exactly *bytes width* **char**s. The **long**s versions of **bits** and **bytes** can be widened similarly.

Here is an example in which a slice is trimmed out of a **bits** value. Note the use of a cast to give strength to what would otherwise have been a weak context (5.5.1.3):

(E8)   **bits** *t* := **1011100**; ¢ for **bits** denotations see next section ¢
            [*1* : *3*] **bool** *b1* := *(* [ ] **bool**: *t)* [*bits width*−*4*: *bits width*−*2*];
            ¢ yields *(***true**, **true**, **true***)* ¢

In the next example, two **bytes** values are concatenated to give a **long bytes** (the method is rather clumsy, but is the only way provided in the language since the operator **leng** (6.7.4) is not provided for **bits** and **bytes**).

(E9)   **bytes** *r* := **ctb** *"ABCD"*, *s* := **ctb** *"EFGH"*;
            long bytes *rr* := **long ctb** *((***string***: r) + (***string***: s));*
                ¢ if *bytes width* is 4 in the implementation,
                this will yield *ABCDEFGH*. Otherwise there may be
                some *null characters* in the middle (6.1.1) ¢

5.7.1. Bases

5.7.1.1. bits denotations

A special form of denotation [R 5.2] is provided for values of mode **bits**:

(E10)   **bits** *bits* := **1011001**;

which means that the value assigned to *bits* is the row-display:

(*false* . . . *false, true, false, true, true, false, false, true*)

Note that the correct number of **falses** is automatically inserted at the left hand end.

If you like quoting your **ints** in binary, you can always write:

(E11)   *i* := **abs 101**   ¢ meaning *i* := *5* ¢

(For the operator **abs**, see 6.1.1).

5.7.1.2. long denotations

There is no coercion provided in the language for converting a **real** into a **long real** or a **long long real**. Therefore the a priori mode of any object must already contain the right number of **longs**. In the case of denotations (**int**, **real**, and **bits**) this is achieved as follows [R 5.1.2]:

(E12)   **long int** *iiiint* := **long** *122333444455555*;
         long long real *reaeal* := **long long** *3.1415926535 8979323846*;
         long long long bits *biiiits* := **long long long 1001010110101010
             0101011010101010100101000101001011111001010101*;

There are no **long** forms of **bool, char, format,** or **string** denotations.

5.7.2. Cohesions − generators

'Generators' [R 8.5.1] are used to make available to the user regions of store where values may be put. They yield the names of those regions. A generator consists of an actual-declarer (2.2.1 and 2.5.2.2), preceded by **loc** or **heap** or nothing (in which case **heap** is implied).

5.7.2.1. loc generators

In the case of **loc** generators, the scope (3.2.2) of the name thus created is the range (3.2.1) in which the generator appears:

(E13)   begin
         [1:n] ref real xx1;
         int i := 1;
         [ ] proc switch = (minus, zero, plus);
loop: switch [2 + sign i1 [i]]; ¢ for the operator sign see 6.1.1 ¢
minus: xx1[i] := x1[i]; join;
zero: xx1[i] := nil; join;
plus: xx1[i] := loc real := 0;
join: if (i plus 1) ≤ n then goto loop fi;
         comment At this point, each element of the multiple value
         xx1 has been set up referring to either an element of x1 (if the
         corresponding element of i1 was negative), or to no value at
         all (if zero), or to some value specially created for the purpose
         by the generator **loc real**, and initially set to zero. The number
         of these special values is determined at run time, according to
         the values of the elements of i1. The only way to gain access
         to them, at the moment, is via the elements of xx1. Because a
         loc generator was used, they will all disappear when we leave
         this range. ¢
         skip
         end
         ¢ At this point, xx1 has disappeared, and so have any locally
         generated values to which it referred ¢

In this example, the generator **loc real**, each time it was encountered, would reserve storage for one **real** value (presumably on the same stack as xx1 and i) and yield the name referring to that value. 0 would then be assigned to that name, and the name itself would be assigned to xx1[i].

However, the range of a **loc** generator is the smallest range in which it can be found, and this leads the way to various pitfalls. For example, you might have tried to achieve the effect of E13 by the following (and you would have failed miserably):

         begin
         [1:n] ref real xx1;
         for i to n do
             xx1[i] := case sign i1[i] +2 in x1[i],
                                              nil,
                                              loc real := 0 esac;
         skip
         end

Ch.5.7.2.1　　　UNITARY CLAUSES　　　　　　　　　241

Here, the range in which **loc real** occurs lies between the ",", and the **esac**, which is far too local for your purpose. The next range outside that one lies between the **do** and the ";", which would not have done either. The range you really wanted lay between the **begin** and the **end**, and example E13 was carefully arranged so that this was also the range of the **loc** generator.

Here then is a complete list of the places which constitute a range:

> serial-clauses (see 3.1.5 for where these can occur) [R 4.1.1.e]
> routine-denotations (see 4.2.2.2)
> case-clauses (3.2.4.3) [R 9.4.c,d]
> the first part of conformity-case-clauses (3.7.3), from
> 　　**case** to **in** [R 9.4.e,f]
> repetitive-statements (3.5.2) [R 9.3]
> certain unitary-clauses, occuring as follows:
> 　　the unitary-statement after **do** (3.5.2) [R 9.3.a,b]
> 　　the controlled unitary-clauses in case- and conformity-case-
> 　　clauses (3.2.4.3 and 3.7.3) [R 9.4.c,d]

loc generators are particularly useful for creating triangular and other oddly-shaped multiples:

(E14)　　**begin**
　　　　　$[1:0$ **flex**] **ref** [ ] **real** *triangle;*
　　　　　mode array = $[1:0$ **flex**] **real**; ¢ *to save ink* ¢
　　　　　triangle := *(* **loc array** := *1*,
　　　　　　　　　　　loc array := *(1,2)*,
　　　　　　　　　　　loc array := *(1,2,3)*,
　　　　　　　　　　　loc array := *(1,2,3,4)* *)*;
　　　　　for *i* **to** *4* **do** *print (triangle* [*i*] [*i*] *)* ¢ *prints the diagonal* ¢
　　　　　end

Outside the range of E14, both *triangle* and the **arrays** to which it referred will have vanished.

The slice *triangle* [*i*] [*i*] is worthy of further examination. *triangle* itself is of mode **ref** [ ] **ref** [ ] **real**. *triangle* [*i*] is a slice of mode **ref ref** [ ] **real** (for the reasons explained in 5.5.1.3). It yields the name of the name of the *i*th row of *triangle* (it is impossible to get hold of the columns). In order to be able to take a further slice out of *triangle* [*i*], we must demonstrate that it is a weak primary of mode **ref** [ ] **real**. Now a base is a primary (5.1.0.1) and a weak base of mode **ref** [ ] **real** can be obtained by dereferencing a base of mode **ref ref** [ ] **real**. A slice, such as *triangle* [*i*], is such a base (5.5.1), and there we are. We can make the further slice *triangle* [*i*] [*i*], and the mode it yields is **ref real**. In E14 this was then dereferenced once more so that a **real** value could be printed.

Now, we shall remind you for the last time that:

(E15)   **real** *x* ;

really stands for:

(E16)   **ref real** *x* = **loc real**;

x is here declared to be of mode **ref real** and to possess the name of the piece of store made available by the generator **loc real**. Since this is a **loc** generator, the piece of store will cease to be available outside the range in which E15 or E16 appeared. Also, outside this range, the identifier *x* cannot occur (or if it does, it identifies something completely different). Thus *x* and the name which it possesses rise and fall together.

5.7.2.2. heap generators

In the case of **heap** generators, the scope (3.2.2) of the name that is created is not restricted to any range:

(E17)   **begin**
          real *w*;
          w := *10.5*;
          xx := **heap real** := *w* ¢ creates an extra instance of *10.5*
                                    on the heap ¢
          end;
                    comment now we are outside the range of *w* and of the
                              first instance of *10.5* to which it referred. However, the
                              second instance of *10.5* is still intact, and is accessible
                              via the variable *xx* ¢
          print (xx); ¢ prints *10.5* (after dereferencing *xx* twice) ¢
          xx := *x*   ¢ the instance of *10.5* on the heap is now quite
                              inaccessible, because no-one now refers to it ¢

In this example, when the **heap** generator **heap real** was encountered, storage for one **real** value was reserved (but not on the main stack such as was used by *w* — thus a different region of store, usually termed the "heap", is involved). The generator yielded the name referring to this piece of storage, the value *10.5* was assigned to it, and it was assigned to *xx* (which is of mode **ref ref real** — see Appendix 2). Both *xx* and this value remained fully available outside the range in which **heap real** occurred, and were used in the *print*. However, after this, *xx* was used for something else and the *10.5* was just left sitting there.

Thus it is very easy to waste large amounts of the heap:

(E18)   to *10000* do **heap real**

this will reserve 10,000 words on the heap, and there will be no way of accessing any of them – they will in fact be "garbage". Therefore it will be necessary for your implementation to include in your run-time program a "garbage collection routine" which will be called in whenever the size of the heap has become embarrassingly large. How this works in detail is your implementor's worry, but it will go something like this:

1) Consider all the values (on the stack) which are names and which are possessed by identifiers (i.e. all identifiers declared with mode **ref ref amode** within the current range, or its surrounding ranges).
2) If any such name refers to a value on the heap, mark that area of the heap as useful (this could be done by a vast array of bits, one for each word on the heap). Since the mode of the name is always known, the size of the value can easily be determined.
3) If the value referred to by any such name contains further names within itself (again, this will be apparent from the known mode of the given name), then consider these names also.
4) Go through the array of bits searching for areas of the heap that have not been marked as useful. These areas can now be made available for further use.

This process will be recognised as being similar to that employed in list-processing languages such as LISP, and it is for applications in which list-processing would otherwise have had to be used that **heap** generators are primarily intended.

You can, if you like, do fairly conventional list-processing in this language:

(E19)   **union** atom = *(* **char, int***)*;
        struct cons = *(* **union** *(* atom, **ref** cons*)* car, **ref** cons *cdr)*;
        proc *list* = *(* [*1*:**either**] **union** *(* atom, **ref** cons*)* item*)* **ref** cons:
            begin
            ref cons *a* := **nil**;
            for *i* **from upb** *item* **by** -1 **to** *1* **do**
                a := **heap** cons := *(item* [*i*], *a)*;
            a
            end;
        ref cons *expression* := *list (("X", "+", list (("Y", "×", 2))))*;

However, if you intend to create many lists with the same layout, it is better to declare them as **structs**, and generate them as such:

(E20)   **union operand** = *(*char, int, ref expression*)*;
struct expression = *(*operand *left*, char *operator*, operand *right)*;
ref expression *expression* := **heap expression** :=
   ("X", "+", **heap expression** := *("Y", "×", 2))*;

This version is more convenient to write, will use less storage space, and will have its garbage collected more speedily (since a complete **expression** can be removed at one go).

As was mentioned in 2.7.3, the contracted declaration:

(E21)   **heap real** *x*;

really stands for [R 9.2.a] :

(E22)   **ref real** *x* = **heap real**;

x is here declared to be of mode **ref real** and to possess the name of the piece of store made available by the generator **heap real**. This piece of store will still be available outside the range in which E21 or E22 appeared, even though the identifier *x* cannot occur there (or if it does, it identifies something completely different). It could be accessed in the following circumstances, which should be compared with E17:

(E23)   **begin**
heap real *w*;
w := *10.5*;
xx := *w*
end;
print (xx); ¢ prints 10.5 ¢
xx := *x*   ¢ the instance of *10.5* on the heap is now garbage ¢

The word **heap** can be omitted from a **heap** generator (since a **loc** generator must always be preceded by **loc**). This was in fact done in 5.6. E5 and 3.7. E11, which illustrated the use of generators in conformity-relations and case conformities. Note that in these particular examples the generators were never elaborated, so that no storage was reserved.

5.7.3. Formulas — order of elaboration of operands

The elaboration of a dyadic-formula involves the elaboration of two operands (these are either other formulas or secondaries). Generally speaking, these two operands are elaborated collaterally (see 3.7.1). The following dangerous example illustrates this, and should be compared with 3.7. E2:

(E24)   **begin int** i;
        proc int $side = (i:=1; i:=2; i)$;
        $print\ (\ side + side\ )$
        end

This will print either 3 or 4, for the reasons given in 3.7.1.

The advantage of this collateral elaboration from the point of view of implementation is that the order of elaboration can be chosen to be that which yields the minimum number of compiled instructions. For example:

(E25) $y := x + a \times b$

Most compilers will choose to fetch and multiply a and b before getting hold of x.

It is possible so to declare an operator that its operands will always be taken in order:

(E26)   **priority plusinorder** = 6;
        op plusinorder = (**real** a; **real** b) **real**: $a + b$;
        $y := x$ **plusinorder** $a \times b$

Note how a semicolon was used in between the two formal-parameters in the routine-denotation (see 4.5.2). The x will now always be elaborated before the $a \times b$. However, none of the operators declared within the standard-prelude (Chapter 6) is declared in this way.

5.7.4. Confrontations – identity relations

Identity-relations are used to detect whether two names are identical:

(E27)   **ref real** $anotherx = x$; **real** y;
        $anotherx :=: x$;   ¢ always yields **true** ¢
        $anotherx :\neq: x$;   ¢ always yields **false** ¢
        $anotherx :=: y$ ¢ always yields **false** ¢

This example is quite trivial, because *anotherx* and x, by virtue of the identity-declaration, both possess the same name.

(E28)   xx := yy := x;
(E29)   xx :=: x ; ¢ yields **true**   ¢
(E30)   x :=: xx; ¢ yields **true**   ¢
(E31)   xx :=: yy   ¢ yields **false** ¢

In E29 and E30, xx was dereferenced to yield the name to which it currently referred (i.e. x). It is permissable to dereference on one side of an identity-relation, but not on both, and it is for this reason that E31 did not work. E31 could never yield **true**, whatever assignments we might make to xx and yy. However, by the use of casts we can achieve the result presumably intended:

(E32)   *(* **ref real**: *xx)* :=: *(* **ref real**: *yy)* ¢ yields **true** (in the context
                                                                    of E28) ¢

The rules governing the use of an identity-relation are the following:

It has two sides — a strong side and a soft side. One of these can stand as the LHS, in which case the other must stand as the RHS. The symbol in between is either ":=:" or ":≠:".

For its strong side:
    a) It must yield a name (i.e. its mode must be **ref amode**).
    b) It must be a tertiary.
    c) Its context is strong (so that dereferencing is allowed,
       and also **nil** (5.7.0.1)).

For its soft side:
    a) It must yield a name, of the same mode as that yielded
       by the strong side.
    b) It must be a tertiary.
    c) Its context is soft (so that deproceduring is the only
       possible coercion, and **nil** is not permitted).

As a whole, an identity-relation yields a **bool** value — **true** if the names match and the symbol in between is ":=:" or if the names do not match and the symbol is ":≠:".

Here is an exceedingly delicately balanced example (cf. the Report at 8.3.3.2):

(E33)   **case** *i* **in** *xx, x* **or** *y* **out nil esac**
         :=:
         case *j* **in** *yy*, **skip, ref real**:=*x* **esac**

First, let us rewrite the example showing the a priori modes of all the items:

Ch.5.7.4   UNITARY CLAUSES   247

```
case i in xx,        ¢ ref ref real   ¢
         x or y      ¢ proc ref real  ¢
      out nil        ¢ wait and see   ¢
esac :=:
case j in yy,        ¢ ref ref real   ¢
         skip,       ¢ wait and see   ¢
         ref real:=x ¢ ref ref real   ¢
esac
```

Which is the soft side, and what is the mode of the name that it yields? Well, to put you out of your misery, the LHS is the soft one and the mode is **ref real**, but to obtain it we have to recall that case-clauses can be balanced (5.2.0.1) so that, even on the soft side, all but one of the items can be strongly coerced. Here then is the example again with all made clear:

```
case i in xx,        ¢ strongly dereferenced ¢
         x or y      ¢ softly deprocedured   ¢
      out nil        ¢ strongly hipped       ¢
esac :=:
case j in yy,        ¢ strongly dereferenced ¢
         skip,       ¢ strongly hipped       ¢
         ref real:=x ¢ strongly dereferenced ¢
esac
```

For an application of identity-relations, let us return to our list processing in E19. Let us assume all the declarations of E19 to have been made, and now continue thus:

(E34)   **op** eql = /union (**atom**, **ref cons**) a, b/ **bool**:
           begin
           char c, d, **int** i, j, **ref cons** rc;
           case c, i, rc ::= a
           in   (d,j::=b | c=d, **false** | b eql c),
                  (j,d::=b | i=j, **false** | b eql i),
                  car of rc eql b
           esac
           end;
           comment this recursively defined (and probably not very
                      efficient) operator compares two *cars* (or *cdrs*)
                      of *conss* and yields **true** if they are, or refer to
                      via a chain of *cars*, identical atoms ¢
ref cons a := list (("A", "X"));

ref cons $b := $ *list (("B", "X"));*
cdr **of** *(***cons:** *a)* **eql** *cdr* **of** *(***cons:** *b);*
¢ yields **true** because both sides refer to the value $"X"$ ¢
cdr **of** *(***cons:** *a)* :=: *cdr* **of** *(***cons:** *b)*
¢ yields **false** because both sides refer to different instances of the value $"X"$ ¢

The distinction here illustrates how, in list processing, it is often important to distinguish between a pointer to a list which is merely a copy of a given one, and a pointer which points to the given list itself. The identity-relation should be used to make this test.

Vertical readers, please turn to 6.7.

6. STANDARD PRELUDE

6.1. Operators

Each particular-program written by a user is presumed to be included within an "outer range", at the head of which is the standard-prelude (1.1) in which various standard declarations are made. These include:
Standard constants (see 6.2 and 6.7)
Standard procedures (see 6.2 and 6.7)
Standard operators (see this section, and 6.3, 6.5 and 6.7)
Additional constants and procedures required for transput (see 7)

Likewise, at the tail of the outer range, is a label *exit*:, to which you may jump in order to terminate the elaboration of your program, and which is followed by the library- and standard-postludes (see 1.1 and Appendix 3).

We now set out, in tabular form, details of all the common operators (for the manner in which they are used in formulas see 5.1.3). The tables include, for completeness, all of the meanings which each operator can have, even though you may not yet be familiar with all of the modes involved. The meaning of each operator is given in the last column for those operators whose meaning is not obvious. If nothing appears in this column, it means that the generally accepted meaning applies, or that a similar operator has already been explained higher up the column.

Note that many operators have more than one representation, in which case they are all given in the first column.

6.1.1. Monadic operators

operator	priority	mode of *a*	mode of result	meaning
¬ ~ not	10	bool bits	bool bits	
+	10	int real compl	int real compl	

operator	priority	mode of a	mode of result	meaning
−	10	int real compl	int real compl	
bin	10	int	bits	the binary digits representing the positive integer a
re	10	compl	real	the real part
im	10	compl	real	the imaginary part
conj	10	compl	compl	re a i −im a
abs	10	bool int real compl bits char	int int real real int int	1 for true and 0 for false $sqrt(re a \uparrow 2 + im a \uparrow 2)$ the opposite of bin a unique integer for each permissable value of char
odd	10	int	bool	true if odd, false if even
sign	10	int real	int int	} yields -1, 0, or $+1$
round	10	real	int	the nearest integer
entier ⌊ lwb	10	real	int	the integer equal to a, or the next integer below (more negative than) a
repr	10	int	char	the opposite of abs of a char
btb	10	[1 :] bool	bits	the multiple a, made up with falses at the left, is turned into bits
ctb	10	string	bytes	the string a, made up with *null characters* (6.2.1) on the right is turned into bytes

Ch.6.1.2   STANDARD PRELUDE   251

6.1.2. Dyadic operators

operator	priority	mode of a	mode of b	mode of result	meaning
i ⊥ !	9	real int int real	real int real int	compl compl compl compl	a plus i times b
↑ ** up ^	8	int real compl bits	int int int int	int real compl bits	a^b where $b \geq 0$ a^b a^b a shifted left b places (or right for b negative)
÷ over	7	int	int	int	abs $(a \div b)$ = entier abs (a/b) i.e. truncation towards zero
mod ÷:	7	int	int	int	$0 \leq a \bmod b < b$
× *	7	int real compl real int compl compl int real	int real compl int real int real compl compl	int real compl real real compl compl compl compl	
	7	int real compl real int compl compl int real	int real compl int real int real compl compl	real real compl real real compl compl compl compl	
elem □	7	int int	bits bytes	bool char	the a th bit of b the a th char of b

operator	priority	mode of a	mode of b	mode of result	meaning
+	6	int	int	int	
		real	real	real	
		compl	compl	compl	
		real	int	real	
		int	real	real	
		compl	int	compl	
		compl	real	compl	
		int	compl	compl	
		real	compl	compl	
		string	string	string	the concatenation
		string	char	string	of a and b
		char	string	string	
−	6	int	int	int	
		real	real	real	
		compl	compl	compl	
		real	int	real	
		int	real	real	
		compl	int	compl	
		compl	real	compl	
		int	compl	compl	
		real	compl	compl	
< lt	5	int	int	bool	
		real	real	bool	
		real	int	bool	
		int	real	bool	
		char	char	bool	true if abs a < abs b
		string	string	bool	true if the first character
		string	char	bool	in a that differs from the
		char	string	bool	corresponding character
		bytes	bytes	bool	in b is less than same
> gt	5	int	int	bool	
		real	real	bool	
		real	int	bool	
		int	real	bool	
		char	char	bool	
		string	string	bool	
		string	char	bool	
		char	string	bool	
		bytes	bytes	bool	

operator	priority	mode of *a*	mode of *b*	mode of result	meaning
≤ <= le	5	int real real int bits	int real int real bits	bool bool bool bool bool	**true** if each bit in *a* implies the corresponding bit in *b*
		char string string char bytes	char string char string bytes	bool bool bool bool bool	
≥ >= ge	5	int real real int bits char string string char bytes	int real int real bits char string char string bytes	bool bool bool bool bool bool bool bool bool bool	
= eq	4	bool int real compl real int compl compl int real bits char string string char bytes	bool int real compl int real int real compl compl bits char string char string bytes	bool bool bool bool bool bool bool bool bool bool bool bool bool bool bool bool	

oper-ator	prior-ity	mode of a	mode of b	mode of result	meaning
≠ ¬= ne	4	bool int real compl real int compl compl int real bits char string string char bytes	bool int real compl int real int real compl compl bits char string char string bytes	bool bool bool bool bool bool bool bool bool bool bool bool bool bool bool bool	
∧ & and	3	bool bits	bool bits	bool bits	
∨ or	2	bool bits	bool bits	bool bits	

Vertical readers, please turn to 7.1.

6.2. Constants and procedures

6.2.1. Constants

With the exception of *pi* (and *last random*), the purpose of these constants is to give information about the implementation upon which the program is being run, and they are therefore called "environment enquiries". They are all declared in the standard-prelude [R 10.1, R 10.3.a], by means of identity-declarations, to be of some mode such as **int** or **real**. Hence they are not names, and hence they cannot be altered by the user.

Some further environment enquiries are given in 6.7.1 (in connection with **long** modes) and in 7.2.2 and 7.5.3 (in connection with transput).

Ch.6.2.2　　　　　　　　STANDARD PRELUDE　　　　　　　　　　　255

identifier of constant	mode	value
max int	**int**	the largest **int** value which can be represented
max real	**real**	the largest **real** value which can be represented
small real	**real**	the smallest **real** value which can be meaningfully added to or subtracted from *1*
bits width	**int**	the number of bits in **bits** (see 2.7.1)
bytes width	**int**	the number of chars in **bytes** (see 2.7.1)
null character	**char**	some character
pi	**real**	π
last random	**ref real**	see 6.2.2

6.2.2. Procedures

The following procedures are all declared within the standard-prelude [R 10.3] to be of some mode **proc amode**, rather than **ref proc amode**. Hence they cannot be altered by the user. Their meanings are those generally accepted, or as specified by the last column of the following table.

Further procedures from the standard-prelude are to be found in 6.7.2, 7.1.1, 7.1.2, 7.2.1, 7.2.3, 7.2.4, 7.2.5, 7.4.3, 7.5.1, 7.6.3 and 7.7.1.

identifier of **proc**	mode	
sqrt	**proc(real) real**	
exp	**proc(real) real**	
ln	**proc(real) real**	
cos	**proc(real) real**	
arccos	**proc(real) real**	$0 \leqslant arccos(x) \leqslant \pi$
sin	**proc(real) real**	
arcsin	**proc(real) real**	$-\pi/2 \leqslant arcsin(x) \leqslant \pi/2$
tan	**proc(real) real**	
arctan	**proc(real) real**	$-\pi/2 \leqslant arctan(x) \leqslant \pi/2$
random	**proc real**	The next **real** value from a pseudo-random sequence uniformly distributed in the range $0 \leqslant$ *random* < 1. The value yielded is also assigned to a **ref real** *last random* which is initially set to the value *0.5*. A different sequence of pseudo-random numbers may be obtained by first assigning to it some different value in the range *0* to *1*.

See 6.7.2 for long(s) versions of these.

Vertical readers, please turn to 7.2.

6.3. Assigning operators

The operators in the following table all have the property that the result of the operation is automatically assigned to the name of the left hand operand, and this name is yielded as the value of the formula. Thus:

(E1)   *a* **plus** *b*   ¢ means the same as *a* := *a+b* ¢
(E2)   *x* := *a* **plus** *b*   ¢ means the same as *x* := *a* := *a+b* ¢
(E3)   *a* **minus** *b* **plus** *c*

E3 has implied bracketing:

(E4)   *(a* **minus** *b)* **plus** *c*   ¢ and therefore means *a* := *a−b; a* := *a+c* ¢
(E5)   *a* **plus** *b* := *x*

E5 is a legitimate example of a formula on the LHS of an assignation, but it is not very sensible since *b* does not enter into the result.

operator	priority	mode of *a*	mode of *b*	mode of result	meaning
times ×:=	1	ref int ref real ref compl ref real ref compl ref compl	int real compl int int real	ref int ref real ref compl ref real ref compl ref compl	*a* := *a*×*b*
overb ÷:=	1	ref int	int	ref int	*a* := *a*÷*b*
div /:=		ref real ref compl ref real ref compl ref compl	real compl int int real	ref real ref compl ref real ref compl ref compl	*a* := *a*/*b*
modb ÷::=	1	ref int	int	ref int	*a* := *a* mod *b*

operator	priority	mode of a	mode of b	mode of result	meaning
plus + :=	1	ref int ref real ref compl ref real ref compl ref compl ref string ref string	int real compl int int real string char	ref int ref real ref compl ref real ref compl ref compl ref string ⎱ ref string ⎰	$a := a+b$ $a := a+b$ (+ implying concatenation)
prus +=:	1	string char	ref string ref string	ref string ref string	$b := a+b$
minus − :=	1	ref int ref real ref compl ref real ref compl ref compl	int real compl int int real	ref int ref real ref compl ref real ref compl ref compl	$a := a-b$

Vertical readers, please turn to 8.3.

6.5. Interrogations

The following table specifies the operators introduced informally in 5.5.3. Note that **nonrow** stands for any mode other than a row-of mode, and ",s" stands for any number of commas (including none).

6.5.1. Dyadic operators

operator	priority	mode of a	mode of b	mode of result	meaning
lwb ⌊ entier	8	int	[,s] nonrow	int	the lower bound of the a th dimension of b
upb ⌈	8	int	[,s] nonrow	int	the upper bound of the a th dimension of b
lws ⌞	8	int	[,s] nonrow	bool	true if the lower state of the a th dimension of b is fixed
ups ⌝	8	int	[,s] nonrow	bool	true if the upper state of the a th descriptor of b is fixed

6.5.2. Monadic operators

operator	priority	mode of a	mode of result	meaning
lwb ⌊ entier	10	[,s] nonrow	int	1 lwb a
upb ⌈	10	[,s] nonrow	int	1 upb a
lws ⌞	10	[,s] nonrow	bool	1 lws a
ups ⌝	10	[,s] nonrow	bool	1 ups a

Vertical readers, please turn to 7.5.

6.7. Long operators

6.7.1. Environment enquiries

The numbers of different lengths of **ints**, **reals**, etc. that are provided may vary between different implementations. Environment enquiries (6.2.1) are therefore provided to indicate these numbers [R 10.1]. Additionally, the environment enquiries introduced in 6.2.1 (*max int*, etc.) and in 7.5.3 (*int width*, etc.) have long versions of themselves [R 10.5.2.1].

identifier of constant	mode	value
int lengths	**int**	the number of different lengths of **ints**
real lengths	**int**	the number of different lengths of **reals** (and of **compls**)
bits widths	**int**	the number of different widths of **bits**
bytes widths	**int**	the number of different widths of **bytes**
long max int	**long int**	the largest **long int** value which can be represented
long long max int	**long long int**	
long long long max int	**long long long int**	

and so on, up to any number of *long*s. For the rest of this table, let us introduce the convention that "*long*(s)" means any number of *long*s and "**long**(s)" means the same number of **long**s.

long(s) *max real*	**long**(s) **real**	the largest **long**(s) **real** value which can be represented
long(s) *small real*	**long**(s) **real**	the smallest **long**(s) **real** value which can be meaningfully added to or subtracted from *1*.
long(s) *bits width*	**int**	the number of bits in **long**(s) **bits**
long(s) *bytes width*	**int**	the number of **char**s in **long**(s) **bytes**
long(s) *int width*	**int**	the number of decimal digits required to represent *long*(s) *max int* − not including sign
long(s) *real width*	**int**	the number of decimal digits required to represent a mantissa, such that *long*(s) *small real* is not neglected in comparison with *1* − not including sign
long(s) *exp width*	**int**	the number of decimal digits required to represent a decimal exponent, such that *long*(s) *max real* can be correctly represented − not including sign
long(s) *pi*	**long**(s) **real**	π

6.7.2. Procedures

The procedures introduced in 6.2.2 [R 10.3] and 7.5.2 [R 10.5.2.1,2] also have their long versions. Note that a procedure with, for example, a **long long real** formal-parameter yields a value whose mode has exactly the same number of **long**s in it.

identifier of **proc**	mode
long sqrt	**proc**(**long real**)**long real**
long long sqrt	**proc**(**long long real**)**long long real**

and so on. We shall adopt the same abbreviation as before.

long(s) *exp*	**proc**(**long**(s) **real**)**long**(s) **real**
long(s) *ln*	**proc**(**long**(s) **real**)**long**(s) **real**
long(s) *cos*	**proc**(**long**(s) **real**)**long**(s) **real**
long(s) *arccos*	**proc**(**long**(s) **real**)**long**(s) **real**
long(s) *sin*	**proc**(**long**(s) **real**)**long**(s) **real**
long(s) *arcsin*	**proc**(**long**(s) **real**)**long**(s) **real**
long(s) *tan*	**proc**(**long**(s) **real**)**long**(s) **real**
long(s) *arctan*	**proc**(**long**(s) **real**)**long**(s) **real**
long(s) *random*	**proc long**(s) **real** .... with which is associated a **ref long**(s) **real** *long*(s) *last random* which is initially set to the value **long**(s) *0.5*: see 6.2.2.
long(s) *int string*	**proc**(**long**(s) **int** *i*, **int** *w*, **int** *r*) **string**
long(s) *real string*	**proc**(**long**(s) **real** *x*, **int** *w*, **int** *d*, **int** *e*) **string**
long(s) *dec string*	**proc**(**long**(s) **real** *x*, **int** *w*, **int** *d*) **string**
long(s) *string int*	**proc**(**string** *x*, **int** *r*)**long**(s) **int**
long(s) *string dec*	**proc**(**string** *x*)**long**(s) **real**
long(s) *string real*	**proc**(**string** *x*)**long**(s) **real**

6.7.3. Operators

Most of the operators introduced in 6.1.1, 6.1.2 and 6.3 have their **long**(s) counterparts [R 10.2]. We shall not list them all here; instead we shall give you a rule for working them out yourself.

Each operator has one or two parameters and a result, each being of some mode. If one or more of these modes is:

int, real, compl, bits or **bytes**

then new versions of that operator can be obtained by inserting **long**(s) in front of each of those modes. However, the modes **bool, char** and **string**, wherever they occur, must be left strictly alone.

For example, one of the versions of the operator "+" can be used to add a **real** to an **int** yielding a **real** (6.1.2). There therefore exists another version which adds a **long long real** to a **long long int** yielding a **long long real** (but not to add a **long long real** to a **long int** yielding a **real** — the number of **longs** added must be the same throughout).

However, there are certain exceptions to this general rule, all of which are concerned with not allowing **long**(s) **ints** in places where they would clearly be ridiculous. Thus:

    The **abs** of a **char** yields a (single) **int**
    The **repr** of a (single) **int** yields a **char**
    long(s) **ints**, **reals** and **compls** can be raised to a (single)
        int power, yielding correspondingly **long**(s) **ints** etc.
    The (single) **int** th element of a **long**(s) **bits** or **bytes**
        yields a **bool** or a **char**
    The **/** (or **its**) of a (single) **int** yields a **sema** (3.7.2)

In all of these, the phrase "(single) **int**" implies **int** where **long**(s) **int** might otherwise have been expected.

The two operators **btb** and **ctb** (6.1.1), which yield **bits** and **bytes** respectively, have long(s) versions known as **long**(s) **btb** and **long**(s) **ctb**, which yield **long**(s) **bits** and **long**(s) **bytes**.

6.7.4. leng and short

There are no coercions provided in the language for converting, for example, **ints** into **long ints** or vice versa. Instead, you are provided with the monadic-operators **leng** and **short** (see 8.4.2 for a meaningful example of their use):

oper-ator	prior-ity	mode of *a*	mode of result	meaning
leng	10	**long**(s) **int** **long**(s) **real** **long**(s) **compl**	**long long**(s) **int** ⎫ **long long**(s) **real** ⎬ **long long**(s) **compl** ⎭	the longer value equivalent to *a*
short	10	**long long**(s) **int** **long long**(s) **real** **long long**(s) **compl**	**long**(s) **int** ⎫ **long**(s) **real** ⎬ **long**(s) **compl** ⎭	the shorter value equivalent to *a*, if it exists

In this table, as usual, "**long**(s)" means **long** repeated zero or more times (but the same number of times in each column). Note that if you try to **shorten**, for example, a **long int** which is greater than *max int* (6.2.1), then the result is undefined.

Note that the operators **leng** and **short** are not provided for **long**(s) **bits** and **long**(s) **bytes** (but see 5.7. E9).

6.7.5. up and down

The operators **up**, **down** and "/" (or **its**), as applied to **semas** were defined in 3.7.2.

Vertical readers, please turn to 7.7.

7. TRANSPUT

7.1. Formatless transput

"Transput" is the name given to all those operations which communicate with the environment. These include input, output and transfers to backing media such as magnetic tape and discs.

There is a large variety of transput facilities provided to suit the user's taste, ranging from the simplest formatless transput described in this section, through the facilities for accessing various types of device (7.2) and for dealing with exceptional situations (7.4.4) up to the formatted transput described in 7.6 and the binary transput in 7.7.

7.1.1. Formatless output

Formatless output is achieved by means of the procedure *print*, e.g.:

(E1)   *print (x); print (i+3); print (p & i<j); print ("A");*
          print ("ABC"); print (x **i** *y); print (101); print (r)*

The modes of the actual-parameters in these examples are, respectively, **real**, **int**, **bool**, **char**, **string**, **compl**, **bits** and **bytes** (for a description of the mode **string** see 2.5.3 and 5.5.1.1, for **compl** see 2.4.4 and 5.4.3 and for **bits** and **bytes** see 2.7.1 and 5.7.1.1). In addition, multiple values (1.5.1, 2.5) and structures (1.4.1, 2.4) made up of any of these modes can be used. The actual-parameter of this procedure is a firm unitary-clause (the firmness arises from the particular way in which it is defined in the standard-prelude), which means that widening is not allowed, but dereferencing is. Note that it is not possible to output names (i.e. modes beginning with **ref**), or **formats** (7.6.2) or routines.

It is possible to output more than one item with one call on *print*:

(E2)   *print ((x, i+3, p&i<j, "A", "ABC" x* **i** *y, 101, r))*

which is equivalent to the series of separate *print*s in E1 above. Note the additional parentheses (these are required because the list of items is really a row-display (see 3.5.1)).

The following layout procedures [R 10.5.1.2.o,p,q,r] may be called upon in between calls of *print*:

identifier of **proc**	mode	
newpage	**proc**(**file**)	continue printing at the beginning of the next page
newline	**proc**(**file**)	continue printing at the beginning of the next line
space	**proc**(**file**)	skip one character (which results in a space character unless cunning use has been made of *backspace*)
backspace	**proc**(**file**)	move back one character (but not beyond the start of the current line). A subsequent call on *print* will overwrite whatever character was previously there (but a call on *space* will not).

These layout procedures (and other **proc**(**file**)s (see 7.2.6) written by the user) may also be called upon within a *print* call. Thus:

(E3)   *print ((newpage, "HEADING", newline, "X$\dot{=}$$\dot{.}$", x))*

means the same as:

(E4)   *newpage (stand out);*
         print ("HEADING");
         newline (stand out);
         print (("X$\dot{=}$$\dot{.}$", x))

Note the denotation ($\dot{.}$) for the space character. The *stand out* parameter specifies the **file** (see 7.2.1) to be affected. The **file** *stand out* is automatically implied by *print*, and is therefore supplied as the parameter of these routines when they occur within it.

When *print* is called, the mode of each item to be printed is identified, and appropriate action taken as follows:

ints, reals, compls:

If there is not room for the item on the current line (page), then *newline* (*newpage*) is called. Then the item is printed, preceded by a space (if not at the beginning of a line), allowing sufficient positions to cope with the largest permissible value of that mode.

Examples are:

```
+123456
   +456
     -1
     +0
+1.23456₁₀+11
-6.54321₁₀ -2
+1.23456₁₀+11-6.54321₁₀ -2
```

chars, bools:

newline or *newpage* is called if necessary as above, and then the item is output with no preceding space. 1 is printed for **true**, 0 for **false**.

strings, bytes:

newline and *newpage* are not called, and if the string will not fit on the remainder of the existing line, then the result is undefined (unless the programmer has provided for this contingency by providing a *physical file end* procedure (see 7.4.4.2)). Otherwise the **string** is output with no preceding space.

If an item is a multiple (structure) (**bits**), then its component elements (fields) (**bools**) are output in turn according to the above rules. This is discussed more fully in 7.5.1 (7.4.1) under the heading of "straightening".

7.1.2. Formatless input

This is achieved by means of the procedure *read* [R 10.5.2.2] . e.g.:

(E5)   *read (x); read (i); read (p); read (c); read (s); read (z);*
        read (t); read (r)

The modes of the actual-parameters in these examples are, respectively:

> **ref real, ref int, ref bool, ref char, ref string, ref compl,**
> **ref bits, ref bytes**

In addition, references to multiples and references to structures made up of any of the modes referred to can be used. The actual-parameter is in fact a firm unitary-clause, which means that

(E6)   *read (xx)*

is allowed, where *xx* is of mode **ref ref real** and must be dereferenced once. The quantity actually input, of course, is of mode **real, int,** etc. The actual-parameter yields the name of the place where it is to be put. Note that it is not possible to input names, or **formats**, or routines or **unions** (1.6, 2.6).

It is possible to input more than one item with one call on read:

(E7)   *read ((x, i, p, c, s, z, t, r))*

which is entirely equivalent to the series of separate *read*s given above. Note the additional parentheses (these are required because the list of items is really a row-display (see 3.5.1)).

The following layout procedures [R 10.5.1.2.o,p,q,r] may be called upon in between calls of *read*:

identifier of **proc**	mode	
newpage	proc(file)	ignore the rest of the current page and start reading the next
newline	proc(file)	ignore the rest of the current line, and start reading the next
space	proc(file)	ignore the next character
backspace	proc(file)	move back one character (but not beyond the start of the current line). A subsequent call on *read* will yield the last character again

These layout procedures (and other **proc** *(file)*s (see 7.2.6) written by the user) may also be called upon within a call of *read*. Thus:

(E8)   *read ((newpage, s, newline, x))*

means the same as:

(E9)   *newpage (stand in);*
       read (s);
       newline (stand in);
       read (x)

The *stand in* parameter specifies the **file** (see 7.2.1) to be affected. The **file** *stand in* is automatically implied by *read*, and is therefore supplied as the parameter of these routines when they occur within it.

When *read* is called, the mode of each item required is identified, and appropriate action taken as follows:

   ints, **real**s, **compl**s, **bool**s:

The input stream is searched for the first character that is not space (*newline* and *newpage* being called as necessary). When it is found, the required item is read in (note that when **real** is called for, an **int** will suffice). If no recognisable item is found, then the result is undefined (unless the user has provided a *char error* procedure (see 7.4.4.5)). The following examples are acceptable:

```
+123456
+    456
   +456
-1
123456
12.3456
-  12.34
1.23456₁₀+11
1.23456e-2
12₁₀12
12.34 ⊥ 1.23456₁₀12
1 (for true)
0 (for false)
```

Any alternative character (i or j perhaps) may be accepted for "⊥", if the user has provided a suitable *char error* procedure (see 7.4.4.5).

    chars:

The next-character (possibly space) is read from the input stream, *newline* or *newpage* being first called if necessary.

    ℓ   **string**s (or other flexible [ ] **char**s):

Characters are read from the current position until either the end of the current line is reached, or (if the user has specified a *term* (see 7.4.2)) one of the terminating characters is found (this character is not yielded as part of the **string**, but will be read by the next *read*). If you do not want to have the **string** stopped by the end of the line (but only by the *term*), you may provide a *physical file end* procedure (7.4.4.2) to call *newline* automatically.

    [*m* : *n*] **char**s (i.e. a multiple with strict bounds) and **byte**s:

The exact number of **char**s needed (i.e. $n-m+1$ or *bytes width*) is read. If the end of the line is reached before this, the action is undefined unless the user has provided a *physical file end* procedure (see 7.4.4.2).

If an item refers to a multiple value (structure) (**bits**), then its component elements (fields) (**bools**) are sought in turn according to the above rules. This is discussed more fully in 7.5.1 (7.4.1) under the heading of "straightening". The number of elements expected in a multiple value (other than a **string**) is the number contained in the existing multiple referred to by the item.

Vertical readers, please turn to 8.1.

7.2. Files

7.2.1. Channels, books and files

Your particular-program communicates with its environment via facilities termed "channels" [R 10.5.1]. A channel may be anything from a keyboard to a wind tunnel, with all the usual peripherals (tape, cards, magnetic tape, discs) coming in between. We distinguish between "character transput" (in which the external representation of the data is potentially readable) and "binary transput" (in which it is not, and which we shall not consider until 7.7).

Confining ourselves, then, to character transput (although some channels may be able to accommodate both varieties), it is convenient to imagine that at the other end of the channel is a "book" (or maybe several books). Some channels permit the program to read the book, and some to write in it. Some very accommodating ones will permit both, and may even allow you to browse through the pages in any order. A program connected to several paper tape readers would be reading several such books through one channel (a channel is thus a type of device, rather than an individual piece of hardware). This channel would presumably permit reading (*get possible*), forbid writing (⌐ *put possible*), would insist that the book be read in strict sequence (⌐ *reset possible* and ⌐*set possible*) but might conceivably agree to provide data in binary (*bin possible*).

A book has pages, lines and characters, the maximum number of each of which (*max page, max line, max char*) may be limited by the channel, although the actual book may be smaller. The "current position" is the position of the character you are about to read or write, identified by its page, line and character number. New readers are advised to start at *(1,1,1)*. If, by some mischance, you find yourself at a current position not permitted by *max page, max line* or *max char*, then you are outside the "physical" book. If the book has been written, but not right up to its end, then the "end of file" is the page, line and character number which were due to be written on next. New writers are recommended to start on an empty book with its end of file at

(1, 1, 1). If by some further mischance you contrive to get your current position beyond your end of file, then you are outside the "logical" book.

A book has a title, its "identification", which you may use to ensure that you get the right one. If the channel does not provide this facility (¬ *idf possible*), then you must rely upon the operator or the operating system to known your requirements in advance, in a manner left undefined by the Report. Some channels may allow you to change the identification of the book (*reidf possible*). For your convenience when referring to the book from within your program, we provide an identifier for it, and with this we associate a record containing useful information (as detailed in 7.4.2). This record is of a special mode called **file** (in actual fact a **file** is a particular form of structure (1.4), and there is no reason why several **files** should not refer to one book, nor why one **file** should not be assigned to another). **files** may be declared thus:

(E1)   **file** *my input, my output;*

The process of causing a **file** to refer to a book is known as "opening" the **file** (see 7.2.3 below). Initially, every particular program is provided with one book to read, one to be written, and one to browse in. These are already opened in the standard-prelude [R 10.5.1.3] (and are closed in the standard-postlude), and are referred to by **files** called:

stand in		*stand in channel*
stand out	the books being accessed	*stand out channel*
stand back	by channels called	*stand back channel*

The properties of these standard channels are given by

	stand in channel	*stand out channel*	*stand back channel*
set possible			true
reset possible			true
get possible	true		true
put possible		true	true
bin possible			true
idf possible			
reidf possible			

You may open further **files** on these and other channels up to a maximum permitted by the implementation:

(E2) open *(my input, "BOOK.1", stand in channel);*
create *(my output, special printer channel)*

The results of the first of these can be represented thus:

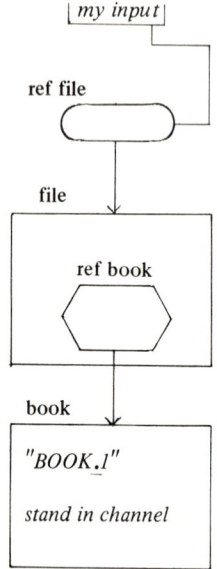

The procedures *print* and *read* introduced in 7.1 automatically use the books referred to by *stand in* and *stand out*. Two further procedures *put* and *get* perform identical functions for other **files**. These must specify some **file**, and are such that:

print (XXXXX) is equivalent to *put (stand out, XXXXX)*
read (XXXXX) is equivalent to *get (stand in, XXXXX)*

7.2.2. Environment enquiries

You will see, therefore, that channels have lots of useful properties. What we need are some more environment enquiries (see 6.2.1) to guide us [R 10.5.1.1]:

identifier of constant	mode	value
nmb channels	**int**	the number of channels (i.e. facilities) recognised
set possible	[*1:nmb channels*] **bool**	**true** if the channel permits random access
reset possible	[*1:nmb channels*] **bool**	**true** if the current position can be reset to *(1,1,1)* (e.g. rewind on magnetic tape)
get possible	[*1:nmb channels*] **bool**	**true** if input is possible through the channel
put possible	[*1:nmb channels*] **bool**	**true** if output is possible through the channel
bin possible	[*1:nmb channels*] **bool**	**true** if binary transput is possible through the channel
idf possible	[*1:nmb channels*] **bool**	**true** if the book required on the channel can be identified by a **string**
reidf possible	[*1:nmb channels*] **bool**	**true** if (*idf* presumably being *possible* also) the **string** which identifies the book can be changed by *reidf* (7.2.3)
max nmb files	[*1:nmb channels*] **int**	the maximum number of books which may simultaneously be read through the channel
max page	[*1:nmb channels*] **int**	the maximum number of pages permitted to a book on the channel
max line	[*1:nmb channels*] **int**	the maximum number of lines to a page in a book on the channel
max char	[*1:nmb channels*] **int**	the maximum number of characters to a line in a book on the channel
stand in channel	**int**	the channel number on which the file *stand in* is opened
stand out channel	**int**	the channel number on which the file *stand out* is opened
stand back channel	**int**	the channel number on which the file *stand back* is opened

Some further environment enquiries will be given in 7.5.3.

Each channel thus has a channel number, peculiar to the implementation. However, implementations will doubtless create, in their library preludes (1.1), identifiers to possess these numbers, on the lines of *stand in channel* etc. Thus users will rarely have to quote actual **int** denotations when opening files.

7.2.3. Procedures for opening and closing
[R 10.5.1.2]

identifier of proc	mode	
open	proc(ref file *file*, string *idf*, int *ch)*	Attach file to an existing book with identification *idf* (or, if *idf* = "", to whatever book (if any) was last closed on channel *ch*, or to one provided by the operator or the system) through channel *ch* (or ignore *idf* if ¬*idf possible* [*ch*]). The book will already contain writing up to some end of file, and it will have some number of pages, lines and characters consistent with the maxima for the channel. Undefined if no such book.
establish	proc(ref file *file*, string *idf*, int *mp, ml, mc*, int *ch)*	Create a new, empty book with identification *idf* and with *mp* pages each of *ml* lines of *mc* characters. Attach *file* to this book through channel *ch* (with which *mp*, *ml* and *mc* must be consistent).
create	proc(ref file *file*, int *ch)*	Create a new, empty book with identification " " (i.e. an empty string), and with the maximum number of pages, lines and characters permitted by the channel *ch*. Attach *file* to this book through *ch*.

Note that in *establish* and *create* an identification is given to the book, even though *idf* may not be *possible* on *ch*. This may still be relevant if the book is subsequently opened on another channel for which *idf* is *possible*.

When an existing book is opened, its current position will be as left when it was last closed (assuming it had been used earlier in the same elaboration of the program). If this is its first opening during the current elaboration, its current position will be as provided by the operating system — i.e. presumably at *(1, 1, 1)*.

identifier of proc	mode	
scratch	proc *(file file)*	detach the book (if any) referred to by *file* and burn it
close	proc *(file file)*	detach the book from *file* (but it may subsequently be opened again via the same channel)
lock	proc *(file file)*	Detach the book from *file*. It may not be re-opened during the same elaboration of the program.
reidf	proc *(file file, string idf)*	change the identification (if any) of the book referred to *idf* (*idf* and *reidf* must be *possible*)

Note that, if two **files** are declared, and one is assigned to the other, then they both refer to the same book. For the application of such assignations, see 7.4.1. However, the **files** *stand in*, *stand out* and *stand back* cannot be assigned to (this is because they are of mode **file** whereas files declared as in E1 are actually of mode **ref file**) [R 10.5.1.3].

7.2.4. Procedures for interrogating **files**.

[R 10.5.1.2]

identifier of proc	mode	
file available	**proc***(***int** *ch)***bool**	**true** if *max nmb files* [*ch*] has not yet been reached (i.e. books may still be opened on the channel)
logical file ended	**proc***(***file** *file)* **bool**	**true** if you have read the book up to (or beyond) its end of file, else **false** (which includes getting there by writing, and which is always yielded if *set possible*, or after the **file** has just been *establish*ed or *reset* (but not yet read)). E.g. reading a magnetic tape beyond the portion that has been written would yield **true**.

identifier of **proc**	mode	
file ended	**proc**(**file** *file*)**bool**	**true** if the current page of the book is outside the physical book (see 7.2.1) E.g. reaching the end-of-tape marker on magnetic tape, or reading it backwards to the start-of-tape marker
page ended	**proc**(**file** *file*)**bool**	**true** if the current line number of the book is outside the physical page
line ended	**proc**(**file** *file*)**bool**	**true** if the current character number of the book is outside the physical line
page number	**proc**(**file** *file*)**int**	the current page number of the book
line number	**proc**(**file** *file*)**int**	the current line number of the book
char number	**proc**(**file** *file*)**int**	the current character number of the book. N.B. the page, line and character number between them define the character position about to be read from or written to.

7.2.5. Procedures for changing the current position
[R 10.5.1.2]

identifier of **proc**	mode	
set	**proc**(**file** *file*, **int** *p, l, c*)	Set the current position of the book referred to to *(p, l, c)*. Only meaningful if *set possible*. See 7.7.1 for applications.
reset	**proc**(**file** *file*)	Reset the current position to *(1, 1, 1)*. Only meaningful if *reset possible*. See 7.7.2 for further effects.
newpage	**proc**(**file** *file*)	see 7.7.1 and 7.1.2
newline	**proc**(**file** *file*)	see 7.1.1 and 7.1.2
space	**proc**(**file** *file*)	see 7.1.1 and 7.1.2
backspace	**proc**(**file** *file*)	see 7.1.1 and 7.1.2

7.2.6. Layout procedures

It will be recalled that procedures of mode **proc** *(file)* (or firmly coerceable thereto) may appear as actual-parameters in calls of *get*, *read* (7.1.2), *put* and *print* (7.1.1). Of course, any procedure of this mode written by the user is acceptable in such positions. Of the procedures defined in the standard-prelude, the following are the relevant ones:

>*backspace*, *space*, *newline*, *newpage*, *reset*, *scratch*, *close*, *lock*.

Note that where such procedures are called from inside *read*, etc. they need no actual-parameter. In other places, the **file** must be specified.

Vertical readers, please turn to 8.2.

7.4. Structures and error situations

7.4.1. Straightening of structures

Given:

(E1)   **struct** *(* **int** *a,* **real** *b,* **compl** *c,* **char** *d, ...) s;*

then *print (s)* (or *put, get, read*, etc.) is equivalent to

(E2)   *print((a* **of** *s, b* **of** *s, c* **of** *s, d* **of** *s, ...))*

In other words, the fields of *s*, taken in the order in which they were declared, are *print*ed (or *put*, or *got*, or *read*) in accordance with whatever rules are applicable to their modes. This is known as straightening [R 10.5.0.2]. If one of the fields is a further structure, then that field itself is also straightened, and so on. Note, however, that although the mode **compl** is a **struct**, it is specifically forbidden from being straightened into two **real**s.

Clearly, since the transput of names and routines and **format**s, and the input of **union**s is forbidden (at least so far as the transput routines declared within the standard-prelude are concerned), it follows that these things cannot appear in **struct**s that are to be transput.

For straightening of multiple values, see 7.5.1.

7.4.2. Files

A **file** is, in reality, a **struct**, being declared in the standard prelude [R 10.5.1.2.a] somewhat like this:

(E3)   **struct file** = (**string** *term*,
                          proc bool *logical file end,*
                                        physical file end,
                                        format end,
                                        value error,
                          proc (**ref char**)**bool** *char error,*
                          proc (**int**)**bool** *other error,*
                          etc, etc, etc)

The "etc, etc, etc" are a series of secret fields, whose selectors are not available to you, so that you cannot make use of them. Essentially, they constitute a reference to the book attached to the **file**. Thus, if you declare two **file**s, open a book on one, and then assign it to the other:

(E4)   **file** *first, second;*
           open (first, "bookname", channel);
           second := first;

you arrive at the situation shown on the next page.
Now, both **file**s must inevitably refer to the same book, and there is no way in which you can change this. However, if you make one of the accessible fields different in the two versions, then you may get different results when you use them:

(E5)   *term* **of** *first* := *"A";*
           term **of** *second* := *"BC";*
           string *s;*
           get (first, s);
           comment will read in a **string** of characters from the current
                     position up to the end of the current line, or up to
                     an *"A"* (whichever occurs first) (see 7.1.1) ¢
           get (second, s);
           comment will read in a **string** from the same book as before,
                     starting from where the previous *get* left off
                     (presumably starting with an *"A"* in this case) and
                     reading up to the end of the line, or until either a
                     "B" or a *"C"* is encountered ¢

Since some of the fields of a **file** are secret, there is no way in which you can set them other than by assigning another complete **file**, or by *open*ing. It is not possible, for example, to assign a structure-display to a **file**, because

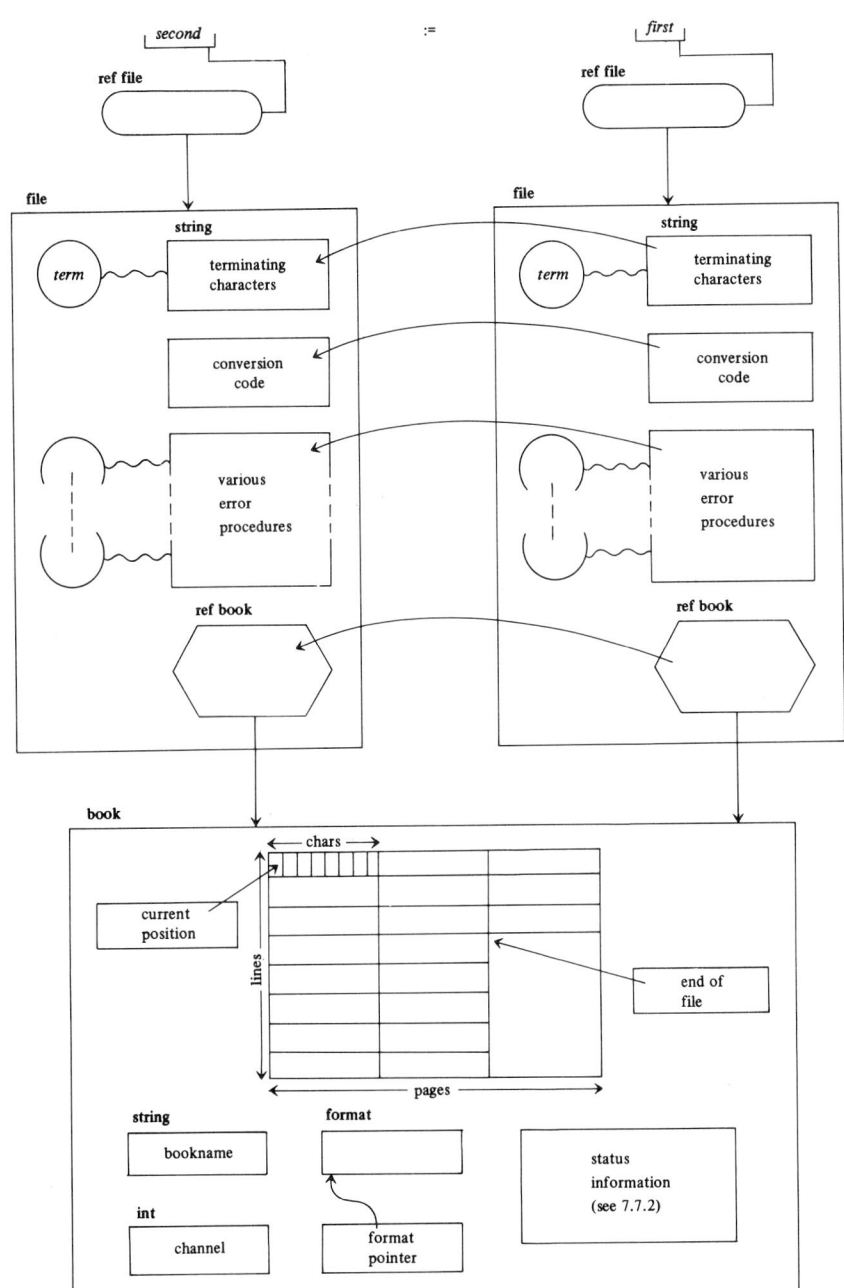

you cannot construct the fields that would be needed to go in it *.

Note, however, that the fields of *stand in*, *stand out* and *stand back* cannot be altered (see 7.2.3).

The use of *term* should be apparent from the above example. The use of the other fields will now be described.

7.4.3. Code conversion

All transput is really a matter of sending **char**s to or from a book. The function of the various transput procedures (*put*, *get*, etc.) is basically to convert the value on hand to or from **string**s of **char**s, and to transput the latter. You will doubtless have observed that internally we have been talking of "chars" — that is the internal objects of mode **char** which can be handled by an ALGOL 68 program. The things which we write in the book (i.e. the external representations) we have been talking of as "characters".

The relationship between these is determined by a conversion rule, and the conversion rule is kept in one of the secret fields of the **file**. A standard conversion rule is provided for each channel, and the intention is that the library-prelude of your implementation will provide additional ones to suit any special codes with with your installation may have to deal.

An environment enquiry (of a sort) [R 10.5.1.m] provides the standard rules, and a procedure [R 10.5.1.2.z] attaches them to the **file**.

identifier	mode	value
stand conv	[*1:nmb channels*] secret	gives the standard conversion for each channel
make conv	**proc** (**ref file** *file*, secret *c*)	associates the conversion rule *c* with *file*

The mode **secret** is not really called **secret**, so you cannot do anything

---

* Pedantically speaking, this is not quite true. Your compiler ought not to complain upon seeing:

>   **file** *f* := (skip, skip, skip, skip, skip, skip,
>   skip, skip, ( ), skip, false, false,
>   false, false, ((**ref char** *a*)**bool**: false),
>   skip)

but we would not like to take any bets on it.

with it, except use it in *make conv*. When a **file** is *open*ed (or *establish*ed or *creat*ed) on a channel, it is set up with the appropriate *stand conv*. When a **file** is assigned, its *conv* goes with it.

(E6) **file** *first, second;*
 open (first, "bookname", stand in channel);
 second := first;
 make conv (second, special conv);
  ¢ supposing that *special conv* is available in the
   particular library-prelude ¢
 get (first, s); ¢ reads a **string** according to the standard ¢
 get (second, s); ¢ reads the next **string** from the same
   book, according to *special conv* ¢
 make conv (second, stand conv [*stand in channel*] *);*
  ¢ restores the original rule ¢
 get (second, s) ¢ now does the same as *get (first, s)*
   would have done ¢

Each conversion rule, on output, yields a certain character for each **char** (possibly the same character for several **char**s). On input, the reverse translation is made [R 10.5.1.2.l,m] . If several **char**s belong to one character, that of the lowest **abs** (see 6.1.1) is yielded.

7.4.4. Error procedures

The remaining fields in **file** are error procedures [R 10.5.1.kk] — not that all the circumstances in which they might be called need be regarded as errors. Rather they are provided to enable some user-defined action to take place when, for example, the end of a page is reached, without the user having to insert a test for this at the end of every transput call.

They all yield some **bool** value, and their default state, as left by *open, create* or *establish*, is to yield the value **false** (except for *other error* which is undefined). If you write some routine of your own, and assign it to one of the procedures **of** your **file**, then you may do what you like inside it, but there are three ways in which you may finish it:
 1) yield **false**. In this case you are asking the transput routine which called you in to continue by taking its default action (which in some cases is left undefined by the Report, but which should then be some sensible system action).
 2) yield **true**. In this case the calling routine will presume that you have corrected the situation to your satisfaction, and it will continue with next business.

3) jump right out of (i.e. terminate) your routine. In this case, the calling routine is terminated also. However, you must be sure that the label to which you jump is in the same reach as that in which your routine was declared, or in a surrounding range (**else** you will be in identification trouble (see 3.2.3)).

In cases 1) and 2), you may alter any of the values associated with the book (e.g. the current position – by *newline*, *reset*, etc. – or the **format**, or the contents) but if you alter the values associated with the **file** (i.e. the *term*, the *con*version code, the error procedures, or the name of the book referred to) the change will not be effective until the routine which called you has itself been completed. This is because the relevant formal-parameter of these routines (*get*, *put*, *in*, *out*, etc.) is of mode **file** rather than **ref file**. However, practical implementations will in fact probably make such changes effective immediately, in which case you could indeed, if you were told by *physical file end* that you had filled up a reel of magnetic tape, immediately open a fresh reel.

Beware of assigning a **proc** to a field **of** a **file** if its scope (4.2.3) is smaller than that of the **file**. If necessary, you must declare a copy of the **file** with the scope of the proposed routine, so that the original **file** can continue to use its original routine outside this scope. A good example of this technique can be found in the Report at 10.5.1.kk.a.

We shall now consider the various routines and their uses.

7.4.4.1. Logical file end

This is called by input routines (*read*, *get*, *inf*, *in* (see 7.6.3) and *get bin* (see 7.7.1) when using channels for which *logical file ended* (7.2.4) could yield **true** (i.e. those with ⌐*set possible*) [R 10.5.1.2.g,l,m] . Input continues right up to the last character present in the book before the end of the file. If a further character is demanded, then the *logical file end* **of** the **file** is called. If this yields **false** (or if no such routine is provided) then the further elaboration is undefined (presumably the implementation halts the program with suitable diagnostics). If it yields **true**, then a further attempt is made to input the character.

The most likely action of the user's routine here is to recognise that his input data is ended, and to take steps to commence the next phase of his program.

7.4.4.2. Physical file end

This is called by all the provided transput routines when, with a character waiting to be transput, *file ended*, *page ended* or *line ended* (7.2.4) would yield **true** [R 10.5.1.2.g,l,m]. The action taken is similar to the previous case — if **false** is yielded the result is undefined (except when reading **strings** (7.1.2)); if **true** the character is tried again.

Thus the user may take the opportunity to call *newline*, or *newpage* (perhaps outputting some heading and page number as he does so).

7.4.4.3. Format end

This is called by the formatted transput routines (*in*, *inf*, *out*, *outf* (see 7.6.3)) when the **format** is exhausted [R 10.5.3.1,2]. It may yield **false** whereupon the previous **format** associated with the book is repeated, or it may provide a fresh **format** and yield **true**. Examples of the use of *format end* are given in 8.6.1.

7.4.4.4. Value error

This is called by the formatted transput routines (7.6.3) when the (internal) value on hand is incompatible with the current picture [R 10.5.3.1,2]. For example, on output the picture may provide too few digits, on input the value yielded may be too large to store (e.g. $>$ *max int*), and in either case the mode of the picture may be wrong. If **true** is yielded, the offending value and picture are skipped; otherwise the result is undefined, except that with *out* and *outf* the value is first output with *put*.

7.4.4.5. Char error

This is called by the input routines (*read*, *get*, *inf*, and *in* (see 7.6.3) when the converted **char** read from the book does not tie up with the sort of value expected (e.g. a letter is found when a number has been called for) or when the character in the book does not correspond to any **char** (e.g. a parity error) [R 10.5.3.2.f]. With the call is provided the name of a **char** which it is proposed to substitute for the offender in order that input may continue. If **false** is yielded, then the implementation will take its own action (e.g. diagnostic message) after which the substitution may duly be made (although the user's routine may nevertheless have taken some note of the error). Alternatively, the user's routine may yield **true**, after possibly having assigned some alternative **char** to be used in place of the suggested one.

The suggestions that will be made in various circumstances are as follows:

Expected	suggestion
a number (unformatted)	0
a digit or supressed zero (formatted)	0
a decimal point (formatted)	
$_{10}$ (formatted)	10
i (for **compl**) (formatted or unformatted)	i
a **bool** value (formatted or unformatted)	**0** (i.e. **false**)

If the user, in this routine, wants to examine the offending character, he has only to backspace the **file** and use *get*. If he decides the offending character should be a candidate for the next input operation, he has only to leave the **file** backspaced.

In the case of an unrecognised character, the suggestion will be "$\underline{\ }$" (i.e. a space).

7.4.4.6. Other error

This routine is never called by the transput routines provided, but it is available for individual implementations to use as they please. Thus it may be used by additional transput routines defined in the library-prelude, or by the provided routines when some situation not covered above (e.g. hardware error) arises.

The routine is provided with an **int** parameter, and must yield a **bool**.

Vertical readers, please turn to 8.4.

7.5. Rows and strings

7.5.1. Straightening of multiple values

Given:

(E1) $\qquad$ [*1:n, 1:4*] **int** *j2;*

then *print(j2)* (or *put, get, read,* etc.) is equivalent to:

(E2) $\qquad$ *print((j2[1,1], j2[1,2], j2[1,3], j2[1,4],*
$\qquad\qquad$ *j2[2,1], j2[2,2], j2[2,3], j2[2,4],*
$\qquad\qquad$ *j2[3,1], j2[3,2], j2[3,3], j2[3,4],*
$\qquad\qquad$ *. . . . .))*

In other words, the rows of *j2*, and within them the elements of each row, are *print*ed (or *put*, or *got*, or *read*) in accordance with whatever rules are applicable to their mode. This is known as straightening [R 10.5.0.2]. If one of the elements is a structure, then it itself is straightened in accordance with 7.4.1 and if a field of a structure is itself a multiple, then it is straightened as above, and so on. Note, however, that a **string** or other [ ] **char** is never straightened into its constituent **char**s. **bytes** is straightened only to [ ] **char**, but **bits** is straightened all the way to its constituent **bool**s.

7.5.2. Conversion procedures

Basically, non-binary transput consists of considering values of various modes and converting these value to or from **string**s. It is the **string**s which are transput across the channel to or from the book.

print, *put*, *read* and *get* provide certain fixed rules for converting **int**s, **real**s, **compl**s, **bool**s, etc. (7.1.1 and 7.1.2). These are quick and easy to use, but they may not always provide the layout you want, in which case you must do-it-yourself (or you might consider formatted transput (7.6)). You can always transput a **string**, and so you use one of the following do-it-yourself procedures [R 10.5.2.1,2] to make (or use) your own **string**:

identifier of **proc**	mode	
int string	**proc**/**int** *i*, **int** *w*, **int** *r*/ **string**	Converts *i* into a **string** of *w* digits, including sign, using radix *r* ($1 < r \leq 16$). The **char**s *a* to *f* are used for the digits *10* to *15*. Yields an empty **string** if *w* digits are not enough or *r* is out of range.
real string	**proc**/**real** *x*, **int** *w*, **int** *d*, **int** *e*/**string**	Converts *x* into a **string** of *w* **char**s consisting of: the sign of the mantissa. the integral part of the mantissa (*w-d-e-4* digits) a decimal point the fractional part of the mantissa (*d* digits, $d \geq 0$) a lowered ten the sign of the exponent the decimal exponent (*e* digits, $e \geq 1$) Yields an empty **string** if the exponent is too large for *e* digits.

identifier of **proc**	mode	
dec string	**proc**(**real** x, **int** w, **int** d)**string**	Converts x into a **string** of w **chars** consisting of: 　the sign 　the integral part (w-d-2 digits) 　a decimal point 　the fractional part (d digits, $d \geq 0$) Yields an empty **string** if w is not enough.
string int	**proc**(**string** x, **int** r)**int**	The **string** x must commence with + or − and must otherwise consist of digits. It is converted to an **int** using radix r ($1 < r \leq 16$). The **chars** a to f are interpreted as the digits 10 to 15. Undefined if x is not correct, or if the result $>$ *max int*.
string dec	**proc**(**string** x)**real**	The **string** x must commence with + or − and must otherwise consist of a decimal integer, or a point followed by a decimal fraction, or both. It is converted to a **real**. Undefined if x is not correct, or if the result $>$ *max real*.
string real	**proc**(**string** x)**real**	The **string** x must be as above, possibly followed by $_{10}$ or e and a signed exponent. It is converted to a **real**. Undefined if x is not correct, or if the result $>$ *max real*.
char in string	**proc**(**char** c, **ref int** i, **string** s)**bool**	Yields **true** if c is contained in s, in which case the index of its first occurrence in s is assigned to i

See 6.7.2 for **long**(**s**) versions of these.

Note that, although *string int*, *string dec* and *string real* are not obliged to work without a "+" or "−" at the beginning, or if leading spaces are present, most implementations will probably convert these cases correctly.
Examples. Given:

(E3)　　　$i := 1023; x := 999.888;$

　　　　　print(int string(i, 7, 10));　　¢ +001023　　　¢
　　　　　print(int string(i, 4, 16));　　¢ +3ff　　　　　¢
　　　　　print(real string(x, 12, 5, 2));　¢ +9.99888$_{10}$+02 ¢
　　　　　print(dec string(x, 8, 2));　　　¢ +1000.00　　　¢
　　　　　print(dec string(x, 8, 2) [2:]);　¢ 1000.00　　　¢

Given, in the book to be read, characters to yield the **string**:

"+123.456.789/A47/999.888*6/"

(E4)   **file** *file* := *stand in*; *term* **of** *file* **plus** "/";
get(file, s);
space; ¢ *to get rid of the* "/" ¢
i := *string int(s[1:4]* +*s[6:8]* +*s[10:12]*, *10)*;
get(file, s); space;
j := *string int("+"* + *s[2:*]*, 10)*;
get(file, s);
x := *string real((char in string(s[1]*, **loc int**, "+−") | "" | "+")
     + *(***int** *i; (char in string("*", i, s)* |
          s[1:i−1]+"$_{10}$"+*s[i+1:*] | *s)))*

After all of which, *i*, *j* and *x* should refer, respectively, to the values

123456789, *47* and *999888000*.

Note the two applications of *char in string* − once to see if a given **char** from the input stream was one of a certain set (in this case so that a "+" could be added if no sign was there already) and secondly to see whether some specific **char** was in the input **string** (in this case an "*" so that, if present, it could be treated as a "$_{10}$". Note also the **loc int** used as an actual-parameter when the index of the found **char**, due to be assigned to it, was not needed.

It will be seen, therefore, that the conversion routines which convert into **string**s are of use for increasing the range of facilities provided by *print* and *put*. The ones which convert from **string**s are useful when the **string** as input requires further processing before it can be converted, or where the **string** is required in both its converted and unconverted forms.

7.5.3. Conversion environment enquiries

print and *put* always output the exact number of digits necessary to represent the largest possible magnitude of the value being output. The user might wish to know what this number of digits is, either when planning the layout of his page, or when using the conversion procedures. Appropriate environment enquiries are therefore provided [R 10.5.2.1].

identifier of constant	mode	value
int width	int	the number of decimal digits required to represent *max int* (6.2.1) – not including sign
real width	int	the number of decimal digits required to represent a mantissa, such that *small real* (6.2.1) is not neglected in comparison with *1* – not including sign
exp width	int	the number of decimal digits required to represent a decimal exponent, such that *max real* (6.2.1) can be correctly represented – not including sign

See 6.7.1 for long(s) versions of these.

Vertical readers, please turn to 8.5.

7.6. Formatted transput

In formatted transput, the information about the values to be transput is presented separately from the information about how they are to be laid out. For example, given, in the book to be read, characters to yield the **string**:

"*+123.456.789/A47/999.888*6/*"

we could achieve an effect similar to example 7.5 E4 by writing:

(E1)   *inf(stand in,*
        $ + 3d x 3d x 3d "/", x 2d "/", 3d . 3d se "" d $,*
        (i, j, x))

Here, *(i, j, x)* is a list of the names to which the values input are to be assigned. In this case they are two **ref int**s and a **ref real**, but they could have been of any of the modes acceptable to *read* (7.1.2) including references to multiples and structures which would require straightening (7.4.1 and 7.5.1). The only things not permitted here are **proc/file**/s such as *newline*, *space*, etc. because these are concerned with the layout rather than the values.

The layout is controlled by the piece between the two "$"s, which is known as a '**format** denotation'. This is made up of various items known as 'frames', 'alignments' and 'literals', and the meaning of each item in this example is as follows:

item	name	effect
$		to introduce the format denotation
+	sign frame	expect a "+" or a "−"
3d	digit frame	read 3 digits
x	alignment	skip one character
3d	digit frame	read 3 digits
x	alignment	skip one character
3d	digit frame	read 3 digits
"/"	literal	the next character must be a "/"
,		This is the end of the 1st "picture". The sign and the 9 digits that have been read are to be converted and assigned to the 1st value, which is i.
x	alignment	skip one character
2d	digit frame	read 2d digits
"/"	literal	the next character must be a "/"
		This is the end of the 2nd picture. The 2 digits that have been read since the last picture are to be converted and assigned to the second value, which is j.
3d	digit frame	read 3 digits
.	point frame	expect a "."
3d	digit frame	read 3 digits
se	exponent frame	because of the s (for suppressed), no character is read for this frame, but the next digit frame will be interpreted as the start of a decimal exponent
"*"	literal	the next character must be an *
d	digit frame	read 1 digit
$		End of the format denotation and of the 3rd picture. The characters read (or implied) by its various frames are to be converted to real and assigned to the 3rd value, which is x.

Thus every character position of the input line is accounted for, and each must contain exactly what the **format** denotation says it should. Example E1 is not therefore an exact equivalent of 7.5 E4, in which a much freer layout is permitted (a "+" or "−" accepted before the 999, and the whole exponent part optional). Formatted input is therefore very suitable for punched card input, where fixed layouts are customary, but less so for paper tape where the free layouts accepted by the unformatted procedures will often be more appropriate.

For output, however, the formatted procedures will always give more control over what is printed, chiefly by their ability to include fixed information (i.e. literals) anywhere amongst the values that are being printed. For example, to print the same line that we read in in E1, we could write:

(E2)   outf(stand out,
         $ + 3d x 3d x 3d "/", "A" 2d "/", 3d . 3d se "*" d $,
         (123456789, 47, 999888000))

You will see that the **format** denotation here is almost exactly the same as before, the only difference being that here we specify the "A" that is to be printed, whereas on input we were prepared to pass over any character that might have been present. On the other hand, the alignment x is quite sufficient to ensure that a space will be output, unless some other piece of transput has tried to put some other character there. In this respect, the x behaves just like a call on *space* (7.1.1).

7.6.1. **format** denotations

A **format** denotation consists of a list of 'pictures' separated by commas, the whole being enclosed between "$"s [R 5.5]. Each picture is obeyed in turn, and if it contains any frames it is matched up against the next value that is to be transput (otherwise its insertions are performed and the next picture is taken).

Within each picture there may be found 'insertions' (which can be further subdivided into 'literals' and 'alignments'), and 'frames'. Insertions, or sequences of insertions, may be put at the beginning or end of the picture, or in between any two frames.

7.6.1.1. Literals

A literal [R 5.5.1.j] consists simply of a **string** denotation (5.5.1.1). On output, when this point in the **format** denotation is reached, the **string** denotation is printed [R 5.5.1.ii]. On input, it is "expected"; i.e. the characters read from the book at this point must match the literal — if they do not, then the result is undefined.

The **string** denotation of a literal is actually preceded by a 'replicator'. These will be described more fully in 7.6.1.4. It will suffice for the moment that a replicator can consist of either "empty" or of an **int** denotation (5.1.1.1), and that we shall indicate the possible presence of one in what follows by an "R".

(E3)   outf(stand out, $ "START" 7"." 3d $, i)

There are two literals in the one and only picture in the **format** denotation in this example. The first has an empty replicator, implying that the **string** "START" is to be printed only once. The replicator in the second shows that

"$\b.$" is to be printed 7 times, so that the characters written to the book should look like this:

   START 987

Note that if two literals occur in succession, then the second one must have a non-empty replicator, for otherwise:

(E4)   *"SMITH" "JONES"*

would be ambiguous. In fact, E4 is a single literal which would be printed out (see 5.5.1.1) as:

   SMITH"JONES

7.6.1.2. Alignments

Alignments [R 5.5.1.e] do not write any characters to the book. Their purpose is to move the current position (7.2.1) to some different page, line or char number, in a similar manner to the procedures *newpage, newline, space* and *backspace* (7.1.1 and 7.1.2) used in formatless transput. The following are the alignments permitted [R 5.5.1.hh, R 10.5.3.1.k]:

alignment	effect
Rx	call *space* the number of times specified by the replicator R. I.e. skip over R characters.
Ry	call *backspace* R times
Rl	call *newline* R times
Rp	call *newpage* R times
Rk	move the current position to char number R of the current line

(E5)   *outf(stand out;*
        $ l "ABCD" 4x 4a, 5k 4a $,
        ("IJKL", "EFGH"))

(in which *4a* is a character frame) will therefore cause to be written, on a new line in the book:

   ABCDEFGHIJKL

7.6.1.3. Frames

(Note that in the following table we have taken some slight liberties with

some of the notions defined in R 5.5. What we shall call a "frame" is, roughly speaking, halfway between the paranotions 'mould' and 'frame'.)
[R 5.5.1.ll,mm]

frame type	syntax	effect on input	effect on output
digit frame [R 5.5.2]	Rd Rsd	expect R digits	print R digits
sign frame [R 5.5.1.l]	+ − Rz+ Rz−	expect $"+"$ or $"-"$ expect $"."$ or $"-"$ pass over up to R spaces (say n), and then expect $"+"$, or $"-"$ or $"."$ as above, followed by R$-n$ digits	print $"+"$ or $"-"$ print $"."$ or $"-"$ replace up to R leading zeroes (say n) by spaces, and then print $"+"$, $"-"$ or $"."$ as above, followed by R$-n$ digits
zero frame [R 5.5.2]	Rz Rsz	expect R digits with leading zeroes replaced by spaces	print R digits with leading zeroes replaced by spaces
point frame [R 5.5.3]	. s.	expect a decimal point	print a decimal point
exponent frame	e se	expect $"_{10}"$ or $"e"$	print $"_{10}"$
complex frame [R 5.5.6]	i si	expect $"i"$	print $"i"$
radix frame [R 5.5.2]	$2r$ $4r$ $8r$ $10r$ $16r$	convert the digits read using the specified radix	convert the int being output using the specified radix, and print in accordance with the rest of the frames
character frame [R 5.5.5,7]	Ra Rsa	expect R characters	print R characters
string frame [R 5.5.7]	t	read characters up to the end of the current line or until a terminating **char** is found, as in *read* (7.1.2)	print as many characters as there are in the **string** being output
boolean frame [R 5.5.4]	b	expect $"0"$ or $"1"$	print $"0"$ or $"1"$

In all the frames listed above, if an *s* is present, then on input the expected characters are not read from the book, but input proceeds as though they had been (and in the case where digits were expected, zeroes are yielded). On output, the characters concerned are not written to the book, but are simply "thrown away".

Note that sign, point, exponent and complex frames serve a dual purpose. They indicate that a certain character is to be expected or printed (unless suppressed), and they also indicate to the conversion routines the significance of the adjacent digit frames. Here are some examples:

(E6) *x := 999888000;*
     *outf(stand out, $ +d.5de2d $, x); ¢* +9.99888$_{10}$08   ¢
     *outf(stand out, $ -5zde-zd $, x); ¢*   999888$_{10}$ 3   ¢
     *outf(stand out, $ .6de+2d $, x); ¢* .999888$_{10}$+09   ¢
     *outf(stand out, $ .5de+2d $, x); ¢* .99989$_{10}$+09   ¢
     outf(stand out, $ +11zd. $, x); ¢ +   999888000.   ¢
     outf(stand out, $ 11z+ds. $, x); ¢   +999888000   ¢
     outf(stand out, $ 9d.3d $, x); ¢   999888000.000   ¢
     outf(stand out, $ 6d3z. $, x); ¢   999888   .   ¢
     outf(stand out, $ 6d3sds. $, x); ¢   999888   ¢

As you will see, any reasonable combination of frames is permissible. Rather than try to list all the permitted cases, we shall instead point out certain compatibility restrictions [R 10.5.3.1.b, R 10.5.3.2.b] which arise with certain modes of the value being transput:

1) A radix frame (*r*) may only be used if the value is **int**.
2) Either a point frame (.) or an exponent frame (*e*) must be present if the value is **real**.
3) A complex frame (*i*) must be present if the value is **compl**, with either a point frame (.) or an exponent frame (*e*) somewhere on each side of it.
4) On output, there is no objection to having point, exponent and complex frames present when the value is **int**, nor to having a complex frame when the value is **real**, since the **int** or **real** can be widened. These cases are not acceptable on input, however.
5) Character frames (*a*) and string frames (*t*) may only be used if the value is **char** or **string** (or some other [ ] **char**).
6) A boolean frame (*b*) may only be used if the value is **bool**.
7) The order in which the various frames, in **int**, **real** or **compl** pictures, if present, must appear is as follows:

radix frame (*r*)
sign frame (+, −, *z*+, *z*−)
zero frames (*z*) and digit frames (*d*)
point frame (.)
zero frames (*z*) and digit frames (*d*)
exponent frame (*e*)
sign frame (+, −, *z*+, *z*−)
zero frames (*z*) and digit frames (*d*)
complex frame (*i*), in which case all the preceding frames may occur again

8) Character frames (*a*) must not be mixed with other types within one picture, but there may be several of them.
9) A string frame (*t*) or a boolean frame (*b*) must be the one and only frame of its picture.

Here are some more examples, illustrating **compls**, **bools** and **strings** (single **chars** are treated exactly like **strings**):

(E7) *outf(stand out,* $ *2z−d.2d i −d.2de−d* $*, 37.2 i −43.4);*
  ¢ 37.20$\underline{1}$−4.34$_{10}$ 1 ¢
  outf(stand out, $ *b,b,b* $*, (* **true, false, true***));*
  ¢ $\underline{101}$ ¢
  outf(stand out, $ *4a x 4a* $*, "ABCDEFGH");*
  ¢ ABCD EFGH ¢
  file *file := stand in; term* **of** *file* **plus** *"F";*
  inf(file, $ *t* $*, s)* ¢ yields *"ABCDE"* from a book containing
  ABCDEFGH ¢

In addition to the various frames introduced above, there are two further types, known as "choices" [R 5.5.2.f, R. 5.5.4], which can be used when the value to be transput is **int** or **bool**:

(E8) *i := 4; j := 5;*
  outf(stand out;
    $ *c("SUN", "MON", "TUES", "WEDNES", "THUS", "FRI", "SATUR") "DAY"* $*,*
    i);
    ¢ prints WEDNESDAY ¢
  outf(stand out,
    $ *b("LESS$\underline{\ }$THAN", "GREATER")* $*,*
    i<j)
    ¢ prints LESS THAN ¢

On output, one of these literals is selected from the list according to the value of the **int** or the **bool**. (Note that a sequence of literals, complete with replicators (7.6.1.1), could be used in place of each of the single literals shown in the examples.) On input, one of the literals listed is expected, and a value is assigned to the **int** or **bool** accordingly. If two or more of the literals match, the earliest one in the list is taken. If it is necessary to look beyond the end of the line when checking for any particular literal, *physical file end* **of** the file (7.4.4.2) will be called.

7.6.1.4. Replicators and collections

Two types of replicator have been introduced already (7.6.1.1). These consist of "empty" and of an **int** denotation. There exists a third type, known as a 'dynamic replication' [R 5.5.1.h], which consists of an *n* followed by a CLOSED **int** clause (3.2.4):

(E9)   **proc** *digits in* = *(* **int** *i)* **int**: **entier***(ln(i)/ln(10)+1)*;
         j := *0*;
         for *i* **to** *4* **do**
            begin
            j **times** *10* **plus** *i;*
            outf(stand out, $ *l n(digits in(j))d* $, *j)*
         end
         ¢ prints :   1
                      12
                      123
                      1234 ¢

All such CLOSED **int** clauses in a **format** denotation together with the values to be transput are elaborated collaterally at the time that *outf* (or *inf*) is called [R 5.8.2.b], so that you may assume nothing about the order in which things happen. If the expression of a dynamic-replication yields a negative value, then zero is assumed.

Replicators may also be used to cause a 'collection' of pictures within a format to be repeated. This is particularly useful when a multiple value of flexible size is to be transput:

(E10)   [*1:0* **flex**] **struct** *(* **int** *i,* **char** *a) ic1* := *((1,"A"), (2,"B"), (3,"C"), (4,"D"))*;
        outf(stand out,
                $ *p   n(*upb *ic1)(4z+d,   2x a l), "TOTAL=" 3z+d* $,
            (ic1, (**int** *i := 0;* **for** *j* **to** upb *ic1* **do**
                i **plus** *i* **of** *ic1*[*j*] *; i)))*

¢ which will print out, on a new page:
```
    +1   A .
    +2   B
    +3   C
    +4   D
 TOTAL=   +10 ¢
```

Such replicated collections can, of course, be nested to any depth. Moreover the grouping of the pictures so defined need not correspond to any natural grouping in the values being transput:

(E11)   [1:4] int j1 := (999,999,999,999), k1 := (888,888,888,888);
outf(stand out,
$ 3d, 3(3"A" 2(3d x) 3x), 3d $,
(j1, k1))
¢ which would print:
999AAA999 999   AAA999.888   AAA888 888   888¢

In this example, j1 and k1 are first straightened (7.5.1). The changeover from the values arising from j1 to those arising from k1 actually takes place half way through the second repetition of the outermost collection — this is slightly odd, but perfectly permissible.

7.6.2. formats

We shall now introduce a new mode, known as **format**. As with the other primitive modes (**real, int, bool, char**), you may declare **format**s, assign them, refer to them, construct multiples and structures and **union**s out of them, invent **proc**s that deliver them, and you could in principle have operators operating upon them, except for the fact that no such operators are in fact defined in the standard prelude, and there is no way in which you could construct your own. About the only thing you cannot do with a **format** is to transput it.

The value of a **format** is the internal object possessed by some **format** denotation (7.6.1). Moreover, since there are no operators for **format**s, the value of any **format** at any stage in the elaboration of a program, unless it is undefined, must be traceable back to a **format** denotation somewhere in that program. A value of mode **format** (or one strongly coerceable thereto) can stand as an actual-parameter of *inf* or *outf*:

(E12)   **format** *f;* ¢ *f* is therefore of mode **ref format** ¢
     f := $ + *n(int width)d* $;
     outf(stand out, f, 999)
     ¢ which will print something like:
     +00000999 ¢

   Because a **format** denotation can contain expressions which in turn may contain objects (e.g. names possessed by identifiers) of limited scope, it should be pointed out that the scope of a **format** denotation is determined by exactly the same rule as is applied to routines (see 4.2.3) [R 2.2.4.2.b], so that the result of the elaboration of the following is not defined:

       format *f;*
         begin
           int *i* := *4;*
           f := $ *n(i)d* $
         end
       outf(stand out, f, j)

7.6.3. The formatted transput procedures

Associated with each book is a **format** and a **format** pointer. The procedures *inf* and *outf* first of all associate a new **format** with the book referred to and set the pointer to its beginning. Then the sequence of pictures of this **format** (as expanded by performing the replication of any collections) is scanned, each picture being matched against the next value yielded by the straightening process. It may be that the sequence of pictures is exhausted before the sequence of values *(format end* **of** the file is then called (7.4.4.3), or by default the same sequence of pictures is scanned again), or vice versa, in which case the **format** pointer is left pointing at the picture which would have matched the next value. If this happens, it is possible to continue transput from this picture by calling one of the procedures *out* and *in* next time. It is also possible to supply a new **format** to the book without doing any transput, by means of the procedure *format*.

[R 10.5.3]

identifier of **proc**	mode	
format	**proc**(**file** *f*, **format** *t*)	all dynamic replications within *t* are elaborated, and the result becomes the **format** associated with the book referred to by *f*, with the format pointer pointing to the beginning of it
in	**proc**(**file** *f*, [ ] **intype** *x*)	input takes place to the names obtained by straightening the elements of *x*, in accordance with the existing **format** and pointer associated with the book referred to by *f*
inf	**proc**(**file** *f*, **format** *t*, [ ] **intype** *x*)	All dynamic replications within *t* are elaborated collaterally with *x*. The resultant **format** is associated with the book referred to by *f*, and input proceeds as in *in*.
out	**proc**(**file** *f*, [ ] **outtype** *x*)	output takes place from the values obtained by straightening the elements of *x*, in accordance with the existing **format** and pointer associated with the book referred to by *f*
outf	**proc**(**file** *f*, **format** *t*, [ ] **outtype** *x*)	All dynamic replications within *t* are elaborated collaterally with *x*. The resultant **format** is associated with the book referred to by *f*, and output proceeds as in *out*.

The modes **intype** and **outtype** (which are not really called this) [R 10.5.0.1] referred to in the table indicate the modes acceptable to *read* (7.1.2) and *print* (7.1.1), with the exception of **proc**(**file**).

7.6.4. Error situations

The various procedures which you can associate with each file in order to trap various errors during transput were described in 7.4.4. We shall now summarise the situations in which each of them can be called during formatted transput.

During both input and output:
1) The various frames, alignments and literals encountered in the **format** may bring the current position outside the physical book (7.2.1) (i.e. *max page*, *max line* or *max char* is exceeded). If a character is read from or written to the book in this situation, *physical file end* **of** the **file** is called.

2) If the end of the **format** associated with the book is reached before the straightened list of values being transput has been exhausted, then *format end* **of the file** is called.
3) If the mode of the value being transput is incompatible with the sequence of frames which occurs in the current picture (the possible causes of this were listed in 7.6.1.3), then *value error* **of the file** is called.

During input:

4) If an attempt is made to read beyond the (logical) end of the book (7.2.1), then *logical file end* **of the file** is called.
5) If the value yielded by conversion of various digits etc, in accordance with the picture, is too great for values of that mode (e.g. an **int** greater than *max int* (6.2.1)), then *value error* **of the file** is called.
6) If the character read from the book in accordance with one of the frames $d, z, +, -, ., e, i$ or b is not as expected, then *char error* **of the file** is called.
7) If a character that has been expected by a literal is not found, then the result is undefined [R 10.5.3.2.j] .
8) If none of the literals of a choice is found, then the result is undefined [R 10.5.3.2.g,h] .

During output:

9) If a value to be output cannot be converted into the number of digits specified in the picture, then *value error* **of the file** is called.
10) If a negative value is to be output, and the picture does not contain a sign frame, then *value error* **of the file** is called [R 10.5.3.1.g] .
11) If the **int** to be output by a choice is zero or negative or greater than the number of literals in the list, then the result is undefined [R 10.5.3.1.h] .

Where the result is said to be undefined, the particular implementation will take some suitable action (e.g. output of some diagnostic information), and the situation is not necessarily irrecoverable.

Vertical readers, please turn to 8.6.

7.7. Binary transput

Binary output may be used where the sole purpose of the material produced is that it should subsequently be read (during the same or some other program) by binary input. Normally, the medium used will be magnetic tape, disc or drum, but paper tape or cards can be used if your implementation permits.

During binary transput, the medium is still divided into pages, lines and chars, but it is not defined how many chars are occupied by each object that is transput, and your implementation may provide some strange values for *max page*, *max line* and *max char* (e.g. a magnetic drum might be regarded as a continuum of chars, all on the one and only line of the one and only page: on magnetic tape, a line might correspond to some block length, and on a disc a page might demarcate a region which could be accessed without head movement). Nevertheless, it will always be true that the current position will be defined by the triple *(page, line, char)*, and that it can always be inspected and manipulated by means of the facilities provided (7.2.4 and 7.2.5). In particular, the procedure *reset* can be used (7.2.5) if *reset* is *possible* (7.2.2) (as on tapes, discs and drums) and *set* can be used if *set* is *possible* (as on discs and drums). All the binary transput routines which are about to be described start from the current position, and then proceed automatically to cover as many chars, lines and pages as the values being transput may demand.

7.7.1. Binary transput procedures

In all of these procedures, the values are first straightened (7.4.1 and 7.5.1), and the straightened values are transput [R 10.5.4]. Thus all information as to how the original values were divided into structures and rows of multiple values is lost, as are the values of any bounds. Nevertheless, if the values output in this way are subsequently read back into a set of structures and multiples identical to that from which they originally came, then the new set will be an exact copy of the old.

(E1)   **struct**(**int** *a, b*)*s1, s2,* [*1:4*] **int** *i1, i2;*
              s1 := (1,2); i1 := (3,4,5,6);
              reset(stand back);
              put bin(stand back, (s1, i1));
              reset(stand back);
              get bin(stand back, (s2, i2));
                     comment we might just as well have said
                            s2 := s1; i2 := i1
                     However, if we want to mix things up: ¢
              reset(stand back);
              get bin(stand back, (i2, s2))
                 ¢ whereupon *i2* has the value *(1,2,3,4)* and *s2*
                has the value *(5,6)* ¢

identifier of proc	mode	
put bin	proc(file f, [ ] outtype x)	x is straightened and the resultant values are output to the book referred to by f, starting at the current position (which is suitably advanced)
write bin	proc([ ] outtype x)	equivalent to *put bin(stand back, x)*
get bin	proc(file f, [ ] intype x)	x is straightened to yield the names to which the values in the book referred to by f, starting at the current position (which is suitably advanced), are read
read bin	proc([ ] intype x)	equivalent to *get bin(stand back, x)*

In this table, **outtype** and **intype** have the meanings given to them in 7.6.3.

7.7.2. Some restrictions

The environment enquiries listed in 7.2.2 show what can and cannot be done with the various channels provided in an implementation. You can only do binary transput if *bin possible*. However, this is not to say that non-binary (i.e. character) transput is forbidden thereby. You are perfectly entitled to *put* and *get* to and from your disc, provided only that you are prepared to tolerate any strange page and line sizes that it may have.

There is an important distinction between channels with *set possible* (i.e. drums and discs) and the rest [R 10.5.4, R 10.5.1.2.l,m]. With *set possible*, you can roam around your book writing characters here, reading them back there, and doing binary transput in between. It is your entire responsibility to keep track of the (page, line, char) where everything has been put, and of course if you try to read back as characters that which has been written in binary, or vice versa, then the result will be quite undefined.

If, on the other hand, *set* is not *possible*, then things are different. Whenever you start off at *(1,1,1)* (after a *reset*, for example, assuming *reset possible*), you have the choice of reading or writing in characters or binary (assuming a suitable combination of *put*, *get* and *bin possible* on the channel). Thus you have 4 possibilities:

    read binary — you must carry on reading in binary.
    write binary — you must carry on writing in binary.

> read characters — you may continue reading characters up to some point, and then change to writing characters. But you must not read beyond the logical end of the file (7.2.1).
> write characters — each time you write, the logical end of the file is set to the new current position, which effectively prevents you from doing anything other than to write characters again.

Thus, with *put*, *get* and *reset possible*, but not *set possible*, the normal behaviour expected with magnetic tape is obtained. If you disobey any of these rules, then the result is undefined [R 10.5.1.2.k]. Note that when *set* is *possible*, the logical end of the file ceases to have any meaning.

The possible properties of the three standard channels were given in 7.2.1. Note that only the minimum requirements are given there, and individual implementations might, for example, allow *bin possible* on *stand in channel*.

Vertical readers, please turn to 8.7.

8. EXAMPLES

8.1. Simple examples

In this chapter, which forms the tail of the columns in our orthogonal plan, we shall show you, column by column, what you can do with the facilities described so far.

However, the language available to us at the end of this first column is rather sparse. We have shown you only the crudest form of conditional statement. **strings** have only been hinted at. You cannot declare **procs**, nor **refs**, nor even constants. Any substantial and worthwhile example within these limitations could never do justice to the expressive power of ALGOL 68, and we must therefore invite you to read further before encountering a real example in 8.2.

If shorter examples of these simple facilities are what you would like to see, then we must refer you back to the early parts of Chapter 0 (the Very Informal Introduction) where you will find many such.

Vertical readers, please turn to 1.2.

8.2. Procedure examples

8.2.1. Easter

The Gregorian Calendar, insofar as it determines upon which day each year shall start, is universally accepted throughout the world. It also fixes the date of Easter as being the next Sunday after the Paschal Full Moon, which is intended to be the first full moon occurring on or after the Vernal Equinox (March 21st). The rules given for computing this are not so widely accepted. For example, the Jewish Passover and the Orthodox Easter are determined from different (and probably more accurate) calendars.

The defining document for these rules was written by one Clavius under a commission from Pope Gregory XIII [1]. Absolute accuracy was not a prime consideration. The Full Moon is considered to occur on the fourteenth day of the lunar month (which commences with the new moon). The rule was carefully devised so that the date predicted for its new moon always fell on, or one or two days after, the true mean new moon of the astronomers — but never before it. This was to ensure that never, under any circumstances, would the Christian Easter fall on the same day as the Jewish Passover (notwithstanding which, this terrible circumstance does occasionally arise, as in 1903).

The following is a complete program for calculating the date of Easter according to the Gregorian rule. For further explanations, see [3] and [4].

    begin
        int *year, date, moon, paschal, easter;*
comment We shall reckon dates by the number of days since the start of the year.
Thus: **comment**
        int *march21st = 31 + 28 + 21;*
comment The Gregorian calendar was introduced into various parts of the world at different dates. In Great Britain, the year was: **comment**
        int *gregory start = 1752* ¢ *or whatever date you prefer* ¢ *;*
loop: read *(year);*
    if   *year < gregory start*
    then *print (("The ͔ Gregorian ͔ calendar͔was͔not͔introduced ͔ until",*
                gregory start, newline))
    else   **int** *century = year ÷ 100,*
           leap = **abs** *(year* **mod** *4 = 0* ∧ *year* **mod** *100* ≠ *0* ∨
           year **mod** *400 = 0);*
comment *leap = 1* for a leap year, and *0* otherwise. **comment**
        print ((newpage,
           year,
           if *leap = 1* **then** *"͔(Leap ͔ year)"* **else** *" "* **fi** *,*
           newline));
comment To calculate the day of the week corresponding to any date, we associate with each year a Dominical Letter, whose position in the alphabet gives the date of the first Sunday in January. **comment**
        int *dominic = 7 – (year + year ÷ 4 – century + century ÷ 4*
               – 1 – leap) **mod** *7;*
        print (("The ͔ Dominical ͔ Letter ͔ is ͔ ",
           case *dominic* **in** *"A", "B", "C", "D", "E", "F", "G"* **esac** *,*
           if   *leap = 1*
           then **case** *(dominic – 2)* **mod** *7 + 1*
               in   *"/A", "/B", "/C", "/D", "/E", "/F", "/G"*
               esac
           else   *" "*
           fi *,*
           newline));

Ch.8.2.1   EXAMPLES   303

   proc *weekday* = *(* **int** *date)* **string**:
      case *(date − dominic)* **mod** *7 + 1*
      in   *"Sunday"*, *"Monday"*, *"Tuesday"*, *"Wednesday"*,
              "Thursday", *"Friday"*, *"Saturday"*
      esac;
   proc *month* = *(* **ref int** *date)* **string**:
comment This **proc** has a **ref int** parameter which it will alter to become the date within the month. **comment**
      if   *date* ⩽ *31*   **then** *"January"*
      elsf *(date := date−31)* ⩽ *28 + leap*   **then** *"February"*
      elsf *(date := date−28−leap)* ⩽ *31*   **then** *"March"*
      elsf *(date := date−31)* ⩽ *30*   **then** *"April"*
      elsf *(date := date−30)* ⩽ *31*   **then** *"May"*
      elsf *(date := date−31)* ⩽ *30*   **then** *"June"*
      elsf *(date := date−30)* ⩽ *31*   **then** *"July"*
      elsf *(date := date−31)* ⩽ *31*   **then** *"August"*
      elsf *(date := date−31)* ⩽ *30*   **then** *"September"*
      elsf *(date := date−30)* ⩽ *31*   **then** *"October"*
      elsf *(date := date−31)* ⩽ *30*   **then** *"November"*
      else *date := date−30;* *"December"*
      fi;
comment The moon revolves around the earth once every 29.530588 days. 235 such lunations last just 1½ hours less than 19 Julian years. The calendar is therefore based on a "Metonic" cycle of 19 years, each year in a cyclic being allotted a "Golden Number" in the range 1 to 19: **comment**
      int *golden* = *year* **mod** *19 + 1*;
      print (("The_Golden_Number_is", golden, newline));
comment However, following this cycle indefinitely would introduce an error of approximately 0.43 days per century. There is therefore a correction which, for convenience, is only allowed to change at the end of a century: **comment**
      int *lilius* ¢ who is a not inherently meaningful identifier ¢
            = *(century − century ÷ 4*   ¢ *for the leap years omitted*
                                              at the start of some centuries ¢
            − *(century−(century−17) ÷ 25) ÷ 3*
                                          ¢ *the 1½ hours error* ¢
            −*8)* **mod** *30*;
comment On the 1st of January of any year, the number of days since the last new moon is given by the "Epact": **comment**

int *epact* = *(11* × *(golden−1)−lilius)* **mod** *30;*
print (("The ͺEpact ͺis", *epact, newline));*

comment If successive new moons were to occur every 30 days, then we should be able to associate with each date a unique epact, one less for each day modulo 30 (then that date would be a new moon in years with that epact). In fact, six times in the year (and once extra at the end of 19 years) we must have a lunation of only 29 days, whereupon the sequence of epacts slips back a day and some date will have two epacts listed against it. These dates have been carefully chosen (it is alleged) so as to minimise the deviation from the true moon. One of them occurs in February and so happenings in March occur exactly 59 days after those in January (or 60 in a leap year, since the intercalary day, if any, in February is automatically added to the lunation in which it occurs). Therefore, there is a new moon on: **comment**

moon := *31−epact + 59 + leap;*
if *(paschal* := *moon + 13)* < *march21st + leap*
then

comment the fourteenth day of this moon falls before the Vernal Equinox and we want the next one. The next date with two epacts against it occurs in April, the critical epact being given by: **comment**

int *clavius* = **if** *golden* > *11* **then** *26* **else** *25* **fi***;*
moon := *moon + (epact* ⩾ *clavius | 30 | 29);*
paschal := *moon + 13*

fi*;*
print (("The ͺPaschal ͺFull ͺMoon ͺfalls ͺupon ͺ.",
weekday (paschal), space,
month (date := *paschal), space));*

comment Note how we have to break off the *print* here and start another one, so that we can use the value of *date*, as calculated therein, in the next *print*. If it had all been done in one *print*, then we might have been using *date* and assigning to it at the same time (i.e. collaterally), and anything might have happened. **comment**

print ((date, newline));
print (("Easter ͺday, ͺbeing ͺthe ͺnext ͺSunday ͺafter ͺthe ͺ
Paschal ͺFull ͺMoon, ͺtherefore ͺfalls ͺupon ͺ.",
month (date := *easter* := *paschal + 7−(paschal − dominic)*
mod *7)));*
print ((date, newline))

fi*;*
go to *loop*
end

The following are the references quoted in this section:
[1] Christophorus Clavius. Kalendarium Gregorianum Perpetuum. Cum Privilegio Summi Pontificis Et Aliorum Principum. Romae, Ex Officina Dominicae Basae. MDLXXXII. Cum Licentia Superiorum. (with attached Papal Bull).
A companion volume was also prepared, and published in 1603:
[2] Christophorus Clavius. Romani Calendarii a Gregorio XIII. Pontifice Maximo restituti Explicatio.
[3] A. de Morgan. A Budget of Paradoxes. Longmans, Green & Co, 1872.
[4] Sir Harris Nicolas. The Chronology of History, containing Tables, Calculations & Statements, indispensable for ascertaining the dates of Historical Events, and of Public and Private Documents from the earliest periods to the present time. Longman, Brown, Green and Longman's, 1838.

Vertical readers, please turn to 1.3.

8.3. Examples of operators

8.3.1. Parallel plus

This example is intended to show how defining your own operators can lead to a considerable simplification of a program, at the same time making it more easy to follow.

It is well known that if two resistors A and B are placed in parallel, their combined resistance is given by:

$$\frac{1}{\frac{1}{A}+\frac{1}{B}}$$

We can now define the operator "parallel plus" (we shall represent it by **pap**) to perform this operation. **pap** is a well behaved operator, being both commutative and associative. For the sake of completeness we shall also define "parallel minus" (**pam**) and assigning versions (6.3) **paplus** and **paminus**.

Consider the following network:

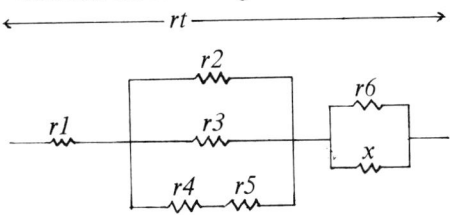

It is required to find the value of *x* such that the resistance of the whole network shall be *rt*. Here is a program to do it:

> **begin**
> **priority** pap = *7*, pam = *7*, paplus = *1*, paminus = *1*;
> **op** pap = *(* **real** *a, b)* **real** : *a* × *b* / *(a + b)*;
> **op** pam = *(* **real** *a, b)* **real** : *a* × *b* / *(b−a)*;
> **op** paplus = *(* **ref real** *a,* **real** *b)* **ref real** : *a* := *a* × *b* / *(a + b)*;
> **op** paminus = *(* **ref real** *a,* **real** *b)* **ref real** : *a* := *a* × *b* / *(b−a)*;
> **real** *rt, r1, r2, r3, r4, r5, r6*;
> *read ((rt, r1, r2, r3, r4, r5, r6))*;
> *print ((rt−(r1+r2* **pap** *r3* **pap** *(r4+r5)))* **pam** *r6)*
> **end**

Electrical engineers will realise that all these operators ought also to be defined for **compl** operands (2.4.4) and for mixed **real** and **compl**.

Vertical readers, please turn to 1.4.

8.4. Two examples of library preludes

A library-prelude (see 1.1) is an expansion of the standard-prelude. It may contain further identity-, mode-, priority- and operation-declarations for use in particular applications. A library-prelude must be throughout consistent with the standard-prelude (i.e. identifiers and indications declared in it may not conflict with those declared in the standard-prelude).

In 8.4.1 we give a library-prelude for the basic operations on vectors in a Euclidean space E_3, the vectors being declared as

> **mode vec** = **struct** *(* **real** *xcoord, ycoord, zcoord)*;

In Section 8.5 we give a library-prelude for the basic operations on vectors in E_n (n arbitrary) which is more general, but also less simple than this one.

In 8.4.2 we give a library-prelude for the basic operations on rational numbers, declared as

> **mode rat** = **struct** *(* **int** *numerator, denominator)*;

The declarations in 8.4.1 and 8.4.2 (and also those in 8.5) are fully consistent with each other and may, therefore, be joined into one library-prelude without any precaution. They may be regarded as one of many possible expansions of the language. Their intention is to demonstrate the expressive power and efficient elegance of the language, and to suggest how to do away

8.4.1. EXAMPLES

in practice with dialects and specific languages for use in particular problems.

8.4.1. Operations on vectors in E_3

mode vec = **struct** (**real** *xcoord* , *ycoord* , *zcoord*) ;

(1)   **priority** parl = 5 , perp = 5 , proj = 6 ;
(2)   **op** x   = (**vec** u) **real**: *xcoord* **of** u ;
(3)   **op** y   = (**vec** u) **real**: *ycoord* **of** u ;
(4)   **op** z   = (**vec** u) **real**: *zcoord* **of** u ;
(5)   **op** +   = (**vec** u) **vec**: u ;
(6)   **op** −   = (**vec** u) **vec**: (−xu , −yu , −zu) ;
(7)   **op** +   = (**vec** u , v) **vec**: (xu + xv , yu + yv , zu + zv) ;
(8)   **op** −   = (**vec** u , v) **vec**: (xu − xv , yu − yv , zu − zv) ;
(9)   **op** ×   = (**real** r , **vec** u) ¢ *the product of a scalar and a vector* ¢
                      vec: (r × xu , r × yu , r × zu) ;
(10) **op** ×   = (**vec** u , **real** r) ¢ *the product of a vector and a scalar* ¢
                      vec: r × u ;
(11) **op** /   = (**vec** u , **real** r) ¢ *the quotient of a vector and a scalar* ¢
                      vec: (xu / r, yu / r, zu / r) ;
(12) **op** ×   = (**vec** u , v) ¢ *the innerproduct* ¢ **real**:
                      xu × xv + yu × yv + zu × zv ;
(13) **op** ××   = (**vec** u , v) ¢ *the vectorproduct* ¢ **vec**:
                      (yu × zv − zu × yv ,
                        zu × xv − xu × zv ,
                        xu × yv − yu × xv) ;
(14) **op** norm   = (**vec** u) **real**: *sqrt* (u × u) ;
(15) **op** e   = (**vec** u) ¢ *the unit vector in the direction of u* ¢ **vec**:
                      (eps u | skip | (1/norm u) × u) ;
(16) **real** *eps* = c *some small enough real number* c ;
(17) **op** eps   = (**real** r) **bool**: abs r < *eps* ;
(18) **op** eps   = (**vec** u) **bool**: eps norm u ;
(19) **op** parl   = (**vec** u , v) ¢ *parallel ?* ¢   **bool**: eps (eu ×× ev) ;
(20) **op** perp   = (**vec** u , v) ¢ *perpendicular ?* ¢ **bool**: eps (eu × ev) ;
(21) **op** proj   = (**vec** u , v) ¢ *the projection of u on a plane*
                      perpendicular to v ¢ **vec**:
                      (**vec** ew = e ((v ×× u) ×× v) ; (u × ew) × ew) ;
(22) **proc** *angle* = (**vec** u , v) ¢ *the angle between u and v* ¢ **real**:
                      arccos (eu × ev) ;

(23) **proc** *plane* = *(* **vec** *u* , *v* , *w* *)* ¢ *in one plane ?* ¢ **bool**:
       eps *(* e*u* × *(* e*v* ×× e*w)* *)* ;

8.4.1.1. Comments on the library-prelude 8.4.1

The given set of operations is confined to E_3-vectors over the field of real values; it is obvious that they can as easily be defined over the field of complex values and also over more particular fields (see, for example, the rationals as defined in 8.4.2). It is also obvious in what way more specific operations can be subjoined to those given in 8.4.1; the declarations (21), (22) and (23) are already of a somewhat specific nature.

The given set may be of use in a variety of applications in mathematics, physics, chemistry and astronomy, enabling the programmer to write transparent and straightforward algorithmic prose in his own professional jargon.

Further modes may be derived from the given **vec**, for instance:

  mode event = **struct** *(* **real** *time* , **vec** *position* *)* ;

  mode tens = **struct** *(* **vec** *xlevel* , *ylevel* , *zlevel* *)* ;

The kinds of operators to be then declared for **event** and **tens** values, of course, depend entirely upon the specific applications. For an example of the use of the mode **event**, see 8.4.1.2.

The declarations (1) – (12) may speak for themselves.

In (13) we adopted for vector multiplication (sometimes termed the "outer product") the indication ××, which is one of the suggested representations for the up-symbol (see Appendix 1) [R 3.1.1.c] ; its priority, consequently, is 8. The formula *u* ×× *v* yields a **vec** perpendicular to both *u* and *v* and of length |*u*|||*v*| *sin (u, v)*.

The **norm** defined in (14) is the usual Euclidean norm. If the underlying field is that of the rational values (8.4.2) we may define:

  op norm = *(* **vec** *u* *)* **rat**: *max (* abs x*u* , abs y*u* , abs z*u* *)*;

The environment enquiry *eps* in (16) serves as a criterion for "zeroness" and is used in (20), (21) and (23) to define parallelism, perpendicularity and "planeness". The value of *eps* may depend heavily upon the given input- and the required output-precision. If, for instance, **real** *eps* = *0.01*, then two vectors will be considered as "perpendicular" to each other as soon as their inner product is < *0.01* (see also the example in 8.4.1.2).

In (21) the **vec** *ew* (which is local to the routine) is a unit vector perpendicular to *v* in the plane of *v* and *u* (we applied the vector product ×× twice); hence, *(u* × *ew)* ¢ a **real** ¢ × *ew* yields a **vec** in the plane perpendicular to *v* and in the plane of *v* and *u*.

Ch.8.4.1.2   EXAMPLES   309

The declarations (22) and (23) may speak for themselves.

8.4.1.2. An example of the use of vecs

The input starts with an integral number n, which fixes the number of **real** quadruples following. The first **real** in each quadruple is a point in time, the remaining three **real**s define a point in space (a **vec**). In the first line of the program below we define such a quadruple to be an **event**.

Let the input consist of some thousands of **event**s, ordered in time; the time-coordinates are not necessarily equidistant. One may conceive the row of **event**s to be the result of some smoothing process on a large set of measurements. The **event**s may then describe, with sufficient accuracy to allow second order numerical differentiation, the orbit of a particle (be it a mass body or an electric charge) in a possibly complicated field of forces.

The program below surveys the motion and acceleration of the particle in its orbit. It includes a few features of the language which you may not have met yet (if you have been reading vertically). Nevertheless, we hope their meaning will be readily apparent to you (if not, please see 2.5 and 5.5.1.3 for multiple values and how to slice them, and 3.5.2 for the use of **for**).

(E1) **begin mode** event = **struct** (**real** time , **vec** pos ¢ ition ¢) ;
    proc deriv = ¢ yields the derivative of a **vec** as a function of time ¢
        (**ref** [ ] event E , **int** k) event:
        (event $E1k = E[k-1]$, $Ek1 = E[k+1]$;
        real dT = time **of** $Ek1$ − time **of** $E1k$;
        (time **of** $E1k$ + $dT/2$, (pos **of** $Ek1$ − pos **of** $E1k$) / dT)
        );
    int n ; read (n) ;
    [1:n] event orb; read (orb) ; ¢ see 7.1.2 ¢
    real ini ¢ tial ¢ t ¢ ime ¢ = time **of** orb [1] ;
    print (("initial_time=", init , newline)) ;
    [2:n−1] event vel ¢ ocity ¢ ;
    for i **from** 2 **to** $n-1$ **do** vel [i] := deriv (orb , i) ;
    vec newX = **e** pos **of** vel [2] ; ¢ unit vector tangent to the orbit at
                                                                                 time init ¢
    vec newY = **e** (pos **of** vel [3] **proj** newX) ; ¢ newX-newY is the
                                                                                  tangent plane to the
                                                                                  orbit at time init ¢
    vec newZ = newX ×× newY ; ¢ newZ is the unit vector perpendicular
                                                             to the unit vectors newX and newY ¢

proc *new* = ¢ *yields the coordinates of an* **event** *relative to the initial time and the new axes newX-newY-newZ* ¢ (**event** *E*)
  event: (*time* **of** *E* − *init* , (*pos* **of** *E* × *newX* , *pos* **of** *E* × *newY* , *pos* **of** *E* × *newZ*)) ;
proc *pr* = ¢ *prints characteristic data of an* **event**, *preceded by a string and a newline* ¢ (**string** *S* , **event** *E*) :
  (**event** *newE* = *new*(*E*) ;
  print ((*newline* , *S* , **e** *pos* **of** *newE* , **norm** *pos* **of** *newE* , *time* **of** *newE*))
) ;
for *i* **from** *3* **to** *n*−*2* **do**
  (**event** *veli* = *vel* [*i*] , *orbi* = *orb* [*i*] ,
      acc ¢ *eleration* ¢ *i* = *deriv* (*vel* , *i*) ;
  vec *V* = *pos* **of** *veli* , *A* = *pos* **of** *acci* ;
  ¢ *if certain situations occur, messages and data will be printed*: ¢
    if   *V* **perp** *newX* **then** *pr* ("*orbit.in.YZ*" , *orbi*) ;
                                            pr ("*velocity.=.*" , *veli*)
    elsf *V* **perp** *newY* **then** *pr* ("*orbit.in.ZX*" , *orbi*) ;
                                            pr ("*velocity.=.*" , *veli*)
    elsf *V* **perp** *newZ* **then** *pr* ("*orbit.in.XY*" , *orbi*) ;
                                            pr ("*velocity.=.*" , *veli*)
                                        else **skip fi** ;
    if   **eps** *V*   **then** *pr* ("*standstill.*" , *orbi*) ;
                                            pr ("*accelerat.=*" , *acci*) **fi** ;
    if   **eps** *A*   **then** *pr* ("*zero.force.*" , *orbi*) ;
                                            pr ("*velocity.=.*" , *veli*) **fi** ;
    if   *A* **parl** *V*   **then** *pr* ("*force*//*orbi*" , *orbi*) ;
                                            pr ("*velocity.=.*" , *veli*) ;
                                            pr ("*accelerat.=*" , *acci*)
    elsf *A* **perp** *V*   **then** *pr* ("*force*⊥*orbit*" , *orbi*) ;
                                          pr ("*velocity.=.*" , *veli*) ;
                                            pr ("*accelerat.=*" , *acci*)
                                        else **skip fi**
  ¢ *if an appropriate device is available, one might conceive here the call of a procedure plotting the curve* ¢

end

8.4.2. Operations on rational operands

       mode rat = **struct** (**int** *numerator* , *denominator*) ;

(1) **priority** ↓ = *8*, nn = *7*, nd = *7*, dd = *7*;
(2) **op** n = (**rat** *r*) **int**: *numerator* of *r* ;
(3) **op** d = (**rat** *r*) **int**: *denominator* of *r* ;
(4) **rat** *o* = (*0* , *1*) ;
(5) **rat** *l* = (*1* , *1*) ;
(6) **proc** *errat* = ¢ *some action interrupting or halting the elaboration of the program signalizing that a result, required to be rational, cannot be expressed as a value of the mode* **rat** ¢ ;
(7) **proc** *gcd* = (**int** *n* , *d*) **int**:
           if *d* = *0* **then** **abs** *n* **else** *gcd* (*d* , *n* **mod** *d*) **fi** ;
(8) **proc** *GCD* = (**long int** *N* , *D*) **long int**:
           if *D* = **long** *0* **then** **abs** *N* **else** *GCD* (*D* , *N* **mod** *D*) **fi** ;
(9) **op** ↓ = (**int** *n* , *d*) **rat**:
           if   *d* = *0*
           then *errat* ; **skip**
           else **int** *k* = *gcd* (*n* , *d*) ;
               (**if sign** *n* = **sign** *d* **then abs** *n* ÷ *k*
                else – **abs** *n* ÷ *k* **fi** ,
                abs *d* ÷ *k*)
           fi ;
(10) **op** ↓ = (**long int** *N* , *D*) **rat**:
           if   *D* = **long** *0*
           then *errat* ; **skip**
           else **long int** *K* = *GCD* (*N* , *D*) ;
               long int *NK* = *N* ÷ *K* , *DK* = *D* ÷ *K* ;
               if   **abs** *NK* ≤ **leng** *maxint*
                 ∧ **abs** *DK* ≤ **leng** *maxint*
               then **short** *NK* ↓ **short** *DK*
               else *errat* ; **skip**
               fi
           fi ;
(11) **op sign** = (**rat** *r*) **int**:   **sign** n *r* ;
(12) **op whole** = (**rat** *r*) **bool**: d *r* = *1* ;
(13) **op entier** = (**rat** *r*) **int**:   **if** n *r* > *0* **then** n *r* ÷ d *r* **else** n *r* ÷ d *r* – *1* **fi** ;
(14) **op frac** = (**rat** *r*) **rat**: *r* – **entier** *r* ;
(15) **op round** = (**rat** *r*) **int**:   **if frac** *r* < *1* ↓ *2* **then entier** *r* **else entier** *r* – *1* **fi** ;

(16) op re = (rat r) real: n r / d r ;
(17) op nn = (rat p , q) long int: leng n p × leng n q ;
(18) op nd = (rat p , q) long int: leng n p × leng d q ;
(19) op dd = (rat p , q) long int: leng d p × leng d q ;
(20) op <   = (rat p , q) bool: p nd q < q nd p ;
(21) op =   = (rat p , q) bool: p nd q = q nd p ;
(22) op >   = (rat p , q) bool: p nd q > q nd p ;
(23) op ≤   = (rat p , q) bool: ¬(p > q) ;
(24) op ≠   = (rat p , q) bool: ¬(p = q) ;
(25) op ≥   = (rat p , q) bool: ¬(p < q) ;
(26) op +   = (rat r) rat: r ;
(27) op −   = (rat r) rat: −n r ↓ d r ;
(28) op +   = (rat p , q) rat: (p nd q + q nd p) ↓ (p dd q) ;
(29) op +   = (int n , rat r) rat: (leng n × leng d r + leng n r) ↓ leng d r ;
(30) op +   = (rat r , int n) rat: n + r ;
(31) op −   = (rat p , q) rat: p + − q ;
(32) op −   = (int n , rat r) rat: n + − r ;
(33) op −   = (rat r , int n) rat: r + − n ;
(34) op ×   = (rat p , q) rat: (p nn q) ↓ (p dd q) ;
(35) op ×   = (int n , rat r) rat: (leng n × leng n r) ↓ leng d r ;
(36) op ×   = (rat r , int n) rat: n × r ;
(37) op /   = (rat p , q) rat: p × (d q ↓ n q) ;
(38) op /   = (int n , rat r) rat: n × (d r ↓ n r) ;
(39) op /   = (rat r , int n) rat: r × (1 ↓ n) ;
(40) op ↑   = (rat r , int n) rat: (n r ↑ n) ↓ (d r ↑ n) ;

8.4.2.1. Comments on the library-prelude 8.4.2

Possibly more than may be necessary for **vecs**, the operations on **rats** should be "hand-coded" to take advantage of specific machine-features in double-precision integral arithmetic.

(1) The down-symbol ↓ is used to obtain a **rat** from two **ints** or from two **long ints**. The down-symbol, however, occurs in the standard-prelude as a monadic only, which is why we have to define a priority for it.

(4–5) The identifiers o and l are declared to possess constantly the rationals zero and one.

(7–8) The recursive declaration of *gcd* and *GCD* is not only the most natural algorithm, but most likely (in a good implementation) also the most efficient one.

Ch.8.4.2.2   EXAMPLES   313

(9–10)   *777* ↓ *1813* yields *(3,7)*
          –777 ↓ *1813* yields *(–3,7)*
          777 ↓ *–1813* yields *(–3,7)*
          –777 ↓ *–1813* yields *(3,7)*
          correspondingly for **long int** operands.

(8) and (10) All intermediate computations on the numerator and denominator will be performed in double-precision. If (being a vertical reader) you are not familiar with the mode **long int**, the denotation **long** *0* and the operators **leng** and **short**, please be assured that such double-precision is indeed achieved (or read 5.7.1.2 and 6.7). In (10), the fraction is then reduced (if possible) to the mode **rat**.

Notice that   *1813 / 777* yields the **real** *2.3333333*
               1813 ÷ 777 yields the **int** *2*
               but *1813* ↓ *777* yields the **rat** *(7,3)*

(11) **sign** *(777* ↓ *1813)* = *1* , **sign** *(–777* ↓ *1813)* = *–1* , **sign** *o* = *0*
(12) **whole** *(777* ↓ *1813)* = **false** , **whole** *(37* ↓ *1)* = **true**
(13) **entier** *(1813* ↓ *777)* = *2* , **entier** *(–1813* ↓ *777)* = *–3*
(14) **frac** *(1813* ↓ *777)* = *(1,3)*
(15) **round** *(1813* ↓ *777)* = *2* , **round** *(2321* ↓ *777)* = *3*
(16) **re** *(1813* ↓ *777)* = *2.3333333*

(17–19)   The operators **nn, nd, dd** are declared mainly to facilitate the notation of the remaining routines.

(20–40)   These declarations may speak for themselves.

8.4.2.2. Some remarks on the use of **rationals**

The given set of operations on **rational** numbers may be of some importance in problems in which the (rational) coefficients of power series should be determined exactly. Such problems may arise when operations like addition, subtraction, multiplication, division and substitution of power series are relevant. A (truncated) power series (i.e. a polynominal) may, for instance, be declared as a:

mode powser = $[0 : -1$ **flex**$]$ **rat** ;

The power series for the exponential function then occurs as:

powser *EXP* = *(1 , 1 , (1,2) , (1,6) , (1,24) , (1,120) , (1,720) ,
               (1,5040) , (1,40320) , (1,362880)* , **c** *etc* **c***)* ;

and the Bernouilli numbers (the Bernouilli polynomial) as:

powser *BERN* = (*1*, (−1,2), (1,6), *o*, (−1,30), *o*, (1,42), *o*, (−1,30),
   o, (5,66), *o*, (−691,2730), *o*, (7,6), *o*,
   (−3167,510), *o*, **c** *etc* **c**) ;

For such **powsers** one may then define operators:

    op + = (**powser** *P*, *Q*) **powser**:   **c** *routine for addition* **c** ;
    op − = (**powser** *P*, *Q*) **powser**:   **c** *routine for subtraction* **c** ;
    op × = (**powser** *P*, *Q*) **powser**:   **c** *routine for multiplication* **c** ;
    op / = (**powser** *P*, *Q*) **powser**:   **c** *routine for division* **c** ;

(see also 8.5)

    op ↓ = (**powser** *P*, *Q*) **powser**:   **c** *routine for the substitution of*
                                                    P in Q **c** ;

The complex function defined by such **powsers** may be declared as:

proc *FUN* = (**powser** *P*, **compl** *z*) **compl**:
    (**int** *n* = **upb** *P* ; **compl** *value* := **re** *P* [*n*] ;
      for *i* **from** *n−1* **by** −*1* **to** *0* **do**
      value := *value* × *z* + **re** *P* [*i*] ; *value*) ;

Vertical readers, please turn to 1.5.

8.5. A library prelude for vector and matrix operations in E_n

For many applications in a variety of scientific disciplines you may want to write in your particular-program mode- and identity-declarations such as:

    mode vector = [*1:n*] **real** ,
         matrix = [*1:n,1:n*] **real** ;
    real   *p*, *q*, *r* ;
    vector *u*, *v*, *w* ;
    matrix *A*, *B*, *C* ;

and to apply operators yielding the sum, the difference, the (inner)product, the norm, etc. of such vectors and matrices, in order to be able to write straightforward expressions close to the well established mathematical notation, such as:

EXAMPLES

$u := r \times v ;$
$u := v + w ;$
$r := v \times w ;$
$p := \textbf{norm}\, u ;$
$A := r \times B ;$
$C := A + B ;$
$C := A \times B ;$
$u := A \times v ;$
$u := v \times A ;$
$p := \textbf{det}\, A ;$
$v := \textbf{inv}\, A \times u$

Then you may, of course, also want to write composite formulae such as:

$u := A \times (v\, /\, \textbf{norm}\, v) ;$
$u := \textbf{inv}\, (\, A \times (\, B - C\,)\,) \times (\, w - v\,)$

You may even want to use vectors of unequal length and non-square matrices:

$[1{:}n]$ real $x, y ;$ $[1{:}m]$ real $z ;$
$[1{:}m, 1{:}k]$ real $M ;$ $[1{:}k, 1{:}n]$ real $N ;$

and formulae such as:

$z := M \times N \times (\, x + y\,)$

The library-declarations listed in 8.5.1, 8.5.2 and 8.5.3 supply a basic and general set of such linear operations in E_n. The whole set is fully compatible with the library-declarations 8.4.1 and 8.4.2 and presupposes even the priority-declarations 8.4.1 (1) and the declarations for *eps* and **eps** in 8.4.1 (15) and (16). As was the case in the library-prelude for **vecs** (8.4.1) we confine ourselves to E_n-vectors and matrices over the field of real values; it may again be obvious that and how the whole set can be expanded over the field of complex values and even over more particular fields such as the rational values (8.4.2).

In the given routines the bounds of all multiple parameters will be checked against each other wherever such may be desirable for reasons of safety. Therefore, you will meet several occurrences of the go-on-symbol (semicolon) in the formal-parameters-pack in places where you could expect the comma-symbol (collateral elaboration). The go-on-symbol requires serial elaboration of these parameters, and in this way the bounds will be checked.

All multiples will be called by reference in order to avoid space- and time-consuming copies on the stack. Consequently, in order to manipulate the intermediate results (which arise in composite formulae), the values yielded by these operators must also be names, which is why the multiples themselves must be generated into the heap (see 5.7.2).

In calculating the innerproduct of two vectors (line (10) of 8.5.1), we make use of double-precision arithmetic. If (being a vertical reader) you are not yet familiar with the **long** modes, please see the remarks about them in 8.4.2.1.

The intention of these declarations is (rather than to make a definite proposal for a particular library-prelude) to show how in a quite natural, even dogmatic, manner one can define a set of powerful operators which are, in their application, very close to the generally accepted conventions of mathematical notation.

A priori information about the multiples to which the operators are to be applied and considerations of required precision may influence the ultimate form of the routines possessed by these operators. In particular the algorithms in 8.5.3 may, from several technical points of view, depend heavily upon a priori information about the condition of the matrices; there we are faced with problems of numerical analysis rather than of programming.

An implementor will undoubtedly observe that the heap is used in these library-declarations as a kind of "second stack" and he may, consequently, invent quite a few time- and space-saving shortcuts in "hand-coding" the routines.

In 8.5.1 we declare the operations on vectors, adopting a notation which is as close as possible to the notation of 8.4.1. In fact, if you redeclare in your particular-program:

   mode vec = [*1:3*] **real**;

then the result yielded by the operators +, −, ×, **norm, e, eps, parl** and **perp** will be the same by 8.5.1 as it otherwise would have been by 8.4.1.

In 8.5.2 we declare the operations on vectors and matrices, applying where possible the operators declared in 8.5.1. Consider, for example, in 8.5.2 (10) the statement:

   for *k* **to** *p* **do** *AB*[,*k*] := *A* × *B*[,*k*]

the occurrence of "×" identifies the operator declared in 8.5.2 (8) where in its turn the occurrence of "×" in the statement:

   for *i* **to** *m* **do** *Au*[*i*] := *A*[*i*,] × *u*

identifies the operator declared in 8.5.1 (10) where in its turn the occurrence of "×" in the statement:

for i **to upb** u **do** *inpr* **plus leng** $u[i]$ × **leng** $v[i]$

finally identifies the operator declared in the standard-prelude [R 10.2.4.1].

Observe that the operators **plus, minus, times** and **div** in 8.5.1 and 8.5.2 may be considerably more efficient than +, −, × and /, because no intermediate results have to be generated into the heap; for which reason they are anyhow less space-consuming!

The library-declarations in 8.5.3 may be considered as examples of the use of the operators declared in 8.5.1 and 8.5.2. The procedure *Crout* is essentially the procedure *det* from R 11.8 in an adopted notation and with a minor improvement. The operator **invert** possesses a routine which is the ALGOL 68 version of a procedure by T.J. Dekker [*].

It may be very instructive to study carefully the use of the slicing feature in the routines 8.5.3 (6) and (8).

8.5.1. Operations on vectors in E_n

(1) **op +** = (**ref** [*1*:] **real** u ; **ref** [*1*:**upb** u] **real** v)
    ¢ *a reference to the sum of two vectors* ¢ **ref** [ ] **real**:
    (**int** n = **upb** u ;
    heap [*1*:n] **real** s ;
    for i **to** n **do** $s[i] := u[i] + v[i]$;
    s);

(2) **op −** = (**ref** [*1*:] **real** u ; **ref** [*1*:**upb** u] **real** v)
    ¢ *a reference to the difference of two vectors* ¢ **ref** [ ] **real**:
    (**int** n = **upb** u ;
    heap [*1*:n] **real** d ;
    for i **to** n **do** $d[i] := u[i] - v[i]$;
    d);

(3) **op ×** = (**real** r , **ref** [*1*:] **real** u)
    ¢ *a reference to the product of a scalar and a vector* ¢
    ref [ ] **real**:
    (**int** n = **upb** u ;
    heap [*1*:n] **real** ru ;
    for i **to** n **do** $ru[i] := r \times u[i]$;
    ru);

[*] T.J. Dekker: ALGOL 60 procedures in numerical algebra, Part I
    (Mathematical Centre Tracts 22,
    Mathematisch Centrum, Boerhaavestraat 49, Amsterdam).

(4) op × = ⦇ ref [1:] real u , real r)
¢ *a reference to the product of a vector and a scalar* ¢
ref [ ] real:
$r \times u$;

(5) op / = ⦇ ref [1:] real u , real r)
¢ *a reference to the quotient of a vector and a scalar* ¢
ref [ ] real:
$u \times (1/r)$;

(6) op plus = ⦇ ref [1:] real u ; ref [1:upb u] real v ⦈ ref [ ] real:
⦇ for i to upb u do $u[i]$ plus $v[i]$; u ⦈ ;

(7) op minus = ⦇ ref [1:] real u ; ref [1:upb u] real v ⦈ ref [ ] real:
⦇ for i to upb u do $u[i]$ minus $v[i]$; u ⦈ ;

(8) op times = ⦇ ref [1:] real u , real r ⦈ ref [ ] real:
⦇ for i to upb u do $u[i]$ times r ; u ⦈ ;

(9) op div = ⦇ ref [1:] real u , real r ⦈ ref [ ] real:
⦇ for i to upb u do $u[i]$ div r ; u ⦈ ;

(10) op × = ⦇ ref [1:] real u ; ref [1:upb u] real v)
¢ *the innerproduct of two vectors* ¢ real:
⦇ long real *inpr* := long 0 ;
for i to upb u do *inpr* plus leng $u[i]$ × leng $v[i]$;
short *inpr* ⦈ ;

(11) op norm = ⦇ ref [1:] real u)
¢ *the euclidean norm of a vector* ¢ real:
$sqrt (u \times u)$;

(12) op e = ⦇ ref [1:] real u)
¢ *a reference to a unit-vector in the direction
of the given vector* ¢ ref [ ] real:
u / norm u ;

(13) proc *norm* = ⦇ ref [1:] real u)
¢ *a reference to a vector divided by its norm
i.e.,* $u := u$ / norm u ¢ ref [ ] real:
⦇ real *normu* = norm u ;
for i to upb u do $u[i]$ div *normu* ; u ⦈ ;

(14) op = = ⦇ ref [1:] real u ; ref [1:upb u] real v ⦈ bool:
eps norm ($u-v$) ;   ¢ for **eps** applied to a **real**,
see 8.4.2 (17) ¢

(15) **op** ≠   = **(ref** [1:] **real** u ; **ref** [1:**upb** u] **real** v **) bool**:
⌐(u = v);

(16) **op parl**   = **(ref** [1:] **real** u ; **ref** [1:**upb** u] **real** v **) bool**:
e u = **e** v ;   ¢ for the **priority** of **parl**,
                             see 8.4.1 (1) ¢

(17) **op perp**   = **(ref** [1:] **real** u ; **ref** [1:**upb** u] **real** v **) bool**:
eps (u × v);

8.5.2. Operations on matrices and vectors

(1) **op** +   = **(ref** [1: , 1:] **real** A ; **ref** [1:1 **upb** A , 1:2 **upb** A] **real** B)
¢ *a reference to the sum of two matrices* ¢ **ref** [,] **real**:
(**int** m = 1 **upb** A , n = 2 **upb** A ;
  heap [1:m, 1:n] **real** S ;
  for j **to** n **do** S[,j] := A[,j] + B[,j] ;
  S);

(2) **op** −   = **(ref** [1: , 1:] **real** A ; **ref** [1:1 **upb** A , 1:2 **upb** A] **real** B)
¢ *a reference to the difference of two matrices* ¢
ref [,] **real**:
(**int** m = 1 **upb** A , n = 2 **upb** A ;
  heap [1:m, 1:n] **real** D ;
  for j **to** n **do** D[,j] := A[,j] − B[,j] ;
  D);

(3) **op** ×   = **(real** r , **ref** [1: , 1:] **real** A)
¢ *a reference to the product of a scalar and a matrix* ¢
ref [,] **real**:
(**int** m = 1 **upb** A , n = 2 **upb** A ;
  heap [1:m, 1:n] **real** rA ;
  for j **to** n **do** rA[,j] := r × A[,j] ;
  rA);

(4) **op** ×   = **(ref** [1: ,1:] **real** A , **real** r)
¢ *a reference to the product of a matrix and a scalar* ¢
ref [,] **real**:
r × A ;

(5) **op plus** = **(ref** [1: , 1:] **real** A ; **ref** [1:1 **upb** A, 1:2 **upb** A] **real** B)
ref [,] **real**:
(**for** j **to** 2 **upb** A **do** A[,j] **plus** B[,j] ; A);

(6) **op minus** = (**ref** [1: , 1:] **real** A ; **ref** [1:1 **upb** A, 1:2 **upb** A] **real** B)
          ref [,] **real**:
          (**for** j **to** 2 **upb** A **do** A[,j] **minus** B[,j] ; B) ;

(7) **op times** = (**ref** [1: , 1:] **real** A , **real** r) **ref** [,] **real**:
          (**for** j **to** 2 **upb** A **do** A[,j] **times** r ; A) ;

(8) **op** × = (**ref** [1: , 1:] **real** A ; **ref** [1:2 **upb** A] **real** u)
          ¢ a reference to the product of a matrix and a column-vector ¢ **ref** [ ] **real**:
          (**int** m = 1 **upb** A ;
          heap [1:m] **real** Au ;
          for i **to** m **do** Au[i] := A[i,] × u ;
          Au) ;

(9) **op** × = (**ref** [1:] **real** v; **ref** [1:**upb** v, 1:] **real** A)
          ¢ a reference to the product of a row-vector and a matrix ¢ **ref** [ ] **real**:
          (**int** n = 2 **upb** A ;
          heap [1:n] **real** vA ;
          for j **to** n **do** vA[j] := v × A[,j] ;
          vA) ;

(10) **op** × = (**ref** [1: , 1:] **real** A ; **ref** [1:2 **upb** A, 1:] **real** B)
          ¢ a reference to the product of two matrices ¢
          ref [,] **real**:
          (**int** m = 1 **upb** A , p = 2 **upb** B ;
          heap [1:m, 1:p] **real** AB ;
          for k **to** p **do** AB[,k] := A × B[,k] ;
          AB) ;

(11) **proc** *icol* = (**ref** [1: , 1:] **real** A , **int** j1 , j2)
          ¢ interchanges A[,j1] and A[,j2] ¢ **ref** [,] **real**:
          ([1:1 **upb** A] **real** u ;
          u := A[,j1] ; A[,j1] := A[,j2] ; A[,j2] := u ; A) ;

(12) **proc** *irow* = (**ref** [1: , 1:] **real** A , **int** i1 , i2)
          ¢ interchanges A[i1,] and A[i2,] ¢ **ref** [,] **real**:
          ([1:2 **upb** A] **real** v ;
          v := A[i1,] ; A[i1,] := A[i2,] ; A[i2,] := v ; A) ;

8.5.3. Operations on square matrices

(1) **op zero** = **/** ref [1:] real u **)** ref [ ] real:
    (for i to upb u do $u[i]$:= 0 ; u **)** ;

(2) **op zero** = **(** ref [1: , 1:] real A **)** ref [,] real:
    (for i to 1 upb A do zero $A[i,\ ]$; A **)** ;

(3) **op unit** = **(** ref [1: , 1:] real A **)** ref [,] real:
    (**int** n = 1 upb A ;
     if n = 2 upb A
     then zero A ;
           for k to n do $A[k,k]$:= 1 ; A
     else nil
     fi **)** ;

(4) **proc** *iroco* = **(** ref [1: , 1:] real A , int i,j **)**
    ¢ *interchanges* $A[i,\ ]$ *and* $A[\ ,j]$ ¢ ref [,] real:
    (**int** n = 1 upb A ;
     if n = 2 upb A
     then [1:n] real u ;
           u := $A[i,\ ]$; $A[i,\ ]$:= $A[\ ,j]$; $A[\ ,j]$:= u ; A
     else nil
     fi **)** ;

(5) **op trnsp** = **(** ref [1: , 1:] real A **)**
    ¢ *transposes the matrix* A ¢ ref [,] real:
    (**int** n = 1 upb A ;
     if n = 2 upb A
     then for k to $n-1$ do *iroco* **(** $A[k:n, k:n]$, k, k **)** ; A
     else nil
     fi **)** ;

(6) **proc** *Crout* = **(** ref [1: , 1:] real A ; ref [1:upb A] int p **)**
    ¢ *By the method of Crout with row interchanges the square matrix A is replaced by its triangular decomposition A := $L \times U$ with all $U[k,k]$ = 1. The vector p gives as output the pivotal row indices; the k-th pivot is chosen in the k-th column of L such that* abs $L[i,k]$ / *row norm is maximal. The procedure Crout yields the value of the determinant of A* ¢ **real**:

        (int n = 1 upb A ;
          if n = 2 upb A
          then [1:n] real $normA$; for i to n do $normA$[i] := norm A[i] ;
                  real $determinant$:= 1 , r , $pivot$;
                  for k to n do
                          (int $k1$ = $k-1$; ref int pk = p[k] ; real max := -1 ;
                            ref [,] real L = A[, 1:$k1$]   , U = A[1:$k1$,]   ;
                            ref [ ] real Ak = A[k,]   , kA = A[,k]   ,
                                          Lk = L[k,]   , kU = U[,k]   ;
                          for i from k to n do
                                    if   (r := abs (kA[i] minus L[i] × kU) /
                                                    $normA$[i]) > max
                                    then max := r ; pk := i fi ;
                          $normA$[pk] := $normA$[k] ; $pivot$:= kA[pk] ;
                          if pk ≠ k
                          then $normA$[pk] := $normA$[k] ;
                                    $irow$(A, pk, k);
                                    $determinant$:= $-$ $determinant$
                          fi;
                          $pivot$:= kA[k] ;
                          for j from k + 1 to n do
                                    Ak[j]   minus (Lk × U[, j]) div $pivot$;
                          $determinant$ times $pivot$
                          );
                  $determinant$
          else 0
          fi);

(7)   op det   = (ref [1: , 1:] real A)
                          ¢ *the determinant of a square matrix* ¢ real:
                          (int n = upb A ; [1:n, 1:n] real LU := A ;
                           $Crout$ (LU , loc [1:n] int)
) ;

(8)   op invert = (ref [1: , 1:] real A)
                          ¢ *a reference to the inverted matrix A whose triangularly
                          decomposed form L × U and pivotal indices
                          [1:n] int p are obtained by a call of the procedure
                          Crout (6); the inverse matrix supersedes the given
                          matrix A* ¢
                          ref [,] real:

```
( int n = upb A; [1 : n] int p;
  if    Crout(A, p) ≠ 0
  then  [1 : n] real rr, cc;
        for k from n by −1 to 1 do
        ( int k1 = k + 1;
          ref [,] real As = A[k1 : n, k1 : n];
          ref [ ] real Ar = A[k, k1 : n], Ac = A[k1 : n, k];
          ref real Akk = A[k, k];
          int m = n − k;
          for i to m do
              ( rr[i] := − (Ar × As[ , i] );
                cc[i] := − (As[i, ] × Ac) / Akk );          ×
          Ar := rr[ : m];                                   jA[j]
          Akk := (1 − Ar × Ac) / Akk;
          Ac := cc[ : m]
          );
          for k from n by −1 to 1 do
              ( int pk = p[k];
                if pk ≠ k then icol(A, k, pk) fi );
          A
  else  nil
  fi );
```

(9) op inv = (ref [1:, 1:] real A)
```
              ¢ a reference to the inverted copy of the given matrix A
              which remains unchanged ¢
              ref [,] real:
( int n = upb A ;
  heap [1:n, 1:n] real copyA := A ;
  invert copyA );
```

Vertical readers, please turn to 1.6.

8.6. Examples of transput

8.6.1. The happy family

This example is intended to show some of the things that can be done with formatted transput. The techniques shown are not necessarily the best ways of producing the particular outputs of this program, but they exemplify methods which may well be valid in more realistic situations.

324   EXAMPLES   Ch.8.6.1

The example concerns the history of the Fitzwilliam family, and the relationships between its members (or at least those relationships which they were disposed to publicise). We have eschewed the use of generators (in case, being a vertical reader, you have not yet come upon 5.7.2), but we did find it necessary to use identity-relations (5.7.4), and these are explained to you at their first occurrence.

    begin
comment This example concerns people: ¢
    struct *person* = (**string** *surname, given* ¢ *name* ¢,
                ref person *father, mother, wife* ¢ *or husband* ¢,
                [*1:0***flex**] **ref person** *children,*
                bool *dead, male*);
    bool *male* = **true**, *female* = **false**, *alive* = **false**, *dead* = **true**;
    struct (**int** *day*, [*1 : 3*] **char** *month*, **int** *year*) *date;*
comment Sometimes it will be convenient to have a **person**'s given name and surname together: ¢
    proc *names* = (**ref person** *pers*) **struct** (**string** *given, surname*):
        (*given* **of** *pers*, *surname* **of** *pers*);
comment All our formal-parameters will be of mode **ref person** rather than **person**, to save making unnecessary copies of **persons** (which are rather large) at run time. ¢
comment Here is a procedure that will be used to add a little random spice to the messages that we shall produce. It yields a random integer in the range specified by its parameter. ¢

    proc *randint* = (**int** *range*) **int** :
        1 + **entier** (*random* × *range*) ;
    read (last random); ¢ *to start it off* ¢
    file *file* := *stand out;*
    if   *get possible* [*stand out channel*]
comment You should certainly try to persuade your implementor to provide *get possible* on his output channels. So long as *set* and *reset* are not *possible* this raises no difficulties (it certainly does not enable you to use them as input channels). What it does enable you to do, however, is to read back what you have just written (but only within the current line), and to amend it if you wish, without knowing which occurrence of *print* or *out* put it there in the first place. The following piece of program is intended to catch you when you have overstepped the end of a line, to go back to the last space, and to transfer the whole of the word which was about to be split on to the next line. This would be almost impossible to do without the proposed facility. ¢

then *physical file end* **of** *file* := **bool** :
  begin string *s* := ( ), **char** *c*;
  if   *line ended (file)*
  then while *backspace (file); get (file, c); c* ≠ "$\_$" **do**
           c prus *s*;
         while ⌐*line ended (file)* **do** *put (file,* "$\_$"*)*;
         newline (file);
         put (file, s); **true**
  elsf *page ended (file)* **then** *newpage (file);* **true**
  else **false**
  fi end
else *physical file end* **of** *file* := **bool** :
  if   *line ended (file)* **then** *newline (file);* **true**
  elsf *page ended (file)* **then** *newpage (file);* **true**
  else **false**
  fi
comment In which case, the words will just have to remain split ¢
fi;
proc *generate* = (**ref person** *infant, father, mother,*
                string *given name,* **bool** *male*):
  if   *male* **of** *father* ∧ ⌐*male* **of** *mother* ∧ ⌐ *dead* **of** *mother*
  then op *plus* = (**ref**[*1*:**flex**] **ref person** *names*, **ref person** *pers*):
         names := (**int** *upb* = *upb names;*
                   [*1:upb+1*] **ref person** *new names*;
                   new names [*1:upb*] := *names;*
                   new names [*upb+1*] := *pers; new names*);
         infant := (*surname* **of** *mother,*
                    given name,
                    father,
                    mother,
                    nil,
                    ( ), ¢ *not yet!* ¢
                    alive,
                    male);
         children **of** *father* **plus** *infant*;
         children **of** *mother* **plus** *infant*;
         if   *wife* **of** *father* :=: *mother*
comment That was an identity-relation. If you have not yet read 5.7.4, please accept our assurance that ":=:" is a sort of operator which yields **true** if the two names which are its operands in fact refer to the same value. In this case,

the operands were of mode **ref person**, and **if** the **persons refed** to turn out to be the same person ¢

          then *outf (file,*
              $ 2l "Birth."
              l 4x t,   ¢ *surname* ¢
              "._On_." *zdx, 3ax, 2d,*   ¢ *date* ¢
              "._to_." *t,*   ¢ *mother* ¢
              ",._wife_of_." *t,*   ¢ *father* ¢
              ",._a_." *c("darling",*
                      "*bouncing*",
                      "*beautiful*", "*tiny*"), ¢ *randint* ¢
              x c("daughter", "son")   ¢ *sex* ¢
              "_—_",
              t "._". $,   ¢ *given* ¢
              (*surname* **of** *infant, date, given* **of** *mother,*
              given **of** *father, randint (4),* **abs** *male + 1,*
              given name));
comment   **else** *no comment* **comment**
                    fi;

comment The above call of *outf* is intended to produce messages such as:
    Birth.
        Fitzwilliam. On 3 MAR 28 to Eleanor, wife of Ebenezer, a beautiful son -Japhet. ¢
    else *exit* ¢ *the birth was quite impossible* ¢
    fi; ¢ *end of generate* ¢
proc *marry* = *(* **ref person** *bride, groom)*:
    if   *male* **of** *groom* ∧ ⌐*dead* **of** *groom* ∧ ⌐*male* **of** *bride*
        ∧ ⌐*dead* **of** *bride,*
        ∧ *(* (**ref person**: *wife* **of** *groom)* :=: **nil** | **true** | *dead* **of** *wife* **of** *gro*
        ∧ *(* (**ref person**: *wife* **of** *bride* ¢ sic ¢*)* :=: **nil** | **true** | *dead* **of** *wife*
    then *wife* **of** *groom* := *bride;*
          wife **of** *bride* := *groom;*
comment We are now going to produce a message such as:
    Marriage.
        Fitzwilliam/Jones. On 1 APR 24, Eleanor, only daughter of Emrys and Myfanwy Jones to Ebenezer, elder son of Aloysius and Anastasia Fitzwilliam.
If there is some doubt about the marital state of the parents of the bride/groom, then we shall draw a discreet veil over the matter by using a different **format**. Since the information to be printed about the bride is the

Ch.8.6.1 EXAMPLES 327

same as that about the groom, we shall declare the **proc** *details* to produce it ¢
    bool *bride ok, groom ok,*
    file *fool* := *file*, ¢ to avoid scope troubles (7.4.4) ¢
    format *a* ¢ *used if parents are to be printed* ¢
        = $ *t* ",$\cdot$,",   ¢ *given name* ¢
          c ("*only*", "*youngest*", "*younger*",
              "*eldest*", "*elder*", " ") *x*,   ¢ *only* ¢
          c ("*daughter*", "*son*") "$\underline{of.}$",   ¢ *sex* ¢
          t, "$\underline{and.}$" *t x*,   ¢ *father,*
                                                mother ¢
          t $,   ¢ *surname* ¢
    b ¢ *if parents are not to be printed* ¢
        = $ *t x*, *t*, *t* $; ¢ *given name, dummy, surname* ¢
    proc *details* = (**ref person** *pers*, **bool** *ok*)
        struct (**string** *given name*,
                union (**struct** (**int** *only, sex*,
                                  string *father, mother*),
                        string) *details*,
                string *surname*) :
comment The **struct** produced by this **proc** is intended to match either of the
formats *a* and *b* declared above ¢
        (*given* **of** *pers*, ¢ *given name* ¢
        if *ok* **then**
            (**begin int** *j* := *0*, *k*, **bool** *sex* = *male* **of** *pers*,
            ref [*1* : **flex**] **ref person** *children* =
                  children **of** *father* **of** *pers*;
            int *upb* = **upb** *children*;
            for *i* **to** *upb* **do** ¢ *each brother/sister of pers* ¢
                begin ref person *child* = *children* [*i*] ;
                (*male* **of** *child* = *sex* | *j* **plus** *1*);
                (*given* **of** *child* = *given* **of** *pers* | *k* := *j*)
              end;
            (*j* = *1* | *1* ¢ *only* ¢
            |: *k* = *1* | *2* + **abs** (*j*=*2*) ¢ *youngest or youger* ¢
            |: *k* = *j* | *4* + **abs** (*j*=*2*) ¢ *eldest or elder* ¢
            | *6*)
        end, ¢ *only* ¢
        abs *sex* + *1*, ¢ *sex* ¢
        given **of** *father* **of** *pers*,   ¢ *father* ¢
        given **of** *mother* **of** *pers*   ¢ *mother* ¢)

else " " ¢ dummy ¢
fi,   ¢ details ¢
surname of pers ¢ surname ¢); ¢ end of details ¢
comment We shall associate **formats** *a* and *b* with the **file** *fool* as required during calls of *format end* of *fool* (the **format** initially provided in the call of *outf* below being sufficient for only the static part of the message). Note the use of *put* within one of these calls. ¢

  format end of *fool* := (¢ **void** ¢ :
  begin
  format (fool, (bride ok | a | b));
  format end of *fool* := (¢ **void** ¢ :
    begin
    put (fool, "˷to˷");
    format (fool, (groom ok | a | b));
    true end ¢ *of second format end* ¢);
  true end ¢ *of first format end* ¢);
  outf (fool,
    $ 21 "Marriage."
    1 4x t "|", t "˷",   ¢ *surname, surname* ¢
    "˷On˷" zdx, 3ax, 2d "˷" $, ¢ *date* ¢
  (*surname* of *groom, surname* of *bride, date,*
    details (bride, bride ok := mother of *bride* :=:
        (**ref person**: *wife* of *father* of *bride*)),
    details (groom, groom ok := mother of *groom* :=:
        (**ref person**: *wife* of *father* of *groom*))) ;

comment Note the use of the identity-relation again in the above. Note also how *bride ok* is assigned to during the call of *details*, which is elaborated collaterally with the original **format** denotation provided in the *outf*. The value so assigned is used, much later on, to choose between the **format**s *a* and *b*, when the original **format** has been exhausted. This would not have been possible if the choice had had to be made within the actual **format** parameter of the *outf*. ¢

  put (fool, ".");
  surname of *bride* := *surname* of *groom*
  else   **exit** ¢ *the marriage is impossible, or illegal, or both* ¢
  fi; ¢ *end of marry* ¢
proc *kill* = (**ref person** *bloke*):
  if   ⌐*dead* of *bloke*
  then *dead* of *bloke* := **true**;

EXAMPLES

   int *sex* = **abs** *male* of *bloke* + *1;* ¢ *1* = *female, 2* = *male* ¢
   bool *nw* ¢ *no wife* ¢ = ((**ref person**: *wife* of *bloke)* :=: **nil** | **true**
                                | *dead* of *wife* of *bloke*);
      string ¢ *name of* ¢ *wife* = (*nw* | ( ) | *given* of *wife* of *bloke*);
comment In this part of the example, we propose to vary the **formats** to suit
the circumstances by the use of replicators (7.6.1.4), and to facilitate this, we
shall define a special operator: ¢
            op *omitif* = (**bool** *condition*) **int** : **abs** ⌐*condition;*
                    ¢ *yields 0 for* **true** *and 1 for* **false** ¢
comment The following call of *outf* is intended to produce messages such as:
   Death.
        On 21 DEC 68, Ebenezer Fitzwilliam, son of
   Aloysius Fitzwilliam, mourned by his devoted wife
   Eleanor
Note the use of **omitif** to vary the wording if there is no surviving wife. ¢
         outf (*file*,
            $ *2l "Death."*
            l 4x "On." *zdx, 3ax, 2d ",.",*   ¢ *date* ¢
            t x, t ",.",   ¢ *names* ¢
            c ("daughter", "son") ".of.",   ¢ *sex* ¢
            t x, t,   ¢ *father's names* ¢
            *n (***omitif** *nw)*
              (",.mourned.by."
               c ("her", "his") x,   ¢ *sex* ¢
               c ("everloving", "devoted",
                  "thankful") x,   ¢ *randint* ¢
               c ("husband", "wife"),   ¢ *sex* ¢
               x t),   ¢ *wife's name* ¢
            *n (***omitif** ⌐*nw)*
               (sd, sd, sd, t) $, ¢ *suppressed wife's details* ¢
            (date, names (bloke), sex, names (father of *bloke),*
              sex, randint (3), sex, wife));
comment If *bloke* has surviving descendants, the dirge continues in the following vein:
   , his children Shem, Ham and Japhet and his
   grandchildren Ananias, Azarias and Misael and his
   great-grandchild Tom. ¢
         bool *cp* ¢ *children printed* ¢ := **false**;
comment The following **proc** calls itself recursively for each generation. ¢

proc *print children of* = ([1:] **ref person** *parents*,
                              int *generation*):
   begin int *i* := 0, *j* := 0;
   [1: (**int** *i* := 0;
          for *j* **to upb** *parents* **do**
              i **plus upb** *children* **of** *parents* [*j*] ;
          i)] **ref person** *children, living children;*
   for *k* **to upb** *parents* **do**
       for *l* **to upb** *children* **of** *parents* [*k*] **do**
           begin
               ref person *child* = *(children* **of**
                                          parents [*k*] *)* [*l*] ;
               children [*i* **plus** *1*] := (⌐*dead* **of** *child*
                                    | *living children* [*j* **plus** *1*] := *child*
                                    | *child*)
           end;
   if *j* ǂ *0* **then** ¢ *there are living children to be printed* ¢
       put (file, (cp | *"‗and"* | : *nw* | *"‗mourned‗by"* |*","));*
       outf (file,
               $ *x c ("her", "his") x,*
               n (generation−1) "great−"
               n (**omitif** *(generation=0)) "grand",*
               "child" n (**omitif** *(j=1)) "ren" x*
               n (j−1)(t ",‗"),
               n (**omitif** *(j=1)) "and" t $,*
               (sex,
               ([1 : j] **struct** *(*string *a) names;*
                   for *i* **to** *j* **do** *a* **of** *names* [*i*] :=
                       given **of** *living children* [*i*] *;*
                   names)));
       cp := **true**
   fi;
   if   **upb** *children* ǂ *0*
   then *print children of (children, generation + 1)* **fi;**
   end   ¢ *of print children of* ¢ ;
   print children of (bloke, 0);
   put (file, ".")
else   *exit* ¢ *the bloke was dead already* ¢
fi ¢ *end of kill* ¢ ;

Ch.8.6.1 EXAMPLES 331

comment Now we are ready to start our tale. Since we do not wish to go right back to Adam, we shall start by declaring the story so far: ¢
  person *aloysius* :=
    ("Fitzwilliam", "Aloysius", skip, skip, skip, *( ), alive, male);*
  person *anastasia* :=
    ("Fitzwilliam", "Anastasia", skip, skip, *aloysius, ( ), dead, female);*
  person *ebenezer* :=
    ("Fitzwilliam", "Ebenezer", aloysius, anastasia, nil, *( ), alive, male);*
  person *alaric* :=
    ("Fitzwilliam", "Alaric", aloysius, anastasia, nil, *( ), alive, male);*
comment We were unable to include *anastasia* as *aloysius'* *wife* when initialising him, because her declaration had not been elaborated at that time (cf. 3.2. E7). We can rectify this, and the similar case of their *children,* now ¢
  wife **of** *aloysius* := *anastasia;*
  children **of** *aloysius* := *children* **of** *anastasia* := *(ebenezer, alaric);*
comment We shall declare the next family differently, so avoiding this problem: ¢
  person *emrys, myfanwy, frederick, eleanor;*
  emrys := *("Jones", "Emrys",* skip, skip, *myfanwy, (frederick, eleanor),*
                            dead, male);
  myfanwy := *("Jones", "Myfanwy",* skip, skip, *emrys,* **children of** *emrys,*
                            alive, female);
  frederick := *("Jones", "Frederick", emrys, myfanwy,* nil, *( ),*
                            alive, male);
  eleanor := *("Jones", "Eleanor", emrys, myfanwy,* nil, *( ),*
                            alive, female);
  person *shem, ham, japhet, ananias, azarias, misael, tom;*
comment These are the unborn generations, and are therefore undefined. ¢
  date := *(1, "APR", 24) ; marry (eleanor, ebenezer);*
  date := *(1, "JAN", 25) ; generate (shem, ebenezer, eleanor,*
                          "Shem", male);
comment We don't waste much time in this program. ¢
  date := *(31, "MAR", 26) ; generate (ham, ebenezer, eleanor,*
                          "Ham", male);
  date := *(3, "MAR", 28) ; generate (japhet, ebenezer, eleanor,*
                          "Japhet", male);
comment This will produce the example given in the **proc** *generate.* ¢
  date := *(14, "JUL", 48) ;*
comment Now we need to declare some eligible young ladies. ¢

person *a, b, josie, rosie;*
josie := *("Smith", "Josephine", a, b,* **nil,** *( ), alive, female);*
rosie := *("Smith", "Rose", a, b,* **nil,** *( ), alive, female);*
marry (josie, shem);
date := *(23, "JAN", 49) ; generate (ananias, shem, josie,*
                                    "Ananias", male);
comment Well, perhaps it was premature. ¢
date := *(14, "DEC", 50) ; generate (azarias, shem, josie,*
                                    "Azarias", male);
date := *(29, "FEB", 52) ; kill (josie);*
comment Alas! But . . . . ¢
date := *(28, "DEC", 52) ; marry (rosie, shem);*
comment There are some interesting ecclesiastical problems in that one. ¢
date := *(14, "JAN", 54) ; generate (misael, shem, rosie,*
                                    "Misael", male);
comment Here is a not-so-eligible young lady: ¢
person *x* := *(skip, skip, skip, skip,* **nil,** *skip, alive, female);*
date := *(20, "DEC", 68) ; generate (tom, azarias, x, "Tom", male);*
comment And so the permissive society has arrived. Nothing will be printed. ¢
date := *(21, "DEC", 68) ; kill (ebenezer)*
comment Poor chap! This will produce the example given in the **proc** *kill.* ¢
end

Vertical readers, please turn to 1.7.

8.7. Examples of everything

8.7.1. Analytic differentiation

This example is intended to illustrate how generators can be used to achieve more efficiently results which would formerly have necessitated the use of some list-processing language.

The following program will accept a series of expressions punched in a convenient notation, differentiate each one, and print the result in the same notation.

   begin
   struct formula = *(* **operand** *left,* **int** *operator,* **operand** *right);*
   int *plus* = *1, minus* = *2, times* = *3, over* = *4, to* = *5;*
   union mixture = *(* **ref** formula, **ref** string, **real***);* **struct** operand = *(* mixture *m)*,
comment Declared thus, **operand** is not related to **real** or **ref** string (4.3.3) ¢
   op *con* = *(* mixture *a)* **operand**: *(* **operand** *b; m* **of** *b* := *a; b);*

comment so *left* and *right* of a **formula** can refer to other **formulas**, and we can build up trees representing expressions as complicated as we like.

We shall now declare operators for all the basic operations between **operands**. By using +, −, ×, / and ↑ for this purpose, we not only make our program easier to follow, but we automatically take advantage of the precedence relations already defined by the priority-declaration for these operators in the standard-prelude (6.1) [R 10.2.0]. Formulas using these operators will yield an **operand**. In cases where further algebraic manipulation is not possible, its **mixture** will simply be a corresponding **formula**, but in singular cases such as "$a-a$", "$a-0$", "$1\times a$", etc. it will be a **real** or a **ref string**. Such singular cases arise quite frequently during differentiation. ¢

    op + = *(*operand *p, q)* operand :
        con begin real *c, d;* **mixture** $a = m$ of *p*, $b = m$ of *q;*
        bool *leftreal* = *c* ::= *a*, *rightreal* = *d* ::= *b;*
comment We declared *leftreal* and *rightreal* to avoid compiling and obeying two copies of the code for *c* ::= *a* and *d* ::= *b*. ¢
        if   *(leftreal* | *c=0* | **false**) **then** *b* ¢ *0+b = b* ¢
              ¢ We could have used *leftreal* ∧ *c=0* , but this would have elaborated *c* every time, even if ⌐ *leftreal* and it were undefined. This would do no harm, but is untidy and would waste time if this case were common. ¢
        elsf *(rightreal* | *d=0* | **false**) **then** *a* ¢ *a+0 = a* ¢
        elsf *(leftreal* ∧ *rightreal)* **then** *c+d*
              ¢ This is the one case where we can use the standard version of + (between two **reals**) to do some real arithmetic. ¢
        else heap formula := *(p, plus, q)*
              ¢ We now have no alternative but to generate a new piece of tree on the heap. ¢
        fi
comment The value of this conditional clause is either a **mixture** (1st 2 cases), a **real** (3rd case) or a **ref formula** (last case). In any event, it is united to the **mixture** which is required by the operator **con**. ¢
        end ¢ *of* + ¢;

    op − = *(*operand *p, q)* operand :
        con begin real *c, d;* **mixture** $a = m$ of *p*, $b = m$ of *q;*
        bool *leftreal* = *c* ::= *a*, *rightreal* = *d* ::= *b;*

if   *(rightreal | d=0 | false)* then *a* ¢ *a−0 = a* ¢
elsf *(leftreal ∧ rightreal | c−d> 0 | false)* then *c−d*
          ¢ We must not permit −ve **reals**, because our system has no provision for a monadic minus. ¢
elsf **ref string** *s, t;*
      *((s ::= a) ∧ (t ::= b) | (**ref string**: s) :=: t | false)*
          ¢ We must be sure to elaborate *s ::= a* and *t ::= b* before *(**ref string**: s) :=: t.* The cast *(**ref string**: s)* was needed because we are not allowed to dereference both sides of an identity-relation (5.7.4). We could have used *s=t,* but this would have wasted time comparing the two **strings** ultimately **referred** to, **char** by **char**. We propose to ensure below that where an expression that we read in contains two instances of one variable, we shall only generate one **string** and yield two **refs** to it. ¢
          then *0.0* ¢ *a−a = 0* ¢
else formula := *(p, minus, q)*
fi
end   ¢ *of* −¢;
op × = *(**operand** p, q)* **operand** :
  con begin real *c, d;* **mixture** *a = m* **of** *p, b = m* **of** *q;*
  bool *leftreal = c ::= a, rightreal = d ::= b;*
  if   *(leftreal | c=0 ∨ c=1 | false)* then *(entier c + 1 | 0.0, b)*
                                                ¢ *0 × b = 0, 1 × b = b* ¢
  elsf *(rightreal | d=0 ∨ d=1 | false)* then *(entier d + 1 | 0.0, a)*
                                                ¢ *a × 0 = 0, a × 1 = a* ¢
  elsf *leftreal ∧ rightreal* then *c × d*
  else formula := *(p, times, q)*
  fi
  end   ¢ *of* × ¢;
op / = *(**operand** p, q)* **operand** :
  con begin real *c, d;* **mixture** *a = m* **of** *p, b = m* **of** *q;*
  bool *leftreal = c ::= a, rightreal = d ::= b;*
  if   *(leftreal | c=0 | false)* then *0.0* ¢ *0/b = 0* ¢
  elsf *(rightreal | d=0 ∨ d=1 | false)*
        then *(entier d + 1 |* **go to** *help, a)* ¢ *a/0 = help, a/1 = a* ¢
  elsf *leftreal ∧ rightreal* then *c/d*
  elsf **ref string** *s, t;*

EXAMPLES

$((s ::= a) \wedge (t ::= b) \mid (\text{ref string } s) :=: t \mid \text{false})$
then $1.0 \; ¢ \; a/a = 1 \; ¢$
else formula := (p, over, q)
fi
end $¢ \, of \mid ¢;$

op ↑ = (**operand** p, q) **operand** :
  con begin real c, d; **mixture** a = m **of** p, b = m **of** q;
  bool leftreal = c ::= a, rightreal = d ::= b;
  if (rightreal $\mid$ d=0 ∨ d=1 $\mid$ **false**)
     then (entier d + 1 $\mid$ 1.0, a) $¢ \, a ↑ 0 = 1, a ↑ 1 = a \, ¢$
  elsf leftreal ∧ rightreal **then** exp (ln (c) × d)
  else formula := (p, to, q)
  fi
  end $¢ \, of ↑ ¢;$

comment We shall now arrange to read in expressions consisting of strings (for variables), constants, the operators +, −, ×, /, and ↑, and pairs of parentheses, each expression being terminated by a semicolon. Spaces and newlines will be ignored in plausible places. Each expression read in is to be stored, on the heap, as an **operand**. $¢$

  file file := stand in;
comment We take a copy of stand in, because we want to modify its term. $¢$
  term **of** file := "+ − × / ↑ ( )$\underline{.}$";
comment These will be regarded as terminating a variable. $¢$
  logical file end **of** file := exit;
comment When we have read all the expressions, we shall have finished the program. $¢$
  [1 : 0 **flex**] **ref string** string list := **loc string** := ( );
comment We shall use this to record all the variables met so far. Initially it refers to one empty string. $¢$
  proc get var or const = (**file** file) **union** (**ref string, real**) :
    begin string s, **real** x, **int** j, up, **file** fool := file, **char** c;
    char error **of** fool := ($¢$ **void** $¢$: (backspace(fool); **go to** notreal));
comment We had to invent fool, for local use, to avoid scope troubles. We are now going to try to read a **real**. If the next thing on the input stream is not a constant, in some readable format (see 7.1.2), char error will be called, and we shall presume it was a variable. $¢$
    get (fool, x);
    x exit $¢$ x is now united to **union** (**ref string, real**) $¢$
    notreal: j := 0;

loop: *get (file* ¢ *or fool* ¢, *c);*
 (c = "." | *loop* | *backspace (file)); * ¢ *ignore initial space* ¢
 get (file, s); ¢ *up to one of the term* **chars**, *or end of line* ¢
 for *i* **to** *up* := **upb** *string list*
     while *string list* [*i*] ≠ *s*
     do *j* := *i;*
comment We see if we have had this **string** before. ¢
     if   *j* ≠ *up* **then** *string list* [*j+1*]
comment We have, so we yield the name of the old copy. ¢
     else *string list* :=
             ([*1:up+1*] **ref string** *ss;*
               ss[*1:up*] := *string list;*
               ss[*up+1*] := **heap string** := *s;*
               ss);
comment It is a newcomer. We have made a copy of it on the heap, and enlarged *string list* to contain its name. ¢
             string list [*up+1*]
     fi
comment The value of this conditional clause is a **ref string** which is now united to **union** *(***ref string***,* **real***).* ¢
   end ¢ *of get var or const* ¢;
comment The next procedure is going to read an **operand**. It reads the first variable or constant itself, with the following operator, and then calls itself recursively to deal with the rest. Its **int** formal-parameter is used to convey the priority of the operator currently being processed. ¢
   proc *read operand* = *(***int** *priority)* **operand** :
       begin operand *operand,* **ref string** *s,* **real** *x,* **char** *c,* **int** *operator;*
       case *x, s* ::= *get var or const(file)*
       in   *operand* := **con** *x,*
             if   **upb** *s* = *0* ¢ *neither var nor const was got* ¢
             then *loop: get(file, c);*
                  if   *c = "."* | *loop*
                  elsf *c* ≠ *"("* | *help*
                  else *operand* := *read operand (0);*
                        loop: get (file, c);
                        (c = "." | *loop* |: *c* ≠ *")"* | *help)*
                  fi
comment If we meet an opening parenthesis, we are to start again at priority zero. ¢

> > **else** *operand* := **con** *s*
> > **fi**
> > **esac** ;
> *loop*: *get(file, c)*;
> **comment** *get* the operator after the first operand. ¢
> > **if** ¬*char in string (c, operator,* $";) \, . + - \times / \uparrow "$ *)* **then** *help* **fi**;
> > **if** *operator* =3 **then go to** *loop* **fi**; ¢ *ignore spaces* ¢
> > *operator* **minus** *3*; ¢ ; = −2
> > >) = −1
> > > + = 1
> > > − = 2
> > > × = 3
> > > / = 4
> > > ↑ = 5 ¢
> > **if**   *operator* < *priority*
> > **then** *backspace(file)*; *operand*
> **comment** If the next operator is of lower priority than the one currently on hand, we ignore it for the time being, and yield what we have got so far. This is, in fact, the only exit from this procedure. Note how ; and) are bound to take this path. ¢
> > **else** *operand* := **case** *operator* **in**
> > > *operand* + *read operand(1)* ,
> > > *operand* − *read operand(2)* ,
> > > *operand* × *read operand(3)* ,
> > > *operand* / *read operand(4)* ,
> > > *operand* ↑ *read operand(5)* **esac**;
> > **go to** *loop*
> > **fi**
> > **end** ¢ *of read operand* ¢;

comment Suppose we were now to write:
> **ref string** *x*;
> *x* ::= *m* **of** *read operand (0)* ;
> **operand** *f* = *read operand(0)*

and suppose that the book being read contained, at its current position:
> ex ;
> ex↑ 2×(ex−2)↑ (fred-bill) ;

then, after elaboration of these phrases, we should have the following situation:

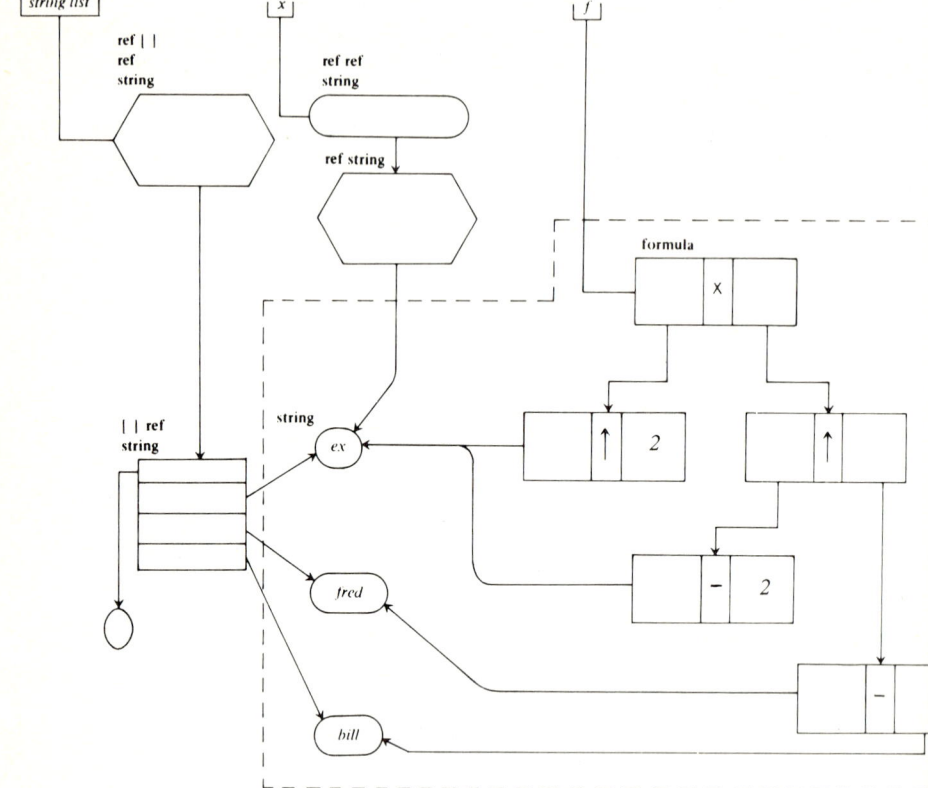

Note that everything inside the dotted line is on the heap.

Now we shall write our procedure to differentiate an **operand** with respect to a variable. ¢

    proc *diff* = *(* **operand** *d,* ¢ *wrt* ¢ **ref string** *x)* **operand** :
        begin ref string *s,* **formula** *form;* **mixture** *f* = *m* **of** *d;*
        if   **real** :: *f* **then con** *0.0*
        elsf *s* ::= *f* **then con** *(s* :=: *x* | *1.0* | *0.0)*
comment The use of an identity-relation is quick and safe here because we ensured, during *get var or const*, that if *s* and *x* refer to identical **strings**, then they do in fact refer to the same **string**. ¢
        else *form* ::= *f;*
            ref operand *left* = *left* **of** *form, right* = *right* **of** *form;*

comment It is important to realise why we did not write **operand** *left* = *left* of *form*, etc. here. Had we done so, the compiler would have had to arrange to take a copy of *left* of *form* for *left* to possess, just in case the value of *left* of *form* should get altered later (which it won't, actually). As things stand, *left* possesses the name referring to *left* of *form*, which it is impossible to change. Thus, no code needs to be compiled for this line, and its sole benefit is to save ink and to improve clarity in what is about to follow. ¢
        case *operator* of *form* in
          ¢ + ¢ *diff(left, x)* + *diff(right, x)*,
          ¢ − ¢ *diff(left, x)* − *diff(right, x)*,
          ¢ × ¢ *diff(left, x)* × *right* + *diff(right, x)* × *left*,
          ¢ / ¢ *(diff(left, x)* − *diff(right, x)* × *d)* / *right*,
          ¢ ↑ ¢ **begin**
              proc *checkforx* = *(***operand** *f,* **ref string** *x)* **bool** :
                begin formula *form,* **ref string** *s;*
                (form, s ::= *m* **of** *f |*
                  checkforx(left **of** *form, x)* ∨
                      checkforx(right **of** *form, x),*
                s :=: *x*
                | **false***)*
comment That was a case conformity, in case you didn't notice. ¢
                end ¢ *of checkforx* ¢;
comment This **proc** yields **true** if *f* is a function of *x*. ¢
            if *checkforx(right, x)* **then** *help*
comment The present program does not purport to cope with this case. ¢
            else *right* × *left* ↑ *(right* − **con** *1.0)* × *diff(left, x)* **fi**
            end
        esac
    fi
    end ¢ *of diff* ¢;
comment Now we ought to have a procedure to print our results. ¢
    proc *print operand* = *(***operand** *operand,* **int** *priority)* :
        begin real *x,* **ref string** *s,* **formula** *f,* **int** *i;*
        case *x, s, f* ::= *m* **of** *operand* in
            outf (stand out, $ *2zd.3d* $, *x)* ,
            print(s) ,
            if   *(i* := **entier** *((operator* **of** *f* + *1)/2))* < *priority*
            then *print("(");*
                *print operand (***con** *f, 0);*
                print(")")

340 EXAMPLES Ch.8.7.1

   else *print operand(left* **of** *f, i);*
     print(" + − × / ↑ " *[operator* **of** *f]);*
     print operand(right **of** *f, i)*
  fi
 esac
 end ¢ *of print operand* ¢;

comment Now we come to the rest of the body of our program (you will have noticed that it actually started when we set *term* **of** *file* a little way back). ¢

 do ¢ ad nauseam, or at least until *logical file end* **of** *file* happens ¢
  begin ref string *x;*
  newline (stand out);
  if ⌐*(x* ::= *m* **of** *read operand (0))* **then** *help*
   ¢ **else** we have read the wrt variable ¢ **fi**;
  print operand(diff(read operand (0), x), 0)
  end;
help: *print("This is not a legitimate case for this program")*
comment In the best circles, the program should here print out some more informative diagnostic message, but to include such in our present example would be tedious rather than instructive. ¢
  end

 Suppose, now, that this program were to be offered as input the piece of text we discussed earlier. Then, during the elaboration of the *print operand*, its formal-parameter *operand* would be as in the scheme on the next page.

 The bottom part of the picture is, of course, that which you saw in the previous diagram.

Note that all the items shown here are on the heap, and that at this instant there is only one of them that is not pointed to, and which is therefore available for garbage collection. As soon as *print operand* has been elaborated, they will all become garbage.

 If you follow through the operation of the program on this example, you will see that the number of items generated would have been much greater had it not been for the facilities for dealing with singular cases (*1×x, a+0*, etc.) in the operation-declarations. When the elaboration of *print operand* is over, it will have printed the following:

  2.000×e×x(ex− 2.000)↑(fred-bill)+(fred-bill)
  x(ex− 2.000)↑(fred-bill− 1.000)×ex↑2

 For a slightly different treatment of problems of this nature, you might now like to study example R 11.11 in the Report.

EXAMPLES

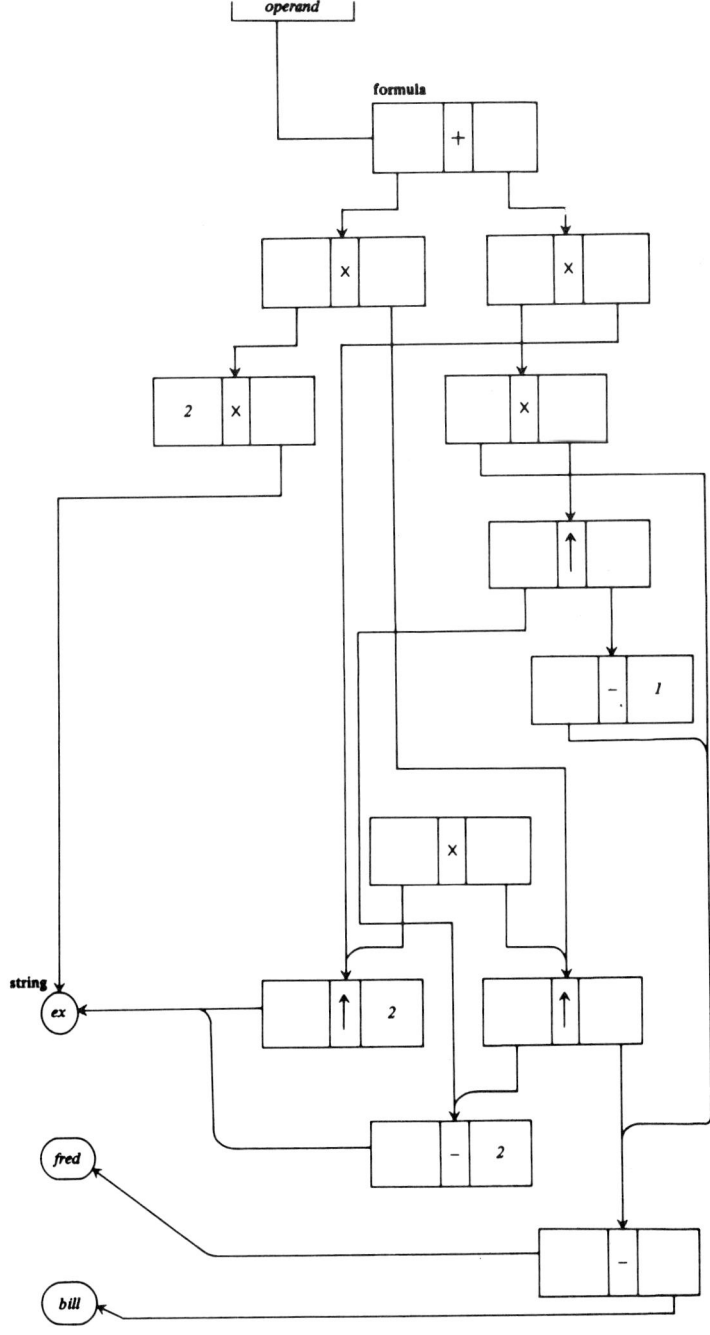

APPENDIX 1. Alternative Representations

As explained in 0.2 and 1.3.1, the Report provides representations for all the symbols needed to construct an ALGOL 68 program, and in this Introduction we have adhered to these (as indeed will most implementations). However, in many cases the Report provides two or more representations for the one symbol, in which case we have chosen the one that we preferred. Here now is a list of all the symbols for which alternatives are provided, giving first in each case the one we have been using.

10	\			5.1.1.1	7.5.2
minus	−:=			6.3	
plus	+:=			6.3	
times	×:=	(*:=)		6.3	
div	/:=			6.3	
overb	÷:=			6.3	
modb	÷::=			6.3	
prus	+=:			6.3	
∨	or			6.1.2	
∧	&	and		6.1.2	
≠	¬=	ne	(~=)	6.1.2	
<		lt		6.1.2	
≤	<=	le		6.1.2	
≥	>=	ge		6.1.2	
>		gt		6.1.2	
÷	over			6.1.2	
mod	÷:			6.1.2	
elem	□			6.1.2	
lwb	⌊	entier		6.5	
upb	⌈			6.5	
lws	⌊			6.5	
ups	⌈			6.5	
entier	⌊	lwb		6.1.1	
i	⊥	!		6.1.2	
¬	~	not		6.1.1	
down	↓			3.7.2	
up	↑	^	**(××)	3.7.2	
↑	**	up	^	6.1.2	
=	eq			6.1.2	

×	*		6.1.2			
:=	..=	.=	5.1.4.1			
::	ct		5.6.4.2			
::=	ctab		5.6.4.2			
:=:	is		5.7.4.2			
:≠:	isnt		5.7.4.2			
:	..		5.1.4.2	3.1.2	2.5.2	5.5.1.3
begin	(	⎫ in matched	⎧ 3.2.4.1			
end	)	⎭ pairs only	⎩ 3.2.4.1			
[	(	(/ ⎫ in matched	⎧ 2.5 5.5.1.3			
]	)	/) ⎭ pairs only	⎩ 2.5 5.5.1.3			
@	at		5.5.1.3			
if	(	case	3.2.4.2			
thef	| :		3.2.4.2			
then	|	in	3.2.4.2			
elsf	| :		3.2.4.2			
else	|	out	3.2.4.2			
fi	)	esac	3.2.4.2			
case	(	if	3.2.4.3	3.7.3		
in	|	then	3.2.4.3			
out	|	else	3.2.4.3			
esac	)	fi	3.2.4.3			
of	→		5.4.2			
;	.,		3.1			
exit	.		3.1.4			
goto	go to		3.1.2			
skip	~		5.1.1.3			
nil	o		5.2.4.1			
"	quote		5.1.1.1	5.5.1.1		
comment	co	¢	#	1.3.2		
pragmat	pr		1.3.2			

The three representations given in brackets (*:=, ~= and ××) are not actually given in the Report, but can reasonably be derived therefrom.

APPENDIX 2. Sample Declarations

The following is a summary of the sample declarations introduced in Chapter 0, with some others from R 1.3.

int *i, j, k, m, n;*
real *a, b, x, y;*
real *e* = c *a real value close to the base of natural logarithms,*
    *i.e. 2.718281828...*c;
bool *p, q, overflow;*
char *c;*
ref real *xx, yy;*
compl *w, z;*
format *f;*
bytes *r;*
bits *t;*
mode vec = struct *(*real *xcoord, ycoord, zcoord);*
vec *v1, v2, v3;*
mode rational = struct *(*int *numerator, denominator);*
rational *r1, r2, r3;*
string *s;*
[*1 : n*] real *x1, y1;*
[*1 : m, 1 : n*] real *x2;*
[*1 : n, 1 : n*] real *y2;*
[*1 : n*] int *i1;*
[*1 : m, 1 : n*] int *i2;*
proc ref real *x or y* = ref real : *(random* <*.5 | x | y);*
proc *ncos* = *(*int *i)* real : *cos (2* × *pi* × *i/n);*
proc *nsin* = *(*int *i)* real : *sin (2* × *pi* × *i/n);*
proc *g* = *(*real *u)* real : *(arctan (u) − a + u − 1);*
proc *stop* = goto *exit;*
op i = *(*int *a)* compl : *(0, a);*
op i = *(*real *a)* compl : *(0, a);*
princeton: *grenoble*: *st pierre de chartreuse*: *kootwijk*:
warsaw: *zandvoort*: *amsterdam*: *tirrenia*: *north berwick*: *munich*:

APPENDIX 3. Glossary

The Report defines a vast number of new technical terms. In this Informal Introduction we have used those of them which we think could or should come into general use within the computing community. We have also invented one or two of our own (we hope they will be acceptable to you — they are marked with an * in the lists below), and occasionally the meaning of one

Ap.3.1   APPENDICES   345

of our terms differs slightly from its meaning in the Report (as marked with
a † below).

We define below the meaning of the principal terms. For the others, you may follow the references given to their "defining occurrences" in our text. Usually, there are two such references — one to the basic concept in Chapter 1, and one to its practical realisation in Chapters 2 through 7.

1. Internal objects and modes

internal object	1.1.1	An object which is stored and manipulated inside the computer; i.e. an instance of a value.
instance (of a value)	1.1.1	$a:=2; b:=2;$ There are now two instances of the value "2". If we assign to b a "3", then we may say "an instance of 2 has been superseded by an instance of 3", but not that "the value of b, which was 2, is now 3". The Report is indeed very strict on this point, but ordinary speech is not so, and neither are we when no ambiguity arises.
mode	1.1.1 1.2.3	The property of a value (and therefore of an instance) which defines the class to which it belongs, i.e. the amount of storage space it requires, its compatibility with other values with which it may be confronted, etc. A mode can also be a property of an external object if that object possesses a value of that mode.

In our text, we use virtual-declarers (e.g. **int**, **ref real**, [ ] **ref compl**) to indicate modes, and also to indicate values of those modes. There is no ambiguity. If we use such a declarer as a noun, it indicates (an instance of) a value. If we use it as an adjective, it is a mode — "The mode of an **int** is **int**".

primitive modes	1.2.3	2.1.1	The built-in modes in terms of which all other modes may be constructed.
int	2.1.1		
real	2.1.1		
bool	2.1.1		
char	2.1.1		
format	7.6.2		
ref	1.2.3		
row-of	1.4.0	2.5.1	Prefixes used to construct declarers (e.g. **ref real**, **union (int, real)**, **proc (real) int**) or to indicate all the modes of the appropriate class (e.g. **proc** modes, **row-of** modes, etc.), or to indicate values of those classes of modes.
rowed			
[ ]			
struct	1.2.3	2.4.1	
union	1.2.3	2.6.1	
proc	1.2.3	4.2.1	
long	1.2.3	2.7.2	
void	4.2.1		When the elaboration of some object yields no value, then **void** is used to describe the mode which that value hasn't got. The concept is useful, but strictly speaking it is not a mode (at least according to the usage of the Report).
string	2.5.3		
bits	2.7.1		Derived modes built into the language.
bytes	2.7.1		
sema	3.7.2		
file	7.2.1		
primitive value			A value of mode **int**, **real**, **bool**, **char** or **format**.
name	1.1.1		A value whose mode is **ref** some other mode, and which refers to a value of that other mode.
† structure	1.4.0	2.4.1	A value consisting of several fields, each being a value of some other mode.
structured value			
struct			
field	1.4.0		
multiple value	1.4.0	1.5.0	A value consisting of a sequence of values, its "elements", of some (same) mode, together with a descriptor.
* multiple			

element	1.4.0	
subvalue	1.5.2.1 5.5.1.3	A subset of the elements of a multiple, as specified by a different descriptor.
descriptor	1.5.1	See under external objects.
routine	1.1.4 4.2.2	The internal equivalent of a clause which is of, or is coerced to, a proc mode.
† constant	1.1.1 1.2.2.2.1	An instance of a value which is immediately possessed by an external object. Therefore, no name refers to it, and it cannot be changed. See also under external objects.
† variable	1.2.2.4.1	An instance of a value to which a name refers (so that it can be changed), together with that name.

2. External objects

Most of the terms defined below are in fact what the Report would class as "paranotions" (see R 1.1.6.c — when you have read that, you will have become truly "initiated"). For this reason, at their defining occurrences in our text they are enclosed between single quotes (e.g. 'serial clause') and at their applied occurrences they are hyphenated, whereas our defining occurences of other technical terms are in double quotes. If you are not initiated, then never mind — the difference does not really matter to you.

external object	1.1.1	A part of a program text, as classified below.
program	1.1	The program text provided by the user, together with the standard- and library-preludes and the standard- and library-postludes.
particular-program	1.1 3.1	The program text provided by the user, on its own.
proper program	1.2.1	A program satisfying the context conditions.
standard-prelude	1.1 6	The declarations already built into the language.
library-prelude	1.1	Additional built in declarations, peculiar to the particular implementation.

library-postlude	1.1	The phrases which need to follow the label *exit*: as a consequence of the library-prelude.
standard-postlude	1.1	The administration of the completion of the program, following the library-postlude.
phrase	1.1.3	A declaration or a clause.
declaration	1.1.3 2	
collateral-declaration	1.1.3 2.2.2	A list of unitary-declarations, separated by commas.
unitary-declaration	2.3.2	
identity-declaration	1.2.2 2.2.1	Causes an identifier to possess a value.
mode-declaration	1.3.3.1 2.3.1	Causes an indicant to possess a mode.
mode-indication	1.3.3.1 2.3.1	An indicant that has been declared to possess a mode.
priority-declaration	1.3.3.3 4.3.1	
operation-declaration	1.3.3.2 4.3.2	Causes an indicant or operator token to possess a routine.
declarer		An external object which specifies some mode.
virtual-declarer	2.5.1	
actual-declarer	2.2.1	
formal-declarer	1.2.2.1 2.2.1	
† descriptor	1.5.1	At run time, an internal object has to be kept for each multiple value and subvalue to record the values of its bounds and whether they are fixed or flexible. This is called, in the Report, a "descriptor". We also apply this term to that external object which conveys the same information, viz. the list of row-of-rowers enclosed between "[" and "]" which appears in the actual-declarer of a row-of mode.
row-of-rower	1.5.1	
bound	1.5.1	
state	1.5.1	
parameter		
formal-parameter	1.2.2 2.2.1	

actual-parameter	1.2.2 2.2.1	
clause	1.1.3	
CLOSED-clause	3.2.4	
closed-clause	1.1.3 3.2.4.1	A serial clause enclosed between **begin** and **end** or "**(**" and "**)**".
collateral-clause	3.7.1	
row-display	3.5.1	
structure-display	3.4	
* parallel-clause	3.7.2	A collateral-void-clause preceded by **par**.
conditional-clause	3.2.4.2	**if** XXXX **then** XXXX **else** XXXX **fi**
case-clause	3.2.4.3	**case** XXXX **in** XXXX, XXXX **out** XXXX **esac**
* case conformity	3.7.3	
serial-clause	1.1.3 3.1 3.1.5	
declaration-preludes	3.1.1	⎫
statement-interlude	3.1.2	⎬ Constituents of serial-clauses.
completer	3.1.4	⎪
label	3.1.2	⎭
go-on-symbol	3.1	A semicolon.
range	1.1.3 3.2.1	A piece of program text (usually a serial-clause) which demarcates the scope of the variables which are locally generated during its elaboration.
reach	3.2.1	A range, with the exclusion of all ranges contained within it.
unitary-clause ⎫ unit ⎭	5.1	
* quaternary	5.1.0.1	A confrontation or a tertiary. The same thing as a unit.
tertiary	5.1.0.1	A formula or a secondary.
secondary	5.1.0.1	A cohesion or a primary.
primary	5.1.0.1	A base or a CLOSED-clause.
coercend	5.1.0.1	
confrontation	5.1.0.1	
assignation	1.1.2.2 5.1.4.1	:=
destination	1.1.2.2	The LHS of an assignation
source	1.1.2.2	The RHS of an assignation

cast	1.2.2.5 5.1.4.2	
conformity-relation	1.6.2 5.6.4.1	:: or ::=
identity-relation	1.7.2 5.7.4	:=: or :≠:
† routine-denotation	4.2.2.2	
formula	1.1.4 5.1.0.1 5.1.3	
operator	1.1.4 6.1	
monadic-operator	1.3.3.2 5.1.3	With one following operand.
dyadic-operator	1.3.3.2 5.1.3	Between two operands.
operand	1.1.4 5.1.3	A secondary or another formula.
cohesion	5.1.0.1	
selection	5.4.2	of
selector	1.4.1 2.4.1	
generator	1.2.2.3 5.7.2	The means of making storage space available for variables.
loc generator	1.2.2.3 5.7.2.1	
heap generator	5.7.2.2	
base	5.1.0.1	
denotation	5.1.1.1	Denotations are provided for **ints**, **reals**, **bools**, **chars**, **strings**, **bits**, **formats**, and the **long**(s) versions (if any) of these.
format denotation	7.6.1	The specification of the layout of the characters produced or expected during transput.
picture	7.6.1	To be matched against a single value.
insertion	7.6.1	
literal	7.6.1.1	
alignment	7.6.1.2	
† frame	7.6.1.3	
replicator	7.6.1.4	
dynamic-replication	7.6.1.4	
† collection	7.6.1.4	A collection of pictures, to be replicated.
identifier	1.1.2 5.1.1.2	
call	5.2.1	Of a procedure with parameters.
slice	1.5.4 5.5.1.3	

† indexer	1.5.2.1	5.5.1.3	
trimscript	1.5.2.2	5.5.1.3	
trimmer	1.5.2.2	5.5.1.3	
subscript	1.5.2.2	5.5.1.3	
† expression	3.1	5.1.0.1	A unitary-clause which yields a value.
† statement	3.1	5.1.0.1	A unitary-clause which yields void.
† constant	1.1.1	1.2.2.2.1	A coercend (usually an identifier) which possesses or yields a value which is not a name. See also under internal objects.
variable	1.2.2.4.1		A coercend (usually an identifier) which possesses or yields a name. See also under internal objects.
procedure	4.2.1		A coercend (usually an identifier or a routine-denotation or a procedured cast) which yields a value of a **proc** mode.
repetitive statement	3.5.2		for XXXX from XXXX by XXXX to XXXX while XXXX do XXXXXXXX.
* LHS	1.1.2.2		The left hand side of a confrontation or identity-declaration.
* RHS	1.1.2.2		The right hand side.
symbol	1.2.1		The smallest external object, out of which all the others are constructed, e.g. a, +, **begin**, etc.
indicant	1.3.2		A symbol, made up of underlined or bold faced characters (or otherwise), invented for the purpose of possessing modes or operators.
comment	1.3.2		May be inserted between any two symbols (except within a **string** denotation).
pragmat	1.3.2		

3. Technical terms

strict language	1.2.1	The language (a sublanguage of ALGOL 68) which is defined by the syntax of the Report.
extended language	1.2.1	The whole of the language ALGOL 68, defined by the Report as comprising the strict language together with extensions which are themselves defined in terms of the strict language.
extension	1.2.1	The process of deriving a construction in the extended language from its strict language counterpart.
sublanguage	Appendix 4	A language (not ALGOL 68) all of whose particular programs are also particular programs of ALGOL 68 and have the same meaning [see R 2.3.c].
* to strop	1.3.2	To construct indicants out of sequences of letters and digits by underlining, enclosing letters between apostrophes, etc.
context conditions	1.2.1	Certain conditions [see R 4.4] which exclude certain programs (otherwise syntactically correct) from being proper programs.
related modes	2.6.1	
instance	1.1.1	Values have instances
occurrence	1.1.5	External objects have occurrences.
defining occurrence	1.1.5 3.2.3	
applied occurrence	1.1.5 3.2.3	
scope	1.1.3 3.2.2	The scope of a value is the range (possibly the whole program) in which it is available for use.
to possess	1.1.1	An external object possesses an internal object.
to refer to	1.1.1	A name refers to a value.

to identify	1.1.5	An applied occurrence identifies a defining occurrence.
to specify	2.2.1	A declarer specifies a mode.
to select	5.4.2	A selector selects a field from a structure.
to develop	1.3.3.1	To derive the mode specified by a mode-indication.
elaboration	1.1.1	The process of inspecting an external object and causing the corresponding actions (as specified by the semantics of the Report) to take place.
actions	1.1.1	The elementary operations (how elementary is not defined) which, when performed in the appropriate sequence, constitute the elaboration of an external object.
collateral elaboration	1.1.2.2 3.7.1	An elaboration in which the actions required to elaborate certain phrases are merged in time, in a manner left undefined.
to supersede	1.1.2.2	To replace an instance of a value by another instance of a value.
to call	1.1.4 4.2.2	To initiate the elaboration of a procedure.
to parametrize	1.2.3.2.1	To substitute actual-parameters for formal ones.
to complete	3.1.4	To finish the elaboration of a serial-clause by yielding a value, or **void** (from its final unit, or from an **exit**).
to terminate	3.1.4	To finish the elaboration of a serial-clause abruptly, as when a jump is made out of it, or when some other elaboration collateral with it is terminated.
to halt	3.7.2	To suspend the elaboration of a serial clause temporarily, as in the operator **down**.
to resume	3.7.2	To resume the elaboration of a clause that had been halted, as in the operator **up**.

coercion	1.1.6 5.1.0	The changing of the mode of a coercend to that required by its context, with a corresponding modification to the actions performed upon elaboration of that coercend.
dereferencing	1.1.6 5.1.0.3	
widening	5.1.0.4	
proceduring	4.2.2.1	
deproceduring	4.2.2.1 5.2.0.3	
rowing	5.5.0	
uniting	5.6.0	
hipping	5.7.0.1	
voiding	5.7.0.1	
balancing	5.2.0.1	
context	5.1.0.2	The context of a coercend is its relationship to the clause in which it occurs. With each such context is associated a strength.
strong	5.1.0.2	
firm	5.1.0.2	
weak	5.1.0.2	
soft	5.1.0.2	
* empty	5.1.0.2	
STOWED	1.4.0	Structured or rowed.
fixed	1.5.1	A property of a bound in a descriptor which prevents the value of that bound from being changed once it has been set up.
flexible	1.5.1	The corresponding property which permits the value of a bound to be changed.
stack (the)	1.2.2.3	That part of the storage of the computer where internal objects created by **loc** generators (other than those containing flexible bounds) are kept.
heap (the)	5.7.2.2	That part of the storage of the computer where internal objects that cannot be held on the stack are kept.

garbage collection	5.7.2.2	The process of recovering storage space on the heap from internal objects that are no longer accessible to the program.
undefined	1.1.2.2	If the result of some elaboration is said to be undefined, then the Report does not oblige an ALGOL 68 implementation to produce any specific result. In practice, implementations may produce the result presumably intended by the user, or produce some diagnostic message, or go completely haywire.
environment enquiry	6.2.1	A constant made available by the standard or library prelude to convey information about some property of a particular implementation.
transput	7.1	Input and output and transfers to backing media.
formatless transput	7.1	
formatted transput	7.6	
binary transput	7.7	
book	7.2.1	The input/output medium in use, together with its contents.
current position	7.2.1	The current page, line and character number of the book.
end of file	7.2.1	The last used page, line and character number of the book.
channel	7.2.1	The facility through which transput to (from) the book takes place.
to open	7.2.1	To attach a book to a **file** through a channel.
to close	7.2.1	To disconnect a book from a **file**.
to straighten	7.4.1 7.5.1	To cause the elements of a multiple value or the fields of a structure to be presented in sequence as a stream of primitive (also **compl** or **string**) values.

APPENDIX 4. Variations

The language realised by a particular implementation may differ from ALGOL 68 as defined by the Report. The differences may be of two sorts:

Sublanguages. If we omit some features of the language, or impose extra restrictions, then we have a "sublanguage" [R 2.3.c]. A particular-program written in a sublanguage should run without further ado on an implementation of the full language.

Superlanguages. If we add new features, or define the results of programs whose results are at present left undefined, then we have a "superlanguage". A particular-program written in canonical ALGOL 68 is therefore automatically correct in any superlanguage.

Any particular implementation is likely to contain variations of both sorts, so that it would be better to speak of "sublanguage features" and "superlanguage features". The documentation accompanying each implementation should state precisely what these features are for its own case. The following notes give an account of some variations which are likely to be found in many implementations.

Sublanguage features

1. No parallel processing

All the features described in 3.7.2 are omitted. Parallel-clauses require a separate stack to be maintained for each parallel branch, and this is not easy to implement efficiently except on a machine with a virtual store.

2. Defining before applying

A compiler for full ALGOL 68 must have at least three passes, the first to build up a table of mode-indications (2.3.1) and the modes that they specify, the second to build up a table of identifiers and the modes of the values they possess, and the third and subsequent ones finally to recognise all of the source text and to generate the object code. The first two of these passes can be omitted if the following restrictions are made:
   a) Defining occurrences of identifiers (except labels) must come before the applied occurrences which identify them (3.2.3).
   b) If the first time that a label identifier occurs is in a (forward) jump (rather than in a label), its **go to** may not be omitted (so that the compiler knows at once that it is a label-identifier).

c) A priority-declaration must come before any operation-declaration which identifies it, and an operation-declaration, in turn, must come before any formula which identifies that (4.3.3).
d) The rule for the identification of mode-indications is not quite so strict. The following is allowed:

> mode a = struct *(*real *p,* ref b *q);*
> mode b = struct *(*int *p,* ref a *q);*

so that recursive pairs (etc.) of modes may be created. However, applied occurrences of mode-indications other than in mode-declarations must not occur until after, not only the mode-declarations that they identify, but also the defining occurrences of other modes used in those mode-declarations. Thus the declaration:

> a *a;*

must come after both of the two mode-declarations given above.

This set of restrictions, and the resultant saving of compile time, are well worth while for installations where the amount of compilation is expected to be comparable with the amount of running. They cause little hardship to the user, the only snag being that it is impossible to declare a pair of procedures (or operators) that call each other recursively. Even this can be avoided, in some implementations, by the use of pragmats (1.3.2).

3. No proceduring

If the first two passes have been saved, as described above, then there may be only one pass left (or there may be more, in which case the object code should be more efficient). If there is only one pass left, it will in general be necessary to make at least two further restrictions:
a) There is to be no proceduring (4.2.2.1) (it is in general impossible to detect that a clause is to be procedured in time to cause it to be compiled as a routine). Instead, a cast is regarded as a new kind of routine-denotation (for a routine without parameters) and if the context does not require a procedure it is immediately deprocedured back into a cast. The only hardship to the user is that everything he would like to be procedured must be written as a cast, which would already be the case on most occasions anyway.
b) Uniting is restricted to strong contexts (cf. 5.6.0). Again, this may require some casts to be written, but straightforward programs are unlikely to be affected.

Superlanguage features

1. The void symbol

This has already been hinted at in 4.2.1. It may be introduced in three places:

a) In **proc** declarers, for routines which yield no value, e.g.:

   proc void
   proc *(*real, int, ref char*)* **void**

b) In routine-denotations, for routines (with parameters) which yield no value, e.g.:

   proc *pqrs* = *(*ref real *a, b)* void: *(i < 0 | a := 3.14 | b := 3.14);*

   (cf. 4.2.2.2. E21).

c) In void-casts, e.g.:

   proc void *q;*
   q := **void** *: x := 3.14*

   (cf. 4.2.2.1. E11). Such a void-cast is a substitute for a void-cast-pack (5.1.4.2), which was an ugly beast with some strange exceptions associated with it.

Note that, in all the examples in the body of this book where we have used the comment ¢ **void** ¢, a **void** symbol can properly be used in this superlanguage.

2. ex

If, as in sublanguage feature 3a) above, a cast (containing a ":") is to be regarded as a routine-denotation, it is desirable in the interests of efficiency to have also a genuine cast (containing a different symbol, such as **ex**):

   *(*ref real **ex** *xx) := a;* ¢ cf. 5.2.4. E22 ¢

In the sublanguage without proceduring, of course, this type of cast can never be procedured into a routine.

3. ouse

On the lines of:

   if   **bool** clause
   then clause

> **elsf** another **bool** clause
> **then** another clause
> **else** an alternative clause
> **fi**

(3.2.4.2), we may have:

> **case** **int** clause
> **in** list of clauses
> **ouse** another **int** clause
> **in** another list of clauses
> **out** an alternative clause
> **esac**

(cf. 3.2.4.3 and also 3.7.3). And, lo and behold, an alternative for the **ouse** symbol is "|:" (or even **elsf**).

4. case

At present the **int** clause following a **case** must be unitary (3.2.4.3), which is to be contrasted with the serial **bool** clause that may follow an **if** (3.2.4.2). Most implementations will permit the serial-clause in both cases.

5. Other variations

At various places in this Introduction we have suggested that your implementation might well be more lenient than the Report requires. These also would really be examples of superlanguage features. The places referred to are:

> 2.5.1, 3.5.1, 3.7.2, 4.2.2.1, 4.2.2.2, 7.4.4, 7.5.2.

INDEX

a, 290
abs, 223, 250, 261, 279
Action, 72, 81, 353
Actual declarer — see declarer, actual
Actual parameter — see parameter, actual
Algol 60, 163, 167, 169, 181, 194, 237
Alignment, 286, 288, 289
amode, 92
and, 254, 342
Applied occurrence, 79, 152, 168, 199, 210, 356
arccos, 255, 260
arcsin, 255, 260
arctan, 255, 260
Array, 109
Assignation, 75, 180, 206, 212, 349
Assignation (example — names), 220
Assignation (of multiples), 230, 235
Assignation (of **unions**), 134
Assignation (scope restriction), 167, 196
Assignation (value yielded), 77
at, 125, 227, 343
b, 290
backspace, 264, 266, 275, 289
Balanced clause — see clause, balanced
Balancing, 172, 174, 176, 206, 215, 246
Base, 205, 350
Base (bits denotation), 239
Base (call), 218
Base (denotation, identifier and **skip**), 209
Base (string denotation, identifier and slice), 225
Base (void cast pack), 215
begin, 76, 165, 170, 176, 180, 343
bin possible, 268, 269, 271
bin, 250
Binary, 239
Binary transput — see transput, binary
bits width, 238, 255, 259
bits widths, 259
bits, 158, 238, 239
bits (input), 267
bits (output), 264
Blank space, 99

Block, 167
Book, 268, 272, 276, 277, 295, 355
bool, 141
bool (input), 266
bool (output), 264
Boundpair, 122
Bounds, 122, 162, 201, 227, 348
Bounds (after rowing), 224
Bounds (binary transput), 298
Bounds (in actual declarer), 153
Bounds (in assignations), 230, 231
Bounds (in formal declarer) 151, 315
Bounds (in **unions**) 235
Bounds (interrogations), 229
Bounds (of row display), 177
Bounds (of string denotation), 225
Bounds, fixed — see fixed
Bounds, flexible — see flexible
btb, 250, 261
by, 178
bytes width, 238, 255, 259
bytes widths, 259
bytes, 137, 158, 238
bytes (input), 267
bytes (output), 264
bytes (straightening), 283
c, 102
Call, 78, 157, 180, 187, 194, 201, 206, 218, 350
Call by name, 194
Call by reference, 96, 194
Call by value, 94, 194, 201
Call, to, 353
Case, 206, 343
Case — see clause, case
Case conformity, 185, 207, 349
Case conformity (example), 339
Case conformity (range), 241
case, 174, 185
Cast, 89, 155, 206, 214, 350, 357
Cast (containing routine denotation), 193
Cast (example), 198, 238
Cast (on LHS of assignation), 213, 220

360

INDEX

Cast (procedured), 191
Chaining, 116
Channel, 268, 277, 355
char error, 267, 276, 281, 297
char error (example), 335
char in string, 284
char number, 274
char, 141
char (input), 267
char (output), 264
Character, 278
Check, 128, 151, 197, 201, 203, 315
Check, run time, 197, 204
Choice, 292, 297
Clause, 76, 349
Clause, case, 170, 173, 216, 349, 359
Clause, case (range), 241
Clause, closed, 76, 166, 170, 212, 224, 349
Clause, CLOSED, 161, 169, 175, 176, 205, 215, 219, 228, 293, 349
Clause, collateral, 170, 180, 349
Clause, conditional, 170, 171, 216, 349
Clause, conformity case − see case comformity
Clause, parallel, 182, 349, 356
Clause, serial, 76, 161, 349
Clause, serial (after **out**), 185
Clause, serial (after **while**), 178
Clause, serial (coercion of), 216
Clause, serial (containing routine denotation), 193
Clause, serial (in closed clause), 170
Clause, serial (in conditional clause), 171
Clause, serial (range), 166, 241
Clause, serial (value of), 163
Clause, serial (where used), 165
Clause, unitary, 205, 216, 349
Clause, unitary (in case clause), 174
Clause, unitary (in case conformity), 185
Clause, unitary (in identity declaration), 143
Clause, unitary (in repetitive statement), 178
Clause, unitary (in serial clause), 161, 163
Clause, unitary (range), 166, 241
Clause, unitary − see also unit

close, 273, 275
Close, to, 355
Closed clause − see clause, closed
CLOSED clause − see clause, CLOSED
co, 343
Code conversion, 278
Coercend, 205, 349
Coercion, 190, 200, 206, 215, 221, 224, 232, 236, 354
Coercion (related modes), 156
Coercion chart, 208
Cohesion, 205, 350
Cohesion (generator) 239
Cohesion (selection) 222
Collateral elaboration, 75, 76, 78, 151, 176, 177, 179, 180, 185, 203, 245, 293, 296, 353
Collection, 293
Column, 177, 227
Comma symbol, 76
Comment, 102, 225, 351
Comment symbol, 225
comment, 343
Common sub-expressions, 182
compl, 149, 221, 223, 275
compl (input), 266
compl (output), 264
Complete, to, 164, 181, 217, 353
Completer, 164
Computer word, 137, 158
Concatenation, 252, 257
Condition, 206
Conditional clause − see clause, conditional
Conformity relation, 134, 148, 156, 185, 207, 232, 233, 350
Confrontation, 193, 205, 349
Confrontation (assignation), 230
Confrontation (conformity relation), 233
Confrontation (deproceduring), 219, 238
Confrontation (identity relation), 245
conj, 223, 250
Constant, 73, 83, 143, 210, 347, 351
Constants (standard prelude), 254
Context, 206, 354

Context conditions, 81, 105, 116, 147, 156, 169, 200, 352
Conversion procedures, 283
cos, 255, 260
create, 272, 279
ct, 343
ctab, 343
ctb, 238, 250, 261
Cube root, 162
Current position, 268, 272, 274, 277, 289, 355
Cyclic permutation, 231
d, 290
dec string, 260, 284
Declaration, 74, 76, 161, 348
Declaration condition, 105, 116, 121, 147
Declaration preludes, 161, 167, 216
Declaration, collateral, 142, 145, 180, 348
Declaration, collateral (extension), 147, 149, 158, 198
Declaration, collateral (formal/actual correspondence), 202
Declaration, **heap**, 159
Declaration, identity, 82, 142, 206, 348
Declaration, identity (and multiples), 126, 129, 150
Declaration, identity (and procedures), 191
Declaration, identity (and structures), 110
Declaration, identity (and **unions**), 131, 157
Declaration, identity (extension), 144, 149, 193
Declaration, identity (formal/actual correspondence), 194
Declaration, initialised, 145
Declaration, mode, 103, 116, 146, 148, 154, 175, 175, 197, 348
Declaration, mode (extension), 149
Declaration, mode (**union**), 158
Declaration, operation, 105, 198, 200, 348
Declaration, operation (example), 305, 333
Declaration, priority, 107, 197, 200, 348
Declaration, procedure, 94, 188

Declaration, row, 150
Declaration, sample, 142
Declaration, simple, 141
Declaration, **struct**, 148
Declaration, **union**, 157
Declaration, unitary, 145, 147, 348
Declarer, 348
Declarer, actual, 122, 144, 146, 155, 239
Declarer, actual (extension), 145
Declarer, actual (row of), 153
Declarer, formal, 143, 151, 154, 155
Declarer, formal (extension), 146
Declarer, formal (row of), 152
Declarer, **proc**, 93, 155, 188
Declarer, row, 150
Declarer, **struct**, 147, 149, 153
Declarer, **union**, 156
Declarer, virtual, 150, 152, 154, 155, 156, 189, 193, 203, 214, 235, 345
Defining occurrence, 79, 167, 200, 356
Delimiters, 165
Denotation, 210, 350
Denotation, bits, 239
Denotation, character, 225
Denotation, format, 286, 288, 294, 350
Denotation, long, 239
Denotation, routine, 350
Denotation, string, 225, 228, 288
Deproceduring, 192, 208, 218, 238
Dereferencing, 208, 209, 216, 222, 228, 234
Descriptor, 122, 151, 202, 226, 347, 348
Destination, 212, 349
develop to, 104, 353
Dijkstra, E.W., 185
Dimension, 109, 150
Disc, 298
Display, row, 176, 180, 217, 224, 263, 266, 349
Display, row (containing routine denotation), 193
Display, structure, 175, 180, 349
Display, structure (containing routine denotation), 193
div, 256, 342

INDEX

363

do, 165, 178, 241
down, 183, 342
Drum, 298
Dummy statement, 210
Dyadic operator — see operator, dyadic
Dynamic replication, 293, 296
e, 290
either, 123, 151, 152, 202, 203
Elaboration, 72, 81, 353
Elaboration, collateral — see collateral elaboration
elem, 251, 261, 342
Element, 109, 122, 150, 153, 176, 224, 231, 347
else, 165, 171, 174, 343
elsf, 165, 173, 343
Empty context, 207, 208, 234
End of file, 268, 272, 273, 277, 300, 355
end, 76, 161, 165, 170, 176, 180, 343
entier, 250, 342
Environment enquiry, 138, 254, 259, 270, 278, 308, 355
Environment enquiry (conversion), 285
eq, 253, 342
Equivalence, 84
Error procedures, 279
Errors (during formatted transput), 296
esac, 165, 174, 185, 343
establish, 272, 273, 279
ex, 358
exit, 165, 249
exit, 164, 217, 343
exp, 255, 260
exp width, 259, 286
Expect, to, 287, 288, 290, 293, 297
Expression, 161, 170, 205, 351
Extended language, 82, 352
Extension, 82, 86, 88, 144, 147, 148, 149, 152, 154, 157, 160, 179, 189, 192, 193, 198, 352
External object, 72, 347
false, 141
fi, 165, 171, 174
Field, 109, 148, 176, 222, 275, 346
file available, 273
file ended, 274, 281

file, 269, 275, 277
Firm context, 206, 208, 212, 233, 263, 264
Fixed, 122, 151, 177, 202, 203, 227, 229, 354
flex, 122, 151, 152, 153, 202, 203, 224
Flexible, 122, 151, 153, 202, 229, 230, 235, 354
Flexible (transput), 293
Flip, 141
Flop, 141
for, 178
Formal declarer — see declarer, formal
Formal parameter — see parameter, formal
format, 296
format end, 276, 281, 295, 297
format end (example), 328
format, 141, 294, 295
format (transput), 263, 266
format denotation — see denotation format
format pointer, 277, 295
Formatless transput — see transput, formatless
Formatted transput — see transput, formatted
Formula, 78, 187, 199, 200, 205, 206, 210, 223, 229, 244, 350
Fortran, 169
Frame, 286, 288, 289
from, 178
Garbage collection, 243, 340, 355
ge, 253, 342
Generator, 186, 234, 239, 350
Generator, **heap**, 160, 242
Generator, **heap** (example), 332
Generator, **loc**, 85, 97, 144, 153, 157, 239
get, 270, 274, 280, 281, 299
get bin, 280, 299
get possible, 268, 269, 271, 324
Go on symbol, 76, 142, 161, 315, 349
go to, 343, 356
go to statement — see statement go to
goto, 343
gt, 252, 342
Halt, to, 183, 353

Heap, 152, 316, 338, 340, 354
heap, 160, 239, 242, 244
heap (example) 317, 333
heap declaration – see declaration, heap
heap generator – see generator, heap
Hipping, 208, 237
i, 290
i, 223, 251, 342, 343, 344
Identification, 167, 356
Identification (of books), 269, 272
Identification (of modes), 175
Identification (of operators), 199
Identifier, 74, 142, 162, 167, 178, 196, 210, 221, 225, 350
Identify, to, 80, 168, 353
Identity declaration – see declaration, identity
Identity relation, 138, 180, 206, 217, 245, 350
Identity relation (example), 325, 334
idf possible, 269, 271, 272
if, 165, 171, 174, 343
im, 223, 250
Implied bracketing, 214, 256
Implies, 253
in, 280, 281, 296
in, 174, 185, 343
Index, 122
Indexer, 124, 128, 226
Indicant, 100, 146, 154, 175, 196, 197, 351
Indication, mode – see mode indication
Indirect addressing, 89
inf, 280, 281, 286, 293, 296
Initialisation, 145
Initialised declaration – see declaration, initialised
Input, formatless, 264
Insertion, 288
Instance, 73, 214, 345, 352
int lengths, 259
int string, 260, 283
int width, 259, 286
int, 141
int (input), 266
int (output), 264
Internal object, 72, 142, 345

Interrogations, 129, 229, 257
intype, 296
is, 138, 343
isnt, 138, 343
its, 183, 261
Jensen's device, 195
Jump, 191, 237
k, 289
l, 289
Label, 162, 164, 168
last random, 255, 260
le, 253, 342
leng, 261
LHS, 351
Library postlude, 249, 348
Library prelude, 72, 211, 271, 278, 282, 306, 314, 347
line ended, 274, 281
line number, 274
Lisp, 243
List, 116
List processing, 243, 247, 332
Literal, 210, 286, 288, 293
ln, 255, 260
loc, 85, 167, 239
Local generator – see generator, loc
lock, 273, 275
Logical book, 269
logical file end, 276, 280, 297
logical file ended, 273, 280
long, 259, 260
long, 92, 259, 261, 346
long modes, 137, 159
long modes (example), 311
long operators, 261
lt, 252, 342
lwb, 129, 229, 236, 258, 342
lws, 129, 229, 258, 342
Magnetic tape, 271, 273, 274, 280, 297, 300
make conv, 278
Matrices, 314
max char, 268, 271, 296, 298
max int, 255, 259, 281, 284, 286
max line, 268, 271, 296, 298
max nmb files, 271, 273
max page, 268, 271, 296, 298
max real, 199, 255, 259, 284, 286

INDEX 365

maze, 195
McCarthy and, 172
Metanotion, 92
min, 198, 199
minus, 257, 342
mod, 251, 342
modb, 256, 342
Mode, 72, 91, 345
Mode declaration – see declaration, mode
Mode indication, 146, 348
Mood, 130
Mould, 290
Multilength arithmetic, 137
Multiple, 346
Multiple value, 108, 122, 150, 162, 177, 346
Multiple value (as parameter), 201, 203
Multiple value (assignation), 230
Multiple value (binary transput), 298
Multiple value (in unions), 235
Multiple value (rowing), 224
Multiple value (slicing), 226
Multiple value (transput), 282
n, 293
Name, 73, 144, 213, 230, 234, 239, 242, 245, 346
Name (dereferencing), 209
Name (example), 316
Name (scope of), 77, 167
Name (transput), 263, 266
Name (variable), 88, 220
Names of fields of structures, 113, 222
Names of slices, 128, 228
ncos, 344
ne, 254, 342
New line, 99
New lower bound, 227
newline, 264, 266, 275, 289
newpage, 264, 266, 275, 289,
nil, 118, 221, 237, 246, 343
nmb channels, 271
nonproc, 208
not, 249, 342
Notion, 91
nsin, 344
null character, 238, 250, 255

Occurrence, 352
odd, 250
of, 222
op, 198
open, 272, 279
Open, to, 269, 273, 355
Operand, 78, 199, 206, 211, 244, 350
Operating system, 269, 272
Operation declaration – see declaration, operation
Operator, 77, 105, 187, 197, 198, 199, 211, 229, 350
Operator, dyadic, 107, 180
Operator, monadic, 184
Operators (assigning), 256
Operators (complex) 223
Operators (standard prelude), 249, 261
Operators, dyadic (standard prelude), 251, 258
Operators, monadic (standard prelude), 249, 258
or, 254, 342
Order of elaboration, 202, 244
other error, 276, 282
ouse, 359
out, 281, 296
out, 165, 174, 185, 217, 343
outf, 281, 288, 293, 296
Output, formatless, 263
outtype, 296
over, 251, 342
overb, 256, 342
p, 289
page ended, 274, 281
page number, 274
Paper tape, 287, 298
par, 182
Parallel clause – see clause, parallel
Parameter, 93, 202, 349
Parameter, actual, 94, 143, 153, 180, 191, 194, 198, 206, 218
Parameter, formal, 77, 82, 143, 193, 245
Parameter, formal (formal/actual correspondence), 194, 201
Parameter, formal (row of), 151
parametrize, to, 94, 353
Paranotion, 347

Parity error, 281
Particular program, 72, 161, 347
Pass, 356
Phrase, 76, 348
Physical book, 268, 274, 296
physical file end, 264, 267, 276, 280, 293, 296
physical file end (example), 325
pi, 255, 259
Picture, 281, 287, 288, 293
pie, 170
plus, 257, 342
possess to, 73, 74, 142, 352
Power, 211
pr, 343
Pragmat, 102, 357
pragmat, 343
Precision, 159
Primary, 170, 205, 206, 219, 226, 349
Primitive modes, 92, 141, 158, 346
Primitive modes (transput), 294
Primitive value, 346
print, 263, 270, 275, 285
Priority, 171, 197, 211
Priority declaration – see declaration, priority
priority, 197
proc, 92, 188, 346
proc declarer – see declarer, **proc**
proc modes, 92
Procedure, 187, 189, 218, 351
Procedure declaration – see declaration, procedure
Procedures (standard prelude), 255, 260, 273, 274, 278, 279, 283, 295, 298
Proceduring, 190, 208, 215, 217, 237, 357
Program, 72, 347
Proper program, 81, 200, 347
prus, 257, 342
Punched cards, 287, 298
put, 270, 274, 285, 299
put bin, 299
put possible, 268, 269, 271
Quaternary, 193, 205, 213, 214, 349
Queue, 116
Quote symbol, 225

quote, 343
r, 290
Radix, 283, 284, 290
Random access, 271
random, 255, 260
Range, 76, 143, 144, 146, 166, 167, 168, 196, 239, 241, 349
Rationals, 311
re, 223, 250
Reach, 167, 168, 349
read, 264, 270, 274, 280, 281
read bin, 299
Real time, 182
real lengths, 259
real string, 260, 283
real width, 259, 286
real, 141
real (input), 266
real (output), 264
Record, 109
Recursion, 195
Recursion (example), 330, 336
ref, 73, 92, 155, 346
Refer, to, 73, 352
reidf, 271, 273
reidf possible, 269, 271, 273
Related modes, 157, 200
Repetitive statement – see statement, repetitive
Replicator, 288, 293
Replicator (example) 329
repr, 250, 261
Representation, 99, 342
reset, 273, 274, 275, 298, 299
reset possible, 268, 269, 271, 274, 298, 299
Resume, to, 183, 353
Rewind, 271
RHS, 351
round, 250
Routine, 77, 93, 187, 188, 189, 237, 347
Routine (and operators), 197, 198
Routine (calling) 218
Routine (recursion), 195
Routine (scope), 196
Routine (transput), 263, 266

INDEX

Routine denotation, 78, 93, 155, 166, 187, 192, 195, 198, 203, 245, 357
Routine denotation (range), 241
Row declaration — see declaration, row
Row declarer — see declarer, row
Row display — see display, row
Row of, 346
Row of rower, 229, 348
Rowed, 346
Rowing, 208, 224, 225, 228
s, 290, 291
Sample declaration — see declaration, sample
Scope, 76, 160, 167, 179, 213, 239, 242, 280, 353
Scope (of formats), 295
Scope (of routines), 196, 327, 335
scratch, 273, 275
Secondary, 205, 207, 222, 229, 349
Select, to, 353
Selection, 207, 222, 229, 350
Selector, 109, 148, 222
sema, 183
Semantics, 81
Semaphore, 183
Semicolon, 76
Serial clause — see clause, serial
set, 274, 298
set possible, 268, 269, 273, 274, 280, 298, 299
Shield, to, 116
Shift, 251
short, 261
Side effect, 75, 181
sign, 250
sin, 255, 260
skip, 98, 210, 237, 343
Slice, 128, 177, 207, 226, 230, 231, 236, 241, 350
Slices, overlapping, 231
small real, 162, 170, 255, 259, 286
Soft context, 207, 208, 213, 219, 234
Source, 213, 349
Space character, 225
space, 264, 266, 275, 288, 289
Specify, to, 353
sqrt, 255, 260

Stack, 240, 243, 354
stand back, 269, 273
stand back channel, 269, 271
stand conv, 278
stand in, 266, 269, 270, 273
stand in channel, 269, 271
stand out, 264, 269, 270, 273
stand out channel, 269, 271
Standard postlude, 249, 269, 348
Standard prelude, 72, 149, 155, 187, 197, 211, 245, 249, 269, 275, 294, 306, 347
State, 153, 202, 229, 236, 348
Statement, 161, 170, 205, 206, 210, 237, 351
Statement interlude, 162, 216
Statement, go to, 162, 237
Statement, repetitive, 177, 351, 358
Statement, repetitive (range), 241
States, 122
STOWED, 354
STOWED value, 108
Straighten, to, 355
Straightening, 264, 268, 286, 298
Straightening (example), 294
Straightening (of multiple values), 282
Straightening (of structures), 275
Strict language, 81, 352
string dec, 260, 284
string int, 260, 284
string real, 260, 284
string, 150, 155, 225, 283
string (input), 267
string (output), 264
string (straightening), 283
strong context, 143, 206, 208, 213, 214, 217, 220, 224, 237, 238, 246
strop, to, 101, 352
struct, 92, 346
struct declaration — see declaration, **struct**
struct declarer — see declarer, **struct**
Structure, 147, 175, 221, 346
Structure (binary transput), 298
Structure (transput), 275
Structure display — see display, structure
Structured value, 108, 109, 346

Sublanguage, 221, 352, 356
Subscript, 124, 226
Subvalue, 124, 227, 228, 230, 347
Superlanguage, 356, 358
Supersede, to, 75, 353
switch, 237
Symbol, 99, 342, 351
Synchronisation, 182
Syntax, 216
t, 290
tan, 255, 260
term, 267, 276, 277
Terminate, to, 165, 169, 181, 249, 353
Tertiary, 151, 152, 153, 185, 205, 207, 212, 213, 227, 234, 246, 349
thef, 165, 172, 343
then, 165, 171, 343
times, 256, 342
to, 178
Transput, 206, 214, 355
Transput procedures, binary, 298
Transput procedures, formatted, 295
Transput, binary, 268, 271, 297
Transput, character, 268
Transput, formatless, 263
Transput, formatted, 286
Transput, formatted (example), 323
Tree, 116
triangle, 241
Trimmer, 124, 226
Trimscript, 124, 206, 226
true, 141
Truncation, 251
Undefined, 75, 171, 174, 181, 189, 210, 236, 262, 267, 272, 279, 280, 281, 284, 288, 297, 299, 300, 355
union, 92, 130, 155, 156, 232, 233, 346
union (example), 332
union (of multiples), 235

union (transput), 266
union declaration — see declaration, **union**
union declarer — see declarer, **union**
Unit, 176, 193, 205, 214, 216, 349
Unit — see also clause, unitary
Unitary clause — see clause, unitary
Unitary declaration — see declaration, unitary
United modes, 130
Uniting, 208, 232, 234, 236, 357
Uniting (example), 333
up, 183, 251, 342
upb, 129, 229, 258, 342
ups, 129, 229, 236, 258, 342
Vacuum, 224
Value, 72, 76, 93
Value (of serial clause), 77
value error, 276, 281, 297
Variable, 88, 141, 142, 144, 347, 351
vec, 344
Vectors, 314
Vectors (example), 307
Virtual declarer — see declarer, virtual
Virtual store, 356
Void cast pack, 191, 215, 358
void, 188, 193, 205, 206, 215, 346, 358
Voiding, 208, 237
Weak context, 207, 208, 222, 226, 228, 246
while, 165, 178
Widening, 206, 208, 209, 212, 216, 221, 233, 238
Word, computer — see computer word
write bin, 299
x, 289
x or y, 344
y, 289
z, 290

QA
76.5
M46
1973

APR 15 1976